the impact of college on students

VOLUME II Summary Tables

Kenneth A. Feldman

Theodore M. Newcomb

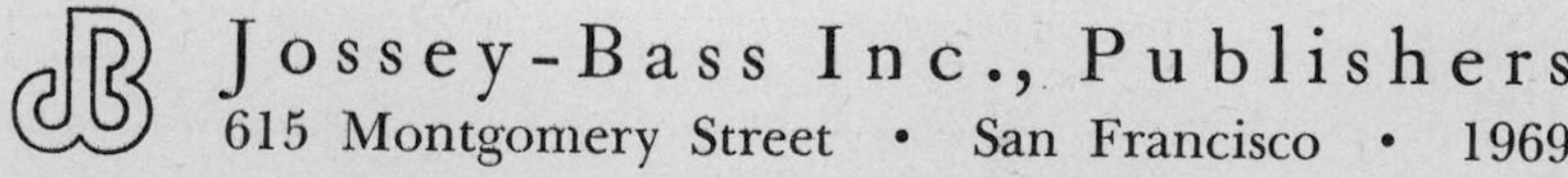

Jossey-Bass Inc., Publishers
615 Montgomery Street • San Francisco • 1969

THE IMPACT OF COLLEGE ON STUDENTS
Volume II: Summary Tables
by Kenneth A. Feldman and Theodore M. Newcomb

Jossey-Bass, Inc., Publishers
615 Montgomery Street
San Francisco, California 94111

Library of Congress Catalog Card Number 79–75940

Standard Book Number SBN 87589-036-9

Manufactured in the United States of America
Printed by Hamilton Printing Company, Rensselaer, New York
Bound by Chas. H. Bohn & Co., Inc., New York
Jacket Design by Willi Baum, San Francisco

FIRST EDITION

Code 6906

Introduction

In each of the tables in Volume Two, we present summaries of studies dealing with a particular topic of interest in the study of the impact of college on students. At the end of many of these tables, under the heading of "other studies," we have included brief descriptions of research in which not enough information was given to warrant inclusion in the more detailed part of the table or whose content was somewhat tangential to the table's primary emphasis.

Full bibliographic references for the studies summarized in this volume may be found in the reference section of Volume One. The tables are numbered to correspond with the chapter in Volume One that each accompanies. For example, Tables 4A and 4B are to be used in conjunction with Chapter Four in the first volume, while Tables 5A and 5B supplement Chapter Five.

These summary tables are, in a very real sense, the "raw" data upon which many of our generalizations in Volume One are built. Since we lay no claims to infallibility, we hope that our readers will use these tables to decide the validity of the inferences we have drawn from them. We hope further that our reader will delve into some of these tables in order to form his own generalizations and to come to his own conclusions.

LIST OF SUMMARY TABLES

	Explanatory Note for Tables 2A–2N	1
2A	Changes in Importance of Different Types of Values (Allport-Vernon-Lindzey Study of Values)	2
2B	Changes in Purposes of College Education Considered Important	10
2C	Changes in Attributes of Job or Career Considered Important	16
2D	Changes in Attitude Toward Political, Economic, Social Issues	19
2E	Changes in Religious Orientation	25
2F	Perceived Changes in Religious Orientation	33
2G	Changes in Intellectual Orientation and Disposition	37
2H	Changes in Authoritarianism, Dogmatism, Ethnocentrism, Prejudice	49

2I Changes in Autonomy, Dominance, and Confidence 57

2J Changes in Readiness to Express Impulses 61

2K Changes in Degree of Masculinity or Femininity of Interests and Attitudes 66

2L Changes in Need for Achievement, Persistence, and Vigor 68

2M Changes in Sociability and Friendliness 71

2N Changes in Psychological Well-Being 75

2O Changes in Occupational Choice and Choice of Major Field 80

2P Net Change in Career Choice and Major Fields 85

2Q Per Cent Defection From Career Choices and Major Fields 89

4A Comparing Expected College Environment and the "Actual" 91

4B Comparing Mean Scores for Different Class Levels on College Characteristics Index 95

5A Diversity of Student Attributes Among Colleges 99

5B Comparing Scores of Male and Female Students on Scales of College Characteristics Index 102

6A Relative Importance of the Spranger Values by Curriculum 104

6B Degree of Politico-Economic and Social Liberalism by Curriculum 111

6C Degree of Religious Orthodoxy or Religious Conventionality by Curriculum 115

6D Degree of Intellectual Ability by Curriculum 117

6E Degree of Intellectual Disposition by Curriculum 123

6F Degree of Authoritarianism and Related Characteristics by Curriculum 127

6G Degree of Masculinity (or Femininity) of Interests and Attitudes by Curriculum 130

6H Degree of Psychological Well-Being by Curriculum 131

6I Degree of Dominance and Confidence, of Impulse Expression, of Sociability, of Achievement Motivation by Curriculum 132

6J Student Descriptions of Environment of Their Major Field 135

6K Differential Change by Major Field 139

7A Comparing Academic Achievement of Students in Various Residence Groupings 144

8A Comparing Student and Faculty Orientations 150

8B Student Ratings of Quality of Instruction and Satisfaction with Courses and Teachers 158

8C Degree of Student Contact with Faculty Outside the Classroom 161

8D Degree Students Feel Faculty are Personally Involved 162

8E Perceived Influence of Various Sources 163

Explanatory Note for Tables 2A-2N

In Tables 2A–2N in this section, we offer capsule summaries of studies in which seniors are compared (either cross-sectionally or longitudinally) with freshmen on a variety of attributes. Our summaries of mean scores, in the columns headed "Comments," present the direction and the statistical significance (if given in the original) of the freshman-senior differences. We have reported the direction of all differences, however slight or "meaningless" taken singly, so that the reader, if he chooses, may note the frequencies with which differences, both great and small, appear among all the studies reported for a given category. We have followed the same practice in commenting on differences in standard deviations, but in this case no information about the significance of differences is included, simply because they are almost never reported by investigators.

For many of the change-areas, we also show results for sophomores and juniors, when available. In those cases, where extreme scores are *not* made by freshmen or seniors, we point this out. We note further between which two contiguous class levels the difference of scores (in the same direction as the freshman-senior difference) is the largest.

Throughout these tables, numbers in parentheses are sample sizes. The following abbreviations have been used:

Fr = freshmen
So = sophomores
Jr = juniors
Sr = seniors

$\overline{X}$ = average (or mean) score
SD = standard deviation

SS = statistically significant
NSS = not statistically significant
PNG = probability level of result(s) not given

Table 2A.--Summaries of studies showing changes in the relative importance of different types of values (Allport-Vernon and Allport-Vernon-Lindzey Study of Values). See explanatory note for Tables 2A-2N.

REFERENCE, SAMPLE, INSTRUMENT	RESULTS	COMMENTS
Whitely (1938). Total sampling of all male students entering Franklin and Marshall Colleges in the fall of 1932. Longitudinal, Fall 1932-Fall 1935. Allport-Vernon Study of Values. (high score = high relative importance of value)	Theoretical Value Fr (84): $\bar{X}$=29.78; SD= 6.70 So (84): $\bar{X}$=30.10; SD= 7.80 Jr (84): $\bar{X}$=30.31; SD= 6.82 Sr (84): $\bar{X}$=30.38; SD= 8.10	Sr are higher than Fr on theoretical value (NSS). Largest difference is between Fr and So. Sr scores are more heterogeneous than Fr scores.
	Economic Value Fr (84): $\bar{X}$=30.99; SD= 7.25 So (84): $\bar{X}$=30.54; SD= 9.00 Jr (84): $\bar{X}$=30.85; SD= 8.46 Sr (84): $\bar{X}$=30.04; SD= 6.97	Sr are lower than Fr on economic value (NSS). Largest difference is between Jr and Sr. Sr scores are less heterogeneous than Fr scores.
	Aesthetic Value Fr (84): $\bar{X}$=24.31; SD= 5.56 So (84): $\bar{X}$=25.10; SD= 8.69 Jr (84): $\bar{X}$=26.62; SD=10.26 Sr (84): $\bar{X}$=26.37; SD= 8.78	Sr are higher than Fr on aesthetic value (SS). Largest difference is between So and Jr. Sr scores are more heterogeneous than Fr scores. Note that the highest score in the junior year.
	Social Value Fr (84): $\bar{X}$=29.21; SD= 6.20 So (84): $\bar{X}$=29.39; SD= 6.77 Jr (84): $\bar{X}$=28.93; SD= 6.48 Sr (84): $\bar{X}$=30.79; SD= 5.23	Sr are higher than Fr on social value (SS). Largest difference is between Jr and Sr. Sr scores are less heterogeneous than Fr scores. Note that the lowest score is in the junior year.
	Political Value Fr (84): $\bar{X}$=32.05; SD= 6.34 So (84): $\bar{X}$=32.20; SD= 6.63 Jr (84): $\bar{X}$=33.11; SD= 8.07 Sr (84): $\bar{X}$=31.91; SD= 8.06	Sr are lower (although So and Jr are higher) than Fr on political value (NSS). Largest difference in increasing direction is between So and Jr, while largest difference in decreasing direction is between Jr and Sr. Sr scores are more heterogeneous than Fr scores. Note that the highest score is in the junior year.
	Religious Value Fr (84): $\bar{X}$=33.65; SD= 9.22 So (84): $\bar{X}$=32.56; SD= 9.56 Jr (84): $\bar{X}$=30.15; SD= 6.93 Sr (84): $\bar{X}$=31.38; SD= 9.73	Sr are lower than Fr on religious value (SS). Largest difference is between So and Jr. Sr scores are more heterogeneous than Fr scores. Note that the lowest score is in the junior year.
Twomey (1962). Random sampling of male and female students (at each class level) at Colorado State College. Cross-sectional, year not given. Allport-Vernon-Lindzey Study of Values. (high score = high relative importance of value)	Theoretical Value Fr (70): $\bar{X}$=39.70; SD= 6.48 So (70): $\bar{X}$=39.36; SD= 5.91 Jr (70): $\bar{X}$=41.79; SD= 5.00 Sr (70): $\bar{X}$=41.68; SD= 7.28	Sr are higher than Fr on theoretical value (NSS). Largest difference is between So and Jr. Sr scores are more heterogeneous than Fr scores. Note that the highest score is in the junior year, and the lowest score is in the sophomore year.
	Economic Value Fr (70): $\bar{X}$=42.75; SD= 9.27 So (70): $\bar{X}$=36.28; SD= 7.48 Jr (70): $\bar{X}$=37.96; SD= 6.92 Sr (70): $\bar{X}$=36.41; SD= 9.21	Sr are lower than Fr on economic value (SS). Largest difference is between Fr and So. Sr scores are less heterogeneous than Fr scores. Note that the lowest score is in the sophomore year.
	Aesthetic Value Fr (70): $\bar{X}$=33.15; SD= 6.55 So (70): $\bar{X}$=40.32; SD= 8.42 Jr (70): $\bar{X}$=42.04; SD=10.24 Sr (70): $\bar{X}$=42.94; SD=10.63	Sr are higher than Fr on aesthetic value (SS). Largest difference is between Fr and So. Sr scores are more heterogeneous than Fr scores.
	Social Value Fr (70): $\bar{X}$=37.40; SD= 5.91 So (70): $\bar{X}$=38.30; SD= 7.81 Jr (70): $\bar{X}$=37.50; SD= 6.16 Sr (70): $\bar{X}$=39.32; SD= 7.28	Sr are higher than Fr on social value (NSS). Largest difference is between Jr and Sr. Sr scores are more heterogeneous than Fr scores.
	Political Value Fr (70): $\bar{X}$=42.05; SD= 4.69 So (70): $\bar{X}$=37.25; SD= 7.28 Jr (70): $\bar{X}$=40.29; SD= 7.07 Sr (70): $\bar{X}$=39.03; SD= 5.47	Sr are lower than Fr on political value (NSS). Largest difference is between Fr and So. Sr scores are more heterogeneous than Fr scores. Note that the lowest score is in the sophomore year.
	Religious Value Fr (70): $\bar{X}$=44.45; SD= 8.48 So (70): $\bar{X}$=46.75; SD= 7.81 Jr (70): $\bar{X}$=40.42; SD=10.67 Sr (70): $\bar{X}$=39.03; SD= 9.21	Sr are lower than Fr on religious value (SS). Largest difference is between So and Jr. Sr scores are more heterogeneous than Fr scores. Note that the highest score is in the sophomore year.

Table 2A.--Changes in the relative importance of different types of values (CONTINUED)

REFERENCE, SAMPLE, INSTRUMENT	RESULTS	COMMENTS
Thompson (1960). Total sampling of all entering male and female freshmen at Macalester College in the fall of 1947. Longitudinal, Fall 1947-Spring 1951. (116 students took the Allport-Vernon test during their freshman, sophomore and senior years. An additional nine students took the test only as freshmen and seniors.) Allport-Vernon Study of Values. (high score = high relative importance of value)	<u>Theoretical Value</u> Fr (125): $\bar{X}$=26.8; SD= 6.0 So (116): $\bar{X}$=26.2; SD= 6.0 Sr (125): $\bar{X}$=26.7; SD= 6.3	Sr are lower than Fr on theoretical value (NSS). Largest difference is between Fr and So. Sr scores are more heterogeneous than Fr scores. Note that the lowest score is in the sophomore year.
	<u>Economic Value</u> Fr (125): $\bar{X}$=26.4; SD= 7.0 So (116): $\bar{X}$=26.8; SD= 5.0 Sr (125): $\bar{X}$=27.5; SD= 7.6	Sr are higher than Fr on economic value (NSS). Largest difference is between So and Sr. Sr scores are more heterogeneous than Fr scores.
	<u>Aesthetic Value</u> Fr (125): $\bar{X}$=26.0; SD= 8.0 So (116): $\bar{X}$=26.4; SD= 7.5 Sr (125): $\bar{X}$=28.2; SD= 7.7	Sr are higher than Fr on aesthetic value (SS). Largest difference is between So and Sr. Sr scores are less heterogeneous than Fr scores.
	<u>Social Value</u> Fr (125): $\bar{X}$=31.4; SD= 5.6 So (116): $\bar{X}$=32.5; SD= 5.7 Sr (125): $\bar{X}$=32.4; SD= 5.3	Sr are higher than Fr on social value (NSS). Largest difference is between Fr and So. Sr scores are less heterogeneous than Fr scores. Note that the highest score is in the sophomore year.
	<u>Political Value</u> Fr (125): $\bar{X}$=29.9; SD= 6.4 So (116): $\bar{X}$=27.9; SD= 5.9 Sr (125): $\bar{X}$=28.1; SD= 5.6	Sr are lower than Fr on political value (NSS). Largest difference is between Fr and So. Sr scores are less heterogeneous than Fr scores. Note that the lowest score is in the sophomore year.
	<u>Religious Value</u> Fr (125): $\bar{X}$=40.6; SD= 7.2 So (116): $\bar{X}$=41.6; SD= 6.9 Sr (125): $\bar{X}$=39.0; SD= 7.1	Sr are lower than Fr on religious value (SS). Largest difference is between So and Sr. Sr scores are less heterogeneous than Fr scores. Note that the highest score is in the sophomore year.
Huntley (1965). Total sampling of all entering male freshmen at Union College during 1956 - 1961. Longitudinal, Freshman year to Senior year. Allport-Vernon-Lindzey Study of Values. (high score = high relative importance of value)	<u>Theoretical Value</u> Fr (1027): $\bar{X}$=45.86; SD= 7.43 Sr (1027): $\bar{X}$=45.95; SD= 7.58	Sr are higher than Fr on theoretical value (NSS). Sr scores are more heterogeneous than Fr scores.
	<u>Economic Value</u> Fr (1027): $\bar{X}$=43.34; SD= 7.49 Sr (1027): $\bar{X}$=41.59; SD=10.01	Sr are lower than Fr on economic value (SS). Sr scores are more heterogeneous than Fr scores.
	<u>Aesthetic Value</u> Fr (1027): $\bar{X}$=33.33; SD= 8.19 Sr (1027): $\bar{X}$=39.86; SD= 9.92	Sr are higher than Fr on aesthetic value (SS). Sr scores are more heterogeneous than Fr scores.
	<u>Social Value</u> Fr (1027): $\bar{X}$=34.78; SD= 6.84 Sr (1027): $\bar{X}$=34.14; SD= 7.51	Sr are lower than Fr on social value (NSS). Sr scores are more heterogeneous than Fr scores.
	<u>Political Value</u> Fr (1027): $\bar{X}$=43.19; SD= 6.65 Sr (1027): $\bar{X}$=43.46; SD= 7.10	Sr are higher than Fr on political value (NSS). Sr scores are more heterogeneous than Fr scores.
	<u>Religious Value</u> Fr (1027): $\bar{X}$=39.52; SD= 8.83 Sr (1027): $\bar{X}$=34.79; SD= 9.97	Sr are lower than Fr on religious value (SS). Sr scores are more heterogeneous than Fr scores.

Table 2A.--Changes in the relative importance of different types of values (CONTINUED)

REFERENCE, SAMPLE, INSTRUMENT	RESULTS	COMMENTS
Arsenian (1943). Total sampling of all entering male freshmen at a men's college in New England during 1938. Longitudinal, Fall 1938-Spring 1942. Allport-Vernon Study of Values. (high score = high relative importance of value)	Health and Physical Education Majors Theoretical Value Fr (47): $\bar{X}$=33.36; SD=6.42 Sr (47): $\bar{X}$=33.32; SD=6.24	Sr are lower than Fr on theoretical value (NSS). Sr scores are less heterogeneous than Fr scores.
	Economic Value Fr (47): $\bar{X}$=29.40; SD=6.26 Sr (47): $\bar{X}$=27.90; SD=5.68	Sr are lower than Fr on economic value (NSS). Sr scores are less heterogeneous than Fr scores.
	Aesthetic Value Fr (47): $\bar{X}$=20.04; SD=6.56 Sr (47): $\bar{X}$=22.92; SD=6.80	Sr are higher than Fr on aesthetic value (SS). Sr scores are more heterogeneous than Fr scores.
	Social Value Fr (47): $\bar{X}$=30.88; SD=5.30 Sr (47): $\bar{X}$=35.02; SD=5.28	Sr are higher than Fr on social value (SS). Sr scores are less heterogeneous than Fr scores.
	Political Value Fr (47): $\bar{X}$=32.54; SD=5.38 Sr (47): $\bar{X}$=32.96; SD=4.66	Sr are higher than Fr on political value (NSS). Sr scores are less heterogeneous than Fr scores.
	Religious Value Fr (47): $\bar{X}$=34.20; SD=7.10 Sr (47): $\bar{X}$=29.36; SD=7.02	Sr are lower than Fr on religious value (SS). Sr scores are less heterogeneous than Fr scores.
	Social Science Majors Theoretical Value Fr (26): $\bar{X}$=30.58; SD=5.86 Sr (26): $\bar{X}$=31.88; SD=5.10	Sr are higher than Fr on theoretical value (NSS). Sr scores are less heterogeneous than Fr scores.
	Economic Value Fr (26): $\bar{X}$=29.04; SD=6.48 Sr (26): $\bar{X}$=24.42; SD=5.40	Sr are lower than Fr on economic value (SS). Sr scores are less heterogeneous than Fr scores.
	Aesthetic Value Fr (26): $\bar{X}$=21.34; SD=5.36 Sr (26): $\bar{X}$=22.12; SD=5.90	Sr are higher than Fr on aesthetic value (NSS). Sr scores are more heterogeneous than Fr scores.
	Social Value Fr (26): $\bar{X}$=32.50; SD=6.44 Sr (26): $\bar{X}$=37.26; SD=4.12	Sr are higher on social value than Fr (SS). Sr scores are less heterogeneous than Fr scores.
	Political Value Fr (26): $\bar{X}$=29.58; SD=6.48 Sr (26): $\bar{X}$=27.80; SD=6.20	Sr are lower than Fr on political value (NSS). Sr scores are less heterogeneous than Fr scores.
	Religious Value Fr (26): $\bar{X}$=38.12; SD=7.72 Sr (26): $\bar{X}$=37.20; SD=7.76	Sr are lower than Fr on religious value (NSS). Sr scores are more heterogeneous than Fr scores.

Table 2A.--Changes in the relative importance of different types of values (CONTINUED)

REFERENCE, SAMPLE, INSTRUMENT	RESULTS	COMMENTS
Stewart (1964, and personal communication to authors of supplementary information). Sampling of entering male and female freshmen at Univ. of California, Berkeley, in the fall of 1957. Longitudinal, Fall 1957-Spring 1961. Allport-Vernon Study of Values. (high score = high relative importance of value)	Theoretical Value Males Fr (47): $\bar{X}$=48.872; SD= 7.424 Sr (47): $\bar{X}$=48.234; SD= 7.559 Females Fr (42): $\bar{X}$=39.952; SD= 8.208 Sr (42): $\bar{X}$=41.929; SD= 8.221	For males, Sr are lower than Fr on theoretical value (NSS), while for females, Sr are higher than Fr on theoretical value (NSS). For each sex, Sr scores are more heterogeneous than Fr scores.
	Economic Value Males Fr (47): $\bar{X}$=39.936; SD= 7.361 Sr (47): $\bar{X}$=37.936; SD= 9.180 Females Fr (42): $\bar{X}$=34.690; SD= 6.701 Sr (42): $\bar{X}$=34.881; SD= 8.529	For males, Sr are lower than Fr on economic value (NSS), while for females, Sr are higher than Fr on economic value (NSS). For each sex, Sr scores are more heterogeneous than Fr scores.
	Aesthetic Value Males Fr (47): $\bar{X}$=37.574; SD= 8.900 Sr (47): $\bar{X}$=41.383; SD= 9.059 Females Fr (42): $\bar{X}$=40.190; SD= 9.397 Sr (42): $\bar{X}$=44.571; SD= 9.526	For each sex, Sr are higher than Fr on aesthetic value (SS). For each sex, Sr scores are more heterogeneous than Fr scores.
	Social Value Total Sample (Male-Female)* Fr (89): $\bar{X}$=37.21; SD= 8.16 Sr (89): $\bar{X}$=37.40; SD= 7.35	For combined male-female sample, Sr are higher than Fr on social value (PNG). Sr scores are less heterogeneous than Fr scores.
	Political Value Males Fr (47): $\bar{X}$=41.553; SD= 7.369 Sr (47): $\bar{X}$=42.298; SD= 7.095 Females Fr (42): $\bar{X}$=39.667; SD= 8.096 Sr (42): $\bar{X}$=41.310; SD= 7.891	For each sex, Sr are higher than Fr on political value (NSS). For each sex, Sr scores are less heterogeneous than Fr scores.
*Data not given separately for males and females.	Religious Value Males Fr (47): $\bar{X}$=37.745; SD= 9.981 Sr (47): $\bar{X}$=34.149; SD= 8.638 Females Fr (42): $\bar{X}$=44.619; SD=11.489 Sr (42): $\bar{X}$=38.119; SD=11.421	For each sex, Sr are lower than Fr on religious value (SS). For each sex, Sr scores are less heterogeneous than Fr scores.

Table 2A.--Changes in the relative importance of different types of values (CONTINUED)

REFERENCE, SAMPLE, INSTRUMENT	RESULTS	COMMENTS
Heath (1968, and personal communication to authors). Random sampling of entering male freshmen at Haverford College. Longitudinal, Fall 1960-Spring 1964, Fall 1961-Spring 1965. Allport-Vernon-Lindzey Study of Values. (high score = high relative importance of value)	Theoretical Value 1960-1964 Fr (24): $\bar{X}$=49.6; SD= 8.4 Sr (24): $\bar{X}$=48.8; SD= 8.2 1961-1965 Fr (24): $\bar{X}$=43.7; SD= 6.5 Sr (24): $\bar{X}$=41.0; SD= 8.1	For each sample, Sr are lower than Fr on theoretical value (NSS). For the first sample, Sr scores are less heterogeneous than Fr scores; for the second sample, Sr scores are more heterogeneous.
	Economic Value 1960-1964 Fr (24): $\bar{X}$=35.8; SD=12.3 Sr (24): $\bar{X}$=35.1; SD=10.9 1961-1965 Fr (24): $\bar{X}$=37.5; SD= 8.5 Sr (24): $\bar{X}$=34.0; SD= 8.9	For each sample, Sr are lower than Fr on economic value (NSS). For the first sample, Sr scores are less heterogeneous than Fr scores; for the second sample, Sr scores are more heterogeneous.
	Aesthetic Value 1960-1964 Fr (24): $\bar{X}$=42.0; SD=10.7 Sr (24): $\bar{X}$=47.0; SD= 9.3 1961-1965 Fr (24): $\bar{X}$=43.0; SD= 8.5 Sr (24): $\bar{X}$=49.7; SD= 7.2	For each sample, Sr are higher than Fr on aesthetic value (SS). For each sample, Sr scores are less heterogeneous than Fr scores.
	Social Value 1960-1964 Fr (24): $\bar{X}$=38.4; SD=10.5 Sr (24): $\bar{X}$=37.2; SD= 9.2 1961-1965 Fr (24): $\bar{X}$=36.8; SD= 9.0 Sr (24): $\bar{X}$=37.3; SD= 8.0	For the first sample, Sr are lower than Fr on social value (NSS), while for the second sample, Sr are higher (NSS). For each sample, Sr scores are less heterogeneous than Fr scores.
	Political Value 1960-1964 Fr (24): $\bar{X}$=40.8; SD= 6.8 Sr (24): $\bar{X}$=40.0; SD= 7.0 1961-1965 Fr (24): $\bar{X}$=43.0; SD= 7.6 Sr (24): $\bar{X}$=40.3; SD= 6.1	For each sample, Sr are lower than Fr on political value (NSS). For the first sample, Sr scores are more heterogeneous than Fr scores, while for the second sample, Sr scores are less heterogeneous.
	Religious Value 1960-1964 Fr (24): $\bar{X}$=33.0; SD=10.7 Sr (24): $\bar{X}$=31.7; SD=11.2 1961-1965 Fr (24): $\bar{X}$=36.1; SD= 8.2 Sr (24): $\bar{X}$=37.9; SD= 8.4	For the first sample, Sr are lower than Fr on religious value (NSS), while for the second sample, Sr are higher on religious value (NSS). For each sample, Sr scores are more heterogeneous than Fr scores.
Burgemeister (1940). Total sampling of entire freshman body (females) at Barnard College, Fall, 1938. Longitudinal, Fall 1938-Spring 1940. Allport-Vernon Study of Values. (high score = high relative importance of value)	Theoretical Value Fr (164): $\bar{X}$=28.47; SD=8.00 So (164): $\bar{X}$=29.95; SD=7.29	So are higher than Fr on theoretical value (NSS).
	Economic Value Fr (164): $\bar{X}$=24.84; SD=7.45 So (164): $\bar{X}$=25.30; SD=7.85	So are higher than Fr on economic value (NSS).
	Aesthetic Value Fr (164): $\bar{X}$=34.15; SD=8.73 So (164): $\bar{X}$=35.79; SD=8.73	So are higher than Fr on aesthetic value (NSS).
	Social Value Fr (164): $\bar{X}$=31.41; SD=6.65 So (164): $\bar{X}$=30.92; SD=6.60	So are lower than Fr on social value (NSS).
	Political Value Fr (164): $\bar{X}$=31.53; SD=8.35 So (164): $\bar{X}$=30.31; SD=6.90	So are lower than Fr on political value (NSS).
	Religious Value Fr (164): $\bar{X}$=32.18; SD=9.35 So (164): $\bar{X}$=30.83; SD=9.80	So are lower than Fr on religious value (NSS).

Table 2A.--Changes in the relative importance of different types of values (CONTINUED)

REFERENCE, SAMPLE, INSTRUMENT	RESULTS	COMMENTS
Klingelhofer (1965). Sampling of entering male and female freshmen at Sacramento State College in the fall of 1960. Longitudinal, Fall 1960-Spring 1962. Allport-Vernon-Lindzey Study of Values. (high score = high relative importance of value)	<u>Theoretical Value</u> Males Fr (46): $\bar{X}$=43.76; SD=10.08 So (46): $\bar{X}$=45.35; SD= 9.75 Females Fr (54): $\bar{X}$=37.39; SD= 6.88 So (54): $\bar{X}$=40.07; SD= 8.91	For each sex, So are higher than Fr on theoretical value (SS for females, NSS for males).*
	<u>Economic Value</u> Males Fr (46): $\bar{X}$=45.09; SD= 3.61 So (46): $\bar{X}$=44.00; SD=10.48 Females Fr (54): $\bar{X}$=35.48; SD= 7.17 So (54): $\bar{X}$=35.15; SD= 7.53	For each sex, So are lower than Fr on economic value (NSS).**
	<u>Aesthetic Value</u> Males Fr (46): $\bar{X}$=31.35; SD= 6.24 So (46): $\bar{X}$=35.02; SD= 7.43 Females Fr (54): $\bar{X}$=39.17; SD= 9.33 So (54): $\bar{X}$=45.37; SD= 9.53	For each sex, So are higher than Fr on aesthetic value (SS).**
	<u>Social Value</u> Males Fr (46): $\bar{X}$=34.04; SD= 8.14 So (46): $\bar{X}$=33.83; SD= 7.45 Females Fr (54): $\bar{X}$=41.22; SD= 6.66 So (54): $\bar{X}$=40.72; SD= 7.07	For each sex, So are lower than Fr on social value (NSS).**
	<u>Political Value</u> Males Fr (46): $\bar{X}$=43.54; SD= 8.64 So (46): $\bar{X}$=44.35; SD= 9.13 Females Fr (54): $\bar{X}$=38.61; SD= 5.63 So (54): $\bar{X}$=37.78; SD= 7.00	For males, So are higher than Fr on political value (NSS), while for females, So are lower than Fr (NSS).***
	<u>Religious Value</u> Males Fr (46): $\bar{X}$=37.43; SD=10.43 So (46): $\bar{X}$=32.17; SD=10.60 Females Fr (54): $\bar{X}$=47.33; SD= 7.14 So (54): $\bar{X}$=40.87; SD=10.73	For each sex, So are lower than Fr on religious value (SS).**

*In a replication study of entering freshmen in the fall of 1961 and retested in the spring of 1963, the direction of the results are the same as presented here, but this time are NSS for females as well as males.

**In a replication study of entering freshmen in the fall of 1961 and retested in the spring of 1963, the direction and significance of the results are the same as presented here.

***In a replication study of entering freshmen in the fall of 1961 and retested in the spring of 1963, for each sex, So are lower on political value (NSS).

Table 2A.--Changes in the relative importance of different types of values (CONTINUED)

REFERENCE, SAMPLE, INSTRUMENT	RESULTS	COMMENTS
Telford and Plant (1963); Plant and Telford (1966). Sampling of entering male and female students at six California public 2-year colleges in the fall of 1960. Longitudinal, Fall 1960-Fall-Spring 1961-1962. Allport-Vernon-Lindzey Study of Values. (high score = high relative importance of value)	Theoretical Value Males Fr (440): $\bar{X}$=45.07; SD=6.75 So (440): $\bar{X}$=44.33; SD=6.89 Females Fr (336): $\bar{X}$=38.72; SD=6.59 So (336): $\bar{X}$=38.66; SD=6.68	For each sex, So are lower than Fr on theoretical value (SS for males, NSS for females).
	Economic Value Males Fr (440): $\bar{X}$=42.63; SD=7.08 So (440): $\bar{X}$=41.78; SD=7.79 Females Fr (336): $\bar{X}$=38.47; SD=6.73 So (336): $\bar{X}$=37.49; SD=6.98	For each sex, So are lower than Fr on economic value (SS).
	Aesthetic Value Males Fr (440): $\bar{X}$=35.17; SD=7.54 So (440): $\bar{X}$=37.21; SD=8.76 Females Fr (336): $\bar{X}$=39.23; SD=7.86 So (336): $\bar{X}$=42.02; SD=8.67	For each sex, So are higher than Fr on aesthetic value (SS).
	Social Value Males Fr (440): $\bar{X}$=35.26; SD=6.30 So (440): $\bar{X}$=36.45; SD=6.80 Females Fr (336): $\bar{X}$=40.44; SD=6.52 So (336): $\bar{X}$=40.72; SD=6.33	For each sex, So are higher than Fr on social value (SS for males, NSS for females).
	Political Value Males Fr (440): $\bar{X}$=42.74; SD=6.05 So (440): $\bar{X}$=42.06; SD=6.68 Females Fr (336): $\bar{X}$=38.55; SD=6.24 So (336): $\bar{X}$=38.07; SD=6.10	For each sex, So are lower than Fr on political value (SS for males, NSS for females).
	Religious Value Males Fr (440): $\bar{X}$=39.03; SD=8.43 So (440): $\bar{X}$=38.07; SD=9.59 Females Fr (336): $\bar{X}$=44.46; SD=8.23 So (336): $\bar{X}$=42.85; SD=8.69	For each sex, So are lower than Fr on religious value (SS).
Todd (1941). Sampling of male seniors in 103 high school and preparatory schools (Sr-hs) in the New England states, New York, New Jersey, and Pennsylvania. Longitudinal from last months of the senior year in high school to the sophomore year in college (years not given). Allport-Vernon Study of Values. (high score = high relative importance of value)	Theoretical Value Sr-hs (94): $\bar{X}$=32.60; SD=6.36 So (94): $\bar{X}$=31.89; SD=6.41	So are lower than seniors in high school on theoretical value (NSS).
	Economic Value Sr-hs (94): $\bar{X}$=31.88; SD=6.36 So (94): $\bar{X}$=33.08; SD=7.05	So are higher than seniors in high school on economic value (SS).
	Aesthetic Value Sr-hs (94): $\bar{X}$=24.00; SD=7.28 So (94): $\bar{X}$=26.38; SD=8.07	So are higher than seniors in high school on aesthetic value (SS).
	Social Value Sr-hs (94): $\bar{X}$=30.77; SD=5.13 So (94): $\bar{X}$=30.83; SD=4.98	So are higher than seniors in high school on social value (NSS).
	Political Value Sr-hs (94): $\bar{X}$=33.53; SD=6.72 So (94): $\bar{X}$=30.78; SD=6.90	So are lower than seniors in high school on political value (SS).
	Religious Value Sr-hs (94): $\bar{X}$=32.48; SD=9.68 So (94): $\bar{X}$=29.28; SD=9.76	So are lower than seniors in high school on religious value (SS).

OTHER STUDIES:

A four-year longitudinal study conducted at the University of Delaware (1965) in the 1960s revealed that for both men and women students at that university there was a statistically significant increase (between the freshman and senior years) in the importance given to aesthetic values and a statistically significant decrease in the importance given to religious values. For men, there was a smaller but still statistically significant increase in importance attached to political values, and for women a decrease in the importance attached to values in the economic area. Comparing a sample of National Merit and Certificate of Merit winners at the end of their freshman and seniors years in college, Tyler (1963) reports statistically significant increases on the Theoretical and Aesthetic Scales and statistically significant decreases on the Economic and Religious Scales (of the Allport-Vernon-Lindzey Study of Values). Discussing only one of the six scales of the Study of Values, Eleanor Miller (1959) notes a statistically nonsignificant decrease on the religious value during the four years of college. For scores on the Study of Values scales administered seven successive times at one-month intervals to ten male seniors at Carnegie Institute of Technology and ten female seniors at the Margaret Morrison Carnegie College for Women, see Hilton and Korn (1964).

Table 2B.--Summaries of studies showing changes in the various purposes of a college education considered to be important. See explanatory note for Tables 2A-2N.

Note: Numbers in brackets indicate rank order of percentages

REFERENCE, SAMPLE	RESULTS					
Goldsen, Rosenberg, Williams, and Suchman (1960).	Percent of students responding that each of the following goals (that an ideal college or university ought to emphasize) is of "first importance" (i.e., most important) and of "high importance"					
			Fr (684)	So (644)	Jr (770)	Sr (761)
Sampling of male students at eleven colleges and universities (Dartmouth, Yale, Harvard, Wesleyan, Cornell, Fisk, Univ. of North Carolina, Univ. of Michigan, Univ. of Texas, UCLA, and Wayne State Univ.).	Provide vocational training, develop skills and techniques directly aplicable to your career	First Imp.	36% [1]	35%	34%	27% [2]
		High Imp.	65%	62%	58%	52%
	Provide a basic general education and appreciation of ideas	First Imp.	25% [2]	28%	34%	42% [1]
		High Imp.	65%	71%	74%	79%
	Develop your ability to get along with different kinds of people	First Imp.	19% [3]	17%	14%	13% [3]
		High Imp.	75%	70%	69%	69%
	Help develop your moral capacities, ethical standards and values	First Imp.	10% [4]	9%	8%	9% [4]
		High Imp.	44%	45%	46%	48%
Cross-sectional, 1952.	Develop your knowledge and interest in community and world problems	First Imp.	3% [5]	3%	3%	4% [5]
		High Imp.	46%	49%	50%	56%
	Prepare you for a happy marriage and family life	First Imp.	1% [6]	1%	2%	1% [6]
		High Imp.	22%	21%	23%	21%
Goldsen (1951).	Percent of students ranking each of the following purposes as "the principal goal" of higher education					
Random sampling of male and female students at Cornell.			Males			
			Fr (515)	So (446)	Jr (450)	Sr (557)
Cross-sectional, Spring 1950.	Provide vocational training, develop skills and techniques applicable to your career		44% [1]	40%	32%	32% [2]
	Provide a basic general education and appreciation of ideas		26% [2]	28%	39%	39% [1]
	Develop your ability to get along with different kinds of people		19% [3]	19%	17%	15% [3]
	Develop your knowledge and interest in community and world problems		5% [4]	4%	3%	6% [4.5]
	Help develop your moral capacities, ethical standards and values		4% [5]	6%	6%	6% [4.5]
	Prepare you for a happy marriage and family life		2% [6]	3%	3%	2% [6]
			Females			
			Fr (211)	So (197)	Jr (183)	Sr (143)
	Provide a basic general education and appreciation of ideas		34% [1]	36%	40%	43% [1]
	Provide vocational training, develop skills and techniques applicable to your career		29% [2]	29%	22%	28% [2]
	Develop your ability to get along with different kinds of people		21% [3]	22%	22%	15% [3]
	Help develop your moral capacities, ethical standards and values		9% [4]	5%	7%	6% [4]
	Develop your knowledge and interest in community and world problems		5% [5]	4%	6%	3% [6]
	Prepare you for a happy marriage and family life		3% [6]	3%	4%	4% [5]

Table 2B.--Changes in the various purposes of a college education (CONTINUED)

REFERENCE, SAMPLE	RESULTS				
DiRenzo (1965). Random sampling of male students at Fairfield University. Cross-sectional, May 1964.	Rank of the average rank given by students to each of the following educational goals (that Fairfield University should emphasize)				
		Fr (54)	So (53)	Jr (48)	Sr (48)
	Provide a basic general education	1.5	2.5	2.5	1.5
	Develop moral and spiritual qualities	1.5	2.5	2.5	1.5
	Provide preparation for advanced education	3	1	1	3
	Provide professional and occupational training	4	4	4	4
	Develop ability to get along with all kinds of people	5	6	5	5
	Develop your knowledge and interest in community and world affairs	6	5	6	6
	Provide a preparation for marriage and family life	7	7	7	7
Rose (1964). Random sampling of male and female students at American International College, Amherst College, Mt. Holyoke College, The College of Our Lady of the Elms, Smith College, Springfield College, Univ. of Massachusetts, and Western State College for Teachers (all in the Connecticut Valley of Western Massachusetts). Cross-sectional, Dec. 1962.	Percent of students responding to each of the following as the "most important" goal (personally) of a college education*				
		Amherst, Mount Holyoke and Smith			
		Fr (112)	So (102)	Jr (106)	Sr (99)
	Provide me with a basic general education and an appreciation of ideas	67% [1]	66%	80%	82% [1]
	Provide me with vocational training, develop skills and techniques directly applicable to a career	9% [2]	7%	7%	7% [2]
		American International College			
		Fr (26)	So (32)	Jr (36)	Sr (25)
	Vocational training	53% [1]	36%	30%	48% [1]
	Basic general education	30% [2]	39%	52%	44% [2]
		The College of Our Lady of the Elms			
		Fr (32)	So (38)	Jr (44)	Sr (33)
	Vocational training	37% [1]	39%	32%	33% [2]
	Basic general education	16% [2]	25%	40%	40% [1]
		Springfield College			
		Fr (30)	So (23)	Jr (21)	Sr (25)
	Vocational training	53% [1]	34%	47%	36% [2]
	Basic general education	13% [2]	47%	33%	44% [1]
		University of Massachusetts			
		Fr (46)	So (40)	Jr (24)	Sr (26)
	Vocational training	58% [1]	40%	33%	20% [2]
	Basic general education	28% [2]	27%	46%	64% [1]
		Western State College for Teachers			
		Fr (51)	So (35)	Jr (25)	Sr (26)
	Vocational training	56% [1]	40%	40%	61% [1]
	Basic general education	19% [2]	23%	44%	23% [2]
	*Rose reports that 9% of those in the overall sample group checked the goal "develop my ability to get along with different kinds of people" as most important; 7% said "help develop my moral capacities, ethical standards and values"; 3% checked "prepare me for a happy marriage and family"; and 2% checked "develop my knowledge and interest in community and world problems." These data are not further broken down by school and class year.				

Table 2B.--Changes in the various purposes of a college education (CONTINUED)

REFERENCE, SAMPLE	RESULTS		
King (nd). Random sampling of male students entering Harvard in the fall of 1960. Longitudinal, Fall 1960-1964.	Percent of students responding that each of the following educational goals (that Harvard ideally ought to emphasize) is of "high importance"		
		Fr (269)	Sr (187)
	Provide a basic general education and appreciation of ideas	86% [1]	91% [1]
	Develop your knowledge and interest in community and world problems	47% [2]	47% [2]
	Develop your ability to get along with different kinds of people	43% [3]	35% [3]
	Provide a highly intensive, specialized understanding of one field of knowledge	27% [4]	21% [5]
	Help develop your moral capacities, ethical standards and values	24% [5]	25% [4]
	Provide vocational training, develop skills and techniques directly applicable to your career	17% [6]	7% [6]
	Prepare you for a happy marriage and family life	3% [7]	2% [7]
Birney, Coplin and Grose (1960). Total sampling of entering male freshmen at Amherst in September 1955. Longitudinal, Sept. 1955-April 1959. (Analysis uses data for all freshmen and for all of these still remaining in senior year; therefore sample size for freshmen and seniors is not identical.)	Percent of students judging each of the following purposes of a college education of "high importance"		
		Fr (234)	Sr (213)
	Provide a basic general education and appreciation of ideas	86.3% [1]	94.4% [1]
	Develop one's ability to get along with different kinds of people	71.4% [2]	41.5% [2]
	Provide vocational training, develop skills and techniques directly applicable to one's career	31.1% [3]	13.6% [5]
	Develop one's knowledge and interest in community and world problems	29.9% [4]	34.1% [3]
	Help develop one's moral capacities, ethical standards and values	29.4% [5]	26.2% [4]
	Prepare one for a happy marriage and family life	7.9% [6]	1.9% [6]
Gaff (1965). Random sampling of male and female students at Univ. of California, Berkeley. Cross-sectional, Summer 1964.	Percent of students ranking each of the following as one of the two most important goals of a college education to them		
		Fr (165)	Sr (124)
	Provide a basic general education and appreciation of ideas	49% [1]	62% [1]
	Provide vocational training, develop skills and techniques directly applicable to your career	43% [2.5]	36% [3]
	To advance learning and stimulate the production of new knowledge	43% [2.5]	44% [2]
	Develop your ability to get along with different people	23% [4]	23% [4]
	Prepare you to serve mankind	17% [5]	8% [7]
	Develop your knowledge and interest in community and world problems	11% [6]	14% [5]
	Help develop your moral capacities, ethical standards and values	9% [7]	10% [6]
	Prepare you for a happy marriage and family life	3% [8]	1% [8]
	Prepare you to serve your immediate community	1% [9]	1% [9]
Gaff (1965). Random sampling of male and female students at Univ. of the Pacific. Cross-sectional, Summer 1964.	Percent of students ranking each of the following as one of the two most important goals of a college education to them		
		Fr (142)	Sr (100)
	Provide vocational training, develop skills and techniques directly applicable to your career	43% [1]	52% [1]
	Provide a basic general education and appreciation of ideas	40% [2]	48% [2]
	Develop your ability to get along with different people	39% [3]	25% [4]
	To advance learning and stimulate the production of new knowledge	36% [4]	35% [3]
	Help develop your moral capacities, ethical standards and values	19% [5]	9% [6]
	Prepare you to serve mankind	13% [6]	17% [5]
	Develop your knowledge and interest in community and world problems	7% [7]	6% [7]
	Prepare you for a happy marriage and family life	1% [8]	1% [8]
	Prepare you to serve your immediate community	0% [9]	3% [9]

Table 2B.--Changes in the various purposes of a college education (CONTINUED)

REFERENCE, SAMPLE	RESULTS				
Trent (1964a). Total sampling of all male and female freshmen and random or representative sampling of male and female senior students at five West Coast Catholic colleges (in 1959-1960). Cross-sectional, freshmen at the beginning and seniors at the end of the school year.	Percent of male and female students reporting each of the following as the first or second most important goal of college				
		Males		Females	
		Fr (505)	Sr (90)	Fr (602)	Sr (90)
	Other practical training	62% [1]	43% [1]	59% [1]	39% [1]
	Knowledge; ideas	18% [2.5]	30% [2]	21% [2]	31% [2]
	Character formation (religious training and family education)	18% [2.5]	25% [3]	18% [3]	27% [3]
McConnell, Clark, Heist, Trow, and Yonge (forthcoming). Sampling of male and female students at Antioch, Reed, Swarthmore, Univ. of Calif. at Berkeley, Univ. of the Pacific, St. Olaf, and Univ. of Portland. Longitudinal; first school, 1958-1963, next two schools, 1958-1962, last four schools, 1959-1963.	Percent of students ranking each of the following as the "most important" college purpose				
		Basic gen. ed.		Vocational Train.	
		Fr	Sr	Fr	Sr
	Antioch	47% [1]	68% [1]	23% [2]	12% [2]
	Reed	71% [1]	75% [1]	15% [2]	14% [2]
	Swarthmore	54% [1]	81% [1]	22% [2]	9% [2]
	Berkeley	39% [2]	65% [1]	45% [1]	16% [2]
	Univ. of the Pacific	24% [2]	48% [1]	62% [1]	32% [2]
	St. Olaf	29% [2]	59% [1]	47% [1]	12% [2]
	Univ. of Portland	22% [2]	40% [1]	57% [1]	34% [2]
McConnell (1961b). Sampling of National Merit Scholars prior to college entrance. Longitudinal, 1956-1958.	Percent of students ranking each of the following as the "most important" objective of an ideal college				
		Fr (504)	Jr (504)		
	General education and appreciation of ideas	50%	71%		
	Vocational training	33%	17%		
Selvin (1963). Sampling of entering male freshmen at Univ. of California at Berkeley, Fall 1959. Longitudinal, Fall 1959-Spring 1961.	Percent of students ranking each of the following as the "most important" or "second most important" goal of college education (for the students themselves)				
		Fr (730)	So (730)		
	Provide vocational training, develop skills and techniques directly applicable to your career	65%	66%		

Table 2B.--Changes in the various purposes of a college education (CONTINUED)

REFERENCE, SAMPLE	RESULTS		
Weiss (1964).	Percent of students ranking each of the following as the "main goal" of a college education		
Total sampling of male and female freshmen, sophomores and seniors at St. Louis University.		When first enrolled*	At present
	Obtaining professional or career training	68.8%	55.4%
	Gaining a liberal education	14.7%	17.8%
Fall 1963.	Providing for greater economic security	10.4%	10.6%
	Acquiring social polish, confidence, poise; learning to get along with different kinds of people; providing contacts for later life	1.9%	6.6%
	Examining important social, political, economic questions; developing deeper religious and moral understanding	1.8%	6.6%
	*Main goal when first enrolled is that recalled by the subject		
Stanfield (1965).	Percent of students reporting each of the following as the "first reason" for their coming or staying in college		
Random sampling of male and female students at the University of Massachusetts.		Reason for coming*	Reason for staying
	Vocational training	71%	55%
	General education	25%	35%
Spring 1964.	Social education	4%	10%
	*Reason for coming to college is that recalled by the subject		
Lehmann and Dressel (1962); Lehmann (1963).	Percent of students endorsing each of the following four statements as coming closest to describing them when they first came to college and "now" as seniors		
Sampling of male and female seniors at Michigan State University.		When first came*	Now as a senior
	For the most part, this person's primary reason for being in college is to obtain vocational or occupational training	41.9% [1]	29.1% [2]
Spring 1962.	For the most part, this person feels that the social life in college is not the most important but is certainly essential for his development	23.1% [2]	39.8% [1]
	For the most part, this person attempts to "make grades" but will rarely go out of his way to do extra or non-assigned readings	19.0% [3]	11.2% [4]
	For the most part, this person would consider himself to be someone who is primarily motivated by intellectual curiosity	16.0% [4]	19.6% [3]
	*Reason when first came to college is that recalled by the subject		
Adams (1965).	Percent of students endorsing each of the following four statements as most accurately describing the kind of philosophy they had when they first came to college and the one they have "at this time"		
Sampling of male senior students at Michigan State University during the school year 1964-1965.		When you first came*	At this time
	Philosophy A: This philosophy emphasizes education essentially as preparation for an occupational future [vocational subcultural identity]	52% [1]	27% [2]
(Note: all of these students were freshmen residents of South Case Residence Hall [Michigan State's first coeducational living-learning residence hall] in the winter term of 1962.)	Philosophy C: ... while not excluding academic activities, this philosophy emphasizes the importance of the extracurricular side of college life [collegiate subcultural identity]	26% [2]	51% [1]
	Philosophy B: ... the philosophy attaches greatest importance to interest in ideas, pursuit of knowledge, and cultivation of the intellect [academic subcultural identity]	18% [3]	12% [3]
	Philosophy D: ... There is often deep involvement with art and ideas ... this philosophy may emphasize individualistic interests and styles, concern for personal identity and often contempt for many aspects of organized society [nonconformist subcultural identity]	4% [4]	10% [4]
	*Philosophy when first came to college is that recalled by the subject		

Table 2B.--Changes in the various purposes of a college education (CONTINUED)

OTHER STUDIES:

Baur (1965) reports that at a state university in the midwest, a majority (55%) of the students showed evidence in interviews (gathered longitudinally) of having changed from narrowly occupational aims to a genuine interest in education. Similarly, Pemberton (1963) reports that the trend from the freshman to the senior year at the University of Delaware is away from the practical and utilitarian concerns and toward theoretical and abstract orientations. When students were asked to rank in order of importance fifteen possible motives for choosing an "ideal" program of study, seniors placed more emphasis than did freshmen and sophomores on intellectual values while attaching less importance to economic, vocational and social-service motives.

In a four-year longitudinal study of students at the State University College in Plattsburgh, New York, the personal educational objective of "application of course material to relevant life and vocational situations" decreased in importance, on the average, to students. "Obtaining of knowledge of facts and material" and "personal independence" also decreased in importance. The objective of acquiring the "skills necessary for orderly thought" remained as important to students when they were seniors as when they were freshmen. Finally, "the ability to communicate effectively" increased in importance to students (Johnson, nd[b]).

Hassenger (1965) asked students at Mundelein (a Catholic women's college in Chicago) to indicate which of eleven "purposes or goals of a college education" they felt was most important to them currently. He notes some decrease of the more pragmatic (e.g., career training) and social goals, and an increase in choice of certain "liberal" goals (e.g., opportunity to read interesting books, opportunity to examine ideas, and political, social and moral questions). However, even with these changes, the former, pragmatic goals remained more important to the students as a group.

Jervis and Congdon (1958) had students rank nine objectives of higher education. The rank-order correlation between the median rank (of each objective) for freshmen and the median rank (of each objective) for seniors is .88. Although the rank-order correlation is very high, it does not represent a perfect correlation. Therefore, two or more of the objectives did change in rank order but we do not know which ones since the actual median ranks for each objective are not given. Also, it is possible that certain median ranks did gain or lose, but not enough to cause a change in rank position of the given objective.

Table 2C.--Summaries of studies showing changes in the attributes of a job or career considered to be important. See explanatory note for Tables 2A-2N.

Note: Numbers in brackets indicate rank order of percentages

REFERENCE, SAMPLE	RESULTS				
Goldsen (1951). Random sampling of male and female students at Cornell. Cross-sectional, Spring 1950.	Percent of students responding that each of the following requirements of an ideal job or career is of "first importance" (i.e., most important)				
		Fr (707)	So (650)	Jr (619)	Sr (683)
	Enable me to look forward to a stable, secure future	30% [1]	23%	21%	21% [2]
	Provide an opportunity to use my special abilities	27% [2]	28%	29%	29% [1]
	Give me an opportunity to work with people rather than things	10% [3]	13%	11%	12% [3.5]
	Permit me to be creative and original	8% [4]	10%	12%	12% [3.5]
	Give me an opportunity to be helpful to others	8% [5]	6%	12%	7% [5.5]
	Provide me with a chance to earn a good deal of money	8% [6]	9%	5%	7% [5.5]
	Leave me relatively free of supervision by others	5% [7]	6%	5%	6% [7.5]
	All other	4% [8]	5%	5%	6% [7.5]
Thielens (1966). Random sampling of male students at Columbia College. Cross-sectional, Spring 1965.	Percent of students responding that each of the following aspects of work is of "high importance"*				
		Fr (45)	So (47)	Jr (40)	Sr (47)
	Give an opportunity to work with people rather than things	69% [3]	64%	60%	51% [4]
	Provide a stable, secure future	56% [5.5]	43%	32%	21% [9]
	Be relatively free of supervision by others	56% [5.5]	53%	72%	64% [3]
	Provide a chance to earn a good deal of money	36% [8.5]	19%	35%	23% [8]
	Give a chance to exercise leadership	36% [8.5]	38%	47%	45% [5.5]
	Give social status and prestige	22% [10]	13%	18%	13% [10]
	*In addition to these results, Thielens reports that seniors and freshmen were substantially alike in attaching importance to jobs that "permit you to be creative and original"--of high importance to approximately 85% [1.5, Fr, Sr], "provide an opportunity to use your special abilities," 85% [1.5, Fr, Sr], "give an opportunity to be helpful to others," 45% [4, Fr] [5.5, Sr], and "provide you with adventure," 40% [6, Fr] [7, Sr].				
Rosenberg (1957). Sampling of male students at eleven colleges and universities (Dartmouth, Yale, Harvard, Wesleyan, Cornell, Fisk, Univ. of North Carolina, Univ. of Michigan, Univ. of Texas, UCLA, and Wayne State Univ.) Cross-sectional, 1952.	Percent of students responding that each of the following requirements of an ideal job or career is "highly important"				
		Fr (1103)	So (1040)	Jr (1181)	Sr (1251)
	Provide an opportunity to use my special abilities or aptitudes	75% [1]	76%	78%	79% [1]
	Enable me to look forward to a stable, secure future	69% [2]	63%	58%	53% [2.5]
	Enable me to be creative and original	43% [3]	45%	48%	53% [2.5]
	Provide me a chance to earn a good deal of money	41% [4]	39%	37%	37% [4]
	Give me social status and prestige	23% [5]	25%	26%	27% [5]

Table 2C.--Changes in the attributes of a job or career considered to be important

REFERENCE, SAMPLE	RESULTS		
Birney, Coplin and Grose (1960).	Percent of students responding that each of the following requirements of an ideal job or profession is "most important"		
Total sampling of entering freshmen at Amherst in September 1955.		Fr (234)	Sr (180)
Longitudinal, Sept. 1955-April 1959.	Provide an opportunity to use my special abilities and aptitudes	32.1% [1]	43.9% [1]
Analysis uses data for all male freshmen and for all of these still remaining in senior year; therefore the sample sizes for freshmen and seniors are not identical.	Enable me to look forward to a stable, secure future	20.9% [2]	4.4% [5]
	Give me an opportunity to be helpful to others	15.0% [3]	12.2% [3]
	Give me an opportunity to work with people rather than things	13.8% [4]	7.8% [4]
	Permit me to be creative and original	9.4% [5]	21.6% [2]
	Provide me with a chance to earn a good deal of money	3.4% [6]	0.6% [9.5]
	Give me a chance to exercise leadership	2.1% [7]	3.9% [6]
	Provide me with adventure	1.7% [8]	2.2% [8]
	Leave me relatively free of supervision	0.8% [9.5]	2.8% [7]
	Give me social status and prestige	0.8% [9.5]	0.6% [9.5]
Krulee, O'Keefe and Goldberg (1966).	Percent of students responding that each of the following requirements of an ideal job is "highly important"		
Total sampling of all entering male freshmen in the College of Liberal Arts at Northwestern in the fall of 1961 and the fall of 1962.		Fr (599)	Sr (220)
Longitudinal, Fall 1961-Fall 1964, Fall 1962-Fall 1965.	Provide me an opportunity to use my special abilities or aptitudes	88.1% [1]	86.4% [1]
Samples are combined in analysis. Since analysis uses data for all freshmen and for all of these still remaining in senior year, the sample sizes for freshmen and seniors are not identical.	Give me an opportunity to be helpful to others	66.8% [2]	55.0% [5]
	Enable me to look forward to a stable, secure future	63.3% [3]	44.0% [6]
	Give me an opportunity to work with people rather than things	58.0% [4]	57.5% [4]
	Permit me to be original and creative	52.4% [5]	59.5% [3]
	Leave me relatively free of supervision by others	49.7% [6]	62.5% [2]
	Give me a chance to exercise leadership	41.1% [7]	43.5% [7]
	Provide me with a chance to earn a good deal of money	39.4% [8]	30.7% [8]
	Provide me with adventure	29.4% [9]	30.2% [9]
	Give me social status and prestige	25.2% [10]	21.3% [10]
Gaff (1965).	Percent of students responding that each of the following is one of the three characteristics most important to them in picking a job or career		
Random sampling of male and female students at Univ. of California at Berkeley.		Fr (165)	Sr (124)
Cross-sectional, Summer 1964.	Opportunity to be helpful to others or useful to society	57% [1]	55% [1]
	Making an above average living	46% [2]	40% [4]
	Opportunity to work with people rather than things	45% [3]	45% [3]
	Opportunity to be original and creative	41% [4]	52% [2]
	Living and working in the world of ideas	25% [5]	24% [5]
	Freedom from supervision in my work	18% [6]	18% [7]
	A chance to exercise leadership	16% [7.5]	23% [6]
	Opportunity to advance an ideal or cause	16% [7.5]	14% [8]
	Opportunities for moderate steady progress rather than chance of extreme success or failure	15% [9]	12% [9]
	Avoiding a high-pressure job	10% [10]	11% [10]

Table 2C.--Changes in the attributes of a job or career considered to be important

REFERENCE, SAMPLE	RESULTS				
Gaff (1965). Random sampling of male and female students at Univ. of the Pacific. Cross-sectional, Summer 1964.	Percent of students responding that each of the following is one of the three characteristics most important to them in picking a job or career				
				Fr (142)	Sr (100)
	Opportunity to be helpful to others or useful to society			56% [1]	70% [1]
	Opportunity to work with people rather than things			54% [2]	45% [3]
	Making an above average living			44% [3]	45% [4]
	Opportunity to be original and creative			40% [4]	50% [2]
	Opportunities for moderate steady progress rather than chance of extreme success or failure			24% [5]	19% [5.5]
	Freedom from supervision in my work			17% [6.5]	13% [7.5]
	Opportunity to advance an ideal or cause			17% [6.5]	10% [9]
	Living and working in the world of ideas			15% [8]	19% [5.5]
	A chance to exercise leadership			13% [9.5]	13% [7.5]
	Avoiding a high-pressure job			13% [9.5]	5% [10]
Trent (1964a). Total sampling of all male and female freshmen and random or representative sampling of male and female senior students at five West Coast Catholic colleges (in 1959-1960). Cross-sectional, freshmen at the beginning and seniors at the end of the school year.	Percent of students responding that each of the following requirements of an ideal job is "first or second most important" to them				
		Males		Females	
		Fr (505)	Sr (90)	Fr (602)	Sr (132)
	Job security	41% [1]	26%	22%	11% [3]
	Use of abilities	26% [2]	34%	24%	33% [2]
	Social contact	21% [3]	26%	46%	46% [1]
	Permits creativity	8% [4]	12%	7%	10% [4]
Rosenberg (1957). Representative sampling of male and female freshmen and sophomore students at Cornell in 1950. Longitudinal, 1950-1952.	Percent of students responding that each of the following requirements of an ideal job or career is "highly important"				
				Fr and So	Jr and Sr
	Provide an opportunity to use my special abilities or aptitudes			79% [1]	79% [1]
	Enable me to look forward to a stable, secure future			63% [2]	46% [3]
	Permit me to be creative and original			46% [3]	51% [2]
	Provide me a chance to earn a good deal of money			33% [4]	33% [4]
	Give me social status and prestige			21% [5]	22% [5]

OTHER STUDIES:

In longitudinal studies of students at eight universities--Antioch, Reed, Swarthmore, San Francisco State, Univ. of California at Berkeley, Univ. of the Pacific, St. Olaf, and Portland Univ.--in all cases, a smaller proportion of seniors than freshmen felt that the "extrinsic" occupational values of money and security were the "most important" to them in their conception of an ideal job (McConnell, Clark, Heist, Trow, and Yonge, forthcoming). At all but one of the colleges a larger percentage of seniors than freshmen endorsed "intrinsic" occupational values (opportunity to be creative, chance to use special abilities and opportunities). With respect to "people-oriented" occupational values (opportunity to work with people, opportunity to be helpful to others), students at four colleges showed small percentage increases, students at three colleges showed no change, and students at one school decreased in percentage endorsement over the college years.

Table 2D.--Summaries of studies showing changes in attitudes toward political, economic and social issues. See explanatory note for Tables 2A-2N.

REFERENCE, SAMPLE	INSTRUMENT	RESULTS	COMMENTS
Nelson (1938). Sampling of male and female students at four state universities (three of which are located in the Mid-West and one in the South); at six colleges affiliated with Lutheran Church groups (three in the Mid-West, two in the East, and one in the South); at three colleges affiliated with the Society of Friends (all in the Mid-West); at University "N," a university (west of the Mississippi) affiliated with the Methodist Church; at College "O," a college (west of the Mississippi) affiliated with the Presbyterian Church; at College "P," a college (west of the Mississippi) affiliated with the Seventh Day Adventist Church; at College "Q," a college (west of the Mississippi) affiliated with the United Brethren Church; and at College "R," a college (west of the Mississippi) affiliated with the Catholic Church. Cross-sectional, May 1936 (So, Jr and Sr) and Aug. 1936 (Fr).	Lantz C-R Opinionaire, Form K (high score = high conservatism with respect to politico-economic, social, and religious matters)	Four State Universities Fr (510): $\bar{X}$=35.86; SD=6.62 So (178): $\bar{X}$=30.87; SD=8.38 Jr (169): $\bar{X}$=31.26; SD=9.14 Sr (175): $\bar{X}$=27.78; SD=8.25	Sr are less conservative than Fr (SS). Largest difference is between Fr and So. Sr scores are more heterogeneous than Fr scores.
		Six Lutheran Colleges Fr (640): $\bar{X}$=36.08; SD=6.26 So (188): $\bar{X}$=36.04; SD=6.53 Jr (140): $\bar{X}$=32.18; SD=6.71 Sr (214): $\bar{X}$=32.71; SD=7.24	Sr are less conservative than Fr (SS). Largest difference is between So and Jr. Sr scores are more heterogeneous than Fr scores. Note that the lowest conservatism score is in the junior year.
		Three Friends Colleges Fr (190): $\bar{X}$=33.05; SD=7.11 So (82): $\bar{X}$=29.33; SD=7.51 Jr (58): $\bar{X}$=25.17; SD=7.95 Sr (57): $\bar{X}$=26.36; SD=8.17	Sr are less conservative than Fr (SS). Largest difference is between So and Jr. Sr scores are more heterogeneous than Fr scores. Note that the lowest conservatism score is in the junior year.
		Methodist University Fr (256): $\bar{X}$=33.59; SD=6.40 So (70): $\bar{X}$=32.36; SD=7.16 Jr (58): $\bar{X}$=28.19; SD=8.06 Sr (53): $\bar{X}$=28.63; SD=6.63	Sr are less conservative than Fr (SS). Largest difference is between So and Jr. Sr scores are more heterogeneous than Fr scores. Note that the lowest conservatism score is in the junior year.
		Presbyterian College Fr (204): $\bar{X}$=35.39; SD=5.98 So (20): $\bar{X}$=35.00; SD=6.02 Jr (31): $\bar{X}$=29.91; SD=7.50 Sr (29): $\bar{X}$=30.60; SD=7.24	Sr are less conservative than Fr (PNG). Largest difference is between So and Jr. Sr scores are more heterogeneous than Fr scores. Note that the lowest conservatism score is in the junior year.
		Adventist College Fr (165): $\bar{X}$=38.11; SD=5.15 Sr (18): $\bar{X}$=34.17; SD=5.55	Sr are less conservative than Fr (PNG). Sr scores are more heterogeneous than Fr scores.
		United Brethren College Fr (101): $\bar{X}$=35.17; SD=7.02 So (30): $\bar{X}$=33.00; SD=6.50 Jr (14): $\bar{X}$=29.29; SD=6.44 Sr (10): $\bar{X}$=32.00; SD=6.98	Sr are less conservative than Fr (PNG). Largest difference (in direction of decreasing conservatism) is between So and Jr. Sr scores are less heterogeneous than Fr scores. Note that the lowest conservatism is in the junior year.
		Catholic College Fr (37): $\bar{X}$=43.44; SD=4.90 So (24): $\bar{X}$=42.08; SD=6.44 Jr (21): $\bar{X}$=41.55; SD=5.26 Sr (16): $\bar{X}$=41.25; SD=5.56	Sr are less conservative than Fr (PNG). Largest difference is between So and Jr. Sr scores are more heterogeneous than Fr scores.
Boldt and Stroud (1934). Random sampling of male and female freshmen at the Kansas State Teachers College of Emporia. Cross-sectional, Fall 1933.	Harper's Test of Social Beliefs and Attitudes (high score = high liberalism with respect to politico-economic, social and religious matters)	Fr (411): $\bar{X}$=42.23; SD=7.12* So (106): $\bar{X}$=45.81; SD=8.76* Jr (98): $\bar{X}$=52.00; SD=7.69* Sr (103): $\bar{X}$=54.32; SD=6.86* * SD's calculated by the authors from the probability of the error of the mean given in original	Sr are more liberal than Fr (SS). Largest difference is between So and Jr. Sr scores are less heterogeneous than Fr scores.

Table 2D.--Changes in attitudes toward political, economic and social issues (CONTINUED)

REFERENCE, SAMPLE	INSTRUMENT	RESULTS	COMMENTS
Fay and Middleton (1939). Sampling of male and female students at De Pauw Univ. Cross-sectional, year not given.	Attitude Toward Communism Scale (Thurstone) (high score = favorable attitude toward communism)	Fr (185): $\bar{X}$=4.48; SD=1.19 So (168): $\bar{X}$=4.54; SD=1.18 Jr (108): $\bar{X}$=4.82; SD= .98 Sr (114): $\bar{X}$=5.13; SD=1.35	Sr are more favorable toward communism (more liberal)* than are Fr (SS).** Largest difference is between Jr and Sr. Sr scores are more heterogeneous than Fr scores.
	Attitude Toward Patriotism Scale (Thurstone) (high score = favorable attitude toward patriotism)	Fr (185): $\bar{X}$=6.47; SD=1.11 So (168): $\bar{X}$=6.38; SD= .96 Jr (108): $\bar{X}$=6.23; SD= .83 Sr (114): $\bar{X}$=5.93; SD= .89	Sr are less favorable toward patriotism (more liberal)* than are Fr (SS).** Largest difference is between Jr and Sr. Sr scores are less heterogeneous than Fr scores.
*As interpreted in original	Attitude Toward the U. S. Constitution Scale (Thurstone) (high score = favorable attitude toward the U.S. Constitution)	Fr (185): $\bar{X}$=6.14; SD= .88 So (169): $\bar{X}$=6.00; SD= .86 Jr (108): $\bar{X}$=5.71; SD= .64 Sr (114): $\bar{X}$=5.53; SD= .92	Sr are less favorable toward U. S. Constitution (more liberal)* than are Fr (SS).** Largest difference is between So and Jr. Sr scores are more heterogeneous than Fr scores.
**Statistical significance determined in original analysis on the differences between the median scores (not the mean scores) of Fr and Sr.	Attitude Toward Law Scale (Thurstone) (high score = favorable attitude toward law)	Fr (185): $\bar{X}$=6.30; SD= .66 So (168): $\bar{X}$=6.12; SD= .74 Jr (108): $\bar{X}$=5.98; SD= .62 Sr (114): $\bar{X}$=5.98; SD= .64	Sr are less favorable toward law (more liberal)* than are Fr (SS).** Largest difference is between Fr and So. Sr scores are less heterogeneous than Fr scores.
	Attitude Toward Censorship Scale (Thurstone) (high score = favorable attitude toward censorship)	Fr (185): $\bar{X}$=5.45; SD=1.41 So (168): $\bar{X}$=5.16; SD=1.38 Jr (108): $\bar{X}$=5.28; SD=1.38 Sr (114): $\bar{X}$=4.94; SD=1.40	Sr are less favorable toward censorship (more liberal)* than are Fr (SS).** Largest difference is between Jr and Sr. Sr scores are less heterogeneous than Fr scores.
Foster *et al*. (1961). Total sampling of entire student body (males) at Univ. of Santa Clara. Cross-sectional, September 1959.	California P.E.C. Scale (high score = high conservatism)	Fr (292): $\bar{X}$=64.2; SD=7.49 So (239): $\bar{X}$=64.3; SD=7.92 Jr (250): $\bar{X}$=64.1; SD=7.86 Sr (233): $\bar{X}$=63.0; SD=8.59	Sr are less conservative than Fr (NSS). Largest difference is between Jr and Sr. Sr scores are more heterogeneous than Fr scores. Note that the highest conservatism score is in the sophomore year.
Foster *et al*. (1961). Total sampling of entire student body (males) at Univ. of Santa Clara. Cross-sectional, May 1961.	California P.E.C. Scale (high score = high conservatism)	Fr (337): $\bar{X}$=64.6; SD=7.21 So (235): $\bar{X}$=61.9; SD=7.77 Jr (197): $\bar{X}$=62.8; SD=9.01 Sr (210): $\bar{X}$=62.3; SD=8.18	Sr are less conservative than Fr (SS). Largest difference is between Fr and So. Sr scores are more heterogeneous than Fr scores. Note that the lowest conservatism score is in the sophomore year.
	McClosky Classical Conservatism Scale (high score = high conservatism)	Fr (336): $\bar{X}$=3.8; SD=1.94 So (235): $\bar{X}$=3.5; SD=1.83 Jr (198): $\bar{X}$=3.3; SD=1.77 Sr (210): $\bar{X}$=3.7; SD=1.85	Sr are less conservative than Fr (NSS). Largest difference is between Fr and So. Sr scores are less heterogeneous than Fr scores. Note that the lowest conservatism score is in the junior year.
Newcomb (1943). Total sampling of female students at Bennington College. Cross-sectional, Fall 1935, Fall 1936, Fall 1937, Spring 1938, Fall 1938, and Spring 1939. (Samples are combined in analysis.)	Political and Economic Progressivism Scale (high score = high conservatism on politico-economic matters)	Fr (276): $\bar{X}$=74.2; SD=12.9* So (241): $\bar{X}$=69.4; SD=12.6* Jr (166): $\bar{X}$=65.9; SD=12.7* Sr (155): $\bar{X}$=62.4; SD=11.2* *SD's are based on somewhat smaller N's than are the means. See Table 49, p. 206, in the original.	Sr are less conservative than Fr (SS). Largest difference is between Fr and So.** Sr scores are less heterogeneous than Fr scores. **Considering the six samples separately, the Fr-So difference is the largest for three of the six samples. For two samples, the So-Jr difference is the largest one. While for one sample, the Jr-Sr is the largest difference.
Flacks (1963). Total sampling of entire student body (females) at Bennington. Cross-sectional, Fall 1959.	Liberalism Scale (derived from earlier measures by McClosky) from an early form of the Omnibus Personality Inventory (high score = high liberalism, favorability to change)	Fr: $\bar{X}$=56.6 So: $\bar{X}$=58.3 Jr: $\bar{X}$=58.8 Sr: $\bar{X}$=61.4	Sr are more liberal (more favorable to change) than Fr (SS). Largest difference is between Jr and Sr.

Table 2D.--Changes in attitudes toward political, economic and social issues (CONTINUED)

REFERENCE, SAMPLE	INSTRUMENT	RESULTS	COMMENTS
Droba (1931b). Sampling of male and female students at Univ. of Chicago. Cross-sectional, year not given.	Droba's Scale of Militarism-Pacifism (high score = high pacifism)	Fr (8): $\bar{X}$=11.23; SD=2.02 So (136): $\bar{X}$=11.32; SD=2.35 Jr (96): $\bar{X}$=11.56; SD=2.05 Sr (66): $\bar{X}$=11.93; SD=2.30	Sr are more pacifistic than Fr (PNG). Largest difference is between Jr and Sr. Sr scores are more heterogeneous than Fr scores.
Droba (1931a). Sampling of students at Univ. of Chicago. Cross-sectional, Fall 1928.	Droba's Scale of Militarism-Pacifism (high score = high pacifism)	Fr (289): $\bar{X}$=11.43; SD=1.98 So (240: $\bar{X}$=11.65; SD=2.09 Jr (145): $\bar{X}$=11.80; SD=1.95 Sr (52): $\bar{X}$=11.52; SD=1.98	Sr are more pacifistic than Fr (NSS). Largest difference (in direction of increasing pacifism) is between Fr and So. Sr scores equal Fr scores in hetereogeneity. Note that the highest pacifism score is in the junior year.
Ericksen (1944). Sampling of male and female students at Univ. of Arkansas. Cross-sectional, May 1942.	Thurstone-Peterson's Attitude Toward War Scale (low score = unfavorable attitude toward war)	Fr (63): $\bar{X}$=5.05; SD=1.37 So (54): $\bar{X}$=4.42; SD=1.17 Jr (51): $\bar{X}$=4.17; SD=1.13 Sr (42): $\bar{X}$=4.01; SD= .73	Sr have a less favorable attitude toward war (NSS). Largest difference is between Fr and So. Sr scores are less heterogeneous than Fr scores.
Moore and Garrison (1932). Sampling of students at North Carolina State College. Cross-sectional, year not given.	Vetter's Measurement of Social and Political Attitudes	Percent selecting liberal or radical alternatives Fr (49) = 34.1% So (62) = 40.0% Jr (68) = 46.3% Sr (31) = 47.8%	Sr are more likely to be liberal or radical with respect to social and political attitudes than are Fr (PNG). Largest difference is between So and Jr.
Norman Miller (1958). Sampling of male students at eleven colleges (Dartmouth, Yale, Harvard, Wesleyan, Cornell, Fisk, Univ. of North Carolina, Univ. of Michigan, Univ. of Texas, UCLA, and Wayne State Univ.) Cross-sectional, April-May 1952.	Civil Rights Score (an index of attitude toward civil rights with scores divided to make a pro- and anti-civil rights category)	Percent scoring as pro-civil rights Fr (1103) = 38% So (1040) = 45% Jr (1181) = 47% Sr (1116) = 52%	Sr are more likely to be pro-civil rights than are Fr (PNG). Largest difference is between Fr and So.
	Labor Score (an index of attitudes toward labor with scores divided to make a pro- and an anti-labor category)	Percent scoring as pro-labor Fr (1103) = 34% So (1040) = 38% Jr (1181) = 40% Sr (1116) = 44%	Sr are more likely to be pro-labor than are Fr (PNG). The Fr-So and the Jr-Sr differences are tied for being the largest difference between contiguous class levels.
	Political-economic Score (an index of orientation toward political-economic matter with scores divided to make a liberal and a conservative category)	Percent scoring as liberal Fr (1103) = 27% So (1040) = 29% Jr (1181) = 32% Sr (1116) = 35%	Sr are more likely to be liberal with respect to political-economic matter than are Fr (PNG). The So-Jr and Jr-Sr differences are tied for being the largest difference between contiguous class levels.
Selvin and Hagstrom (1960). Sampling of male and female students at the Univ. of California, Berkeley. Cross-sectional, December 1957.	Selvin and Hagstrom's Libertarianism Index (high score = high libertarianism, high support for the Bill of Rights)	Percent scoring as highly libertarian Fr (131) = 21% So (226) = 29% Jr (216) = 34% Sr (266) = 40%	Sr are more likely to be highly libertarian (more supportive of the Bill of Rights) than are Fr (PNG). Largest difference is between Fr and So.

Table 2D.--Changes in attitudes toward political, economic and social issues (CONTINUED)

REFERENCE, SAMPLE	INSTRUMENT	RESULTS	COMMENTS
Finney (forthcoming). Total sampling of entering male students at the Univ. of California at Berkeley. Longitudinal, Fall 1959-Spring 1963. Analysis is for the 792 freshmen who were still at the college in the spring of 1961 and for a sample of these students (N=159) in the college in the spring of 1963.)	5-item Libertarianism Index constructed by Finney (high score = high social or civil liberalism)	Percent scoring as highly libertarian Fr (792) = 10% So (792) = 19% Sr (159) = 34%	Sr are more likely to be highly libertarian (higher in social or civil liberalism) than are Fr (PNG).
Hunter (1942a). Total sampling of entering freshmen at a small, southern liberal arts college for women in 1934, 1935, 1936, and 1937. Longitudinal, 1934-1938, 1935-1939, 1936-1940, and 1937-1941. (Samples are combined in analysis.)	Hunter Test of Attitudes--War Subscale (positive score = liberalism)	Fr (185): $\bar{X}$= -0.40; SD=8.06 Sr (185): $\bar{X}$= +0.98; SD=7.72	Sr are less favorable to war (more liberal) than are Fr (SS). Sr scores are less heterogeneous than Fr scores.
	Hunter Test of Attitudes--Economics and Labor Subscale (positive score = liberalism)	Fr (185): $\bar{X}$= +0.13; SD=7.17 Sr (185): $\bar{X}$= +1.99; SD=6.89	Sr are more liberal with respect to attitudes toward economics and labor than are Fr (SS). Sr scores are less heterogeneous than Fr scores.
	Hunter Test of Attitudes--Social Life and Convention Subscale (positive score = liberalism)	Fr (185): $\bar{X}$= +1.38; SD=4.97 Sr (185): $\bar{X}$= +2.61; SD=4.35	Sr are more liberal with respect to attitudes toward social life and convention than are Fr (SS). Sr scores are less heterogeneous than Fr scores.
	Hunter Test of Attitudes--Government Subscale (positive score = liberalism)	Fr (185): $\bar{X}$= -4.23; SD=4.25 Sr (185): $\bar{X}$= -2.48; SD=4.86	Sr are more liberal with respect to attitudes toward the government than are Fr (SS). Sr scores are more heterogeneous than Fr scores.
Jones (1938a, 1938b). Total sampling of entire freshman classes (males) of 1930 and 1931 at College X, a "rather small New England liberal arts college for men." Longitudinal, 1930-1934 and 1931-1935. (Samples are combined in analysis.)	Droba's Attitude Toward War Scale, No. 2, Form A--ed. by Thurstone (high score = unfavorable attitude toward war)	Fr (77): $\bar{X}$=6.53; SD= .89 Sr (77): $\bar{X}$=7.20; SD=1.11	Sr are less favorable toward war (more pacifistic) than are Fr (SS). Sr scores are more heterogeneous than Fr scores.
Bugelski and Lester (1940). Representative sampling of graduating male and female seniors (1931, 1933 and 1934) in the College of Arts and Sciences and the School of Business Administration at Univ. of Buffalo. Longitudinal, 1927-1931, 1929-1933, and 1930-1934. (Samples are combined in analysis.)	Opinion Test, consisting of items formulated by E.S. Jones (high score = high liberalism with repect to politico-economic, social and religious matters)	Males Fr (124): $\bar{X}$=65.58; SD=11.2 Sr (124): $\bar{X}$=84.49; SD=10.4 Females Fr (97): $\bar{X}$=64.70; SD=11.4 Sr (97): X=88.10; SD= 9.3	For each sex, Sr are more liberal than Fr (SS). Sr scores* are less heterogeneous than Fr scores. *These results are similar to those for each of the six samples taken separately, with one exception. The male Sr graduating in 1933 were more heterogeneous than they were as Fr.

Table 2D. -Changes in attitudes toward political, economic and social issues (CONTINUED)

REFERENCE, SAMPLE	INSTRUMENT	RESULTS	COMMENTS
Sowards (1934). Sampling of male and female freshmen and seniors at Kansas State Teachers College at Pittsburgh, Kansas. Cross-sectional, May 1933.	Thurstone's Attitude Toward War Test, Form A (high score = unfavorable attitude toward war)	Fr (179): $\bar{X}$=6.64; SD=2.11 Sr (106): $\bar{X}$=6.76; SD=1.94	Sr are less favorable toward war (more pacifistic) than are Fr (NSS). Sr scores are less heterogeneous than Fr scores.
Farnsworth (1937). Sampling of male freshmen at Stanford in the fall of 1932. Longitudinal, Fall 1932-Fall 1936.	Peterson's Attitude Toward War Scale, Forms A and B (high score = favorable attitude toward war)	Fr (50): $\bar{X}$=3.72 Sr (50): $\bar{X}$=3.43	Sr have less favorable attitude toward war (more pacifistic) than are Fr (SS).* * $p < .05$. In original, difference was reported as not significant because a more stringent probability level was used.
Peterson (1965b). Sampling of male and female students at 16 colleges (Appalachian State Teachers College, Bellarmine College, Brown Univ., Pembroke College, C.I.T., Clarkson College, East Carolina College, Flint Junior College, Fordham Univ., Georgia Southern College, Kutztown State College, Orange Coast College, Pomona College, Univ. of Connecticut, Univ. of Delaware, and Whitman College. Cross-sectional, Spring 1963.	Liberalism Scale from the ETS College Student Questionnaire (high score = high political-economic-social liberalism)	Fr (327): $\bar{X}$=25.9 Sr (121): $\bar{X}$=27.0	Sr are more liberal than Fr (SS).
McConnell, Clark, Heist, Trow, and Yonge (forthcoming). Sampling of male and female freshmen at Antioch, Reed, Swarthmore, San Francisco State, Univ. of Calif. at Berkeley, Univ. of the Pacific, St. Olaf, and Univ. of Portland. Longitudinal; first school, 1958-1963; next three schools, 1958-1962; last four schools, 1959-1963.	Index of Civil Libertarianism (high libertarianism = tending to not want the exclusion of past or present communists from teaching; disapproval of legislative investigation of political beliefs of academic personnel)	<u>Percent scoring as high in civil libertarianism</u> Antioch Fr = 32% Sr = 58% Reed Fr = 47% Sr = 70% Swarthmore Fr = 32% Sr = 59% San Francisco State Fr = 5% Sr = 22% Berkeley Fr = 14% Sr = 31% Univ. of the Pacific Fr = 6% Sr = 13% St. Olaf Fr = 6% Sr = 18% Univ. of Portland Fr = 1% Sr = 3%	In all cases, but in varying degrees, Sr are more likely than Fr to be high in civil libertarianism.

Table 2D.--Changes in attitudes toward political, economic and social issues (CONTINUED)

OTHER STUDIES:

Goldsen, Rosenberg, Williams, and Suchman (1960) present cross-sectional data for male students at ten colleges and universities with respect to the philosophy of government held by these students (see Table 5-9 and Appendix 16). They found that for most of these colleges, seniors were more likely than freshmen to accept statements reflecting a laissez-faire philosophy of government. This is interpreted as showing increases in conservatism. McClintock and Turner (1962) sampled freshman and senior students at 10 colleges in Southern California. For both males and females, there was no statistically significant difference between the two class levels on an index of attitudes toward Federal power nor on an overall index of political liberalism-conservatism. (Direction of trends, if any, was not given.) For females, there also was no statistically significant difference between freshmen and seniors on an index of attitudes toward civil rights. Male seniors, however, were more liberal with respect to civil rights than were male freshmen (SS).

There are a number of investigations that cross-sectionally compare students at different class levels on a variety of questionnaire items dealing with political, economic and social issues: Brameld (1934); Garrison and Mann (1931); Jones (1926); McConnell (1962a); Rose (1964); Willoughby (1930); and Wilner and Fearing (1950-51). In these studies, the items are not combined into indices but are analyzed separately. While results are not absolutely consistent across items and across studies, in each study seniors are somewhat more liberal than freshmen on most items. In a longitudinal study of National Merit Scholars, Webster, Freedman and Heist (1962) report that as juniors these students were more liberal than they were as freshmen with respect to government provision of medical and dental care for citizens.

Other longitudinal analyses compare scores of students early in their freshman year and one to two years later on various measures of liberality. Results of these studies are not always consistent. Hassenger (1965, 1966) writes that sophomore students at a Catholic women's college in a midwestern city were more "libertarian" (on Selvin and Hagstrom's Bill of Rights Scale) than they were as freshmen (SS). Using a sample of female students at the University of Wisconsin, Corey (1940) found that students scored more liberally as sophomores than as freshmen on scales measuring attitudes toward communism, patriotism and war. Only in the first attitudinal area, however, were differences statistically significant. In another study, while women at a southern women's college were more liberal at the end of their freshman year than at the beginning with respect to issues involving law and war, they were less liberal with respect to issues involving the Constitution (Barkley, 1942b). Finally, Blau (1953) did not find that Cornell undergraduates became, in general, less war-minded over a two-year period. Moreover, there was a trend during these years away from considering world government as an important factor in preventing "another great war." (Also, see Goldsen, Rosenberg, Williams, and Suchman, 1960.)

Table 2E.--Summaries of studies showing changes in religious orientation. See explanatory note for Tables 2A-2N.

REFERENCE, SAMPLE	INSTRUMENT	RESULTS	COMMENTS
Nelson (1940). Sampling of male and female students at four state universities (three of which are located in the Mid-West and one in the South); at six colleges affiliated with Lutheran Church groups (three in the Mid-West, two in the East, and one in the South); at three colleges affiliated with the Society of Friends (all in the Mid-West); at University "N," a university (west of the Mississippi) affiliated with the Methodist Church; at College "O," a college (west of the Mississippi) affiliated with the Presbyterian Church; at College "P," a college (west of the Mississippi) affiliated with the Seventh Day Adventist Church; at College "Q," a college (west of the Mississippi) affiliated with the United Brethren Church; and at College "R," a college (west of the Mississippi) affiliated with the Catholic Church.	Thurstone-Chave's Attitude Toward the Church Scale (high score = favorable attitude toward the church [Nelson uses a reversed scoring])	Four State Universities Fr (512): $\bar{X}$=8.75; SD=1.20 So (178): $\bar{X}$=8.36; SD=1.40 Jr (167): $\bar{X}$=8.38; SD=1.48 Sr (174): $\bar{X}$=8.20; SD=1.65	Sr are less favorable toward the church than are Fr (SS). Largest difference is between Fr and So. Sr scores are more heterogeneous than Fr scores.
		Six Lutheran Colleges Fr (617): $\bar{X}$=9.07; SD= .96 So (186): $\bar{X}$=8.87; SD= .95 Jr (139): $\bar{X}$=9.06; SD= .78 Sr (214): $\bar{X}$=8.94; SD= .98	Sr are less favorable toward the church than are Fr (NSS). Largest difference is between Fr and So. Sr scores are more heterogeneous than Fr scores. Note that the least favorable score is in the sophomore year.
		Three Friends Colleges Fr (190): $\bar{X}$=8.77; SD=1.04 So (81): $\bar{X}$=9.02; SD= .88 Jr (58): $\bar{X}$=8.41; SD=1.39 Fr (57): $\bar{X}$=8.50; SD=1.46	Sr are less favorable toward the church than are Fr (NSS). Largest difference is between So and Jr. Sr scores are more heterogeneous than Fr scores. Note that the least favorable score is in the junior year, and the most favorable in the sophomore year.
		Methodist University Fr: $\bar{X}$=8.89; SD=1.10 So: $\bar{X}$=9.10; SD= .92 Jr: $\bar{X}$=8.56; SD=1.05 Sr: $\bar{X}$=8.82; SD= .86	Sr are less favorable toward the church than are Fr (NSS). Largest difference is between So and Jr. Sr scores are less heterogeneous than Fr scores. Note that the least favorable score is in the junior year, and the most favorable in the sophomore year.
		Presbyterian College Fr: $\bar{X}$=8.93; SD= .87 So: $\bar{X}$=8.83; SD=1.44 Jr: $\bar{X}$=8.96; SD=1.12 Sr: $\bar{X}$=9.28; SD= .42	Sr are more favorable toward the church than are Fr (PNG). Largest difference (in increasing favorableness) is between Jr and Sr. Sr scores are less heterogeneous than Fr scores. Note that the least favorable score is in the sophomore year.
		Adventist College Fr: $\bar{X}$=9.34; SD= .84 Sr: $\bar{X}$=9.32; SD= .78	Sr are less favorable toward the church than are Fr (PNG). Sr scores are less heterogeneous than Fr scores.
		United Brethren College Fr: $\bar{X}$=9.20; SD= .78 So: $\bar{X}$=8.97; SD=1.18 Jr: $\bar{X}$=9.07; SD= .73 Sr: $\bar{X}$=8.70; SD=1.17	Sr are less favorable toward the church than are Fr (PNG). Largest difference is between Jr and Sr. Sr scores are more heterogeneous than Fr scores.
		Catholic College Fr: $\bar{X}$= 9.85; SD= .74 So: $\bar{X}$= 9.96; SD= .71 Jr: $\bar{X}$=10.12; SD= .58 Sr: $\bar{X}$=10.13; SD= .48	Sr are more favorable toward the church than are Fr (PNG). Largest difference (in increasing favorableness) is between So and Jr. Sr scores are less favorable than Fr scores.
Cross-sectional, May 1936 (So, Jr and Sr) and August 1936 (Fr).	Thurstone-Chave's Attitude Toward the Reality of God Scale (high score = favorable attitude toward or belief in the reality of God)	Four State Universities Fr (498): $\bar{X}$=7.79; SD=1.35 So (175): $\bar{X}$=7.44; SD=1.48 Jr (167): $\bar{X}$=7.50; SD=1.55 Sr (633): $\bar{X}$=7.28; SD=1.62	Sr have a less favorable attitude toward (less belief in) the reality of God than do Fr (SS). Largest difference is between Fr and So. Sr scores are more heterogeneous than Fr scores.
		Six Lutheran Colleges Fr (663): $\bar{X}$=7.99; SD=1.34 So (184): $\bar{X}$=8.01; SD=1.42 Jr (137): $\bar{X}$=8.24; SD=1.18 Sr (214): $\bar{X}$=8.09; SD= .99	Sr have a more favorable attitude toward (more belief in) the reality of God than do Fr (NSS). Largest difference (in increasing belief) is between So and Jr. Sr scores are less heterogeneous than Fr scores. Note that the most favorable score is in the junior year.
		Three Friends Colleges Fr (188): $\bar{X}$=8.05; SD=1.30 So (81): $\bar{X}$=8.02; SD=1.29 Jr (58): $\bar{X}$=7.93; SD=1.45 Sr (56): $\bar{X}$=7.84; SD=1.55	Sr have a less favorable attitude toward (less belief in) the reality of God than do Fr (NSS). The So-Jr and the Jr-Sr differences are tied for being the largest difference. Sr scores are more heterogeneous than Fr scores.
		Methodist University Fr: $\bar{X}$=7.98; SD=1.20 So: $\bar{X}$=7.80; SD=1.27 Jr: $\bar{X}$=7.72; SD=1.38 Sr: $\bar{X}$=7.76; SD=1.07	Sr have a less favorable attitude toward (less belief in) the reality of God than do Fr (NSS). The largest difference is between Fr and So. Sr scores are less heterogeneous than Fr scores. Note that the least favorable score is in the junior year.
		Presbyterian College Fr: $\bar{X}$=7.99; SD=1.23 So: $\bar{X}$=7.88; SD= .70 Jr: $\bar{X}$=8.58; SD= .64 Sr: $\bar{X}$=7.77; SD= .96	Sr have a less favorable attitude toward (less belief in) the reality of God than do Fr (PNG). The largest difference is between Jr and Sr. Sr scores are less heterogeneous than Fr scores. Note that the most favorable score is in the junior year.

Table 2E.--Changes in religious orientation (CONTINUED)

REFERENCE, SAMPLE	INSTRUMENT	RESULTS	COMMENTS
Nelson (continued).	Thurstone-Chave's Attitude Toward the Reality of God Scale (continued)	Adventist College Fr: $\bar{X}$=8.58; SD=1.05 Sr: $\bar{X}$=8.57; SD=1.06	Sr have a less favorable attitude toward (less belief in) the reality of God than do Fr (PNG). Sr scores are more heterogeneous than Fr scores.
		United Brethren College Fr: $\bar{X}$=7.99; SD=1.37 So: $\bar{X}$=8.03; SD=1.36 Jr: $\bar{X}$=7.71; SD=1.52 Sr: $\bar{X}$=7.30; SD=2.07	Sr have a less favorable attitude toward (less belief in) the reality of God than do Fr (PNG). Largest difference is between Jr and Sr. Sr scores are more heterogeneous than Fr scores. Note that the most favorable score is in the sophomore year.
		Catholic College Fr: $\bar{X}$=8.77; SD=1.00 So: $\bar{X}$=8.96; SD= .64 Jr: $\bar{X}$=8.45; SD=1.07 Sr: $\bar{X}$=8.69; SD= .63	Sr have a less favorable attitude toward (less belief in) the reality of God than do Fr (PNG). Largest difference is between So and Jr. Sr scores are less heterogeneous than Fr scores. Note that the least favorable score is in the junior year, and the most favorable is in the sophomore year.
	Thurstone-Chave's Attitude Toward God as an Influence on Conduct Scale (high score = favorable attitude toward or belief in God having an influence on one's own conduct [Nelson uses a reversed scoring])	Four State Universities Fr (471): $\bar{X}$=7.65; SD=1.92 So (167): $\bar{X}$=7.08; SD=2.19 Jr (165): $\bar{X}$=7.25; SD=2.19 Sr (167): $\bar{X}$=7.17; SD=2.22	Sr have a less favorable attitude toward (less belief in) God having an influence on their conduct than do Fr (SS). Largest difference is between Fr and So. Sr scores are more heterogeneous than Fr scores. Note that the least favorable score is in the sophomore year.
		Six Lutheran Colleges Fr (625): $\bar{X}$=8.40; SD=1.58 So (181): $\bar{X}$=8.38; SD=1.52 Jr (138): $\bar{X}$=8.41; SD=1.57 Sr (213): $\bar{X}$=8.03; SD=1.74	Sr have a less favorable attitude toward (less belief in) God having an influence on their conduct than do Fr (SS). Largest difference is between Jr and Sr. Sr scores are more heterogeneous than Fr scores. Note that the most favorable score is in the junior year.
		Three Friends Colleges Fr (187): $\bar{X}$=8.17; SD=1.89 So (81): $\bar{X}$=8.18; SD=1.68 Jr (58): $\bar{X}$=7.64; SD=2.13 Sr (56): $\bar{X}$=8.43; SD=1.65	Sr have a more favorable attitude toward (more belief in) God having an influence on their conduct than do Fr (NSS). Largest difference is between Jr and Sr. Sr scores are less heterogeneous than Fr scores. Note that the least favorable score is in the junior year.
		Methodist University Fr: $\bar{X}$=8.09; SD=1.64 So: $\bar{X}$=8.34; SD=1.53 Jr: $\bar{X}$=7.66; SD=1.67 Sr: $\bar{X}$=7.88; SD=1.70	Sr have a less favorable attitude toward (less belief in) God having an influence on their conduct than do Fr (NSS). Largest difference is between So and Jr. Sr scores are more heterogeneous than Fr scores. Note that the least favorable score is in the junior year, and the most favorable in the sophomore year.
		Presbyterian College Fr: $\bar{X}$=8.05; SD=1.81 So: $\bar{X}$=8.00; SD=1.71 Jr: $\bar{X}$=9.50; SD=1.26 Sr: $\bar{X}$=8.63; SD=1.53	Sr have a more favorable attitude toward (more belief in) God having an influence on their conduct than do Fr (PNG). Largest difference is between So and Jr. Sr scores are less heterogeneous than Fr. Note that the most favorable score is in the junior year, and the least favorable in the sophomore year.
		Adventist College Fr: $\bar{X}$=9.19; SD=1.16 Sr: $\bar{X}$=9.57; SD=1.10	Sr have a more favorable attitude toward (more belief in) God having an influence on their conduct than do Fr (PNG). Sr scores are less heterogeneous than Fr scores.
		United Brethren College Fr: $\bar{X}$=8.59; SD=1.37 So: $\bar{X}$=8.00; SD=1.84 Jr: $\bar{X}$=8.42; SD=1.77 Sr: $\bar{X}$=7.60; SD=1.76	Sr have a less favorable attitude toward (less belief in) God having an influence on their conduct than do Fr (PNG). Largest difference is between Jr and Sr. Sr scores are more heterogeneous than Fr scores.
		Catholic College Fr: $\bar{X}$=9.28; SD= .74 So: $\bar{X}$=9.33; SD= .90 Jr: $\bar{X}$=9.20; SD= .95 Sr: $\bar{X}$=9.10; SD= .94	Sr have a less favorable attitude toward (less belief in) God having an influence on their conduct than do Fr (PNG). Largest difference is between So and Jr. Sr scores are more heterogeneous than Fr scores. Note that the most favorable score is in the sophomore year.

Table 2E.--Changes in religious orientation (CONTINUED)

REFERENCE, SAMPLE	INSTRUMENT	RESULTS	COMMENTS
Nelson (continued).	Wang-Thurstone's Scale for Attitude Toward Sunday Observance (high score = favorable attitude toward Sunday observance)	<u>Four State Universities</u> Fr (512): $\bar{X}$=5.29; SD=1.47 So (178): $\bar{X}$=4.73; SD=1.26 Jr (168): $\bar{X}$=5.06; SD=1.56 Sr (175): $\bar{X}$=4.89; SD=1.45	Sr are less favorable toward Sunday observance than are Fr (SS). Largest difference is between Fr and So. Sr scores are less heterogeneous than Fr scores. Note that the least favorable score is in the So year.
		<u>Six Lutheran Colleges</u> Fr (638): $\bar{X}$=6.09; SD=1.50 So (186): $\bar{X}$=6.31; SD=1.49 Jr (140): $\bar{X}$=6.42; SD=1.52 Sr (214): $\bar{X}$=5.84; SD=1.61	Sr are less favorable toward Sunday observance than are Fr (SS). Largest difference is between Jr and Sr. Sr scores are more heterogeneous than Fr scores. Note that the most favorable score is in the junior year.
		<u>Three Friends Colleges</u> Fr (190): $\bar{X}$=5.88; SD=1.48 So (82): $\bar{X}$=5.87; SD=1.43 Jr (58): $\bar{X}$=5.59; SD=1.62 Sr (57): $\bar{X}$=6.13; SD=1.41	Sr are more favorable toward Sunday observance than are Fr (NSS). Largest difference (in direction of increasing favorableness) is between Jr and Sr. Sr scores are less heterogeneous than Fr scores. Note that the least favorable score is in the junior year.
		<u>Methodist University</u> Fr: $\bar{X}$=5.98; SD=1.51 So: $\bar{X}$=5.93; SD=1.31 Jr: $\bar{X}$=5.35; SD=1.54 Sr: $\bar{X}$=5.39; SD=1.42	Sr are less favorable toward Sunday observance than are Fr (SS). Largest difference is between So and Jr. Sr scores are less heterogeneous than Fr. Note that the least favorable score is in the junior year.
		<u>Presbyterian College</u> Fr: $\bar{X}$=5.59; SD=1.49 So: $\bar{X}$=6.18; SD=1.03 Jr: $\bar{X}$=6.47; SD=1.51 Sr: $\bar{X}$=5.58; SD=1.45	Sr are less favorable toward Sunday observance than are Fr (PNG). Largest difference (in direction of decreasing favorableness) is between Jr and Sr. Largest difference (in direction of increasing favorableness) is between Fr and So. Sr scores are less heterogeneous than Fr scores. Note that the most favorable score is in the junior year.
		<u>Adventist College</u> Fr: $\bar{X}$=6.46; SD=1.32 Sr: $\bar{X}$=6.44; SD=1.47	Sr are less favorable toward Sunday observance than are Fr (PNG). Sr scores are more heterogeneous than Fr scores.
		<u>United Brethren College</u> Fr: $\bar{X}$=6.33; SD=1.43 So: $\bar{X}$=6.07; SD=1.50 Jr: $\bar{X}$=6.14; SD=1.39 Sr: $\bar{X}$=5.70; SD=1.40	Sr are less favorable toward Sunday observance than are Fr (PNG). Largest difference is between Jr and Sr. Sr scores are less heterogeneous than Fr scores.
		<u>Catholic College</u> Fr: $\bar{X}$=5.91; SD=1.36 So: $\bar{X}$=6.38; SD= .97 Jr: $\bar{X}$=6.31; SD=1.56 Sr: $\bar{X}$=6.25; SD=1.35	Sr are more favorable toward Sunday observance than are Fr (PNG). Largest difference is between Fr and So. Sr scores are less heterogeneous than Fr scores. Note that the most favorable score is in the sophomore year.
Gilliland (1940). Sampling of students at Northwestern Univ. Cross-sectional, year not given.	Thurstone-Chave's Attitude Toward the Church Scale (high score = unfavorable attitude toward the church)	Fr (59): $\bar{X}$=4.4; SD=1.79 So (158): $\bar{X}$=4.3; SD=1.91 Jr (76): $\bar{X}$=4.6; SD=2.03 Sr (56): $\bar{X}$=5.1; SD=2.15	Sr are less favorable in attitude toward the church than are Fr (NSS). Largest difference is between Jr and Sr. Sr scores are more heterogeneous than Fr scores. Note that the most favorable attitude is in the sophomore year.
	Thurstone-Chave's Attitude Toward the Reality of God Scale (high score = favorable attitude toward or belief in the reality of God)	Fr (59): $\bar{X}$=6.3; SD=2.07 So (158): $\bar{X}$=6.8; SD=1.62 Jr (76): $\bar{X}$=6.2; SD=2.02 Sr (56): $\bar{X}$=6.4; SD=1.74	Sr have a more favorable attitude toward (more belief in) the reality of God than do Fr (NSS). Largest difference in increasing favorableness is between Fr and So; largest difference in decreasing favorableness is between So and Jr. Sr scores are less heterogeneous than Fr scores. Note that the most favorable attitude is in the sophomore year, and the least favorable in the junior year.
	Thurstone-Chave's Attitude Toward God as an Influence on Conduct Scale (high score = unfavorable attitude toward or disbelief in God having an influence on one's own conduct)	Fr (59): $\bar{X}$=4.4; SD=2.32 So (158): $\bar{X}$=4.4; SD=2.13 Jr (76): $\bar{X}$=5.3; SD=2.52 Sr (56): $\bar{X}$=5.1; SD=1.89	Sr have a less favorable attitude toward (less belief in) God having an influence on their conduct than do Fr (NSS). Largest difference is between So and Jr. Sr scores are less heterogeneous than Fr scores. Note that the least favorable attitude is in the junior year.

Table 2E.--Changes in religious orientation (CONTINUED)

REFERENCE, SAMPLE	INSTRUMENT	RESULTS	COMMENTS
Gilliland (1940). Sampling of male and female students at Northwestern Univ. Cross-sectional, year not given.	Thurstone-Chave's Attitude Toward the Reality of God Scale (high score = favorable attitude toward or belief in the reality of God)	Fr (150): $\bar{X}$=6.75; SD=1.64 So (197): $\bar{X}$=6.67; SD=1.71 Jr (66): $\bar{X}$=6.63; SD=1.79 Sr (36): $\bar{X}$=6.26; SD=2.06	Sr have a less favorable attitude toward (less belief in) the reality of God than do Fr (PNG). Largest difference is between Jr and Sr. Sr scores are more heterogeneous than Fr scores.
Thurstone and Chave (1929). Sampling of male and female students at Univ. of Chicago. Cross-sectional, year not given.	Thurstone-Chave's Attitude Toward the Church Scale (high score = unfavorable attitude toward the church)	Fr (548): $\bar{X}$=4.42; SD=2.07 So (127): $\bar{X}$=5.04; SD=1.93 Jr (107): $\bar{X}$=4.57; SD=2.02 Sr (107): $\bar{X}$=4.78; SD=1.93	Sr are less favorable toward the church than are Fr (PNG). Largest difference is between Fr and So. Sr scores are less heterogeneous than Fr scores. Note that the least favorable score is in the sophomore year.
Brown and Lowe (1951). Sampling of Protestant male and female students at Univ. of Denver. Cross-sectional, Spring 1948.	Brown and Lowe's Inventory of Religious Belief (high score = acceptance of Christian dogma)	Fr (236): $\bar{X}$=49.95; SD=11.58 So (239): $\bar{X}$=46.56; SD=11.49 Jr (101): $\bar{X}$=43.11; SD=13.56 Sr (37): $\bar{X}$=43.38; SD=14.70	Sr are less accepting of Christian dogma than are Fr (SS). Largest difference is between So and Jr. Sr scores are more heterogeneous than Fr scores. Note that the score of lowest acceptance is in the junior year.
Flacks (1963). Total sampling of entire student body (females) at Bennington College. Cross-sectional, Fall 1959.	Atheism-Agnosticism Scale from an early form of the Omnibus Personality Inventory (high score = high religious liberalism, skepticism or rejection of orthodox or fundamentalistic religious beliefs)	Fr: $\bar{X}$=33.4 So: $\bar{X}$=36.6 Jr: $\bar{X}$=35.9 Sr: $\bar{X}$=35.4	Sr are more religiously liberal (more skeptical of religious orthodoxy and fundamentalism) than Fr (NSS). Largest difference is between Fr and So. Note that most liberal score is in the sophomore year.
Burchard (1964). Sampling of male and female students at Northern Illinois Univ. Cross-sectional, Spring 1962.	Burchard's Fundamentalism Scale (low score = religious fundamentalism)	Fr (612): $\bar{X}$=2.748 So (213): $\bar{X}$=2.771 Jr (189): $\bar{X}$=2.874 Sr (178): $\bar{X}$=3.024	Sr are less fundamentalistic religiously than are Fr (SS). Largest difference is between Jr and Sr.
Young, Dustin and Holtzman (1966). Random sampling of male and female students at Univ. of Texas. Cross-sectional, Spring 1958 and Spring 1964	R Scale (high score = positive attitude toward organized religion)	Spring 1958 Fr (128): $\bar{X}$=65.2 So (100): $\bar{X}$=64.0 Jr (104): $\bar{X}$=62.7 Sr (120): $\bar{X}$=59.4 Spring 1964 Fr (146): $\bar{X}$=57.1 So (122): $\bar{X}$=53.8 Jr (139): $\bar{X}$=55.9 Sr (131): $\bar{X}$=54.4	For the sample of 1958, Sr have a less positive attitude toward organized religion than do Fr (SS). Largest difference is between Jr and Sr. For the sample of 1964, Sr have a less positive attitude toward organized religion than do Fr (NSS). Largest difference is between Fr and So. Note that the least favorable attitude is in the sophomore year.

Table 2E.--Changes in religious orientation (CONTINUED)

REFERENCE, SAMPLE	INSTRUMENT	RESULTS	COMMENTS
Jones (1938a, 1938b). Total sampling of entire freshman classes (males) of 1930 and 1931 at College X, a "rather small New England liberal arts college for men." Longitudinal, 1930-1934 and 1931-1935. (Samples are combined in analysis.)	Thurstone-Chave's Attitude Toward the Church Scale (high score = unfavorable attitude toward the church)	Fr (77): X̄=3.97; SD=2.12 Sr (77): X̄=5.12; SD=2.28	Sr are less favorable toward the church than are Fr (SS). Sr scores are more heterogeneous than Fr scores.
	Thurstone-Chave's Attitude Toward the Reality of God Scale (high score = favorable attitude toward or belief in the reality of God)	Fr (77): X̄=7.07; SD=1.61 Sr (77): X̄=5.54; SD=2.18	Sr have a less favorable attitude toward (less belief in) the reality of God than do Fr (SS). Sr scores are more heterogeneous than Fr scores.
	Thurstone-Chave's Attitude Toward God as an Influence on Conduct Scale (high score = unfavorable attitude toward or disbelief in God having an influence on one's own conduct)	Fr (77): X̄=4.06; SD=2.15 Sr (77): X̄=5.92; SD=2.73	Sr have a less favorable attitude toward (less belief in) God having an influence on their conduct than do Fr (SS). Sr scores are more heterogeneous than Fr scores.
McConnell, Clark, Heist, Trow, and Yonge (forthcoming). Sampling of male and female students at Antioch, Reed, Swarthmore, San Francisco State, Univ. of Calif. at Berkeley, Univ. of the Pacific, St. Olaf, and Univ. of Portland. Longitudinal; first school, 1958-1963; next three schools, 1958-1962; last four schools, 1959-1963.	Religious Liberalism Scale from the Omnibus Personality Inventory (high score = high religious liberalism, skepticism, or rejection of orthodox or fundamentalist beliefs and practices)	Antioch Males Fr (85): X̄=17.44; SD=6.49 Sr (85): X̄=20.24; SD=5.30 Females Fr (70): X̄=17.43; SD=5.76 Sr (70): X̄=21.73; SD=3.90	For each sex, Sr are more religiously liberal than Fr (SS). For each sex, Sr scores are less heterogeneous than Fr scores.
		Reed Males Fr (38): X̄=18.66; SD=6.30 Sr (38): X̄=21.84; SD=7.38 Females Fr (11): X̄=21.00; SD=3.25 Sr (11): X̄=22.18; SD=2.25	For each sex, Sr are more religiously liberal than Fr (SS for males, NSS for females). For males, Sr scores are more heterogeneous than Fr scores, while for females, Sr scores are less heterogeneous.
		Swarthmore Males Fr (77): X̄=17.04; SD=6.65 Sr (77): X̄=20.96; SD=5.03 Females Fr (83): X̄=17.16; SD=5.70 Sr (83): XX̄=21.01; SD=4.86	For each sex, Sr are more religiously liberal than Fr (SS). For each sex, Sr scores are less heterogeneous than Fr scores.
		San Francisco State Males Fr (19): X̄=14.05; SD=5.48 Sr (19): X̄=18.47; SD=6.17 Females Fr (45): X̄=11.24; SD=5.84 Sr (45): X̄=13.67; SD=5.75	For each sex, Sr are more religiously liberal than Fr (SS). For males, Sr scores are more heterogeneous than Fr scores; for females, Sr scores are less heterogeneous.
		Berkeley Males Fr (173): X̄=15.85; SD=6.71 Sr (173): X̄=19.05; SD=6.52 Females Fr (181): X̄=14.10; SD=6.02 Sr (181): X̄=17.49; SD=5.96	For each sex, Sr are more religiously liberal than Fr (SS). For each sex, Sr scores are less heterogeneous than Fr scores.
		Univ. of the Pacific Males Fr (45): X̄=13.51; SD=5.62 Sr (45): X̄=15.84; SD=5.46 Females Fr (63): X̄=10.46; SD=5.23 Sr (63): X̄=14.05; SD=4.58	For each sex, Sr are more religiously liberal than Fr (NSS for males, SS for females). For each sex, Sr scores are less heterogeneous than Fr scores.
		St. Olaf Males Fr (126): X̄= 8.08; SD=3.84 Sr (126): X̄=11.06; SD=4.34 Females Fr (164): X̄= 7.32; SD=5.15 Sr (164): X̄= 9.62; SD=4.13	For each sex, Sr are more religiously liberal than Fr (SS). For males, Sr scores are more heterogeneous than Fr scores, while for females, Sr scores are less heterogeneous.
		Univ. of Portland Males Fr (35): X̄= 8.57; SD=5.23 Sr (35): X̄= 8.42; SD=4.58 Females Fr (54): X̄= 5.26; SD=2.61 Sr (54): X̄= 6.22; SD=2.58	For males, Sr are less religiously liberal than Fr (NSS). For females, Sr are more religiously liberal than Fr (SS). For each sex, Sr scores are less heterogeneous than Fr scores.

Table 2E.--Changes in religious orientation (CONTINUED))

REFERENCE, SAMPLE	INSTRUMENT	RESULTS	COMMENTS
Burchard (1965). Sampling of male and female freshman students at Northern Illinois Univ. in the spring of 1962. Longitudinal, Spring 1962-Spring 1965.	Burchard's Religious Belief and Attitude Questionnaire (high score = religious liberalism or non-fundamentalism)	Males Fr (66): $\bar{X}$=2.89 Sr (66): $\bar{X}$=3.16 Females Fr (106): $\bar{X}$=2.62 Sr (106): $\bar{X}$=2.83	For each sex, Sr are more liberal religiously (less fundamentalistic) than are Fr (SS).
Hunter (1942a). Total sampling of entering female freshmen at a "small, southern liberal college for women" in 1934, 1935, 1936, and 1937. Longitudinal, 1934-1938, 1935-1939, 1936-1940, 1937-1941. (Samples are combined in analysis.)	Hunter Test of Attitudes--Religion Subscale (positive score = liberalism; negative score = conservatism)	Fr (185): $\bar{X}$= -6.74; SD=3.68 Sr (185): $\bar{X}$= -6.45; SD=3.94	Sr are less conservative with respect to religion than are Fr (NSS). Sr scores are more heterogeneous than Fr scores.
Trent (1967). Total sampling of all male and female freshmen at five West Coast Catholic colleges in 1959. Longitudinal, 1959-1963.	Religious Liberalism Scale from the Omnibus Personality Inventory (high score = high religious liberalism, skepticism, or rejection of orthodox or fundamentalist beliefs and practices)	$\bar{X}$=35.5 $\bar{X}$=37.8	Sr are more religiously liberal than Fr (SS).
Gilliland (1940). Sampling of students at a "medium-sized denominational college." Cross-sectional, year not given.	Thurstone-Chave's Attitude Toward the Reality of God Scale (high score = favorable attitude toward or belief in the reality of God)	Fr (116): $\bar{X}$=7.7; SD= .92 Sr (67): $\bar{X}$=7.8; SD=1.04	Sr have a more favorable attitude toward (greater belief in) the reality of God than do Fr (PNG). Sr scores are more heterogeneous than Fr scores.
Trent (1964a). Total sampling of all male and female freshmen and random or representative sampling of male and female senior students at five West Coast Catholic colleges (in 1959-1960). Cross-sectional, freshmen at the beginning and seniors at the end of the school year.	Religious Liberalism Scale from the Omnibus Personality Inventory (high score = high religious liberalism, skepticism, or rejection of orthodox or fundamentalist beliefs and practices)	Males Fr: $\bar{X}$=8; SD=4.8 Sr: $\bar{X}$=8; SD=4.9 Females Fr: $\bar{X}$=5; SD=3.3 Sr: $\bar{X}$=5; SD=2.6	For each sex, Sr are no more religiously liberal than Fr. For males, Sr scores are more heterogeneous than Fr scores, while for females, Sr scores are less heterogeneous.
	Farwell-Trent's Religious Concepts Inventory (high score = high religious fundamentalism)	Males Fr: $\bar{X}$=35; SD=4.6 Sr: $\bar{X}$=34; SD=4.9 Females Fr: $\bar{X}$=36; SD=2.6 Sr: $\bar{X}$=36; SD=1.8	For males, Sr are less religiously fundamentalistic than are Fr (NSS). For females, there is no difference between Sr and Fr. For males, Sr scores are more heterogeneous than Fr scores, while for females, Sr scores are less heterogeneous.
Havens (1964). Sampling of students at Carleton College. Cross-sectional, 1959 and 1962.	McClean's Religious Concepts Scale (high score = religious orthodoxy or liberalism within a Christian context)	1959 Fr (68): $\bar{X}$=52.0 Sr (36): $\bar{X}$=38.2 1962 Fr (62): $\bar{X}$=50.5 Sr (39): $\bar{X}$=40.5	Sr are less religiously orthodox or liberal than are Fr (PNG).

Table 2E.--Changes in religious orientation (CONTINUED)

REFERENCE, SAMPLE	INSTRUMENT	RESULTS	COMMENTS
Hall (1951). Representative sampling of male and female freshmen and senior students at Syracuse Univ. Cross-sectional, Spring 1950.	Hall's You And The Universe Inventory (high score = conviction of the existence of a Supreme Being)	Fr (735): $\bar{X}$=166.5; SD=28.99 Sr (941): $\bar{X}$=166.6; SD=29.62	Sr are more convinced of the existence of a Supreme Being than are Fr (NSS). Sr scores are more heterogeneous than Fr scores.
Bryant (1958). Sampling of male and female students at the Univ. of Nebraska. Cross-sectional, 1956-1957.	25-item questionnaire developed by Bryant (scored for number of liberal responses)	Intellectually Superior Students Fr (26): $\bar{X}$= 9.96 Sr (26): $\bar{X}$= 9.96 Students of Average Intelligence Fr (26): $\bar{X}$= 8.26 Sr (26): $\bar{X}$=10.50	There is no change for intellectually superior students. For students of average intelligence, Sr are more religiously liberal than Fr (SS).* *The questionnaire was also scored for number of conservative responses. In this instance, both types of students showed decreases in religious conservatism (SS only for students of average intelligence).
Hassenger (1965, 1966). Random sampling of entering female students at Mundelein College, a Catholic women's college in Chicago, in September 1963. Longitudinal, Sept. 1963-March 1965.	Religious Liberalism Scale from the Omnibus Personality Inventory (high score = high religious liberalism, skepticism or rejection of orthodox or fundamentalistic beliefs and practices)	Fr (40): $\bar{X}$=8.0; SD=2.6 So (37): $\bar{X}$=9.3; SD=3.0	So are more religiously liberal (more skeptical of religious orthodoxy and fundamentalism) than Fr (SS).
Corey (1940). Sampling of freshmen female students at the Univ. of Wisconsin in December 1934. Longitudinal, Dec. 1934-Fall 1935.	Thurstone-Chave's Attitude Toward the Church Scale (high score = unfavorable attitude toward the church)	Fr (100): $\bar{X}$=2.24; SD=1.00 So (100): $\bar{X}$=2.30; SD=1.18	So are less favorable in attitude toward the church than are Fr (NSS).
	Thurstone-Chave's Attitude Toward the Reality of God Scale (high score = favorable attitude or belief in the reality of God)	Fr (100): $\bar{X}$=8.13; SD= .98 So (100): $\bar{X}$=7.96; SD= .98	So have a less favorable attitude toward (less belief in) the reality of God than do Fr (NSS).
Barkley (1942b). Random sampling of entering female students in a 1-year commercial curriculum in a southern women's college (year not given). Longitudinal, from beginning of the year (Fr-b) to the end of the year (Fr-e).	Thurstone-Chave's Attitude Toward the Church Scale (high score = unfavorable atttitude toward the church)	Fr-b (68): $\bar{X}$=1.98; SD=.60 Fr-e (68): $\bar{X}$=2.14; SD=.85	Fr-e are less favorable toward the church than are Fr-b (NSS).
	Thurstone-Chave's Attitude Toward the Reality of God Scale (high score = favorable attitude or belief in the reality of God)	Fr-b (68): $\bar{X}$=8.03; SD=.21 Fr-e (68): $\bar{X}$=7.93; SD=.96	Fr-e have a less favorable attitude toward (less belief in) the reality of God than do Fr-b (NSS).

OTHER STUDIES:

King (1967) reports that in two separate longitudinal samples of Harvard students, seniors manifested less religious conventionalism and less reliance on traditional religious values than they did as freshmen. Similarly, Lane (University of Delaware, 1965) reports that upperclassmen at the University of Delaware are less orthodoxly, religiously and ethically rigid than freshmen. Comparing senior and freshmen scores on three factors obtained from a number of questionnaire items on religious orientation, Hites (1965) found that seniors at Birmingham Southern College had less acceptance of certain functions of religion, had a less literal acceptance of the Bible, and had less belief in immortality. Symington (1935) found upperclassmen to be more religiously liberal than lowerclassmen. Mull (1947) found the religious thinking of seniors to be "of a higher order" than that of freshmen, but the difference was not statistically significant. A sample of students at Cornell were classified as high or low on a scale of three items dealing with religious faith, relative importance of religion as a source of satisfaction in life, and belief in a divine God (Ferman, 1960). During the first two years of college, 50.9% of the students started and remained low on this index, 27.3% started and remained high, while 12.5% became less religious, and 9.5% became more religious.

Other studies report cross-sectional differences or longitudinal changes on either a single questionnaire item or a series of such items not combined into a scale: Allport, Gillespie and Young (1948); Bain (1927); Dudycha (1933b); Gaff (1965); Garrison and Mann (1931); Hassenger (1965); Jones (1926); Katz and Allport (1931); MacNaughton (1966); Trent (1964a); Webster (1958); Webster, Freedman and Heist (1962); Wickenden (1932); and Willoughby (1930). These studies show that, in general, as a group seniors are somewhat less likely to believe in God and more likely to be indifferent or opposed to religion, are somewhat more likely to conceive of God in impersonal terms, are somewhat less orthodox or fundamentalistic in religious orientation, and are somewhat more religiously liberal. There are, however, a number of items showing no differences between seniors and freshmen, and there are a few items revealing religious changes in reverse directions.

Table 2F.--Summaries of studies showing perceived changes in religous orientation. See explanatory note for Tables 2A-2N.

REFERENCE, SAMPLE	RESULTS
Jacobson and Sharp (1966). Random sampling of male and female students from all class levels at Univ. of Wisconsin, Dec. 1965. (N = 764)	Perceived change in the importance of religion in the student's life since entering college Protestant* (N=332) Increased importance: 33% — Net change: 7% (increased importance) Decreased importance: 26% No change in importance: 41% Catholic* (N=162) Increased importance: 32% — Net change: 8% (increased importance) Decreased importance: 24% No change in importance: 44% Jewish* (N=106) Increased importance: 11% — Net change: 22% (decreased importance) Decreased importance: 33% No change in importance: 56% No preference* (N=128) Increased importance: 6% — Net change: 33% (decreased importance) Decreased importance: 39% No change in importance: 55% All Students (N=764) Increased importance: 24% — Net change: 5% (decreased importance) Decreased importance: 29% No change in importance: 47% *The respondents' religious preference at the time of answering the question on perceived change in the importance of religion
MacGregor (1967). Sampling of male and female students from all class levels at Brooklyn College. Year (or years) not given. (N = 2414)	Perceived effect of student's experience at Brooklyn College on his concern with religious questions Jewish* (N=2071) Increased concern with religious questions: 19.4% — Net change: 15% (increased concern with religious questions) Decreased concern with religious questions: 4.4% Not affected concern with religious questions: 74.7% Catholic* (N=292) Increased concern with religious questions: 36.5% — Net change: 29% (increased concern with religious questions) Decreased concern with religious questions: 7.5% Not affected concern with religious questions: 51.9% Protestant* (N=51) Increased concern with religious questions: 36.5% — Net change: 30.8% (increased concern with religious questions) Decreased concern with religious questions: 5.7% Not affected concern with religious questions: 55.7% *Author does not explain why percentages do not add to 100%
Trent (1967); Trent and Medsker (1967). Sampling of male and female seniors at a number of colleges, 1963.	Perceived change in student's valuing of religion during college Catholic students at Catholic colleges (N=99) Value religion more: 82% — Net change: 79% (valuing religion more) Value religion less: 3% No change: 15% Catholic students at non-Catholic colleges (N=183) Value religion more: 42% — Net change: 13% (valuing religion more) Value religion less: 29% No change: 27% No response: 2% Non-Catholic students (N=1124) Value religion more: 47% — Net change: 20% (valuing religion more) Value religion less: 27% No change: 25% No response: 1% Males Value religion more: 47% — Net change: 21% (valuing religion more) Value religion less: 26% No change or no response: 7% Females Value religion more: 50% — Net change: 26% (valuing religion more) Value religion less: 24% No change or no response: 26%

Table 2F.--Perceived changes in religious orientation (CONTINUED)

REFERENCE, SAMPLE	RESULTS
Lehmann and Dressel (1962); Lehmann (1963). Sampling of male and female senior students at Michigan State University, Spring 1962. (N=1084)	Perceived change in student's commitment to a set of religious beliefs since entering college Males (N=645) Increased commitment: 20% — Net change: 14% (decreased commitment) Decreased commitment: 34% Same: 46% Females (N=439) Increased commitment: 24% — Net change: 9% (decreased commitment) Decreased commitment: 33% Same: 43% --- Perceived change in student's attachment to a religious sect or denomination that he can believe in and defend Males (N=645) Increased attachment to a religious sect or denomination: 12% — Net change: 25% (decreased attachment to a religious sect or denomination) Decreased attachment: 37% Same: 51% Females (N=439) Increased attachment: 17% — Net change: 17% (decreased attachment to a religious sect or denomination Decreased attachment: 34% Same: 49% --- Perceived change in student's acceptance of the Bible as a guide to modern living Males (N=645) Increased acceptance of the Bible: 11% — Net change: 23% (decreased acceptance of the Bible) Decreased acceptance: 34% Same: 55% Females (N=439) Increased acceptance of the Bible: 13% — Net change: 18% (decreased acceptance of the Bible) Decreased acceptance: 31% Same: 56% --- Perceived change in student's feeling of the necessity for religious faith for living in modern times since entering college Males (N=645) Increased feeling of the necessity for religious faith: 33% — Net change: 4% (increased feeling of the necessity for religious faith) Decreased feeling of the necessity for religious faith: 29% Same: 38% Females (N=439) Increased feeling of the necessity for religious faith: 40% — Net change: 17% (increased feeling of the necessity for religious faith) Decreased feeling of the necessity for religious faith: 23% Same: 37%
Burchard (1965). Sampling of male and female senior students at Northern Illinois University, Spring 1962. (N = 222)	Perceived effect of college experience on student's religious beliefs Males* (N=96) Strengthened religious beliefs: 18% — Net change: 23% (weakened religious beliefs) Weakened religious beliefs: 41% Left religious beliefs unchanged: 39% Females* (N=126) Strengthened religious beliefs: 40% — Net change: 17% (strengthened religious beliefs) Weakened religious beliefs: 23% Left religious beliefs unchanged: 32% *Author does not explain why percentages do not add to 100%

Table 2F.--Perceived changes in religious orientation (CONTINUED)

REFERENCE, SAMPLE	RESULTS
Jacob (1957). Random sampling of male students from all class levels at ten colleges, Spring 1952.	Perceived change in student's evaluation of religion since coming to college
	<u>UCLA</u> Value ɜligion more: 22% Value religion less: 17% No change: 61% Net change: 5% (value religion more)
	<u>Cornell</u> Value religion more: 32% Value religion less: 15% No change: 53% Net change: 17% (value religion more)
	<u>Dartmouth</u> Value religion more: 36% Value religion less: 18% No change: 46% Net change: 18% (value religion more)
	<u>Harvard</u> Value religion more: 30% Value religion less: 22% No change: 48% Net change: 8% (value religion more)
	<u>Univ. of Michigan</u> Value religion more: 32% Value religion less: 20% No change: 48% Net change: 12% (value religion more)
	<u>Univ. of North Carolina</u> Value religion more: 34% Value religion less: 12% No change: 54% Net change: 22% (value religion more)
	<u>Univ. of Texas</u> Value religion more: 33% Value religion less: 14% No change: 53% Net change: 17% (value religion more)
	<u>Wayne State Univ</u>. Value religion more: 24% Value religion less: 15% No change: 61% Net change: 9% (value religion more)
	<u>Wesleyan</u> Value religion more: 49% Value religion less: 16% No change: 35% Net change: 33% (value religion more)
	<u>Yale</u> Value religion more: 36% Value religion less: 19% No change: 45% Net change: 17% (value religion more)
Arsenian (1943). Sampling of male seniors at a "men's college in New England," Spring 1942. (N = 76)	Perceived change in student's attitudes toward religion during his four years at college Attitude has become more favorable: 66% Attitude has become less favorable: 12% Attitude has remained unchanged: 22% Net change: 54% (attitude has become more favorable)
Newcomb, Koenig, Flacks, and Warwick (1967). Sampling of female students at all class levels at Bennington College, Spring 1962. (N = 309)	Perceived change in student's commitment to religious beliefs since entering college "Very much" or "much" more committed to religious beliefs: 6% "Very much" or "much" less committed to religious beliefs: 20% Intermediate change (includes no change, "somewhat" more and "somewhat" less committed to religious beliefs): 74% Net change: 14% ("very much" or "much" less committed to religious beliefs)

Table 2F.--Perceived changes in religious orientation (CONTINUED)

REFERENCE, SAMPLE	RESULTS
Morgenstern, Gussow, Woodward, and Russin (1965). Sampling of male and female seniors at 22 colleges representing a cross section of America's colleges and universities, 1965.	Perceived effect of campus experience on student's religious faith Intensified religious faith: 20% Raised doubts about religious faith: 45% No change: 34% Net change: 25% (raised doubts about faith)
Blau, Pitts, Nosanchuk, and Russell (1966). Sampling of male and female students at all class levels at University of Michigan, year not given. (N = 185)	Perceived change in degree of religiosity of the student since coming to the University of Michigan More religious: 13% Less religious: 20% Same: 67% Net change: 7% (less religious)

<u>OTHER STUDIES</u>:

In one study, students at twelve schools (Educational Reviewer, 1963) were asked if (and when) they had experienced any sudden resurgence of religious faith and interest. The following percentages indicate the proportion of students answering that they had experienced such a resurgence in college: Sarah Lawrence (36%), Williams College (27%), Yale (25%), Marquette Univ. (47%), Boston Univ. (34%), Indiana Univ. (36%), Univ. of South Carolina (31%), Harvard Univ. (35%), Reed (20%), Davidson College (30%), Brandeis (10%), and Stanford (22%). For perceived changes in religious orientation of students in a Psychology of Religion Class at Morningside College, see Emme (1941).

Table 2G.--Summaries of studies showing changes in intellectual orientation and disposition. See explanatory note for Tables 2A-2N.

REFERENCE, SAMPLE	INSTRUMENT	RESULTS	COMMENTS
Rowe (1964). Total sampling of entire student bodies (females) at three women's colleges in Virginia (Hollins, Randolph-Macon, and Sweet Briar). Cross-sectional, 1962.	Humanism (Humanities, Social Science) Scale from Stern's Activities Index (high score = interest in the manipulation of external social objects or artifacts through empirical analysis, reflection and discussion; interest in the Humanities and the Social Sciences)	College No. 1 Fr (161): $\bar{X}$=6.97; SD=2.57 So (123): $\bar{X}$=7.59; SD=2.45 Jr (83): $\bar{X}$=7.61; SD=2.17 Sr (101): $\bar{X}$=8.53; SD=1.72 College No. 2. Fr (196): $\bar{X}$=6.91; SD=2.47 So (123): $\bar{X}$=7.15; SD=2.37 Jr (83): $\bar{X}$=7.11; SD=2.49 Sr (101): $\bar{X}$=7.83; SD=2.08 College No. 3 Fr (118): $\bar{X}$=7.00; SD=1.50 So (136): $\bar{X}$=7.79; SD=1.90 Jr (87): $\bar{X}$=7.49; SD=1.63 Sr (79): $\bar{X}$=7.34; SD=2.18	In all three colleges, Sr are more interested in the Humanities and the Social Sciences (are more interested in the manipulation of external social objects or artifacts through empirical analysis, reflection, and discussion) than are Fr (PNG). In Colleges No. 1 and No. 2, the largest difference is between Jr and Sr; in College No. 3, it is between Fr and So. In Colleges No. 1 and No. 2, Sr scores are less heterogeneous than Fr scores; in College No. 3, they are more heterogeneous. Note that in College No. 3, the highest score is in the sophomore year.
	Understanding Scale from Stern's Activities Index (high score = preference for detached intellectualization and for problem-solving, analysis, or abstraction as an end in itself)	College No. 1 Fr (161): $\bar{X}$=6.59; SD=2.19 So (123): $\bar{X}$=6.98; SD=2.19 Jr (83): $\bar{X}$=7.31; SD=2.02 Sr (101): $\bar{X}$=7.29; SD=2.17 College No. 2 Fr (196): $\bar{X}$=6.34; SD=2.33 So (123): $\bar{X}$=6.31; SD=2.28 Jr (83): $\bar{X}$=6.52; SD=2.57 Sr (101): $\bar{X}$=6.27; SD=2.30 College No. 3 Fr (118): $\bar{X}$=6.76; SD=1.66 So (136): $\bar{X}$=7.02; SD=1.75 Jr (87): $\bar{X}$=7.00; SD=1.83 Sr (79): $\bar{X}$=6.72; SD=2.28	In College No. 1, Sr have a higher preference for detached intellectualization than do Fr (PNG). In Colleges No. 2 and No. 3, they have a lower preference for this (PNG). In College No. 1, the largest difference is between Fr and So. In the other two colleges, the largest difference (in direction of decrease) is between Jr and Sr. In the first two colleges, Sr scores are less heterogeneous than Fr scores; in the last college, they are more heterogeneous. Note that in Colleges No. 1 and No. 2, the highest score is in the junior year; in College No. 3, the highest score is in the sophomore year.
	Scientism (Science) Scale from Stern's Activities Index (high score = interest in the manipulation of external physical objects through empirical analysis, reflection and discussion; interest in Natural Sciences)	College No. 1 Fr (161): $\bar{X}$=3.76; SD=3.04 So (123): $\bar{X}$=4.14; SD=3.10 Jr (83): $\bar{X}$=3.97; SD=3.06 Sr (101): $\bar{X}$=4.36; SD=2.94 College No. 2 Fr (196): $\bar{X}$=3.66; SD=2.90 So (123): $\bar{X}$=3.27; SD=2.87 Jr (83): $\bar{X}$=2.95; SD=3.07 Sr (101): $\bar{X}$=3.08; SD=2.89 College No. 3 Fr (118): $\bar{X}$=4.03; SD=2.17 So (136): $\bar{X}$=4.19; SD=1.98 Jr (87): $\bar{X}$=3.94; SD=1.86 Sr (79): $\bar{X}$=3.75; SD=2.31	In College No. 1, Sr are more interested in the Natural Sciences (are more interested in the manipulation of external physical objects through empirical analysis, reflection, and discussion) than are Fr (PNG). In the other two colleges, Sr are less interested in this (PNG). In College No. 1, the largest difference (in direction of increase) is between Jr and Sr. In College No. 2, the largest difference (in direction of decrease) is between Fr and So. In College No. 3, the largest difference (in direction of decrease) is between So and Jr. In the first two colleges, Sr scores are less heterogeneous than Fr scores; in the last college they are more heterogeneous. Note that in College No. 2, the lowest score is in the junior year.
	Reflectiveness Scale from Stern's Activities Index (high score = liking of intraceptive activities; introspective preoccupation with private psychological, spiritual, esthetic, or metaphysical experience)	College No. 1 Fr (161): $\bar{X}$=6.95; SD=1.90 So (123): $\bar{X}$=6.95; SD=2.04 Jr (83): $\bar{X}$=6.81; SD=2.01 Sr (101): $\bar{X}$=7.03; SD=1.84 College No. 2 Fr (196): $\bar{X}$=7.17; SD=1.85 So (123): $\bar{X}$=6.84; SD=2.15 Jr (83): $\bar{X}$=6.39; SD=2.27 Sr (101): $\bar{X}$=6.24; SD=2.26 College No. 3 Fr (118): $\bar{X}$=7.42; SD=1.72 So (136): $\bar{X}$=6.99; SD=2.11 Jr (87): $\bar{X}$=6.60; SD=1.81 Sr (79): $\bar{X}$=6.08; SD=2.18	In College No. 1, Sr have more liking for intraceptive activities than do Fr (PNG). In Colleges No. 2 and No. 3, they have less liking for intraceptive activities (PNG). In the first college, the largest difference (in the direction of increase) is between Jr and Sr. In the last two colleges, the largest difference (in the direction of decrease) is between Jr and Sr. In College No. 1, Sr scores are less heterogeneous than Fr scores. In Colleges No. 2 and No. 3, they are more heterogeneous. Note that in College No. 1, the lowest score is in the junior year.

Table 2G.--Changes in intellectual orientation and disposition (CONTINUED)

REFERENCE, SAMPLE	INSTRUMENT	RESULTS	COMMENTS
Yuker and Block (1967). Sampling of students at Hofstra Univ. Cross-sectional, year not given.	Yuker-Block I-P Scale (high score = high intellectualism-liberalism; low score = high pragmatism-conservatism)	Fr (66): $\bar{X}$=118.5; SD=20.6 So (191): $\bar{X}$=119.6; SD=18.4 Jr (255): $\bar{X}$=122.8; SD=19.0 Sr (316): $\bar{X}$=123.4; SD=21.1	Sr are more intellectual-liberal than Fr (NSS). Largest difference is between So and Sr. Sr scores are more heterogeneous than Fr scores.
Flacks (1963). Total sampling of entire student body (females) at Bennington. Cross-sectional, Fall 1959.	Theoretical Orientation Scale from the Omnibus Personality Inventory (high score = high interest in science and scientific activities; high scorers are generally logical, rational and critical in their approach to problems)	Fr: $\bar{X}$=35.7 So: $\bar{X}$=38.2 Jr: $\bar{X}$=36.5 Sr: $\bar{X}$=38.2	Sr are more interested in science and scientific activities (are generally more logical, rational, and critical in their approach to problems) than are Fr (SS). Largest difference is between Fr and So.
	Originality Scale from an early form of the Omnibus Personality Inventory (high score = high independence of thought, freedom of expression, and novelty of insight)	Fr: $\bar{X}$=63.0 So: $\bar{X}$=65.4 Jr: $\bar{X}$=65.7 Sr: $\bar{X}$=67.5	Sr show more independence of thought, freedom of expression and novelty of insight than do Fr (SS). Largest difference is between Fr and So.
	Estheticism Scale from the Omnibus Personality Inventory (high score = diverse interests in artistic matters and activities)	Fr: $\bar{X}$=33.6 So: $\bar{X}$=36.2 Jr: $\bar{X}$=34.2 Sr: $\bar{X}$=37.4	Sr are more interested in artistic matters and activities than are Fr (SS). Largest difference is between Fr and So.
Chickering (nd [a]). Sampling of male and female freshman students at Goddard College in 1960 and 1961. Longitudinal, 1960-1964 and 1961-1965.	Theoretical Orientation Scale from the Omnibus Personality Inventory (high score = high interest in science and scientific activities; high scorers are generally logical, rational and critical in their approach to problems)	1960-1964 Fr: $\bar{X}$=22; SD= 6 So: $\bar{X}$=24; SD= 4 Sr: $\bar{X}$=19; SD= 3 1961-1965 Fr: $\bar{X}$=24; SD= 5 So: $\bar{X}$=22; SD= 5 Sr: $\bar{X}$=20; SD= 5	For both samples, Sr have less liking for reflective thought, particularly of an abstract nature, than do Fr (SS). For the first sample, the largest difference is between So and Sr; in the second sample, the Fr-So and So-Sr differences are tied. In the first sample, Sr scores are less heterogeneous than Fr scores, while in the second sample, they are the same. Note that in the first sample the highest score on theoretical orientation is in the sophomore year.
	Originality Scale from an early form of the Omnibus Personality Inventory (high score = high independence of thought, freedom of expression and novelty of insight)	1960-1964 Fr: $\bar{X}$=63; SD=11 So: $\bar{X}$=67; SD= 9 Sr: $\bar{X}$=67; SD= 9 1961-1965 Fr: $\bar{X}$=63; SD=13 So: $\bar{X}$=65; SD=11 Sr: $\bar{X}$=65; SD=16	For both samples, Sr show more independence of thought, freedom of expression and novelty of insight than do Fr (SS for the first sample, NSS for the second sample). For both samples, the largest difference is between Fr and So. For the first sample, Sr scores are less heterogeneous than Fr scores, while in the second sample, they are more heterogeneous.

Table 2G.--Changes in intellectual orientation and disposition (CONTINUED)

REFERENCE, SAMPLE	INSTRUMENT	RESULTS	COMMENTS
Stewart (1964, and personal communication to authors of supplementary information). Sampling of entering male and female freshmen at Univ. of Calif. at Berkeley in the fall of 1957. Longitudinal, Fall 1957-Spring 1961.	Thinking Introversion Scale from the Omnibus Personality Inventory (high score = high liking for reflective thought, particularly of an abstract nature; low score = evaluation of ideas on the basis of their practical, immediate application)	Males Fr (47): $\bar{X}$=38.128; SD=9.249 Sr (47): $\bar{X}$=40.362; SD=8.862 Females Fr (42): $\bar{X}$=39.429; SD=9.600 Sr (42): $\bar{X}$=43.762; SD=8.048	For each sex, Sr have more liking for reflective thought, particularly of an abstract nature, than do Fr (NSS for males, SS for females). For each sex, Sr scores are less heterogeneous than Fr scores.
	Complexity of Outlook Scale from the Omnibus Personality Inventory (high score = high independence and creativity; low score = high conservatism, compliance and readiness to accept authority and tradition)	Males Fr (47): $\bar{X}$=14.745; SD=3.756 Sr (47): $\bar{X}$=16.021; SD=3.819 Females Fr (42): $\bar{X}$=13.143; SD=4.280 Sr (42): $\bar{X}$=16.595; SD=4.334	For each sex, Sr are more independent and creative than are Fr (SS). Sr scores are more heterogeneous than Fr scores.
	Originality Scale from an early form of the Omnibus Personality Inventory (high score = high independence of thought, freedom of expression, and novelty of insight)	Males Fr (47): $\bar{X}$=24.681; SD=4.092 Sr (47): $\bar{X}$=24.851; SD=3.776 Females Fr (42): $\bar{X}$=23.857; SD=4.535 Sr (42): $\bar{X}$=25.428; SD=3.617	For each sex, Sr show more independence of thought, freedom of expression, and novelty of insight than do Fr (NSS for males, SS for females). For each sex, Sr scores are less heterogeneous than Fr scores.
Nichols (1965, (1967). Sampling of male and female National Merit Finalists Longitudinal, 1958-1962.	Autia Scale (Factor M) from the Sixteen Personality Factor Test (high score = highly imaginative, bohemian, nonpractical, self-absorbed, interested in art and basic beliefs)	Males Fr (432): $\bar{X}$=11.46 Sr (432): $\bar{X}$=12.18 Females Fr (204): $\bar{X}$=13.08 Sr (204): $\bar{X}$=13.39	For each sex, Sr are more imaginative, more interested in art and basic beliefs, and are less practical than are Fr (SS for males, NSS for females).
	Radicalism Scale (Factor Q_1) from the Sixteen Personality Factor Test (high score = highly experimenting, critical, liberal, analytic, and free-thinking)	Males Fr (432): $\bar{X}$=11.65 Sr (432): $\bar{X}$=12.42 Females Fr (204): $\bar{X}$=11.06 Sr (204): $\bar{X}$=11.31	For each sex, Sr are more experimenting, free-thinking, critical, and analytic than are Fr (SS for males, NSS for females).

Table 2G.--Changes in intellectual orientation and disposition (CONTINUED)

REFERENCE, SAMPLE	INSTRUMENT	RESULTS	COMMENTS
McConnell, Clark, Heist, Trow, and Yonge (forthcoming). Sampling of male and female freshmen at Antioch, Reed, Swarthmore, San Francisco State, Univ. of the Pacific, Univ. of California at Berkeley, St. Olaf, and Univ. of Portland. Longitudinal; first school, 1958-1963; next three schools, 1958-1962; last four schools, 1959-1963.	Thinking Introversion Scale from the Omnibus Personality Inventory (high score = high liking for reflective thought, particularly of an abstract nature; low score = evaluation of ideas on the basis of their practical, immediate application)	Antioch Males Fr (85): $\bar{X}$=38.11; SD= 9.03 Sr (85): $\bar{X}$=41.13; SD= 9.97 Females Fr (70): $\bar{X}$=41.76; SD= 9.13 Sr (70): $\bar{X}$=42.91; SD= 9.40	For each sex, Sr have more liking for reflective thought than do Fr (SS for males, NSS for females). For each sex, Sr scores are more heterogeneous than Fr scores.
		Reed Males Fr (38): $\bar{X}$=44.03; SD= 9.03 Sr (38): $\bar{X}$=43.45; SD= 7.56 Females Fr (11): $\bar{X}$=46.91; SD= 7.08 Sr (11): $\bar{X}$=44.18; SD= 5.67	For each sex, Sr have less liking for reflective thought than do Fr (NSS for males, SS for females). For each sex, Sr scores are less heterogeneous than Fr scores.
		Swarthmore Males Fr (73): $\bar{X}$=39.70; SD= 9.75 Sr (73): $\bar{X}$=42.34; SD= 9.65 Females Fr (83): $\bar{X}$=42.76; SD= 8.23 Sr (83): $\bar{X}$=44.64; SD= 8.31	For each sex, Sr have more liking for reflective thought than do Fr (SS). For males, Sr scores are less heterogeneous than Fr scores, while for females, they are more heterogeneous.
		San Francisco State Males Fr (19): $\bar{X}$=34.00; SD=10.07 Sr (19): $\bar{X}$=39.68; SD=11.15 Females Fr (45): $\bar{X}$=28.73; SD= 9.30 Sr (45): $\bar{X}$=34.02; SD=10.32	For each sex, Sr have more liking for reflective thought than do Fr (SS). For each sex, Sr scores are more heterogeneous than Fr scores.
		Berkeley Males Fr (173): $\bar{X}$=35.60; SD= 9.63 Sr (173): $\bar{X}$=39.42; SD= 9.75 Females Fr (181): $\bar{X}$=34.96; SD= 9.52 Sr (181): $\bar{X}$=38.69; SD= 9.87	For each sex, Sr have more liking for reflective thought than do Fr (SS). For each sex, Sr scores are more heterogeneous than Fr scores.
		Univ. of the Pacific Males Fr (45): $\bar{X}$=29.91; SD= 9.91 Sr (45): $\bar{X}$=33.27; SD=10.89 Females Fr (63): $\bar{X}$=33.29; SD= 9.06 Sr (63): $\bar{X}$=36.19; SD= 8.59	For each sex, Sr have more liking for reflective thought than do Fr (SS). For males, Sr scores are more heterogeneous than Fr scores, while for females, they are less heterogeneous.
		St. Olaf Males Fr (126): $\bar{X}$=33.82; SD= 8.92 Sr (126): $\bar{X}$=37.42; SD= 9.51 Females Fr (164): $\bar{X}$=35.06; SD= 9.40 Sr (164): $\bar{X}$=37.68; SD= 8.44	For each sex, Sr have more liking for reflective thought than do Fr (SS). For males, Sr scores are more heter-geneous than Fr scores, while for females, they are less heterogeneous.
		Univ. of Portland Males Fr (35): $\bar{X}$=26.20; SD= 8.86 Sr (35): $\bar{X}$=32.74; SD= 8.35 Females Fr (54): $\bar{X}$=29.28; SD= 8.61 Sr (54): $\bar{X}$=33.33; SD= 9.36	For each sex, Sr have more liking for reflective thought than do Fr (SS). For males, Sr scores are less heterogeneous than Fr scores, while for females, they are more heterogeneous.

Table 2G.--Changes in intellectual orientation and disposition (CONTINUED)

REFERENCE, SAMPLE	INSTRUMENT	RESULTS	COMMENTS
McConnell, Clark, Heist, Trow, and Yonge (continued).	Thinking Orientation Scale from the Omnibus Personality Inventory (high score = high interest in science and scientific activities; high scorers are generally logical, rational and critical in their approach to problems).	Antioch Males Fr (85): $\bar{X}$=21.12; SD=5.26 Sr (85): $\bar{X}$=21.59; SD=4.84 Females Fr (70): $\bar{X}$=19.86; SD=4.82 Sr (70): $\bar{X}$=21.01; SD=5.73	For each sex, Sr score higher on theoretical orientation than do Fr (NSS for males, SS for females). For males, Sr scores are less heterogeneous than Fr scores, while for females, they are more heterogeneous.
		Reed Males Fr (38): $\bar{X}$=24.95; SD=4.40 Sr (38): $\bar{X}$=24.68; SD=4.05 Females Fr (11): $\bar{X}$=24.36; SD=3.82 Sr (11): $\bar{X}$=22.00; SD=4.61	For each sex, Sr score lower on theoretical orientation than do Fr (NSS). For males, Sr scores are less heterogeneous than Fr scores, while for females, they are more heterogeneous.
		Swarthmore Males Fr (77): $\bar{X}$=22.90; SD=4.57 Sr (77): $\bar{X}$=22.35; SD=5.00 Females Fr (83): $\bar{X}$=20.84; SD=5.04 Sr (83): $\bar{X}$=21.04; SD=4.76	For males, Sr score lower on theoretical orientation than do Fr (NSS), while for females, Sr score higher (NSS). For males, Sr scores are more heterogeneous than Fr scores, while for females, they are less heterogeneous.
		San Francisco State Males Fr (19): $\bar{X}$=18.74; SD=5.34 Sr (19): $\bar{X}$=20.53; SD=5.20 Females Fr (45): $\bar{X}$=13.56; SD=4.92 Sr (45): $\bar{X}$=16.53; SD=5.88	For each sex, Sr score higher on theoretical orientation than do Fr (SS). For males, Sr scores are less heterogeneous than Fr scores, while for females, Sr scores are more heterogeneous.
		Berkeley Males Fr (173): $\bar{X}$=21.32; SD=4.83 Sr (173): $\bar{X}$=21.61; SD=4.56 Females Fr (181): $\bar{X}$=17.86; SD=5.00 Sr (181): $\bar{X}$=18.49; SD=4.77	For each sex, Sr score higher on theoretical orientation than do Fr (NSS for males, SS for females). For each sex, Sr scores are less heterogeneous than Fr scores.
		Univ. of the Pacific Males Fr (45): $\bar{X}$=17.24; SD=5.07 Sr (45): $\bar{X}$=18.62; SD=5.38 Females Fr (63): $\bar{X}$=16.00; SD=4.64 Sr (63): $\bar{X}$=16.62; SD=4.67	For each sex, Sr score higher on theoretical orientation than do Fr (SS for males, NSS for females). For each sex, Sr scores are more heterogeneous than Fr scores.
		St. Olaf Males Fr (126): $\bar{X}$=18.87; SD=6.30 Sr (126): $\bar{X}$=19.41; SD=4.73 Females Fr (164): $\bar{X}$=16.27; SD=4.81 Sr (164): $\bar{X}$=16.76; SD=4.63	For each sex, Sr score higher on theoretical orientation than do Fr (NSS for males, SS for females). For each sex, Sr scores are less heterogeneous than Fr scores.
		Univ. of Portland Males Fr (35): $\bar{X}$=16.03; SD=3.62 Sr (35): $\bar{X}$=18.17; SD=4.96 Females Fr (54): $\bar{X}$=14.13; SD=4.55 Sr (54): $\bar{X}$=14.50; SD=4.96	For each sex, Sr score higher on theoretical orientation than do Fr (SS for males, NSS for females). For each sex, Sr scores are more heterogeneous than Fr scores.

Table 2G.--Changes in intellectual orientation and disposition (CONTINUED)

REFERENCE, SAMPLE	INSTRUMENT	RESULTS	COMMENTS
McConnell, Clark, Heist, Trow, and Yonge (continued).	Complexity of Outlook Scale from the Omnibus Personality Inventory (high score = high independence and creativity; low score = high conservatism, compliance and readiness to accept authority and tradition)	Antioch Males Fr (85): $\bar{X}$=13.66; SD=4.34 Sr (85): $\bar{X}$=15.54; SD=4.79 Females Fr (70): $\bar{X}$=13.66; SD=4.62 Sr (70): $\bar{X}$=16.39; SD=4.28	For each sex, Sr are more independent and creative than are Fr (SS). For males, Sr scores are more heterogeneous than Fr scores, while for females, they are less heterogeneous.
		Reed Males Fr (38): $\bar{X}$=16.11; SD=4.78 Sr (38): $\bar{X}$=16.00; SD=3.80 Females Fr (11): $\bar{X}$=16.00; SD=5.58 Sr (11): $\bar{X}$=16.09; SD=5.20	For males, Sr are less independent and creative than are Fr (NSS), while for females, Sr are more independent and creative (NSS). For each sex, Sr scores are less heterogeneous.
		Swarthmore Males Fr (77): $\bar{X}$=13.21; SD=4.92 Sr (77): $\bar{X}$=14.94; SD=5.24 Females Fr (83): $\bar{X}$=13.48; SD=4.34 Sr (83): $\bar{X}$=15.51; SD=4.71	For each sex, Sr are more independent and creative than are Fr (SS). For each sex, Sr scores are more heterogeneous than Fr scores.
		San Francisco State Males Fr (19): $\bar{X}$=10.37; SD=3.99 Sr (19): $\bar{X}$=13.84; SD=4.39 Females Fr (45): $\bar{X}$= 9.49; SD=4.32 Sr (45): $\bar{X}$=10.67; SD=4.83	For each sex, Sr are more independent and creative than are Fr (SS). For each sex, Sr scores are more heterogeneous than Fr scores.
		Berkeley Males Fr (173): $\bar{X}$=11.79; SD=4.53 Sr (173): $\bar{X}$=13.72; SD=5.03 Females Fr (181): $\bar{X}$=11.11; SD=4.65 Sr (181): $\bar{X}$=12.42; SD=4.76	For each sex, Sr are more independent and creative than are Fr (SS). For each sex, Sr scores are more heterogeneous than Fr scores.
		Univ. of the Pacific Males Fr (45): $\bar{X}$=10.11; SD=4.25 Sr (45): $\bar{X}$=11.29; SD=4.55 Females Fr (63): $\bar{X}$= 9.94; SD=4.27 Sr (63): $\bar{X}$=10.92; SD=4.44	For each sex, Sr are more independent and creative than are Fr (NSS for males, SS for females). For each sex, Sr scores are more heterogeneous than Fr scores.
		St. Olaf Males Fr (127): $\bar{X}$=11.38; SD=4.32 Sr (127): $\bar{X}$=13.27; SD=4.90 Females Fr (164): $\bar{X}$=10.99; SD=6.56 Sr (164): $\bar{X}$=12.45; SD=4.67	For each sex, Sr are more independent and creative than are Fr (SS). For males, Sr scores are more heterogeneous than are Fr scores, while for females, they are less heterogeneous.
		Univ. of Portland Males Fr (35): $\bar{X}$= 9.91; SD=4.08 Sr (35): $\bar{X}$=10.43; SD=4.77 Females Fr (54): $\bar{X}$= 9.70; SD=3.93 Sr (54): $\bar{X}$= 9.61; SD=4.54	For males, Sr are more independent and creative than are Fr (NSS), while for females Sr are less independent and creative (NSS). For each sex, they are more heterogeneous than Fr scores.

Table 2G.--Changes in intellectual orientation and disposition (CONTINUED)

REFERENCE, SAMPLE	INSTRUMENT	RESULTS	COMMENTS
McConnell, Clark, Heist, Trow, and Yonge (continued).	Estheticism Scale from the Omnibus Personality Inventory (high score = diverse interests in artistic matters and activities)	Antioch Males Fr (85): $\bar{X}$=12.77; SD=4.35 Sr (85): $\bar{X}$=12.71; SD=5.12 Females Fr (70): $\bar{X}$=15.44; SD=4.51 Sr (70): $\bar{X}$=16.66; SD=3.67	For males, Sr are less interested in artistic matters and activities than are Fr (NSS), while for females, Sr are more interested in artistic matters and activities (SS). For males, Sr scores are more heterogeneous than Fr scores, while for females, they are less heterogeneous.
		Reed Males Fr (38): $\bar{X}$=12.29; SD=5.42 Sr (38): $\bar{X}$=12.68; SD=5.02 Females Fr (11): $\bar{X}$=17.91; SD=4.27 Sr (11): $\bar{X}$=17.09; SD=3.45	For males, Sr are more interested in artistic matters and activities than are Fr (NSS), while for females, Sr are less interested in artistic matters and activities (NSS). For each sex, Sr scores are less heterogeneous than Fr scores.
		Swarthmore Males Fr (77): $\bar{X}$=13.12; SD=5.54 Sr (77): $\bar{X}$=14.57; SD=5.25 Females Fr (83): $\bar{X}$=15.03; SD=4.05 Sr (83): $\bar{X}$=16.97; SD=3.97	For each sex, Sr are more interested in artistic matters and activities than are Fr (SS). For each sex, Sr Sr scores are less heterogeneous than Fr scores.
		San Francisco State Males Fr (19): $\bar{X}$=10.32; SD=4.70 Sr (19): $\bar{X}$=13.32; SD=5.97 Females Fr (45): $\bar{X}$=11.84; SD=4.60 Sr (45): $\bar{X}$=12.98; SD=4.14	For each sex, Sr are more interested in artistic matters and activities than are Fr (SS). For males, Sr scores are more heterogeneous than Fr scores, while for females, they are less heterogeneous.
		Berkeley Males Fr (173): $\bar{X}$=10.40; SD=5.00 Sr (173): $\bar{X}$=11.62; SD=5.54 Females Fr (181): $\bar{X}$=12.92; SD=4.71 Sr (181): $\bar{X}$=14.33; SD=4.68	For each sex, Sr are more interested in artistic matters and activities than are Fr (SS). For males, Sr scores are more heterogeneous than Fr scores, while for females, they are less heterogeneous.
		Univ. of the Pacific Males Fr (45): $\bar{X}$= 9.87; SD=4.99 Sr (45): $\bar{X}$=10.24; SD=4.97 Females Fr (63): $\bar{X}$=12.27; SD=4.43 Sr (63): $\bar{X}$=13.49; SD=5.13	For each sex, Sr are more interested in artistic matters and activities than are Fr (NSS for males, SS for females). For males, Sr scores are less heterogeneous than Fr scores, while for females, they are more heterogeneous.
		St. Olaf Males Fr (126): $\bar{X}$= 9.95; SD=4.49 Sr (126): $\bar{X}$=12.18; SD=5.24 Females Fr (164): $\bar{X}$=13.70; SD=6.51 Sr (164): $\bar{X}$=15.32; SD=3.92	For each sex, Sr are more interested in artistic matters and activities than are Fr (SS). For males, Sr scores are more heterogeneous than Fr scores, while for females, they are less heterogeneous.
		Univ. of Portland Males Fr (35): $\bar{X}$= 8.69; SD=4.60 Sr (35): $\bar{X}$= 8.57; SD=4.40 Females Fr (54): $\bar{X}$=10.82; SD=4.09 Sr (54): $\bar{X}$=12.52; SD=4.62	For males, Sr are less interested in artistic matters and activities than are Fr (NSS), while for females, Sr are more interested in artistic matters and activities (SS). For males, Sr scores are less heterogeneous than Fr scores, while for females, they are more heterogeneous.

Table 2G.--Changes in intellectual orientation and disposition (CONTINUED)

REFERENCE, SAMPLE	INSTRUMENT	RESULTS	COMMENTS
Trent and Medsker (1967). Sampling of high school graduates in sixteen communities in the Midwest, Calif., and Pennsylvania in 1959. Longitudinal, 1959-1963. (Analysis is for those students who entered and remained in college.)	Thinking Introversion Scale from the Omnibus Personality Inventory (high score = high liking for reflective thought, particularly of an abstract nature; low score = evaluation of ideas on the basis of their practical, immediate application)	Males Fr (723): $\bar{X}$=48.61 Sr (723): $\bar{X}$=51.76 Females Fr (578): $\bar{X}$=50.24 Sr (578): $\bar{X}$=53.74	For each sex, Sr have more liking for reflective thought than do Fr (SS).
	Complexity of Outlook Scale from the Omnibus Personality Inventory (high score = high independence and creativity; low score = high conservatism, compliance and readiness to accept authority and tradition)	Males Fr (723): $\bar{X}$=50.69 Sr (723): $\bar{X}$=51.28 Females Fr (578): $\bar{X}$=48.79 Sr (578): $\bar{X}$=50.61	For each sex, Sr are more independent and creative than are Fr (SS).
Trent (1967). Total sampling of all male and female freshmen at five West Coast Catholic colleges in 1959. Longitudinal, 1959-1963.	Thinking Introversion Scale from the Omnibus Personality Inventory (high score = high liking for reflective thought, particularly of an abstract nature; low score = evaluation of ideas on the basis of their practical, immediate application)	Fr (243): $\bar{X}$=45.7 Sr (243): $\bar{X}$=50.2	Sr have more liking for reflective thought than do Fr (SS).
	Theoretical Orientation Scale from the Omnibus Personality Inventory (high score = high interest in science and scientific activities; high scorers are generally logical, rational and critical in their approach to problems)	Fr (243): $\bar{X}$=42.4 Sr (243): $\bar{X}$=45.3	Sr have scores higher on theoretical orientation than do Fr (SS).
	Complexity of Outlook Scale from the Omnibus Personality Inventory (high score = high independence and creativity; low score = high conservatism, compliance and readiness to accept authority and tradition)	Fr (243): $\bar{X}$=44.3 Sr (243): $\bar{X}$=48.5	Sr are more independent and creative than are Fr (SS).
	Estheticism Scale from the Omnibus Personality Inventory (high score = diverse interests in artistic matters and activities)	Fr (243): $\bar{X}$=48.3 Sr (243): $\bar{X}$=52.3	Sr are more interested in artistic matters and activities than are Fr (SS).

Table 2G.--Changes in intellectual orientation and disposition (CONTINUED)

REFERENCE, SAMPLE	INSTRUMENT	RESULTS	COMMENTS
Trent (1964a). Total sampling of all male and female freshmen and random or representative sampling of male and female senior students at five West Coast Catholic colleges in 1959-1960. Cross-sectional, freshmen at the beginning and seniors at the end of the school year.	Thinking Introversion Scale from the Omnibus Personality Inventory (high score = high liking for reflective thought, particularly of an abstract nature; low score = evaluation of ideas on the basis of their practical, immediate application)	Males Fr (490): $\bar{X}$=29; SD= 9.3 Sr (86): $\bar{X}$=36; SD=10.1 Females Fr (561): $\bar{X}$=31; SD= 9.2 Sr (120): $\bar{X}$=37; SD= 9.7	For each sex, Sr have more liking for reflective thought, particularly of an abstract nature, than do Fr (SS). For each sex, Sr scores are more heterogeneous than Fr scores.
	Theoretical Orientation Scale from the Omnibus Personality Inventory (high score = high interest in science and scientific activities; high scorers are generally logical, rational and critical in their approach to problems)	Males Fr (490): $\bar{X}$=16; SD= 4.4 Sr (86): $\bar{X}$=18; SD= 4.9 Females Fr (561): $\bar{X}$=14; SD= 4.6 Sr (120): $\bar{X}$=15; SD= 5.0	For each sex, Sr are more interested in science and scientific activities (are generally more logical, rational and critical in their approach to problems) than are Fr (SS for males, NSS for females). For each sex, Sr scores are more heterogeneous than Fr scores.
	Complexity of Outlook Scale from the Omnibus Personality Inventory (high score = high independence and creativity; low score = high conservatism, compliance and readiness to accept authority and tradition)	Males Fr (490): $\bar{X}$=10; SD= 4.1 Sr (86): $\bar{X}$=10; SD= 4.1 Females Fr (561): $\bar{X}$=10; SD= 4.4 Sr (120): $\bar{X}$=10; SD= 4.4	For each sex, Sr are no more independent and creative than are Fr. For each sex, Sr scores are no more or less heterogeneous than Fr scores.
	Estheticism Scale from the Omnibus Personality Inventory (high score = diverse interests in artistic matters and activities)	Males Fr (490): $\bar{X}$= 9; SD= 5.2 Sr (86): $\bar{X}$=10; SD= 5.9 Females Fr (561): $\bar{X}$=12; SD= 4.5 Sr (120): $\bar{X}$=14; SD= 4.4	For each sex, Sr are more interested in artistic matters and activities than are Fr (NSS for males, SS for females). For males, Sr scores are more heterogeneous than Fr scores, while for females, Sr scores are less heterogeneous.
Korn (1967a). Sampling of nearly the entire freshman class at Stanford and nearly two-thirds of the entering freshman class at Univ. of California at Berkeley. Longitudinal, Fall 1961-Spring 1965.	Estheticism Scale from the Omnibus Personality Inventory (high score = diverse interests in artistic matters and activities)	Stanford Males Fr (185): $\bar{X}$=50; SD=10.3 Sr (185): $\bar{X}$=52; SD=11.0 Females Fr (148): $\bar{X}$=49; SD=10.9 Sr (148): $\bar{X}$=52; SD=11.4 Berkeley Males Fr (286): $\bar{X}$=50; SD= 9.8 Sr (286): $\bar{X}$=52; SD=11.6 Females Fr (265): $\bar{X}$=50; SD=10.1 Sr (265): $\bar{X}$=53; SD=10.4	For each sex, Sr are more interested in artistic matters and activities than are are Fr (SS). For each sex, Sr score are more heterogeneous than Fr scores. For each sex, Sr are more interested in artistic matters and activities than are Fr (SS). For each sex, Sr scores are more heterogeneous than Fr scores.

Table 2G.--Changes in intellectual orientation and disposition (CONTINUED)

REFERENCE, SAMPLE	INSTRUMENT	RESULTS	COMMENTS
Stern (1966b). Sampling of male freshmen and seniors at two liberal arts colleges (Antioch and Oberlin), of female freshmen and seniors at three liberal arts colleges (Bennington, Oberlin and Sarah Lawrence), of male freshmen and seniors at eight engineering schools (Arkansas, Detroit, Drexel, General Motors Institute, Georgia Institute of Technology, Illinois, Michigan, and Purdue) and of male freshmen and seniors at three schools of business administration (Cincinnati, Drexel, and Ohio State). All cross-sectional, year not given.	Intellectual Interests Scale from Stern's Activities Index (First-Order Factor 3) (high score = high interest in the arts as well as the sciences, both abstract and empirical)	Males at two liberal arts colleges Fr (72): $\bar{X}$=28.0; SD=7.5 Sr (78): $\bar{X}$=30.2; SD=7.5	Sr are higher in intellectual interests than are Fr (PNG). Sr scores are no more or less heterogeneous than Fr scores.
		Females at three liberal arts colleges Fr (123): $\bar{X}$=28.4; SD=6.5 Sr (117): $\bar{X}$=27.9; SD=7.3	Sr are lower in intellectual interests than are Fr (PNG). Sr scores are more heterogeneous than Fr scores.
		Males at eight engineering schools Fr (358): $\bar{X}$=24.8; SD=8.5 Sr (410): $\bar{X}$=25.2; SD=8.2	Sr are higher in intellectual interests than are Fr (PNG). Sr scores are less heterogeneous than Fr scores.
		Males at three schools of business adminis. Fr (111): $\bar{X}$=21.8; SD=7.9 Sr (78): $\bar{X}$=21.8; SD=7.8	Sr have the same level of intellectual interests as Fr. Sr scores are less heterogeneous than Fr scores.
Brewer (1963). Random sampling of male and female freshmen and seniors at Huston-Tillotson College (a Negro liberal arts college). Cross-sectional, Spring 1961.	Humanism (Humanities, Social Science) Scale from Stern's Activities Index (high score = interest in the manipulation of external social objects or artifacts through empirical analysis, reflection and discussion; interest in the Humanities and the Social Sciences)	Fr (40): $\bar{X}$=7.00; SD=2.29 Sr (40): $\bar{X}$=7.43; SD=1.66	Sr are more interested in the Humanities and the Social Sciences (are more interested in the manipulation of external social objects or artifacts through empirical analysis, reflection, and discussion) than are Fr (NSS). Sr scores are less heterogeneous than Fr scores.
	Understanding Scale from Stern's Activities Index (high score = preference for detached intellectualization and for problem-solving, analysis, or abstraction as an end in itself)	Fr (40): $\bar{X}$=6.68; SD=1.80 Sr (40): $\bar{X}$=6.38; SD=2.25	Sr have a lower preference for detached intellectualization than do Fr (NSS). Sr scores are more heterogeneous than Fr scores.
	Scientism (Science) Scale from Stern's Activities Index (high score = interest in the manipulation of external physical objects through empirical analysis, reflection, and discussion; interest in Natural Sciences)	Fr (40): $\bar{X}$=6.28; SD=2.90 Sr (40): $\bar{X}$=5.98; SD=2.87	Sr are less interested in the Natural Sciences (are less interested in the manipulation of external physical objects through empirical analysis, reflection, and discussion) than are Fr (NSS). Sr scores are less heterogeneous than Fr scores.
	Reflectiveness Scale from Stern's Activities Index (high score = liking of intraceptive activities; introspective preoccupation with private psychological, spiritual, aesthetic, or metaphysical experience)	Fr (40): $\bar{X}$=6.38; SD=2.00 Sr (40): $\bar{X}$=5.83; SD=1.76	Sr have less liking for intraceptive activities than do Fr (NSS). Sr scores are less heterogeneous than Fr scores.

Table 2G.--Changes in intellectual orientation and disposition (CONTINUED)

REFERENCE, SAMPLE	INSTRUMENT	RESULTS	COMMENTS
Webb and Crowder (1961b). Representative sampling of male and female students at Emory College. Cross-sectional, Spring 1959.	Humanism (Humanities, Social Science) Scale from Stern's Activities Index (high score = interest in the manipulation of external social objects or artifacts through empirical analysis, reflection and discussion; interest in the Humanities and the Social Sciences)	Lower division students (116): $\bar{X}$=5.91; SD=3.02 Upper division students (128): $\bar{X}$=6.91; SD=2.59	Upper division students are more interested in the Humanities and the Social Sciences (are more interested in the manipulation of external social objects or artifacts through empirical analysis, reflection, and discussion) than are lower division students (SS). Scores of the former group are less heterogeneous than scores of the latter group. (Note: on scores for the Humanism Scale, upper division students rank 3 out of the 30 scale scores while scores of lower division students rank 15.)
	Understanding Scale from Stern's Activities Index (high score = preference for detached intellectualization and for problem-solving, analysis, or abstraction as an end in itself)	Lower division students (116): $\bar{X}$=6.29; SD=2.59 Upper division students (128): $\bar{X}$=7.04; SD=1.25	Upper division students have a higher preference for detached intellectualization than do lower division students (SS). Scores of the former group are less heterogeneous than scores of the latter group. (Note: on scores, for the Understanding Scale, scores of the upper division students rank 2 out of the 30 scale scores while scores of lower division students rank 9.)
	Scientism (Science) Scale from Stern's Activities Index (high score = interest in the manipulation of external physical objects through empirical analysis, reflection, and discussion; interest in Natural Sciences)	Lower division students (116): $\bar{X}$=5.37; SD=2.99 Upper division students (128): $\bar{X}$=5.72; SD=3.36	Upper division students are more interested in the Natural Sciences (are more interested in the manipulation of external physical objects through empirical analysis, reflection, and discussion) than are lower division students (NSS). Scores of the former group are more heterogeneous than scores of the latter group. (Note: on scores for the Scientism Scale, scores of upper division students rank 16 out of 30, while scores of lower division students rank 20.)
	Reflectiveness Scale from Stern's Activities Index (high score = liking of intraceptive activities; introspective preoccupation with private psychological, spiritual, esthetic, or metaphysical experience)	Lower division students (116): $\bar{X}$=6.92; SD=2.15 Upper division students (128): $\bar{X}$=6.80; SD=2.80	Upper division students have less liking for intraceptive activities than do lower division students (NSS). Scores of the former group are more heterogeneous than scores of the latter. (Note: on scores for the Reflectiveness Scale, scores of upper division students rank 4 out of 30, while scores of lower division students rank 3.)

OTHER STUDIES:

Three other studies--a longitudinal study of high-ability students in various colleges (Tyler, 1963), a cross-sectional investigation of students at Carnegie Institute of Technology (Kirk, 1965) and a cross-sectional study at Mundelein College (Hassenger, 1965)--show that upperclassmen are usually more intellectually reflective and intraceptive, more independent and original in thought, and more logical and rational than are freshmen (as measured by the "intellectuality" scales of either the Omnibus Personality Inventory or the Stern Activities Index). Similarly, sophomore students at Morgan State College and at San Jose scored higher than did freshmen on the Intellectual Efficiency Scale from the Personality Inventory which purports to measure such traits as clear thinking, resourcefulness, alertness, and favorableness toward cognitive and intellectual matters (see Morgan State College, 1961; Telford and Plant, 1963; and Plant and Telford, 1966). Only at San Jose State was the difference statistically significant.

Interestingly enough, students at Goddard enter with high scores on the "intellectuality" scales of the Activities Index, and leave scoring lower (personal communication from Arthur Chickering). Also Snyder (1967) reports that students entering MIT score relatively high on the Complexity and on the Theoretical Introversion scales of the OPI; after four years of study at the school, the mean for seniors on the first scale is about the same as it was at entrance, while for the second scale, the mean has decreased.

One study at Yale has shown that students engage in more "self-propelled intellectual activities" as juniors and seniors than they do as freshmen and sophomores (Rust and Davie, 1963). In a study of students at the University of Delaware, seniors were more likely than sophomores to attend university-sponsored film showings and lectures, to make extensive use of the library, and to be more regular readers of newspapers, news magazines and literary periodicals (University of Delaware, 1965; Lane, 1966). By the time they are seniors, male and female students at Antioch, Reed, Swarthmore, San Francisco State, Univ. of California, Univ. of the Pacific, St. Olaf, and Univ. of Portland are more likely than they were as freshmen to own a large number of books, and to like classical music (McConnell et al., forthcoming). Similarly, Trent (1964a), reports that senior women at five Catholic colleges on the West Coast are more likely than freshman women to own a large number of books, to read poetry for enjoyment, and to like classical music. For men, seniors do not differ from freshmen in these areas. In a longitudinal study of a sample of students who graduated from high schools in sixteen communities and who attended and graduated from college, a slightly larger percentage of these students as seniors than as freshmen showed interest in cultural and news magazines and in classical music (Trent and Medsker, 1967). Thielens (1966) notes that senior upperclassmen at Columbia are more likely than lowerclassmen to read essays and scholarly journals "on their own." From a sample of students at a number of liberal arts, engineering and business schools, it was discovered that seniors were somewhat more likely than freshmen to withdraw unassigned books and journals from the library and to read unassigned materials in their major field, but were no more likely to read unassigned materials outside of their major field (see Wilson and Lyons, 1961, Appendix 6, Table 43).

Table 2H.--Summaries of studies showing changes in authoritarianism, dogmatism, ethnocentrism, and prejudice. See explanatory note for Tables 2A-2N.

REFERENCE, SAMPLE	INSTRUMENT	RESULTS	COMMENTS
Lehmann and Dressel (1962); Lehmann (1963). Total sampling of beginning male and female freshmen (Fr-b) at Michigan State Univ., in the fall of 1958. Longitudinal, follow-up at end of freshman year (Fr-e) 1959, and at end of senior year, 1962. Supplementary random sample of juniors, Spring 1961.	Inventory of Beliefs, Form I (high score indicates a person who is flexible, adaptive and democratic in his relationships with others, and nonstereotypic in beliefs)	Males Fr-b (590): $\bar{X}$=64.77; SD=14.18 Fr-e (590): $\bar{X}$=67.00; SD=14.68 Jr (235): $\bar{X}$=73.68; SD=13.67 Sr (590): $\bar{X}$=73.08; SD=15.10 Females Fr-b (461): $\bar{X}$=65.99; SD=13.11 Fr-e (461): $\bar{X}$=69.32; SD=14.86 Jr (189): $\bar{X}$=75.92; SD=15.51 Sr (461): $\bar{X}$=78.67; SD=14.91	For each sex, Sr are more flexible, less rigid and less authoritarian than Fr (SS). For each sex, largest difference is between Fr-e and Jr. For each sex, Sr scores are more heterogeneous than Fr scores. Note that for males, the highest score on the Inventory of Beliefs is in the junior year.
Lehmann and Dressel (1962); Lehmann (1963). Total sampling of beginning male and female freshmen at Michigan State Univ. in the fall of 1958. Longitudinal, follow-up at end of senior year, 1962. Supplementary random sample of sophomores, Spring 1960.	Rokeach's Dogmatism Scale, Form E (high score = high dogmatism)	Males Fr (590): $\bar{X}$=166.85; SD=25.61 So (197): $\bar{X}$=156.31; SD=24.21 Sr (590): $\bar{X}$=153.98; SD=22.94 Females Fr (461): $\bar{X}$=162.87; SD=25.14 So (217): $\bar{X}$=151.03; SD=24.04 Sr (461): $\bar{X}$=146.69; SD=24.16	For each sex, Sr are less dogmatic than Fr (SS). For each sex, largest difference is between Fr and So. For each sex, Sr scores are less heterogeneous than Fr scores.
Foster et al. (1961). Total sampling of entire student body (males) at Univ. of Santa Clara. Cross-sectional, September 1959.	Rokeach's Dogmatism Scale, Form D (high score = high dogmatism)	Fr (287): $\bar{X}$=166.0; SD=21.62 So (237): $\bar{X}$=158.4; SD=21.82 Jr (249): $\bar{X}$=158.2; SD=22.44 Sr (232): $\bar{X}$=155.6; SD=20.88	Sr are less dogmatic than Fr (SS). Largest difference is between Fr and So. Sr scores are less heterogeneous than Fr scores.
Foster et al. (1961). Total sampling of entire student body (males) at Univ. of Santa Clara. Cross-sectional, May 1961.	Rokeach's Dogmatism Scale, Form D (high score = high dogmatism)	Fr (335): $\bar{X}$=171.0; SD=22.53 So (235): $\bar{X}$=158.3; SD=22.10 Jr (196): $\bar{X}$=156.1; SD=23.83 Sr (211): $\bar{X}$=155.8; SD=22.80	Sr are less dogmatic than Fr (SS). Largest difference is between Fr and So. Sr scores are more heterogeneous than Fr scores.
	Gough revision of the California F Scale (high score = high authoritarianism)	Fr (333): $\bar{X}$=126.8; SD=19.14 So (230): $\bar{X}$=119.8; SD=20.05 Jr (194): $\bar{X}$=116.9; SD=21.11 Sr (209): $\bar{X}$=117.2; SD=20.30	Sr are less authoritarian than Fr (SS). Largest difference is between Fr and So. Sr scores are more heterogeneous than Fr scores. Note that the lowest authoritarianism score is in the junior year.
	California E Scale (high score = high ethnocentrism)	Fr (335): $\bar{X}$= 97.2; SD=23.89 So (231): $\bar{X}$= 89.9; SD=20.98 Jr (193): $\bar{X}$= 86.7; SD=21.81 Sr (209): $\bar{X}$= 88.7; SD=22.16	Sr are less ethnocentric than Fr (SS). Largest difference is between Fr and So. Sr scores are less heterogeneous than Fr scores. Note that the lowest ethnocentrism score is in the junior year.
Webster, Freedman and Heist (1962). Sampling of female students at Bennington. Cross-sectional, year not given.	Social Maturity Scale from the Vassar College Attitude Inventory (high score = low authoritarianism, high social maturity)	Fr (50): $\bar{X}$= 94.08; SD=13.80 So (51): $\bar{X}$= 97.88; SD=12.90 Jr (49): $\bar{X}$= 98.48; SD=11.20 Sr (50): $\bar{X}$=104.86; SD=12.70	Sr are more socially mature (less authoritarian) than Fr (PNG). Largest difference is between Jr and Sr. Sr scores are less heterogeneous than Fr scores.

Table 2H.--Changes in authoritarianism, dogmatism, ethnocentrism, and prejudice (CONTINUED)

REFERENCE, SAMPLE	INSTRUMENT	RESULTS	COMMENTS
William V. D'Antonio (personal communication to authors). Random sampling of students (male) at Notre Dame. Cross-sectional, 1962.	Rokeach's Dogmatism Scale (high score = high dogmatism)	Fr (94): $\bar{X}$=154.9; SD=2.39 So (79): $\bar{X}$=156.0; SD=2.23 Jr (51): $\bar{X}$=156.0; SD=2.48 Sr (41): $\bar{X}$=144.5; SD=3.03	Sr are less dogmatic than Fr (PNG). Largest difference is between Jr and Sr. Sr scores are more heterogeneous than Fr. Note that the highest dogmatism scores are in the sophomore and junior years.
Flacks (1963). Total sampling of entire student body (females) at Bennington. Cross-sectional, Fall 1959.	Nonauthoritarian Scale from an early form of the Omnibus Personality Inventory (high score = high nonauthoritarianism)	Fr: $\bar{X}$=13.4 So: $\bar{X}$=13.8 Jr: $\bar{X}$=13.8 Sr: $\bar{X}$=13.9	Sr are more nonauthoritarian than Fr (NSS). Largest difference is between Fr and So.
Garrison (1961). Sampling of male and female students at Univ. of Georgia. Cross-sectional, year not given.	Sampson and Smiths' Worldminded Attitudes Test (high score = pro-worldminded)	Males: Fr: $\bar{X}$= 99.3; So: $\bar{X}$=100.5; Jr: $\bar{X}$=102.8; Sr: $\bar{X}$=108.1 Females: Fr: $\bar{X}$= 99.9; So: $\bar{X}$=100.8; Jr: $\bar{X}$=106.4; Sr: $\bar{X}$=110.3	For each sex, Sr are more worldminded (less ethnocentric ?) than Fr (PNG). For males, the largest difference is between Jr and Sr, while for females, the largest difference is between So and Jr.
Holtzman (1956). Random sampling of male students at the Univ. of Texas. Cross-sectional, April 1952.	Holtzman's Tolerance of Non-Segregation Scale (scored for a tolerant vs. an intolerant category)	Percent in intolerant classification Fr (65) = 66% So (40) = 58% Jr (78) = 51% Sr (115)= 44%	Sr are less likely to be intolerant than Fr (SS). Largest difference is between Fr and So.
Freehill (1955). Sampling of male and female college students, name of college not given. Cross-sectional, year not given.	Problems in Human Relations Test (scored for type of orientation toward others and toward relationships between persons)	Test scored for "democratic" attitude Males: Fr: $\bar{X}$=13.55; So/Jr: $\bar{X}$=15.28; Sr: $\bar{X}$=16.78 Females: Fr: $\bar{X}$=16.90; So/Jr: $\bar{X}$=18.31; Sr: $\bar{X}$=18.66 Test scored for "hard-boiled" autocracy Males: Fr: $\bar{X}$= 5.31; So/Jr: $\bar{X}$= 4.68; Sr: $\bar{X}$= 4.30 Females: Fr: $\bar{X}$= 4.47; So/Jr: $\bar{X}$= 3.67; Sr: $\bar{X}$= 3.58	For each sex, Sr are more democratically oriented and are characterized less by "hard-boiled autocracy" than are Fr (with the exception of the decrease in "hard-boiled autocracy" among women, differences are SS). For each sex, largest difference is between Fr and combined So-Jr category.
Chickering (nd[a]). Sampling of male and female freshman students at Goddard College in 1960 and 1961. Longitudinal, 1960-1964 and 1961-1965.	Social Maturity Scale from the Omnibus Personality Inventory (high score = high social maturity, low authoritarianism)	1960-1964 Fr: $\bar{X}$=100; SD=20 So: $\bar{X}$=107; SD=15 Sr: $\bar{X}$=107; SD=14 1961-1965 Fr: $\bar{X}$=105; SD=17 So: $\bar{X}$=107; SD=14 Sr: $\bar{X}$=108; SD=18	For both samples, Sr are more socially mature (less authoritarian) than Fr (SS for first sample, NSS for second sample). For both samples, largest difference is between Fr and So. In the first sample, Sr scores are less heterogeneous than Fr scores, while in the second sample, they are more heterogeneous.
	Nonauthoritarianism Scale from an early form of the Omnibus Personality Inventory (high score = high nonauthoritarianism)	1960-1964 Fr: $\bar{X}$= 14; SD= 3 So: $\bar{X}$= 15; SD= 2 Sr: $\bar{X}$= 14; SD= 2 1961-1965 Fr: $\bar{X}$= 14; SD= 3 So: $\bar{X}$= 14; SD= 3 Sr: $\bar{X}$= 14; SD= 3	In both samples, seniors are neither more nor less authoritarian than Fr. In the first sample, Sr scores are less heterogeneous than Fr scores, while in the second sample, they are the same. Note that in the first sample the highest nonauthoritarianism score is in the sophomore year.

Table 2H.--Changes in authoritarianism, dogmatism, ethnocentrism, and prejudice (CONTINUED)

REFERENCE, SAMPLE	INSTRUMENT	RESULTS	COMMENTS
Beach (1966). Random sampling of male and female freshmen at Whitworth College, in the fall of 1961. Longitudinal, Fall 1961-Spring 1965.	California F Scale (high score = high authoritarianism)	Males Fr (17): $\bar{X}$=109.3; SD=16.6 So (17): $\bar{X}$=102.6; SD=15.2 Sr (17): $\bar{X}$= 94.5; SD=15.4 Females Fr (21): $\bar{X}$=116.3; SD=17.4 So (21): $\bar{X}$= 97.6; SD=15.0 Sr (21): $\bar{X}$= 96.4; SD=18.9	For each sex, Sr are less authoritarian than Fr (SS). For males, the largest difference is between So and Sr, while for females, it is between Fr and So. For males, Sr scores are less heterogeneous than Fr scores, while for females, Sr scores are more heterogeneous.
	Social Maturity Scale from the Omnibus Personality Inventory (high score = high social maturity, low authoritarianism)	Males Fr (17): $\bar{X}$= 70.6; SD=13.0 So (17): $\bar{X}$= 82.0; SD=13.0 Sr (17): $\bar{X}$= 85.8; SD=13.2 Females Fr (21): $\bar{X}$= 70.8; SD=14.8 So (21): $\bar{X}$= 82.7; SD=16.3 Sr (21): $\bar{X}$= 82.0; SD=17.8	For each sex, Sr are more socially mature (less authoritari) than Fr (SS). For each sex, the largest difference is between Fr and So. For each sex, Sr scores are more heterogeneous than Fr scores. Note that for females the highest score on the Social Maturity Scale is in the sophomore year.
	California E Scale (high score = high ethnocentrism)	Males Fr (17): $\bar{X}$= 56.6; SD=13.8 So (17): $\bar{X}$= 54.0; SD=16.8 Sr (17): $\bar{X}$= 46.6; SD=10.4 Females Fr (21): $\bar{X}$= 53.6; SD=13.6 So (21): $\bar{X}$= 43.2; SD=10.2 Sr (21): $\bar{X}$= 42.0; SD=10.2	For each sex, Sr are less ethnocentric than Fr (SS). For males, the largest difference is between So and Sr, while for females, it is between Fr and So. For each sex, Sr scores are less heterogeneous than Fr scores.
Beach (1967). Sampling of male and female freshmen and seniors at Whitworth College. Cross-sectional, Fall 1961.	California F Scale (high score = high authoritarianism)	Males Fr (53): $\bar{X}$=112.1; SD=17.0 Sr (39): $\bar{X}$= 99.6; SD=17.4 Females Fr (78): $\bar{X}$=110.5; SD=17.0 Sr (30): $\bar{X}$=100.9; SD=17.1	For each sex, Sr are less authoritarian than Fr (SS). For each sex, Sr scores are more heterogeneous than Fr scores.
	Social Maturity Scale from the Omnibus Personality Inventory (high score = high social maturity, low authoritarianism)	Males Fr (53): $\bar{X}$= 72.8; SD=14.0 Sr (39): $\bar{X}$= 82.9; SD=15.1 Females Fr (78): $\bar{X}$= 73.1; SD=16.9 Sr (30): $\bar{X}$= 77.6; SD=13.5	For each sex, Sr are more socially mature (less authoritarian) than Fr (SS for males, NSS for females). For males, Sr scores are more heterogeneous than Fr scores, while for females, they are less heterogeneous.
	California E Scale (high score = high ethnocentrism)	Males Fr (53): $\bar{X}$= 55.7; SD=13.1 Sr (39): $\bar{X}$= 46.4; SD=12.8 Females Fr (78): $\bar{X}$= 50.3; SD=19.6 Sr (30): $\bar{X}$= 47.9; SD=11.8	For each sex, Sr are less ethnocentric than Fr (SS for males, NSS for females). For each sex, Sr scores are less heterogeneous than Fr scores.
Plant (1958a). Total sampling of entire freshmen body (males and females) at San Jose State College in the spring of 1953. Longitudinal, Spring 1953-Spring 1957.	California E Scale (high score = high ethnocentrism)	Males Fr (137): $\bar{X}$=92.02; SD=22.96 Sr (137): $\bar{X}$=77.13; SD=25.28 Females Fr (134): $\bar{X}$=86.96; SD=26.04 Sr (134): $\bar{X}$=66.40; SD=25.15	For each sex, Sr are less ethnocentric than Fr (SS). For males, Sr scores are more heterogeneous than Fr scores, while for females, Sr scores are less heterogeneous.
Plant (1962, 1965). Total sampling of entire freshmen body (males and females) at San Jose State College in the spring, summer, and fall of 1958 (when applying for admission). Longitudinal, Spring-Summer-Fall 1958-Spring 1962.	Gough revision of the California F Scale (high score = high authoritarianism)	Males Fr (282): $\bar{X}$=121.93; SD=19.12 Sr (282): $\bar{X}$=104.10; SD=21.62 Females Fr (449): $\bar{X}$=120.69; SD=22.47 Sr (449): $\bar{X}$=101.45; SD=22.95	For each sex, Sr are less authoritarian than Fr (SS). For each sex, Sr scores are more heterogeneous than Fr scores.
	Rokeach's Dogmatism Scale, Form E (high score = high dogmatism)	Males Fr (282): $\bar{X}$=157.48; SD=23.95 Sr (282): $\bar{X}$=144.17; SD=25.17 Females Fr (449): $\bar{X}$=153.79; SD=25.11 Sr (449): $\bar{X}$=138.94; SD=24.99	For each sex, Sr are less dogmatic than Fr (SS). For males, Sr scores are more heterogeneous than Fr [illegible] for females, Sr scores are less heterogeneous.
	California E Scale (high score = high ethnocentrism)	Males Fr (282): $\bar{X}$= 84.93; SD=21.07 Sr (282): $\bar{X}$= 75.85; SD=21.64 Females Fr (449): $\bar{X}$= 80.11; SD=22.27 Sr (449): $\bar{X}$= 69.29; SD=20.00	For each sex, Sr are less ethnocentric than Fr (SS). For males, Sr scores are more heterogeneous than Fr scores, while for females, Sr scores are less heterogeneous.

Table 2H.--Changes in authoritarianism, dogmatism, ethnocentrism, and prejudice (CONTINUED)

REFERENCE, SAMPLE	INSTRUMENT	RESULTS	COMMENTS
McConnell, Clark, Heist, Trow, and Yonge (forthcoming). Sampling of male and female freshmen at Antioch, Reed, Swarthmore, San Francisco State, Univ. of California at Berkeley, Univ. of the Pacific, St. Olaf, and Univ. of Portland. Longitudinal; first school, 1958-1963; next three schools, 1958-1962; last four schools, 1959-1963.	Social Maturity Scale from the Omnibus Personality Inventory (high score = low authoritarianism, high social maturity)	Antioch Males Fr (85): $\bar{X}$= 89.66; SD=18.38 Sr (85): $\bar{X}$=105.73; SD=16.99 Females Fr (70): $\bar{X}$= 96.16; SD=17.34 Sr (70): $\bar{X}$=113.17; SD=12.21	For each sex, Sr are more socially mature (less authoritarian) than are Fr (PNG). For each sex, Sr scores are less heterogeneous than Fr scores.
		Reed Males Fr (38): $\bar{X}$=101.40; SD=15.81 Sr (38): $\bar{X}$=119.26; SD=11.53 Females Fr (11): $\bar{X}$=109.55; SD=13.23 Sr (11): $\bar{X}$=112.91; SD= 8.89	For each sex, Sr are more socially mature (less authoritarian) than are Fr (PNG). For each sex, Sr scores are less heterogeneous than Fr scores.
		Swarthmore Males Fr (77): $\bar{X}$= 93.81; SD=18.26 Sr (77): $\bar{X}$=105.40; SD=16.31 Females Fr (83): $\bar{X}$= 98.45; SD=15.09 Sr (83): $\bar{X}$=110.95; SD=13.33	For each sex, Sr are more socially mature (less authoritarian) than are Fr (PNG). For each sex, Sr scores are less heterogeneous than Fr scores.
		San Francisco State Males Fr (19): $\bar{X}$= 71.16; SD=22.28 Sr (19): $\bar{X}$= 85.07; SD=22.68 Females Fr (45): $\bar{X}$= 76.95; SD=19.48 Sr (45): $\bar{X}$= 94.95; SD=20.59	For each sex, Sr are more socially mature (less authoritarian) than are Fr (PNG). For each sex, Sr scores are more heterogeneous than Fr scores.
		Berkeley Males Fr (173): $\bar{X}$=83.20; SD=18.53 Sr (173): $\bar{X}$=98.23; SD=18.32 Females Fr (181): $\bar{X}$=81.11; SD=18.42 Sr (181): $\bar{X}$=96.59; SD=17.59	For each sex, Sr are more socially mature (less authoritarian) than are Fr (PNG). For each sex, Sr scores are less heterogeneous than Fr scores.
		Univ. of the Pacific Males Fr (45): $\bar{X}$= 68.67; SD=17.24 Sr (45): $\bar{X}$= 84.29; SD=19.82 Females Fr (63): $\bar{X}$= 68.73; SD=16.86 Sr (63): $\bar{X}$= 84.67; SD=18.36	For each sex, Sr are more socially mature (less authoritarian) than are Fr (PNG). For each sex, Sr scores are more heterogeneous than Fr scores.
		St. Olaf Males Fr (126): $\bar{X}$=71.96; SD=15.82 Sr (126): $\bar{X}$=89.19; SD=18.46 Females Fr (164): $\bar{X}$=71.21; SD=15.31 Sr (164): $\bar{X}$=89.38; SD=15.84	For each sex, Sr are more socially mature (less authoritarian) than are Fr (PNG). For each sex, Sr scores are more heterogeneous than Fr scores.
		Univ. of Portland Males Fr (35): $\bar{X}$= 60.69; SD=13.26 Sr (35): $\bar{X}$= 71.69; SD=16.82 Females Fr (54): $\bar{X}$= 61.15; SD=13.90 Sr (54): $\bar{X}$= 74.46; SD=15.22	For each sex, Sr are more socially mature (less authoritarian) than are Fr (PNG). For each sex, Sr scores are more heterogeneous than Fr scores.
Stewart (1964, and personal communication to authors of supplementary information). Sampling of entering male and female freshmen at Univ. of California at Berkeley in the fall of 1957. Longitudinal, Fall 1957-Spring 1961.	Modified version of the California F Scale (high score = high authoritarianism)	Males Fr (47): $\bar{X}$= 9.191; SD=4.417 Sr (47): $\bar{X}$= 7.085; SD=4.338 Females Fr (42): $\bar{X}$= 8.190; SD=4.026 Sr (42): $\bar{X}$= 5.095; SD=3.051	For each sex, Sr are less authoritarian than are Fr (SS). For each sex, Sr scores are less heterogeneous than Fr scores.
	Social Maturity Scale from the Omnibus Personality Inventory (high score = low authoritarianism, high social maturity)	Males Fr (47): $\bar{X}$=33.340; SD=7.041 Sr (47): $\bar{X}$=29.638; SD=6.138 Females Fr (42): $\bar{X}$=34.429; SD=6.398 Sr (42): $\bar{X}$=31.810; SD=4.608	For each sex, Sr are less socially mature (more authoritarian) than are Fr (SS). For each sex, Sr scores are less heterogeneous than Fr scores.

Table 2H.--Changes in authoritarianism, dogmatism, ethnocentrism, and prejudice (CONTINUED)

REFERENCE, SAMPLE	INSTRUMENT	RESULTS	COMMENTS
Korn (1967a). Sampling of nearly the entire entering freshman class at Stanford and nearly two-thirds of the entering freshman class at Univ. of California at Berkeley. Longitudinal, Fall 1961-Spring 1965.	Modified version of the California F Scale (high score = high authoritarianism)	Stanford Males Fr (185): $\bar{X}$=110; SD=24.2 Sr (185): $\bar{X}$= 94; SD=25.8 Females Fr (148): $\bar{X}$=103; SD=21.8 Sr (148): $\bar{X}$= 90; SD=25.9	For each sex, Sr are less authoritarian than are Fr (SS). For each sex, Sr scores are more heterogeneous than Fr scores.
		Berkeley Males Fr (286): $\bar{X}$=115; SD=25.78 Sr (286): $\bar{X}$= 96; SD=26.15 Females Fr (265): $\bar{X}$=112; SD=26.5 Sr (265): $\bar{X}$= 89; SD=26.3	For each sex, Sr are less authoritarian than are Fr (SS). For males, Sr scores are more heterogeneous than Fr scores, while for females, Sr scores are less heterogeneous.
	Modified version of the California E Scale (high score = high ethnocentrism)	Stanford Males Fr (185): $\bar{X}$= 51; SD=18.2 Sr (185): $\bar{X}$= 44; SD=17.0 Females Fr (148): $\bar{X}$= 45; SD=14.5 Sr (148): $\bar{X}$= 42; SD=16.8	For each sex, Sr are less ethnocentric than are Fr (SS). For males, Sr scores are less heterogeneous than Fr scores, while for females, Sr scores are more heterogeneous.
		Berkeley Males Fr (286): $\bar{X}$= 56; SD=20.43 Sr (286): $\bar{X}$= 44; SD=17.54 Females Fr (265): $\bar{X}$= 49; SD=17.7 Sr (265): $\bar{X}$= 39; SD=15.7	For each sex, Sr are less ethnocentric than are Fr (SS). For each sex, Sr scores are less heterogeneous than Fr scores.
	Social Maturity Scale from the Omnibus Personality Inventory (high score = low authoritarianism, high social maturity)	Stanford Males Fr (185): $\bar{X}$= 50; SD=10.0 Sr (185): $\bar{X}$= 58; SD=11.0 Females Fr (148): $\bar{X}$= 50; SD=10.8 Sr (148): $\bar{X}$= 57; SD=11.3	For each sex, Sr are more socially mature (less authoritarian) than are Fr (SS). For each sex, Sr scores are more heterogeneous.
		Berkeley Males Fr (286): $\bar{X}$= 50; SD=10.17 Sr (286): $\bar{X}$= 57; SD=11.15 Females Fr (265): $\bar{X}$= 50; SD=10.5 Sr (265): $\bar{X}$= 58; SD=10.0	For each sex, Sr are more socially mature (less authoritarian) than are Fr (SS). For males, Sr scores are more heterogeneous than Fr scores, while for females, Sr scores are less heterogeneous.
Trent and Medsker (1967). Sampling of high school graduates in sixteen communities in the Midwest, Calif., and Pennsylvania in 1959. Longitudinal, 1959-1963. (Analysis is for those students who entered and remained in college.)	Nonauthoritarianism Scale from an early form of the Omnibus Personality Inventory (high score = high nonauthoritarianism)	Males Fr (723): $\bar{X}$=46.26 Sr (723): $\bar{X}$=52.28 Females Fr (578): $\bar{X}$=44.52 Sr (578): $\bar{X}$=52.60	For each sex, Sr are more nonauthoritarian than Fr (SS).
	Social Maturity Scale from the Omnibus Personality Inventory (high score = low authoritarianism, high social maturity)	Males Fr (723): $\bar{X}$=53.34 Sr (723): $\bar{X}$=61.25 Females Fr (578): $\bar{X}$=52.85 Sr (578): $\bar{X}$=63.37	For both males and females, Sr are more socially mature (less authoritarian) than Fr (SS).

Table 2H.--Changes in authoritarianism, dogmatism, ethnocentrism, and prejudice (CONTINUED)

REFERENCE, SAMPLE	INSTRUMENT	RESULTS	COMMENTS
Trent (1967). Total sampling of all male and female freshmen at five West Coast Catholic colleges in 1959. Longitudinal, 1959-1963.	Nonauthoritarianism Scale from the Omnibus Personality Inventory (high score = high nonauthoritarianism)	Fr (243): $\bar{X}$=39.5 Sr (243): $\bar{X}$=46.5	Sr are more nonauthoritarian than Fr (SS).
Hunter (1942a). Total sampling of entering female freshmen at a "small, southern liberal arts college for women" in 1934, 1935, 1936, and 1937. Longitudinal, 1934-1938, 1935-1939, 1936-1940, 1937-1941. (Samples are combined in analysis.)	Hunter Test of Attitudes--The Negro Subscale (high positive score = favorable attitude toward Negroes)	Fr (185): $\bar{X}$= -6.58; SD=10.47 Sr (185): $\bar{X}$= +3.47; SD=11.94	Sr are more favorable to Negroes than are Fr (SS). Sr scores are more heterogeneous than Fr scores.
Jones (1938a, 1938b). Total sampling of entire male freshman classes of 1930 and 1931 at College X, a "rather small New England liberal arts college for men." Longitudinal, 1930-1934 and 1931-1935. (Samples are combined in analysis.)	Hinckley's Attitude Toward the Negro Scale, No. 3, Form A--ed. by Thurstone (high score = favorable attitude toward the Negro)	Fr (77): $\bar{X}$=7.23; SD= .94 Sr (77): $\bar{X}$=7.21; SD=1.20	Sr are less favorable toward Negroes than are Fr (NSS). Sr scores are more heterogeneous than Fr scores.
Trent (1964a). Total sampling of all male and female freshmen and random or representative sampling of senior students at five West Coast Catholic colleges (in 1959-1960). Cross-sectional, freshmen at the beginning and seniors at the end of the school year.	Nonauthoritarian Scale from the Omnibus Personality Inventory (high score = high nonauthoritarianism)	<u>Males</u> Fr (490): $\bar{X}$= 9; SD=2.6 Sr (86): $\bar{X}$= 9; SD=3.1 <u>Females</u> Fr (561): $\bar{X}$= 9; SD=2.6 Sr (120): $\bar{X}$=10; SD=2.6	For males, there is no difference between Fr and Sr with respect to nonauthoritarianism. Sr scores are more heterogeneous than Fr scores. For females, Sr are more nonauthoritarian than Fr (PNG). There is no difference in heterogeneity between Fr and Sr scores.
Webster, Freedman and Heist (1962). Sampling of female freshmen and seniors at Vassar. Cross-sectional, year not given.	Social Maturity Scale from the Vassar College Attitude Inventory (high score = low authoritarianism, high social maturity)	Fr (321): $\bar{X}$=82.13; SD=15.15 Sr (197): $\bar{X}$=92.99; SD=15.01	Sr are more socially mature (less authoritarian) than Fr (PNG). Sr scores are less heterogeneous than Fr scores.
Fox (1965). Sampling of freshmen and seniors at St. Ambrose College. Cross-sectional, year not given.	Omnibus Opinion Survey --constructed by Fox along the lines of the F Scale (high positive score = high authoritarianism)	Fr (61): $\bar{X}$=+17.74; SD=20.70 Sr (80): $\bar{X}$= -9.21; SD=33.30	Sr are less authoritarian than Fr (SS). Sr scores are more heterogeneous than Fr scores.

Table 2H.--Changes in authoritarianism, dogmatism, ethnocentrism, and prejudice (CONTINUED)

REFERENCE, SAMPLE	INSTRUMENT	RESULTS	COMMENTS
Krick (1963). Sampling of male and female students at Indiana Central College. Cross-sectional, Spring 1962. (Note: freshmen and seniors are matched on certain demographic variables.)	Inventory of Beliefs (high score indicates a person who is flexible, adaptive and democratic in his relationships with others, and does not accept stereotypes)	Fr (91): $\bar{X}$=75.2; SD=12.6 Sr (91): $\bar{X}$=61.0; SD=14.0	Sr are more flexible, less rigid and less authoritarian than Fr (SS). Sr scores are more heterogeneous than Fr scores.
Brown and Datta (1959). Random sampling of freshmen and seniors (females) at Vassar. Cross-sectional, year not given.	F_4 Scale--a modified version of the California F Scale; scores are corrected for response set (high score = high authoritarianism)	Fr (135): $\bar{X}$=40.5 Sr (135): $\bar{X}$=31.4	Sr are less authoritarian than Fr (SS).
Brown and Bystryn (1956). Random sampling of female freshmen and seniors at College A ("a small, Eastern liberal arts graduate and undergraduate college for women"), at College B ("a large Eastern co-ed university located in a city") and at College C (a small "upper middle class Catholic liberal arts college for women"). All cross-sectional, Fall 1951.	Modified version of the California F Scale (high score = high authoritarianism)	<u>College A</u> Fr (76): $\bar{X}$=196.330 Sr (69): $\bar{X}$=162.504 <u>College B</u> Fr (34): $\bar{X}$=202.176 Sr (57): $\bar{X}$=192.840 <u>College C</u> Fr (31)*: $\bar{X}$=243.692 Sr (26): $\bar{X}$=231.710 *Note: N's are from Table 1 in original. Table 2 in original has N's reversed.	Sr are less authoritarian than Fr (SS). Sr are less authoritarian than Fr (NSS). Sr are less authoritarian than Fr (SS).
Stephenson (1952). Sampling of male and female freshman and senior students in the College of Arts and Sciences, the School of Business Administration, and the School of Education of Miami Univ. (Oxford, Ohio). Cross-sectional, December 1948.	Hinckley's Attitude Toward the Negro Scale (high score = favorable attitude toward Negroes)	<u>Males*</u> Fr (202): $\bar{X}$=7.36 Sr (217): $\bar{X}$=7.64 <u>Females*</u> Fr (219): $\bar{X}$=7.61 Sr (136): $\bar{X}$=7.93 *Means calculated by averaging the means given separately for samples from the College of Arts and Sciences, the School of Business Administration, and the School of Education.	For each sex, Sr are more favorable to Negroes than are Fr (PNG).
Webster, Freedman and Heist (1962). Sampling of freshmen (females) at Vassar in the fall of 1955 and 1956. Longitudinal, 1955-1958 and 1956-1959.	Social Maturity Scale from the Vassar College Atttitude Inventory (high score = low authoritarianism, high social maturity)	<u>1955-1958 longitudinal</u> Fr (53): $\bar{X}$=85.26; SD=10.83 Jr (53): $\bar{X}$=96.38; SD=11.58 <u>1956-1959 longitudinal</u> Fr (59): $\bar{X}$=85.31; SD=15.35 Jr (59): $\bar{X}$=94.27; SD=16.62	For both longitudinal samples, Jr are more socially mature (less authoritarian) than Fr (PNG).

OTHER STUDIES:

There are three reports that are not included in the above because actual mean data are not given in them although change during the college years is described. All are four-year longitudinal studies. One reports on students at Vassar (Webster, 1956), another on Harvard students (King, 1967), and the third on a sample of National Merit Scholars and Certificate of Merit recipients at whatever school they did their college work (Tyler, 1963). All of these report that seniors are either less authoritarian or less dogmatic than they were as freshmen. Other studies, longitudinal in design (Hassenger, 1965, 1966, 1967b; Plant 1958b, 1958c, 1962, 1965; and Telford and Plant, 1963), report freshman-sophomore differences on the California F and E Scales and on Rokeach's Dogmatism Scale. In all instances, sophomores are, on the average, significantly less authoritarian, dogmatic and ethnocentric than they were as freshmen. Using the Inventory of Beliefs and the Problem in Human Relations Test to study changes in the freshman year, Dressel and Mayhew (1954) found that students become less stereotyped in beliefs and more adaptive and flexible in their thinking in 11 out of 13 educational institutions under investigation, and more democratic in their orientation toward others in 8 out of 9 institutions studied (PNG). Also, using the Inventory of Beliefs, Klingelhofer (1965) found that in two separate longitudinal studies sophomore males and females were more adaptive and flexible in their thinking, and more democratic in their orientation, than they were when they entered college (SS). Using a cross-sectional sample of students at Carnegie Institute of Technology, Kirk (1965) found that upperclassmen score less authoritarian (on a modified version of the Social Maturity Scale of the Omnibus Personality Inventory) than do freshmen. Differences in percentage endorsement (by various class levels at Antioch, Colgate and Michigan State) of selected, individual items of the Inventory of Beliefs are given by Jacob (1957, Table 14).

Some early, cross-sectional studies (Cantey and Mull, 1942; Garrison and Mann, 1931; and Jones, 1926) compare students of different class levels on a series of items that are not combined to form scales or indices. Some of these items appear to tap into the authoritarianism-dogmatism syndrome. Again, seniors are less likely than freshmen to endorse authoritarian statements.

Four studies dealing with prejudice are not included in the above. The first (Barkley, 1942b) compares the same female freshmen in the fall and in the spring on Hinckley's Attitudes Toward the Negro Scale. In the nine months these women spent at a southern women's college, they decreased in favorableness toward Negroes, although the result was not statistically significant. In a cross-sectional study, Kelly, Ferson and Holtzman (1958) report that the University of Texas seniors manifest more favorable attitudes toward Negroes than freshmen (NSS). The other two studies are cross-sectional in design and employ a number of items not combined into indices. In one (Garrison and Burch, 1933), seniors at North Carolina State are less prejudiced toward Negroes than are freshmen on most of the items. The other (Stember, 1961), comparing freshmen and seniors at a number of colleges, reports that seniors are not consistently less prejudiced toward Jews or Negroes. Differences on various items between the two classes are small, and in a few cases, freshmen express slightly less prejudice.

Table 2I.--Summaries of studies showing changes in autonomy, dominance and confidence. See explanatory note for Tables 2A-2N.

REFERENCE, SAMPLE	VARIABLE	COMPARISON GROUP	RESULTS
Stewart (1964). Univ. of California at Berkeley. Longitudinal, 1957-1961.	Dominance and Confidence Scale (VCAI)[1]	Males: Sr vs. Fr	Sr are more dominant and confident (NSS). Sr SD larger.*
		Females: Sr vs. Fr	Sr are more dominant and confident (SS). Sr SD smaller.* *Information about SD's supplied by Stewart in personal communication to authors.
Webster, Freedman and Heist (1962). Vassar College. Cross-sectional, year not given.	Dominance and Confidence Scale (VCAI)[1]	Females: Sr vs. Fr	Sr are more dominant and confident (PNG). Sr SD larger.
Webster, Freedman and Heist (1962). Bennington College. Cross-sectional, year not given.	Dominance and Confidence Scale (VCAI)[1]	Females: Sr vs. Fr	Sr are more dominant and confident (PNG). Sr SD larger.
Nichols (1965, 1967). 4-year longitudinal study of a sample of National Merit Finalists, 1958-1962.	Dominance Scale, Factor E (16 PF)[2]	Males: Sr vs. Fr	Sr are more dominant (NSS).
		Females: Sr vs. Fr	Sr are more dominant (SS).
	Self-Sufficiency Scale Factor Q2, (16 PF)[3]	Males: Sr vs. Fr	Sr are more self-sufficient (SS).
		Females: Sr vs. Fr	Sr are more self-sufficient (SS).
	Dominance Scale[4]	Males: Sr vs. Fr	Sr are less dominant (SS).
		Females: Sr vs. Fr	Sr are less dominant (SS).
	Dependence Scale[5]	Males: Sr vs. Fr	Sr are less dependent (SS).
		Females: Sr vs. Fr	Sr are less dependent (SS).
Farnsworth (1938). Stanford Univ. Longitudinal, 1932-1936.	Dominance-Submission Scale (BPI)[6]	Males: Sr vs. Fr	Sr are more dominant (NSS).
	Self-sufficiency Scale (BPI)[7]	Males: Sr vs. Fr	Sr are more self-sufficient (NSS).
	Self-confidence Scale (BPI)[8]	Males: Sr vs. Fr	Sr are more confident (NSS).
Harrington (1965). Purdue Univ. Longitudinal, 1960-1963.	Dominance Scale (EPPS)[9]	Males (engineering): Sr vs. Fr	Sr have a higher need for dominance (SS). Sr SD smaller.
	Autonomy Scale (EPPS)[10]	Males (engineering): Sr vs. Fr	Sr have a higher need for autonomy (SS). Sr SD smaller.
	Deference Scale (EPPS)[11]	Males (engineering): Sr vs. Fr	Sr have a lower need for deference (SS). Sr SD smaller.
	Abasement Scale (EPPS)[12]	Males (engineering): Sr vs. Fr	Sr have a lower need for abasement (SS). Sr SD smaller.
	Succorance Scale (EPPS)[13]	Males (engineering): Sr vs. Fr	Sr have a lower need for succorance (NSS). Sr SD same.
	Ascendance Scale (GZTS)[14]	Males (engineering): Sr vs. Fr	Sr are more ascendant (SS). Sr SD larger.
Burton (1945). Univ. of Arizona. Longitudinal, 1939-1943.	Dominance-Submission Scale (BPI)[6]	Males and females: Sr vs. Fr	Sr are more dominant (PNG).
	Self-sufficiency Scale (BPI)[7]	Males and females: Sr vs. Fr	Sr are more self-sufficient (PNG).
	Self-confidence Scale (BPI)[8]	Males and females: Sr vs. Fr	Sr are more self-confident (PNG).
Webster (1956). Vassar College. Longitudinal, years not given.	Social Presence Scale (CPI)[15]	Females: Sr vs. Fr	Sr have more social presence, are more poised and self-confident (SS).

Table 21.--Changes in autonomy, dominance and confidence (CONTINUED)

REFERENCE, SAMPLE	VARIABLE	COMPARISON GROUP	RESULTS
Izard (1962a, 1962b). Vanderbilt Univ. Longitudinal, 1957-1961.	Dominance Scale (EPPS)[9]	Males (liberal arts): Sr vs. Fr	No statistically significant change.
		Females (liberal arts): Sr vs. Fr	Sr have a lower need for dominance (SS).
		Males (engineering): Sr vs. Fr	Sr have a higher need for dominance (SS).
		Females (nursing): Sr vs. Fr	No statistically significant change.
	Autonomy Scale (EPPS)[10]	Males (liberal arts): Sr vs. Fr	No statistically significant change.
		Females (liberal arts): Sr vs. Fr	Sr have a higher need for autonomy (SS).
		Males (engineering): Sr vs. Fr	Sr have a higher need for autonomy (SS).
		Females (nursing): Sr vs. Fr	Sr have a higher need for autonomy (SS).
	Deference Scale (EPPS)[11]	Males (liberal arts): Sr vs. Fr	No statistically significant change.
		Females (liberal arts): Sr vs. Fr	Sr have a lower need for deference (SS).
		Males (engineering): Sr vs. Fr	Sr have a lower need for deference (SS).
		Females (nursing): Sr vs. Fr	Sr have a lower need for deference (SS).
	Abasement Scale (EPPS)[12]	Males (liberal arts): Sr vs Fr.	Sr have a lower need for abasement (SS).
		Females (liberal arts): Sr vs. Fr	Sr have a lower need for abasement (SS).
		Males (engineering): Sr vs. Fr	Sr have a lower need for abasement (SS).
		Females (nursing): Sr vs. Fr	Sr have a lower need for abasement (SS).
	Succorance Scale (EPPS)[13]	Males (liberal arts): Sr vs. Fr	No statistically significant change.
		Females (liberal arts): Sr vs. Fr	No statistically significant change.
		Males (engineering): Sr vs. Fr	Sr have a lower need for succorance (SS).
		Females (nursing): Sr vs. Fr	No statistically significant change.
Stern (1966b). Four cross-sectional samples (year not given) as follows: (1) Liberal Arts, Men: Antioch, Oberlin. (2) Liberal Arts, Women: Bennington, Oberlin, Sarah Lawrence. (3) Engineering, Men: Arkansas, Detroit, Drexel, General Motors Institute, Georgia Institute of Technology, Illinois, Michigan, Purdue. (4) Business Administration, Men: Cincinnati, Drexel, Ohio State.	Submissiveness Scale Factor 7 (AI)[16]	Males (liberal arts): Sr vs. Fr	Sr are more submissive (PNG). Sr SD smaller.
		Females (liberal arts): Sr vs. Fr	Sr are less submissive (PNG). Sr SD larger.
		Males (engineering): Sr vs. Fr	Sr are less submissive (PNG). Sr SD smaller.
		Males (bus. ad.): Sr vs. Fr	Sr are less submissive (PNG). Sr SD smaller.

Table 21.--Changes in autonomy, dominance and confidence (CONTINUED)

REFERENCE, SAMPLE	VARIABLE	COMPARISON GROUP	RESULTS
Rowe (1964). Three women's colleges in Virginia (Hollins, Randolph-Macon, Sweet Briar). Cross-sectional, 1961-62.	Dominance-Tolerance Scale (AI)[17]	Females (College No. 1): Sr vs. Fr Females (College No. 2): Sr vs. Fr Females (College No. 3): Sr vs. Fr	Sr have a lower need for dominance (PNG). Sr SD smaller. Sr have a lower need for dominance (PNG). Sr SD smaller. Sr have a lower need for dominance (PNG). Sr SD larger.
	Abasement-Assurance Scale (AI)[18]	Females (College No. 1): Sr vs. Fr Females (College No. 2): Sr vs. Fr Females (College No. 3): Sr vs. Fr	Sr have a lower need for abasement (PNG). Sr SD smaller. Sr have a lower need for abasement (PNG). Sr SD smaller. Sr have a lower need for abasement (PNG). Sr SD larger.
	Deference-Restiveness Scale (AI)[19]	Females (College No. 1): Sr vs. Fr Females (College No. 2): Sr vs. Fr Females (College No. 3): Sr vs. Fr	Sr have a lower need for deference (PNG). Sr SD smaller. Sr have a lower need for deference (PNG). Sr SD larger. Sr have a lower need for deference (PNG). Sr SD larger.
	Succorance (Supplication-Autonomy) Scale (AI)[20]	Females (College No. 1): Sr vs. Fr Females (College No. 2): Sr vs. Fr Females (College No. 3): Sr vs. Fr	Sr have a higher need for succorance (PNG). Sr SD smaller. Sr have a lower need for succorance (PNG). Sr SD larger. Sr have a lower need for succorance (PNG). Sr SD larger.
Brewer (1963). Huston-Tillotson College. Cross-sectional, 1961.	Dominance-Tolerance Scale (AI)[17]	Males and females: Sr vs. Fr	Sr have a higher need for dominance (NSS). Sr SD smaller.
	Abasement-Assurance Scale (AI)[18]	Males and females: Sr vs. Fr	Sr have a lower need for abasement (NSS). Sr SD smaller.
	Deference-Restiveness Scale (AI)[19]	Males and females: Sr vs. Fr	Sr have a higher need for deference (NSS). Sr SD smaller.
	Succorance (Supplication-Autonomy) Scale (AI)[20]	Males and females: Sr vs. Fr	Sr have a higher need for succorance (NSS). Sr SD larger.
Webb and Crowder (1961b). Emory College. Cross-sectional, 1959.	Dominance-Tolerance Scale (AI)[17]	Males and females: Upper division students vs. Lower division students	Upper division students have a higher need for dominance (NSS). Upper division SD larger.
	Abasement-Assurance Scale (AI)[18]	Males and females: Upper division students vs. Lower division students	Upper division students have a lower need for abasement (NSS). Upper division SD same.
	Deference-Restiveness Scale (AI)[19]	Males and females: Upper division students vs. Lower division students	Upper division students have a lower need for deference (NSS). Upper divison SD larger.
	Succorance (Supplication-Autonomy) Scale (AI)[20]	Males and females: Upper division students vs. Lower division students	Upper division students have a higher need for succorance (NSS). Upper divison SD smaller.
Chickering (nd[a]). Goddard College. Longitudinal, 1960-1964 and 1961-1965.	Abasement-Assurance Scale (AI)[18]	Males and females, 1960-1964: Sr vs. Fr Males and females: 1961-1965: Sr vs. Fr	Sr have a lower need for abasement (SS). Sr have a lower need for abasement (SS).
	Deference Scale (AI)[19]	Males and females: 1960-1964: Sr vs. Fr Males and females, 1961-1965: Sr vs. Fr	Sr have a lower need for deference (SS). Sr have a lower need for deference (SS).
	Succorance (Supplication-Autonomy) Scale (AI)[20]	Males and females, 1960-1964: Sr vs. Fr Males and females, 1961-1965: Sr vs. Fr	Sr have a lower need for succorance (SS). Sr have a lower need for succorance (NSS).

Table 21.--Changes in autonomy, dominance and confidence (CONTINUED)

[1] Dominance and Confidence Scale (Vassar College Attitude Inventory): perception of self as a leader within groups and in various social situations, imperturbability.

[2] Dominance Scale, Factor E (Sixteen Personality Factor Questionnaire): dominant, ascendant, assertive, self-assured, independent, aggressive, stubborn.

[3] Self-Sufficiency Scale, Factor Q_2 (Sixteen Personality Factor Questionnaire): self-sufficient, preferring to make own decisions, resourceful.

[4] Dominance Scale: an internally consistent scale from the National Merit Student Survey, no further description given.

[5] Dependence Scale: an internally consistent scale from the National Merit Student Survey, no further description given.

[6] Dominance-Submission Scale (Bernreuter Personality Inventory): tendency to dominate others in face-to-face situations.

[7] Self-sufficiency Scale (Bernreuter Personality Inventory): preference to be alone and not ask for sympathy and encouragement, tendency to ignore the advice of others.

[8] Self-confidence Scale (Bernreuter Personality Inventory): tendency to be wholesomely self-confident and well adjusted to environment.

[9] Dominance Scale (Edwards Personal Preference Schedule): need to argue for one's point of view, to be a leader, to make group decisions, to persuade and influence others to do what one wants, to supervise and direct the actions of others.

[10] Autonomy Scale (Edwards Personal Preference Schedule): need to be able to come and go as desired, to say what one thinks about things, to be free of others in making decisions, to feel free to do what one wants.

[11] Deference Scale (Edwards Personal Preference Schedule): need to get suggestions from others, to follow instructions and do what is expected, to praise others, to accept the leadership of others, to let others make decisions.

[12] Abasement Scale (Edwards Personal Preference Schedule): need to feel guilty when one does something wrong, to feel better when giving in and avoiding a fight than when having one's own way, to feel depressed by inability to handle situations, to feel timid in the presence of superiors, to feel inferior to others in most respects.

[13] Succorance Scale (Edwards Personal Preference Schedule): need to have others provide help when in trouble, to seek encouragement from others, to have others be kindly, to be helped by others when depressed.

[14] Ascendance Scale (Guilford-Zimmerman Temperament Survey): self-defense, leadership habits, able to speak with others and in public, persuasive.

[15] Social Presence Scale (California Personality Inventory): poise, spontaneity and self-confidence in personal and social interaction.

[16] Submissiveness Scale, Factor 7 (Activities Index): high level of control based on social conformity and other-directedness.

[17] Dominance-Tolerance Scale (Activities Index): need for ascendancy and assertive or manipulative control over others.

[18] Abasement-Assurance Scale (Activities Index): need for self-depreciation and devaluation.

[19] Deference-Restiveness Scale (Activities Index): need to submit to the opinions and preferences of others perceived as superior.

[20] Succorance (Supplication-Autonomy) Scale (Activities Index): need to depend on others for love, assistance and protection.

Table 2J.--Summaries of studies showing changes in readiness to express impulses. See explanatory note for Tables 2A-2N.

REFERENCE, SAMPLE	VARIABLE	COMPARISON GROUP	RESULTS
Sanford, Webster and Freedman (1957). Vassar College. Cross-sectional, year not given.	Impulse Expression Scale (VCAI)[1]	Females: Sr vs. Fr	Sr are more ready to express impulses (SS). Sr SD smaller.
Webster, Freedman and Heist (1962). Vassar College. Cross-sectional, year not given	Impulse Expression Scale (VCAI)[1]	Females: Sr vs. Fr	Sr are more ready to express impulses (PNG). Sr SD larger.
Webster, Freedman and Heist (1962). Bennington College. Cross-sectional, year not given.	Impulse Expression Scale (VCAI)[1]	Females: Sr vs. Fr	Sr are more ready to express impulses (PNG). Sr SD smaller.
Webster, Freedman and Heist (1962) Vassar College. Longitudinal, 1953-1956 and 1954-1957.	Impulse Expression Scale (VCAI)[1]	Females: Jr vs. Fr (1953-1956) Females: Jr vs. Fr (1954-1957)	Jr are more ready to express impulses (SS). Jr are more ready to express impulses (SS).
	Flexibility Scale (CPI)[2]	Females: Jr vs. Fr (1953-1956) Females: Jr vs. Fr (1954-1957)	Jr are more flexible, less deliberate and cautious (SS). Jr are more flexible, less deliberate and cautious (SS).
McConnell, Clark, Heist, Trow, and Yonge (forthcoming). Antioch, Reed, Swarthmore, San Francisco State, Univ. of California at Berkeley, Univ. of the Pacific, St. Olaf, and Univ. of Portland. Longitudinal; first school, 1958-1963; next three schools, 1958-1962; last four schools, 1959-1963.	Impulse Expression Scale (OPI)[3]	Antioch Males: Sr vs. Fr Females: Sr vs. Fr Reed Males: Sr vs. Fr Females: Sr vs. Fr Swarthmore Males: Sr vs. Fr Females: Sr vs. Fr San Francisco Males: Sr vs. Fr Females: Sr vs. Fr Berkeley Males: Sr vs. Fr Females: Sr vs. Fr Univ. of Pacific Males: Sr vs. Fr Females: Sr vs. Fr St. Olaf Males: Sr vs. Fr Females: Sr vs. Fr Univ. of Portland Males: Sr vs. Fr Females: Sr vs. Fr	 Sr are more ready to express impulses (SS). Sr SD larger. Sr are more ready to express impulses (SS). Sr SD larger. Sr are less ready to express impulses (SS). Sr SD larger. Sr are more ready to express impulses (SS). Sr SD smaller. Sr are more ready to express impulses (SS). Sr SD smaller. Sr are more ready to express impulses (SS). Sr SD larger. Sr are more ready to express impulses (SS). Sr SD larger. Sr are more ready to express impulses (SS). Sr SD larger. Sr are more ready to express impulses (SS). Sr SD larger. Sr are more ready to express impulses (SS). Sr SD larger. Sr are more ready to express impulses (NSS). Sr SD smaller Sr are more ready to express impulses (SS). Sr SD larger. Sr are more ready to express impulses (SS). Sr SD larger. Sr are more ready to express impulses (SS). Sr SD larger. Sr are less ready to express impulses (SS). Sr SD smaller. Sr are more ready to express impulses (NSS). Sr SD smaller.

Table 2J.--Changes in readiness to express impulses (CONTINUED)

REFERENCE, SAMPLE	VARIABLE	COMPARISON GROUP	RESULTS
Korn (1967a). Stanford and Univ. of California at Berkeley. Longitudinal, 1961-1965.	Impulse Expression Scale (OPI)[3]	Stanford Males: Sr vs. Fr Females: Sr vs. Fr Berkeley Males: Sr vs. Fr Females: Sr vs. Fr	 Sr are more ready to express impulses (SS). Sr SD smaller. Sr are more ready to express impulses (SS). Sr SD larger. Sr are more ready to express impulses (SS). Sr SD larger. Sr are more ready to express impulses (SS). Sr SD larger.
Snyder (1967). Massachusetts Institute of Technology. Longitudinal, years not given.	Impulse Expression Scale (OPI)[3]	Males: Sr vs. Fr	Sr are more ready to express impulses (SS).
Tyler (1963). 4-year longitudinal study of a sample of National Merit Scholarship winners and Certificate of Merit winners, years not given.	Impulse Expression Scale (OPI)[3]	Males and females: Sr vs. Fr	Sr are more ready to express impulses (SS).
Trent (1964a). Selected state and private colleges. Longitudinal, years not given.	Impulse Expression Scale (OPI)[3]	Males and females (non-Catholic students): Sr vs. Fr	Sr are more ready to express impulses (SS).
Trent (1964a). Five West Coast Catholic colleges. Cross-sectional, 1959 (freshmen) and 1960 (seniors).	Impulse Expression Scale (OPI)[3]	Males: Sr vs. Fr Females: Sr vs. Fr	Sr are less ready to express impulses (SS). Sr SD smaller. Sr are less ready to express impulses (SS). Sr SD smaller.
Beach (1966). Whitworth College, a church-related college. Longitudinal, 1961-1965.	Impulse Expression Scale (OPI)[3]	Males: Sr vs. Fr Females: Sr vs. Fr	Sr are more ready to express impulses (SS). Sr SD smaller. Sr are more ready to express impulses (NSS). Sr SD larger.
Beach (1967). Whitworth College, a church-related college. Cross-sectional, 1961.	Impulse Expression Scale (OPI)[3]	Males: Sr vs. Fr Females: Sr vs. Fr	Sr are less ready to express impulses (NSS). Sr SD larger. Sr are less ready to express impulses (SS). Sr SD smaller.
Stewart (1964). Univ. of California, Berkeley. Longitudinal, 1957-1961.	Impulse Expression Scale (OPI)[3]	Males: Sr vs. Fr Females: Sr vs. Fr	Sr are less ready to express impulses (SS). Sr SD larger.* Sr are less ready to express impulses (NSS). Sr SD smaller.*
	Responsibility Scale (OPI)[4]	Males: Sr vs. Fr Females: Sr vs. Fr	Sr are more responsible (SS). Sr SD smaller.* Sr are more responsible (NSS). Sr SD smaller.* *Information about SD's supplied by Stewart in personal communication to authors.

Table 2J.--Changes in readiness to express impulses (CONTINUED)

REFERENCE, SAMPLE	VARIABLE	COMPARISON GROUP	RESULTS
King (1967). Harvard Univ. Longitudinal, 1960-1964 and 1961-1965.	Need-Determined Assertiveness Scale (BVPT)[5]	Males: Sr vs. Fr (1960-1964)	Sr are more ready to express impulses (SS).
		Males: Sr vs. Fr (1961-1965)	Sr are more ready to express impulses (SS).
Nichols (1965, 1967). 4-year longitudinal study of a sample of National Merit Finalists, 1958-1962.	Deferred Gratification Scale[6]	Males: Sr vs. Fr	Sr are less ready to defer gratification (SS).
		Females: Sr vs. Fr	Sr are less ready to defer gratification (SS)
	Self-Control or High Self-sentiment Formation Scale, Factor Q_3 (16 PF)[7]	Males: Sr vs. Fr	Sr are less self-controlled (NSS).
		Females: Sr vs. Fr	Sr are less self-controlled (NSS).
	Character or Super-Ego Strength Scale, Factor G (16 PF)[8]	Males: Sr vs. Fr	Sr have less superego strength (SS).
		Females: Sr vs. Fr	Sr have less superego strength (SS).
	Superego Scale[9]	Males: Sr vs. Fr	Sr score lower on Superego Scale (SS).
		Females: Sr vs. Fr	Sr score lower on Superego Scale (SS).
Harrington (1965). Purdue Univ. Longitudinal, 1960-1963.	Change Scale (EPPS)[10]	Males (engineering): Sr vs. Fr	Sr have a higher need for change (NSS). Sr SD larger.
	Restraint Scale (GZTS)[11]	Males (engineering): Sr vs. Fr	Sr are less restrained and self-controlled (NSS). Sr SD smaller.
	Order Scale (EPPS)[12]	Males (engineering): Sr vs. Fr	Sr have a lower need for order (SS). Sr SD larger.
Izard (1962a, 1962b). Vanderbilt Univ. Longitudinal, 1957-1961.	Change Scale (EPPS)[10]	Males (liberal arts): Sr vs. Fr	No statistically significant change.
		Females (liberal arts): Sr vs. Fr	No statistically significant change.
		Males (engineering): Sr vs. Fr	No statistically significant change.
		Females (nursing): Sr vs. Fr	No statistically significant change.
	Order Scale (EPPS)[12]	Males (liberal arts): Sr vs. Fr	No statistically significant change.
		Females (liberal arts): Sr vs. Fr	No statistically significant change.
		Males (engineering): Sr vs. Fr	No statistically significant change.
		Females (nursing): Sr vs. Fr	Sr have a lower need for order (SS).
Webster (1956). Vassar College. Cross-sectional, year not given.	Responsibility Scale (CPI)[4]	Females: Sr vs. Fr	Sr are less responsible (SS).
Stern (1966b). Four cross-sectional samples (year not given) as follows: (1) Liberal Arts, Men: Antioch, Oberlin. (2) Liberal Arts, Women: Bennington, Oberlin, Sarah Lawrence. (3) Engineering, Men: Arkansas, Detroit, Drexel, General Motors Institute, Georgia Institute of Technology, Illinois, Michigan, Purdue. (4) Business administration, Men: Cincinnati, Drexel, Ohio State.	Orderliness Scale, Factor 6 (AI)[13]	Males (liberal arts): Sr vs. Fr	Sr are less orderly (NSS). Sr SD smaller.
		Females (liberal arts): Sr vs. Fr	Sr have same degree of orderliness (NSS). Sr SD smaller.
		Males (engineering): Sr vs. Fr	Sr are less orderly (NSS). Sr SD smaller.
		Males (bus. ad.): Sr vs. Fr	Sr are less orderly (NSS). Sr SD larger.
	Sensuousness Scale, Factor 9 (AI)[14]	Males (liberal arts): Sr vs. Fr	Sr are less sensuous (NSS). Sr SD larger.
		Females (liberal arts): Sr vs. Fr	Sr are less sensous (NSS). Sr SD larger.
		Males (engineering): Sr vs. Fr	Sr are less sensuous (NSS). Sr SD smaller.
		Males (bus. ad.): Sr vs. Fr	Sr are less sensuous (NSS). Sr SD smaller.
	Expressiveness-Constraint Scale, Factor 11 (AI)[15]	Males (liberal arts): Sr vs. Fr	Sr are less expressive, more constrained (NSS). Sr SD larger.
		Females (liberal arts): Sr vs. Fr	Sr are less expressive, more constrained (NSS). Sr SD smaller.
		Males (engineering): Sr vs. Fr	Sr are less expressive, more constrained (NSS). Sr SD same.
		Males (bus. ad.): Sr vs. Fr	Sr are more expressive, less constrained (NSS). Sr SD same.

Table 2J.--Changes in readiness to express impulses (CONTINUED)

REFERENCE, SAMPLE	VARIABLE	COMPARISON GROUP	RESULTS
Webb and Crowder (1961b). Emory College. Cross-sectional, 1959.	Impulsion (Impulsiveness) Scale (AI)[16]	Males and females: Upper division students vs. Lower division students	Upper division students have a lower need for impulsiveness (NSS). Upper division SD larger.
	Change Scale (AI)[17]	Males and females: Upper division students vs. Lower division students	Upper division students have a higher need for change and unroutinized behavior (SS). Upper division SD larger.
	Emotionality Scale (AI)[18]	Males and females: Upper division students vs. Lower division students	Upper division students have a lower need for active emotional expression (NSS). Upper division SD smaller.
	Sentience (Sensuality) Scale (AI)[19]	Males and females: Upper division students vs. Lower division students	Upper division students have a lower need for sensuous experiences (NSS). Upper division SD smaller.
	Play Scale (AI)[20]	Males and females: Upper division students vs. Lower division students	Upper division students have a lower need for pleasure-seeking (NSS). Upper division SD larger.
	Order Scale (AI)[21]	Males and females: Upper division students vs. Lower division students	Upper division students have a lower need for order (SS). Upper division SD larger.
	Conjunctivity Scale (AI)[22]	Males and females: Upper division students vs. Lower division students	Upper division students have a higher need for planfulness (NSS). Upper division SD smaller.
Rowe (1964. Three women's colleges in Virginia (Hollins, Randolph-Macon, and Sweet Briar). Cross-sectional, 1962.	Impulsion (Impulsiveness) Scale (AI)[16]	Females (College No. 1): Sr vs. Fr Females (College No. 2): Sr vs. Fr Females (College No. 3): Sr vs. Fr	Sr have a lower need for impulsiveness (PNG). Sr SD smaller. Sr have a lower need for impulsiveness (PNG). Sr SD larger. Sr have a lower need for impulsiveness (PNG). Sr SD larger.
	Change Scale (AI)[17]	Females (College No. 1): Sr vs. Fr Females (College No. 2): Sr vs. Fr Females (College No. 3): Sr vs. Fr	Sr have a lower need for change and unroutinized behavior (PNG). Sr SD smaller. Sr have a lower need for change and unroutinized behavior (PNG). Sr SD smaller. Sr have a lower need for change and unroutinized behavior (PNG). Sr SD larger.
	Emotionality Scale (AI)[18]	Females (College No. 1): Sr vs. Fr Females (College No. 2): Sr vs. Fr Females (College No. 3): Sr vs. Fr	Sr have a lower need for active emotional expression (PNG). Sr SD larger. Sr have a lower need for active emotional expression (PNG). Sr SD larger. Sr have a lower need for active emotional expression (PNG). Sr SD larger.
	Sentience (Sensuality) Scale (AI)[19]	Females (College No. 1): Sr vs. Fr Females (College No. 2): Sr vs. Fr Females (College No. 3): Sr vs. Fr	Sr have a lower need for sensuous experiences (PNG). Sr SD smaller. Sr have a lower need for sensuous experiences (PNG). Sr SD larger. Sr have a lower need for sensuous experiences (PNG). Sr SD larger.
	Play Scale (AI)[20]	Females (College No. 1): Sr vs. Fr Females (College No. 2): Sr vs. Fr Females (College No. 3): Sr vs. Fr	Sr have a lower need for pleasure-seeking (PNG). Sr SD smaller. Sr have a higher need for pleasure-seeking (PNG). Sr SD same. Sr have a lower need for pleasure-seeking (PNG). Sr SD larger.
	Order Scale (AI)[21]	Females (College No. 1): Sr vs. Fr Females (College No. 2): Sr vs. Fr Females (College No. 3): Sr vs. Fr	Sr have a higher need for order (PNG). Sr SD smaller. Sr have a lower need for order (PNG). Sr SD smaller. Sr have a lower need for order (PNG). Sr SD larger.
	Conjunctivity Scale (AI)[22]	Females (College No. 1): Sr vs. Fr Females (College No. 2): Sr vs. Fr Females (College No. 3): Sr vs. Fr	Sr have a higher need for planfulness (PNG). Sr SD larger. Sr have a lower need for planfulness (PNG). Sr SD smaller. Sr have a lower need for planfulness (PNG). Sr SD larger.

Table 2J.--Changes in readiness to express impulses (CONTINUED)

REFERENCE, SAMPLE	VARIABLE	COMPARISON GROUP	RESULTS
Brewer (1963). Huston-Tillotson College. Cross-sectional, 1961.	Impulsion (Impulsiveness) Scale (AI)[16]	Males and females: Sr vs. Fr	Sr have a lower need for impulsiveness (NSS). Sr SD same.
	Change Scale (AI)[17]	Males and females: Sr vs. Fr	Sr have a lower need for change and unroutinized behavior (NSS). Sr SD smaller.
	Emotionality Scale (AI)[18]	Males and females: Sr vs. Fr	Sr have a lower need for active emotional expression (NSS). Sr SD smaller.
	Sentience (Sensuality) Scale (AI)[19]	Males and females: Sr vs. Fr	Sr have a lower need for pleasure-seeking (NSS). Sr SD larger.
	Play Scale (AI)[20]	Males and females: Sr vs. Fr	Sr have a lower need for play (NSS). Sr SD larger.
	Order Scale (AI)[21]	Males and females: Sr vs. Fr	Sr have a lower need for order (NSS). Sr SD larger.
	Conjunctivity Scale (AI)[22]	Males and females: Sr vs. Fr	Sr have a higher need for planfulness (NSS). Sr SD larger.

[1] Impulse Expression Scale (Vassar College Attitude Inventory): general readiness to express impulses and to seek gratification either in conscious thought or in overt action; not reserved or dignified.

[2] Flexibility Scale (California Psychological Inventory): flexibility and adaptibility of thinking and social behavior; insightful, informal and adventurous, not deliberate, cautious or worrying.

[3] Impulse Expression Scale (Omnibus Personality Inventory): general readiness to express impulses and to seek gratification either in conscious thought or in overt action; not reserved or dignified.

[4] Responsibility Scale (from an early form of the Omnibus Personality Inventory): planful, resourceful, and concerned with social and moral issues; not immature, lazy and impulsive.

[5] Need-Determined Assertiveness Scale (Bales' Value Profile Test): impulse expression.

[6] Deferred Gratification Scale: an internally consistent scale from the National Merit Student Survey, no further description given.

[7] Self-Control or High Self-Sentiment Formation Scale, Factor Q_3 (Sixteen Personality Factor Questionnaire): controlled, socially-precise, self-disciplined, compulsive.

[8] Character or Super-Ego Strength Scale, Factor G (Sixteen Personality Factor Questionnaire): conscientious, persistent, responsible, emotionally mature, consistently ordered.

[9] Superego Scale: an internally consistent scale from the National Merit Student Survey, no further description given.

[10] Change Scale (Edwards Personal Preference Schedule): need to do new and different things, to experience novelty and change in daily routine, to experiment.

[11] Restraint Scale (Guilford-Zimmerman Temperament Survey): serious-minded, deliberate, persistent, self-controlled; not happy-go-lucky, carefree or impulsive.

[12] Order Scale (Edwards Personal Preference Schedule): need to have written work neat and organized, to make plans before starting on a difficult task, to have things organized, to keep things neat and orderly.

[13] Orderliness Scale, Factor 6 (Activities Index): marked interest in activities stressing personal organization and deliberativeness, avoidance of impulsive behavior.

[14] Sensuousness Scale, Factor 9 (Activities Index): self-indulgence, delight in the gratification which may be obtained through the senses.

[15] Expressiveness-Constraint Scale, Factor 11 (Activities Index): emotional lability, freedom from self-imposed controls, impulsive and uninhibited; not guarded, emotionally constricted, defensive, or rigid.

[16] Impulsion (Impulsiveness) Scale (Activities Index): need for impulsive, spontaneous, impetuous, unreflected behavior.

[17] Change Scale (Activities Index): need for unroutinized, changeable behavior, need for flexibility.

[18] Emotionality Scale (Activities Index): need for intensive, active emotional expression.

[19] Sentience (Sensuality) Scale (Activities Index): need for sensuous or voluptuous experiences and self-gratification.

[20] Play Scale (Activities Index): need for pleasure-seeking (vs. need for purposefulness).

[21] Order Scale (Activities Index): need for compulsive organization of details--preoccupation with neatness, order, and arrangement of the physical environment.

[22] Conjunctivity Scale (Activities Index): need for planfulness and organization of cognitive activities.

Table 2K.--Summaries of studies showing changes in the degree of masculinity or femininity of interests and attitudes. See explanatory note for Tables 2A-2N.

REFERENCE, SAMPLE	VARIABLE	COMPARISON GROUP	RESULTS
Stewart (1964). Univ. of California, Berkeley. Longitudinal, 1957-1961.	Masculinity-Femininity (MF) Scale (SVIB)[1]	Males: Sr vs. Fr Females: Sr vs. Fr	Male Sr have less masculine interests (SS). Sr SD smaller.* Female Sr have more feminine interests (NSS). Sr SD smaller.* *Information about SD's supplied by Stewart in personal communication to authors.
Finnie (1966). Harvard. Longitudinal, 1960-1964.	Masculinity-Femininity (MF) Scale (SVIB)[1]	Males: Sr vs. Fr	Male Sr have less masculine interests (PNG).
Lebold and Salvo (1964). Univ. of Purdue. Longitudinal, 1959-1963.	Masculinity-Femininity (MF) Scale (SVIB)[1]	Males (engineering):* Sr vs. Fr Males (non-engineering):** Sr vs. Fr	Male Sr have less masculine interests (SS). Sr SD smaller. Male Sr have less masculine interests (SS). Sr SD smaller. *Started and remained in the engineering dept. **Started in engineering dept. but graduated from some other department
Mills (1954). Macalester College. Longitudinal, 1947-1951.	Interest or Masculinity-Femininity (MF) Scale (MMPI)[2]	Males: Sr vs. Fr Females: Sr vs. Fr	Male Sr have less masculine interests (PNG). Sr SD smaller. Female Sr have more feminine interests (PNG). Sr SD smaller.
McConnell, Clark, Heist, Trow, and Yonge (forthcoming). Antioch, Reed, Swarthmore, San Francisco State, Univ. of Calif., Berkeley, Univ. of the Pacific, St. Olaf, and Univ. of Portland. Longitudinal; first school, 1958-1963; next three schools, 1958-1962; last four schools, 1959-1963.	Masculinity-Femininity (MF) Scale (OPI)[3]	Antioch Males: Sr vs. Fr Females: Sr vs. Fr	Male Sr are more masculine in interests and attitudes (PNG). Sr SD larger. Female Sr are more masculine in interests and attitudes (PNG). Sr SD larger.
		Reed Males: Sr vs. Fr Females: Sr vs. Fr	Male Sr are less masculine in interests and attitudes (PNG). Sr SD larger. Female Sr are more masculine in interests and attitudes (PNG). Sr SD smaller.
		Swarthmore Males: Sr vs. Fr Females: Sr vs. Fr	Male Sr are less masculine in interests and attitudes (PNG). Sr SD smaller. Female Sr are more masculine in interests and attitudes (PNG). Sr SD smaller.
		San Francisco Males: Sr vs. Fr Females: Sr vs. Fr	Male Sr are less masculine in interests and attitudes (PNG). Sr SD smaller. Female Sr are more masculine in interests and attitudes (PNG). Sr SD smaller.
		Berkeley Males: Sr vs. Fr Females: Sr vs Fr	Male Sr are less masculine in interests and attitudes (PNG). Sr SD smaller. Female Sr are more masculine in interests and attitudes (PNG). Sr SD smaller.
		Univ. of Pacific Males: Sr vs. Fr Females: Sr vs. Fr	Male Sr are more masculine in interests and attitudes (PNG). Sr SD smaller. Female Sr are more masculine in interests and attitudes (PNG). Sr SD smaller.
		St. Olaf Males: Sr vs. Fr Females: Sr vs. Fr	Male Sr are less masculine in interests and attitudes (PNG). Sr SD smaller. Female Sr are less masculine in interests and attitudes (PNG). Sr SD smaller.
		Univ. of Portland Males: Sr vs. Fr Females: Sr vs. Fr	Male Sr are less masculine in interests and attitudes (PNG). Sr SD smaller. Female Sr are less masculine in interests and attitudes (PNG). Sr SD larger.

Table 2K.--Changes in the degree of masculinity or femininity of interests (CONTINUED)

REFERENCE, SAMPLE	VARIABLE	COMPARISON GROUP	RESULTS
Korn (1967a). Stanford and Univ. of California at Berkeley. Longitudinal, 1961-1965.	Masculinity-Femininity (MF) Scale (OPI)[3]	Stanford Males: Sr vs. Fr Females: Sr vs. Fr Berkeley Males: Sr vs. Fr Females: Sr vs. Fr	Male Sr are less masculine in interests and attitudes (SS). Sr SD larger. Female Sr are less masculine in interests and attitudes (SS). Sr SD larger. Male Sr are less masculine in interests and attitudes (SS). Sr SD larger. Female Sr are less masculine in interests and attitudes (SS). Sr SD larger.
Webster, Freedman and Heist (1962). Vassar College. Cross-sectional, year not given.	Masculine Role Scale (VCAI)[4]	Females: Sr vs. Fr	Female Sr have more masculine interests and are less conventionally feminine (PNG). Sr SD larger.
Webster, Freedman and Heist (1962). Bennington College. Cross-sectional, year not given.	Masculine Role Scale (VCAI)[4]	Females: Sr vs. Fr	Female Sr have more masculine interests and are less conventionally feminine (PNG). Sr SD smaller.
Harrington (1965). Purdue Univ. Longitudinal, 1960-1963.	Masculinity Scale (GZTS)[5]	Males (engineering): Sr vs. Fr	Male Sr have more interest in masculine activities (NSS). Sr SD larger.
Nichols (1965, 1967). 4-year longitudinal study of a sample of National Merit Finalists, 1958-1962.	Premsia Scale, Factor I (16 PF)[6]	Males: Sr vs. Fr Females: Sr vs. Fr	Male Sr are more "effeminate" and emotionally sensitive (SS). Female Sr are less "effeminate" and emotionally sensitive (NSS).

[1]Masculinity-Femininity (MF) Scale (Strong Vocational Interest Blank): similarity of person's interests to the average of his own sex.

[2]Interest or Masculinity-Femininity (MF) Scale (Minnesota Multiphasic Personality Inventory): deviation of the basic interest pattern in the direction of the opposite sex.

[3]Masculinity-Femininity (MF) Scale (Omnibus Personality Inventory): expressing interest in science and problem-solving; admitting few adjustment problems, feelings of anxiety or personal inadequacies; not very aesthetic or sociable.

[4]Masculine Role Scale (Vassar College Attitude Inventory): active, having interests and attitudes characteristic of men in the American culture; not passive, acquiescent or conventionally feminine.

[5]Masculinity Scale (Guilford-Zimmerman Temperament Survey): interest in masculine activities and vocations, not easily disgusted, hard-boiled, resistant to fear, little interest in clothes and styles.

[6]Premsia Scale, Factor I (Sixteen Personality Factor Questionnaire): effeminate, emotionally sensitive, dependent, demanding, impatient, subjective, kindly, gentle, tender-minded, over protected.

Table 2L.--Summaries of studies showing changes in need for achievement, persistence, and vigor. See explanatory note for Tables 2A-2N.

REFERENCE, SAMPLE	VARIABLE	COMPARISON GROUP	RESULTS
Webb and Crowder (1961b). Emory College. Cross-sectional, 1959.	Achievement Scale (AI)[1]	Males and females: Upper division students vs. Lower division students	Upper division students have a higher need for achievement (NSS). Upper division SD smaller.
	Ego Achievement Scale (AI)[2]	Males and females: Upper division students vs. Lower division students	Upper division students have a higher need for ego achievement (SS). Upper division SD smaller.
	Fantasied Achievement Scale (AI)[3]	Males and females: Upper divison students vs. Lower division students	Upper division students have a higher need for fantasied achievement (NSS). Upper division SD smaller.
	Counteraction-Inferiority Avoidance Scale (AI)[4]	Males and females: Upper division students vs. Lower division students	Upper division students have a higher need for counteraction (NSS). Upper division SD larger.
	Pragmatism (Practicalness-Impracticalness) Scale (AI)[5]	Males and females: Upper division students vs. Lower division students	Upper division students have a lower need for practical, concrete achievement (NSS). Upper division SD larger.
	Energy-Passivity Scale (AI)[6]	Males and females: Upper division students vs. Lower division students	Upper division students have a higher need for intense, sustained, and vigorous effort (NSS). Upper division SD smaller.
Rowe (1964). Three women's colleges in Virginia (Hollins, Randolph-Macon, Sweet Briar). Cross-sectional, 1961-62.	Achievement Scale (AI)[1]	Females (College No. 1): Sr vs. Fr Females (College No. 2): Sr vs. Fr Females (Colleges No. 3): Sr vs. Fr	Sr have a lower need for achievement (PNG). Sr SD larger. Sr have a lower need for achievement (PNG). Sr SD larger. Sr have a lower need for achievement (PNG). Sr SD larger.
	Ego Achievement Scale (AI)[2]	Females (College No. 1): Sr vs. Fr Females (College No. 2): Sr vs. Fr Females (College No. 3): Sr vs. Fr	Sr have a lower need for ego achievement (PNG). Sr SD larger. Sr have a lower need for ego achievement (PNG). Sr SD smaller. Sr have a lower need for ego achievement (PNG). Sr SD larger.
	Fantasied Achievement Scale (AI)[3]	Females (College No. 1): Sr vs. Fr Females (College No. 2): Sr vs. Fr Females (College No. 3): Sr vs. Fr	Sr have a lower need for fantasied achievement (PNG). Sr SD larger. Sr have a lower need for fantasied achievement (PNG). Sr SD smaller. Sr have a lower need for fantasied achievement (PNG). Sr SD larger.
	Counteraction-Inferiority Avoidance Scale (AI)[4]	Females (College No. 1): Sr vs. Fr Females (College No. 2): Sr vs. Fr Females (College No. 3): Xr vs. Fr	Sr have a lower need for counteraction (PNG). Sr SD larger. Sr have a higher need for counteraction (PNG) Sr SD smaller. Sr have a lower need for counteraction (PNG). Sr SD larger.
	Pragmatism (Practicalness-Impracticalness) Scale (AI)[5]	Females (College No. 1): Sr vs. Fr Females (College No. 2): Sr vs. Fr Females (College No. 3): Sr vs. Fr	Sr have a higher need for practical, concrete achievement (PNG). Sr SD larger. Sr have a lower need for practical, concrete achievement (PNG). Sr SD smaller. Sr have a higher need for practical, concrete achievement (PNG). Sr SD larger.
	Energy-Passivity Scale (AI)[6]	Females (College No. 1): Sr vs. Fr Females (College No. 2): Sr vs. Fr Females (College No. 3): Sr vs. Fr	Sr have a higher need for intense, sustained, vigorous effort (PNG). Sr SD larger. Sr have a lower need for intense, sustained, vigorous effort (PNG). Sr SD larger. Sr have a lower need for intense, sustained, vigorous effort (PNG). Sr SD larger.

Table 2L.--Changes in need for achievement, persistence, and vigor (CONTINUED)

REFERENCE, SAMPLE	VARIABLE	COMPARISON GROUP	RESULTS
Brewer (1963). Huston-Tillotson College. Cross-sectional, 1961.	Achievement Scale (AI)[1]	Males and females: Sr vs. Fr	Sr have a lower need for achievement (NSS). Sr SD larger.
	Ego Achievement Scale (AI)[2]	Males and females: Sr vs. Fr	Sr have a higher need for ego achievement (NSS). Sr SD larger.
	Fantasied Achievement Scale (AI)[3]	Males and females: Sr vs. Fr	Sr have a lower need for fantasied achievement (NSS). Sr SD larger.
	Counteraction-Inferiority Avoidance Scale (AI)[4]	Males and females: Sr vs. Fr	Sr have a higher need for counteraction (NSS). Sr SD larger.
	Pragmatism (Practicalness-Impracticalness) Scale (AI)[5]	Males and females: Sr vs. Fr	Sr have a lower need for practical, concrete achievement (NSS). Sr SD larger.
	Energy-Passivity Scale (AI)[6]	Males and females: Sr vs. Fr	Sr have a lower need for intense, sustained and vigorous effort (NSS). Sr SD smaller.
Stern (1966b). Four cross-sectional samples (year not given) as follows: (1) Liberal Arts, Men: Antioch, Oberlin. (2) Liberal Arts, Women: Bennington, Oberlin, Sarah Lawrence. (3) Engineering, Men: Arkansas, Detroit, Drexel, General Motors Institute, Georgia Institute of Technology, Illinois, Michigan, Purdue. (4) Business Administration, Men: Cincinnati, Drexel, Ohio State.	Motivation Scale, Factor 4 (AI)[7]	Males (liberal arts): Sr vs. Fr	Sr are less motivated (PNG). Sr SD larger.
		Females (liberal arts): Sr vs. Fr	Sr are more motivated (PNG). Sr SD larger.
		Males (engineering): Sr vs. Fr	Sr are less motivated (PNG). Sr SD smaller.
Izard (1962a, 1962b). Vanderbilt Univ. Longitudinal, 1957-1961.	Achievement Scale (EPPS)[8]	Males (liberal arts): Sr vs. Fr	Sr have a higher need for achievement (SS).
		Females (liberal arts): Sr vs. Fr	No statistically significant change.
		Males (engineering): Sr vs. Fr	No statistically significant change.
		Females (nursing): Sr vs. Fr	No statistically significant change.
	Endurance Scale (EPPS)[9]	Males (liberal arts): Sr vs. Fr	No statistically significant change.
		Females (liberal arts): Sr vs. Fr	Sr have a lower need for endurance (NSS).
		Males (engineering): Sr vs. Fr	Sr have a lower need for endurance (SS).
		Females (nursing): Sr vs. Fr	Sr have a lower need for endurance (SS).
Harrington (1965). Purdue Univ. Longitudinal, 1960-1963.	Achievement Scale (EPPS)[8]	Males (engineering): Sr vs. Fr	Sr have a higher need for achievement (NSS). Sr SD same.
	Endurance Scale (EPPS)[9]	Males (engineering): Sr vs. Fr	Sr have a lower need for endurance (NSS). Sr SD larger.
	General Activity Scale (GZTS)[10]	Males (engineering): Sr vs. Fr	Sr are more generally active, have more energy and vitality (SS). Sr SD larger.

Table 2M.--Changes in sociability and friendliness (CONTINUED)

REFERENCE, SAMPLE	VARIABLE	COMPARISON GROUP	RESULTS
Webster, Freedman and Heist (1962). Vassar College. Cross-sectional, year not given.	Social Integration Scale (VCAI)[5]	Females: Sr vs. Fr	Sr are less socially integrated (PNG). Sr SD smaller.
Webster, Freedman and Heist (1962). Bennington College. Cross-sectional, year not given.	Social Integration Scale (VCAI)[5]	Females: Sr vs. Fr	Sr are more socially integrated (PNG). Sr SD smaller.
Palubinskas (1952). Iowa State College. Longitudinal, 1947-1951.	Social Adjustment Scale (Darley and McNamara's Minnesota Personality Scale)[6]	Females (majoring in home economics): Sr vs. Fr	Sr are more gregarious and socially mature (SS).
Harrington (1965). Purdue Univ. Longitudinal, 1960-1963.	Sociability Scale (GZTS)[7]	Males (engineering): Sr vs. Fr	Sr are less sociable (NSS). Sr SD smaller.
	Personal Relations Scale (GZTS)[8]	Males (engineering): Sr vs. Fr	Sr are less tolerant of others, less able to get along with others (NSS). Sr SD larger.
	Friendliness Scale (GZTS)[9]	Males (engineering): Sr vs. Fr	Sr are less friendly--i.e., more belligerant, more ready to fight, and less ready to be dominated (SS). Sr SD smaller.
	Affiliation Scale (EPPS)[10]	Males (engineering): Sr vs. Fr	Sr have a lower need for affiliation (SS). Sr SD smaller.
	Nurturance Scale (EPPS)[11]	Males (engineering): Sr vs. Fr	Sr have a lower need to be nurturant to others (SS). Sr SD smaller.
	Aggression Scale (EPPS)[12]	Males (engineering): Sr vs. Fr	Sr have a higher need to be aggressive toward others (SS). Sr SD smaller.
Izard (1962a, 1962b). Vanderbilt Univ. Longitudinal, 1957-1961.	Affiliation Scale (EPPS)[10]	Males (liberal arts): Sr vs. Fr Females (liberal arts): Sr vs. Fr Males (engineering): Sr vs. Fr Females (nursing): Sr vs. Fr	No statistically significant change. No statistically significant change. No statistically significant change. Sr have a lower need for affiliation (SS).
	Nurturance Scale (EPPS)[11]	Males (liberal arts): Sr vs. Fr Females (liberal arts): Sr vs. Fr Males (engineering): Sr vs. Fr Females (nursing): Sr vs. Fr	Sr have a lower need to be nurturant to others (SS). No statistically significant change. No statistically significant change. No statistically significant change.
	Aggression Scale (EPPS)[12]	Males (liberal arts): Sr vs. Fr Females (liberal arts): Sr vs. Fr Males (engineering): Sr vs. Fr Females (nursing): Sr vs. Fr	Sr have a higher need to be aggressive toward others (SS). No statistically significant change. Sr have a higher need to be aggressive toward others (SS). Sr have a higher need to be aggressive toward others (SS).

Table 2M.--Changes in sociability and friendliness (CONTINUED)

REFERENCE, SAMPLE	VARIABLE	COMPARISON GROUP	RESULTS
Stern (1966b). Four cross-sectional samples (year not given) as follows: (1) Liberal Arts, Men: Antioch, Oberlin. (2) Liberal Arts, Women: Bennington, Oberlin, Sarah Lawrence. (3) Enginering, Men: Arkansas, Detroit, Drexel, General Motors Institute, Georgia Institute of Technology, Illinois, Michigan, Purdue. (4) Business Administration, Men: Cincinnati, Drexel, Ohio State.	Friendliness Scale, Factor 10 (AI)[13]	Males (liberal arts): Sr vs. Fr	Sr are less friendly (PNG). Sr SD smaller.
		Females (liberal arts): Sr vs. Fr	Sr are more friendly (PNG). Sr SD smaller.
		Males (engineering): Sr vs. Fr	Sr are less friendly (PNG). Sr SD smaller.
		Males (bus. ad.): Sr vs. Fr	Sr are more friendly (PNG). Sr SD smaller.
Rowe (1964). Three women's colleges in Virginia (Hollins, Randolph-Macon, Sweet Briar). Cross-sectional, 1961-1962.	Affiliation-Rejection Scale (AI)[14]	Females (College No. 1): Sr vs. Fr	Sr have a lower need for affiliation with others (PNG). Sr SD larger.
		Females (College No. 2): Sr vs. Fr	Sr have a lower need for affiliation with others (PNG). Sr SD larger.
		Females (College No. 3): Sr vs. Fr	Sr have a lower need for affiliation with others (PNG). Sr SD larger.
	Nurturance-Rejection Scale (AI)[15]	Females (College No. 1): Sr vs. Fr	Sr have a lower need to be nurturant to others (PNG). Sr SD larger.
		Females (College No. 2): Sr vs. Fr	Sr have a lower need to be nurturant to others (PNG). Sr SD larger.
		Females (College No. 3): Sr vs. Fr	Sr have a lower need to be nurturant to others (PNG). Sr SD larger.
	Aggression-Blame Avoidance Scale (AI)[16]	Females (College No. 1): Sr vs. Fr	Sr have a lower need to be aggressive toward others (PNG). Sr SD smaller.
		Females (College No. 2): Sr vs. Fr	Sr have a lower need to be aggressive toward others (PNG). Sr SD larger.
		Females (College No. 3): Sr vs. Fr	Sr have a lower need to be aggressive toward others (PNG). Sr SD larger.
Brewer (1963). Huston-Tillotson College. Cross-sectional, 1961.	Affiliation Rejection Scale (AI)[14]	Males and females: Sr vs. Fr	Sr have a lower need for affiliation with others (NSS). Sr SD larger.
	Nurturance-Rejection Scale (AI)[15]	Males and females: Sr vs. Fr	Sr have a lower need to be nurturant to others (NSS). Sr SD larger.
	Aggression-Blame Avoidance Scale (AI)[16]	Males and females: Sr vs. Fr	Sr have a higher need to be aggressive toward others (NSS). Sr SD smaller.
Webb and Crowder (1961b). Emory College. Cross-sectional, 1959.	Affiliation-Rejection Scale (AI)[14]	Males and females: Upper division students vs. Lower division students	Upper division students have a lower need for affiliation with others (NSS). Upper division SD larger.
	Nurturance-Rejection Scale (AI)[15]	Males and females: Upper division students vs. Lower division students	Upper division students have a higher need to be nurturant to others (NSS). Upper division SD smaller.
	Aggression-Avoidance Scale (AI)[16]	Males and females: Upper division students vs. Lower division students	Upper division students have a lower need to be aggressive toward others (NSS). Upper division SD smaller.

[1]Social Introversion Scale (Omnibus Personality Inventory): withdrawing from social contacts and responsibilities; displaying little interest in people or in being with them.

[2]Sociability Scale (Bernreuter Personality Inventory): tendency to be sociable and gregarious.

[3]Cyclothymia or Sociability Scale, Factor A (Sixteen Personality Factor Questionnaire): sociable, warmhearted, outgoing, easy going, participating, ready to cooperate, attentive to people.

[4]Parmia or Adventurousness Scale, Factor H (Sixteen Personality Factor Questionnaire): socially adventurous, liking to meet people, overt interest in opposite sex, responsive, genial, friendly, socially bold, uninhibited.

[5]Social Integration Scale (Vassar Attitude Inventory Scale): not socially alienated or socially isolated.

[6]Social Adjustment Scale (Darley and McNamara's Minnesota Personality Scale): gregarious, socially mature in relations with other people.

[7]Sociability Scale (Guilford-Zimmerman Temperament Survey): social extraversion, at ease with others, enjoys others company, has many friends and acquaintances, enters into social conversations, likes social activities.

[8]Personal Relations Scale (Guilford-Zimmerman Temperament Survey): getting along with others, tolerance of people, faith in social institutions, unsuspicious of others.

[9]Friendliness Scale (Guilford-Zimmerman Temperament Survey): lack of fighting tendencies, urge to please others and be liked, toleration of hostile action, acceptance of domination.

[10]Affiliation Scale (Edwards Personal Preference Schedule): need to be loyal to and do things for friends, to participate in friendly groups, to form new friendships, to do things with friends rather than alone.

[11]Nurturance Scale (Edwards Personal Preference Schedule): need to help friends when they are troubled, to assist others less fortunate, to treat others with kindness and sympathy, to show affection toward others, to have others confide in one about personal problems.

[12]Aggression Scale (Edwards Personal Preference Schedule): need to attack contrary points of view, to tell others what one thinks about them, to get revenge for insults, to become angry, to blame others when things go wrong.

[13]Friendliness Scale, Factor 10 (Activities Index): interest in playful, friendly relationships with other people, enjoying simple and uncomplicated forms of amusement in a group setting.

[14]Affiliation-Rejection Scale (Activities Index): need for close, friendly, reciprocal associations with others.

[15]Nurturance-Rejection Scale (Activities Index): need to help or support others by providing love, assistance and protection.

[16]Aggression-Blame Avoidance Scale (Activities Index): need for overt or covert hostility toward others.

Table 2N.--Summaries of studies showing changes in psychological well-being. See explanatory note for Tables 2A-2N.

REFERENCE, SAMPLE	VARIABLE	COMPARISON GROUP	RESULTS
Nichols (1965, 1967). 4-year longitudinal study of a sample of National Merit Finalists, 1958-1962.	Emotional Stability or Ego Strength Scale, Factor C (16 PF)[1]	Males: Sr vs. Fr Females: Sr vs. Fr	Sr are less emotionally mature and stable (SS). Sr are less emotionally mature and stable (SS).
	Guilt Proneness Scale, Factor O (16 PF)[2]	Males: Sr vs. Fr Females: Sr vs. Fr	Sr are more anxious (NSS). Sr are more anxious (SS).
	Ergic Tension Scale, Factor Q4 (16 PF)[3]	Males: Sr vs. Fr Females: Sr vs. Fr	Sr are more tense (NSS). Sr are more tense (NSS).
	Surgency Scale, Factor F (16 PF)[4]	Males: Sr vs. Fr Females: Sr vs. Fr	Sr are less happy-go-lucky (NSS). Sr are less happy-go-lucky (SS).
Harrington (1965). Purdue Univ. Longitudinal, 1960-1963.	Emotional Stability Scale (GZTS)[5]	Males (engineering): Sr vs. Fr	Sr are less emotionally stable (NSS). Sr SD larger.
Palubinskas (1952). Iowa State College. Longitudinal, 1947-1951.	Emotionality Scale (Darley and McNamara's Minnesota Personality Scale)[6]	Females (majoring in home economics): Sr vs. Fr	Sr are more stable and self-possessed (SS).
Phillips (1966). Dartmouth College. Cross-sectional, year not given.	22 Item Mental Health Scale (Srole)[7]	Males: Sr vs. Fr	Sr have poorer mental health (PNG).
Stone (1951). State College of Washington. Cross-sectional, 1942.	Bell Adjustment Inventory[8]	Females not in sororities: Jr and Sr vs. Fr and So Females in sororities: Jr and Sr vs. Fr and So	A smaller percentage of Jr and Sr score as "well adjusted" (NSS). A larger percentage of Jr and Sr score as "well adjusted" (NSS).
Robertson and Stromberg (1939). Oklahoma Agricultural and Mechanical College. Longitudinal, 1935-1938.	Royer Personality Inventory[9]	Females: Jr vs. Fr	Jr are more dominant, extroverted and non-neurotic (SS).
Burton (1945). Univ. of Arizona. Longitudinal, 1939-1943.	Neurotic Tendency Scale (BPI)[10]	Males and females: Sr vs. Fr	Sr are less neurotic in tendency and emotionally unstable* (PNG). *See note at the end of table
Farnsworth (1938). Stanford Univ. Longitudinal, 1932-1936.	Neurotic Tendency Scale (BPI)[10]	Males: Sr vs. Fr	Sr are less neurotic in tendency and emotionally unstable* (SS). *See note at end of table
Pressey (1946); Pressey and Jones (1955). Ohio State Univ. Cross-sectional, 1933, 1943 and 1953.	Pressey "X-O" Test 2, Anxieties: scored for number of worries	Males (1933): Sr vs. Fr (1943): Sr vs. Fr (1953): Sr vs. Fr Females (1933): Sr vs. Fr (1943): Sr vs. Fr (1953): Sr vs. Fr	 Sr have less worries (PNG). Sr have less worries (PNG). Sr have more worries (PNG). Sr have more worries (PNG). Sr have less worries (PNG). Sr have more worries (PNG).

Table 2N.--Changes in psychological well-being (CONTINUED)

REFERENCE, SAMPLE	VARIABLE	COMPARISON GROUP	RESULTS
Kuhlen (1941). Ohio State Univ. Longitudinal, 1934-1938.	Pressey Interest-Attitude Test, Worries: scored for number of worries	Males (College of Education): Sr vs. Fr	Sr have less worries (NSS).
		Females (College of Education): Sr vs. Fr	Sr have less worries (NSS).
Constantinople (1965). Sampling of male and female students at Univ. of Rochester. Cross-sectional, year not given.	Wessman and Rick's Elation-Depression Scale[11]	Males: Sr vs. Fr	Sr are happier (PNG). Sr SD smaller.
		Females: Sr vs. Fr	Sr are happier (PNG). Sr SD larger.
McConnell, Clark, Heist, Trow, and Yonge (forthcoming). Antioch, Reed, Swarthmore, San Francisco State, Univ. of Calif., Berkeley, Univ. of the Pacific, St. Olaf, and Univ. of Portland. Longitudinal; first school, 1958-1963; next three schools, 1958-1962; last four schools, 1959-1963.	Schizoid Functioning (SF) Scale (OPI)[12]	Antioch Males: Sr vs. Fr	Sr score lower on SF Scale (SS). Sr SD larger.
		Females: Sr vs. Fr	Sr score lower on SF Scale (SS). Sr SD larger.
		Reed Males: Sr vs. Fr	Sr score lower on SF Scale (NSS). Sr SD larger.
		Females: Sr vs. Fr	Sr score lower on SF Scale (NSS). Sr SD smaller.
		Swarthmore Males: Sr vs. Fr	Sr score lower on SF Scale (SS). Sr SD larger.
		Females: Sr vs. Fr	Sr score lower on SF Scale (NSS). Sr SD larger.
		San Francisco Males: Sr vs. Fr	Sr score lower on SF Scale (SS). Sr SD smaller.
		Females: Sr vs. Fr	Sr score lower on SF Scale (SS). Sr SD larger.
		Berkeley Males: Sr vs. Fr	Sr score lower on SF Scale (SS). Sr SD smaller.
		Females: Sr vs. Fr	Sr score lower on SF Scale (SS). Sr SD smaller.
		Univ. of Pacific Males: Sr vs. Fr	Sr score lower on SF Scale (SS). Sr SD smaller.
		Females: Sr vs. Fr	Sr score lower on SF Scale (SS). Sr SD smaller.
		St. Olaf Males: Sr vs. Fr	Sr score lower on SF Scale (SS). Sr SD smaller.
		Females: Sr vs. Fr	Sr score lower on SF Scale (SS). Sr SD smaller.
		Univ. of Portland Males: Sr vs. Fr	Sr score lower on SF Scale (SS). Sr SD larger.
		Females: Sr vs. Fr	Sr score lower on SF Scale (SS). Sr SD larger.
Korn (1967a). Stanford and Univ. of California, Berkeley. Longitudinal, 1961-1965.	Schizoid Functioning (SF) Scale (OPI)[12]	Stanford Males: Sr vs. Fr	Sr score lower on SF Scale (SS). Sr SD smaller.
		Females: Sr vs. Fr	Sr score lower on SF Scale (SS). Sr SD larger.
		Berkeley Males: Sr vs. Fr	Sr score lower on SF Scale (SS). Sr SD larger.
		Females: Sr vs. Fr	Sr score lower on SF Scale (SS). Sr SD larger.
Beach (1966). Whitworth College. Longitudinal, 1961-1965.	Schizoid Functioning (SF) Scale (OPI)[12]	Males: Sr vs. Fr	Sr score lower on SF Scale (NSS). Sr SD smaller.
		Females: Sr vs. Fr	Sr score lower on SF Scale (NSS). Sr SD smaller.

Table 2N.--Changes in psychological well-being (CONTINUED)

REFERENCE, SAMPLE	VARIABLE	COMPARISON GROUP	RESULTS
Beach (1967). Whitworth College. Cross-sectional, 1961.	Schizoid Functioning (SF) Scale (OPI)[12]	Males: Sr vs. Fr Females: Sr vs. Fr	Sr score lower on SF Scale (NSS). Sr SD smaller. Sr score lower on SF Scale (SS). Sr SD smaller.
Romine and Gehman (1966). Duke University College of Engineering. Cross-sectional, 1965.	S-R Inventory of Anxiousness[13]	Males (engineering): Sr vs. Fr	Sr are less tense than Fr (NSS).
Webster (1956). Vassar College. Not clear whether cross-sectional or longitudinal, years not given.	Hypocondriasis (Hs) Scale (MMPI)[14]	Females: Sr vs. Fr	Sr score higher on Hs Scale (SS).
	Depression (D) Scale (MMPI)[15]	Females: Sr vs. Fr	Sr score higher on D Scale (SS).
	Hysteria (Hy) Scale (MMPI)[16]	Females: Sr vs. Fr	Sr score higher on Hy Scale (SS).
	Psychopathic Deviate (Pd) Scale (MMPI)[17]	Females: Sr vs. Fr	Sr score higher on Pd Scale (SS).
	Paranoia (Pa) Scale (MMPI)[18]	Females: Sr vs. Fr	Sr score higher on Pa Scale (SS).
	Psychasthenia (Pt) Scale (MMPI)[19]	Females: Sr vs. Fr	Sr score higher on Pt Scale (SS).
	Schizophrenia (Sc) Scale (MMPI)[20]	Females: Sr vs. Fr	Sr score higher on Sc Scale (SS).
	Hypomania (Ma) Scale (MMPI)[21]	Females: Sr vs. Fr	Sr score higher on Ma Scale (SS).
Mills (1954). Macalester College. Longitudinal, 1947-1951.	Hypocondriasis (Hs) Scale (MMPI)[14]	Males: Sr vs. Fr Females: Sr vs. Fr	Sr score lower on Hs Scale (PNG). Sr SD larger. Sr score higher on Hs Scale (PNG). Sr SD smaller.
	Depression (D) Scale (MMPI)[15]	Males: Sr vs. Fr Females: Sr vs. Fr	Sr score lower on D Scale (PNG). Sr SD smaller. Sr score lower on D Scale (PNG). Sr SD smaller.
	Hysteria (Hy) Scale (MMPI)[16]	Males: Sr vs. Fr Females: Sr vs. Fr	Sr score lower on Hy Scale (PNG). Sr SD smaller. Sr score higher on Hy Scale (PNG). Sr SD larger.
	Psychopathic Deviate (Pd) Scale (MMPI)[17]	Males: Sr vs. Fr Females: Sr vs. Fr	Sr score higher on Pd Scale (PNG). Sr SD smaller. Sr score higher on Pd Scale (PNG). Sr SD larger.
	Paranoia (Pa) Scale (MMPI)[18]	Males: Sr vs. Fr Females: Sr vs. Fr	Sr score lower on Pa Scale (PNG). Sr SD smaller. Sr score higher on Pa Scale (PNG). Sr SD smaller.
	Psychasthenia (Pt) Scale (MMPI)[19]	Males: Sr vs. Fr Females: Sr vs. Fr	Sr score higher on Pt Scale (PNG). Sr SD smaller. Sr score higher on Pt Scale (PNG). Sr SD smaller.
	Schizophrenia (Sc) Scale (MMPI)[20]	Males: Sr vs. Fr Females: Sr vs. Fr	Sr score higher on Sc Scale (PNG). Sr SD smaller. Sr score higher on Sc Scale (PNG). Sr SD smaller.
	Hypomania (Ma) Scale (MMPI)[21]	Males: Sr vs. Fr Females: Sr vs. Fr	Sr score higher on Ma Scale (PNG). Sr SD larger. Sr score higher on Ma Scale (PNG). Sr SD larger.

Table 2N.--Changes in psychological well-being (CONTINUED)

REFERENCE, SAMPLE	VARIABLE	COMPARISON GROUP	RESULTS
Stewart (1964). Univ. of California at Berkeley. Longitudinal, 1957-1961.	Hysteria (Hy) Scale (MMPI)[16]	Males: Sr vs. Fr Females: Sr vs. Fr	Sr score higher on Hy Scale (NSS). Sr SD larger.* Sr score lower on Hy Scale (NSS). Sr SD smaller.*
	Psychopathic Deviate (Pd) Scale (MMPI)[17]	Males: Sr vs. Fr Females: Sr vs. Fr	Sr score higher on Pd Scale (NSS). Sr SD smaller.* Sr score lower on Pd Scale (NSS). Sr SD smaller.*
	Schizophrenia (Sc) Scale (MMPI)[20]	Males: Sr vs. Fr Females: Sr vs. Fr	Sr score higher on Sc Scale (NSS). Sr SD larger.* Sr score lower on Sc Scale (SS). Sr SD smaller.*
	Hypomania (Ma) Scale (MMPI)[21]	Males: Sr vs. Fr Females: Sr vs. Fr	Sr score lower on Ma Scale (NSS). Sr SD smaller.* Sr score lower on Ma Scale (SS). Sr SD smaller.* *Information about SD's supplied by Stewart in personal communication to authors.
Tyler (1963). 4-year longitudinal study of a sample of National Merit Scholar winners and Certificate of Merit winners, years not given.	Hysteria (Hy) Scale (MMPI)[16]	Males: Sr vs. Fr Females: Sr vs. Fr	Sr score higher on Ma Scale (SS). No statistically significant change.
	Psychopathic Deviate (Pd) Scale (MMPI)[17]	Males: Sr vs. Fr Females: Sr vs. Fr	No statistically significant change. No statistically significant change.
	Schizophrenia (Sc) Scale (MMPI)[20]	Males: Sr vs. Fr Females: Sr vs. Fr	Sr score lower on Sc Scale (SS). Sr score lower on Sc Scale (SS).
	Hypomania (Ma) Scale (MMPI)[21]	Males: Sr vs. Fr Females: Sr vs. Fr	No statistically significant change. No statistically significant change.
Heath (1968, and personal communication to authors). Haverford College. Longitudinal, 1960-1964 and 1961-1965.	Sum total of eight MMPI scales: Hs[14]; D[15]; Hy[16]; Pd[17]; Pa[18]; Pt[19]; Sc[20]; Ma[21].	1960-1964 Males: Sr vs. Fr 1961-1965 Males: Sr vs. Fr	Sr have lower total score (NSS). Sr have lower total score (SS).

[1]Emotional Stability or Ego Strength Scale, Factor C (Sixteen Personality Factor Questionnaire): emotionally mature, emotionally stable, calm, facing reality, absence of neurotic fatigue.

[2]Guilt Proneness Scale, Factor O (Sixteen Personality Factor Questionnaire): anxious, worrying, apprehensive, depressed, easily upset, moody.

[3]Ergic Tension Scale, Factor Q4 (Sixteen Personality Factor Questionnaire): tense, driven, overwrought, fretful, excitable.

[4]Surgency Scale, Factor F (Sixteen Personality Factor Questionnaire): happy-go-lucky, enthusiastic, heedless, gay, talkative, cheerful.

[5]Emotional Stability Scale (Guilford-Zimmerman Temperament Survey): optimism, cheerfulness; evenness of moods, interests and energy; composure, feeling in good health.

[6]Emotionality Scale (Darley and McNamara's Minnesota Personality Scale): stable, self-possessed, not anxious nor over-reactive.

[7]22 Item Mental Health Scale (developed by Srole and associates): high score = poor mental health.

[8]Bell Adjustment Inventory: measures the home, health, social and emotional adjustment of the respondent.

[9]Royer Personality Inventory: high score = a dominant, extroverted and non-neurotic person.

[10]Neurotic Tendency Scale (Bernreuter Personality Inventory)*: emotionally unstable.

[11]Wessman and Rick's Elation-Depression Scale: high score = elation, happiness.

Table 2N.--Changes in psychological well-being (CONTINUED)

[12]Schizoid Functioning (SF) Scale (Omnibus Personality Inventory): feelings of isolation, loneliness and rejection, intentionally avoiding others, having such ego weaknesses as identity confusion, day dreaming, disorientation, feelings of impotence, and fear of loss of control.

[13]S-R Inventory of Anxiousness (Endler, Hunt and Rosenstein): anxiousness, tenseness.

[14]Hypocondriasis (Hs) Scale (Minnesota Multiphasic Personality Inventory): measures the amount of abnormal concern about bodily functions.

[15]Depression (D) Scale (Minnesota Multiphasic Personality Inventory): measures the depth of the clinically recognized symptom or symptom-complex, depression.

[16]Hysteria (Hy) Scale (Minnesota Multiphasic Personality Inventory): measures the degree to which the respondent is like psychiatric patients who have developed conversion-type hysteria symptoms.

[17]Psychopathic Deviate (Pd) Scale (Minnesota Multiphasic Personality Inventory): measures the similarity of the subject to a group of persons whose main difficulty lies in their absence of deep emotional response, their inability to profit from experience, and their disregard of social mores.

[18]Paranois (Pa) Scale (Minnesota Multiphasic Personality Inventory): measures the degree to which the respondent is like psychiatric patients characterized by suspiciousness, oversensitivity and delusions of persecution, with or without expansive egotism.

[19]Psychasthenia (Pt) Scale (Minnesota Multiphasic Personality Inventory): measures the similarity of the respondent to psychiatric patients who are troubled by phobias or compulsive behavior.

[20]Schizophrenia (Sc) Scale (Minnesota Multiphasic Personality Inventory): measures the similarity of the respondent to psychiatric patients characterized by bizarre and unusual thoughts or behavior.

[21]Hypomania (Ma) Scale (Minnesota Multiphasic Personality Inventory): measures the personality factor characteristic of persons with marked overproductivity in thought and action.

---

*Reviewing published and unpublished evidence, some investigators (LaPiere and Farnsworth, 1936, p. 357; Farnsworth, 1938) argue that decreases on the Neurotic Tendency Scale of the Bernreuter Personality Inventory actually represent increases in neuroticism when such decreases are changes away from an average score. Since such is the case in Burton (1945) and Farnsworth (1938), it may be that the results in these studies would be more correctly interpreted as showing increasing neuroticism.

Table 20.--Summaries of studies showing changes in occupational choice and choice of major field of study.

REFERENCE, SAMPLE	DESCRIPTION OF ANALYSIS	RESULTS
Darley (1962). Sampling of entering male freshmen at Univ. of Minnesota (College of Science, Literature, and the Arts) in the fall of 1952. Longitudinal, Fall 1952-Fall 1956.	Comparison is between occupational choice for each of 446 male students as freshmen and as graduating seniors. Classification of occupational choices: biological science/medicine; physical science/engineering; semi-professional, social science/service, business, law/other verbal, none given (7 categories)	61% of the male students changed occupational choice
Sampling of entering male freshmen at seven private coeducational colleges in Minnesota in the fall of 1952. Longitudinal, Fall 1952-Fall 1956.	Comparison is between occupational choice for each of 528 male students as freshmen and as graduating seniors. Classification of occupational choices: biological science/medicine; physical science/engineering; semi-professional, social science/service, business, law/other verbal, none given (7 categories)	64% of the male students changed occupational choice
Sampling of entering male freshmen at 29 colleges in Minnesota in the fall of 1952. Longitudinal, Fall 1952-Fall 1956.	Comparison is between occupational choice for each of 1856 male students as freshmen and as graduating seniors. Classification of occupational choices: biological sciences and medicine, physical sciences and engineering, semi-professional, social sciences, high-school teaching, business, verbal (7 categories)	46% of the male students changed occupational choice
Sampling of entering female freshmen at 29 colleges in Minnesota in the fall of 1952. Longitudinal, Fall 1952-Fall 1956.	Comparison is between occupational choice for each of 1470 female students as freshmen and as graduating seniors. Classification of occupational choices: biological sciences and medicine, physical sciences and engineering, semi-professional, social sciences, high-school teaching, business, verbal (7 categories)	43% of the female students changed occupational choice
Ellis and Lane (1966). Probability sampling of entering male freshmen at Stanford Univ. in 1958. Longitudinal, 1958-1962. (Note: Analysis is limited to students whose initial occupational choices were sufficiently well articulated to permit later classification, and to students for whom occupational information was available for each of the four years.)	Comparison is between career choice for each of 55 students when a sophomore, a junior, and a senior, and his initial career choice. Classification of career choices not given.	25% of the male students as sophomores, 56% as juniors, and 53% as seniors stated a career choice other than the one initially chosen
Katz (1967a). Sampling of entering male freshmen at Stanford Univ. in 1961. Longitudinal, 1961-1965.	Comparison is between occupational choice given in the application for each of 48 entering students and the occupation they say they plan to enter as seniors. Classification of occupational choices not given.	31% of the male students showed "much change" and another 17% showed "moderate change" in occupational choice
Akenson and Beecher (1967). Total sampling of Harvard graduating class of 1965. Longitudinal from time of entrance.	Career choice for each of 824 male graduates is compared with the one at entrance. (N does not include 25 students for whom there was no information at one or the other time.) Classification of career choices: all education, scientific research, law, medicine, business, creative arts and journalism, government, engineering and technical, and miscellaneous (9 categories)	61% of the male students changed career choice
Sisson (1938). Sampling of the male graduates of the classes of 1929-1932 at Wesleyan Univ. Longitudinal from time of entrance.	Vocational choice for each of 252 seniors is compared with the one at the time of entrance. Classification of vocational choices not given. (Note: in an earlier report by Sisson (1937), he uses a classification consisting of 25 categories. We are not able to tell from the later study whether or not he used the same ones.)	40% of the male students either made a change in vocational preference or changed from "no choice" to some actual preference
Wightwick (1945). Sampling of freshman women attending a small college "situated near New York City ... [attracting] a student body from the upper middle economic class" in the fall of 1933. Longitudinal, Fall 1933-Spring 1937.	Comparison is between vocational choice for each of 115 female students as freshmen and as seniors. Classification of vocational choices: teaching, stenography, clerical work, social work, "non-paying work," retail sales, library work, laboratory work, psychological work, art, writing-literary, writing-journalism, costume designing, dietetics, economics, nursing, medicine, law, acting, bacteriology, occupational therapy, vocational guidance, chemistry, undecided (24 categories)	38% of the female students changed vocational goals

Table 20.--Changes in occupational choice and choice of major field of study (CONTINUED)

REFERENCE, SAMPLE	DESCRIPTION OF ANALYSIS	RESULTS
Davis (1965). Sampling of male and female senior graduates at 135 colleges and universities, Spring 1961.	Anticipated future career for each of 49,817 seniors is compared with his recall of career aspirations when a freshman. Classification of careers: physical sciences, biological sciences, social sciences, humanities and fine arts, education, engineering, medicine, law, other professional fields, business (10 categories)	37% of the male and female seniors had changed career plans. Another 8% who said they had no career aspirations as a freshman decided on a career by their senior year. In total, 45% of the seniors had changed.
Thielens (1966). Random sampling of male seniors at Columbia College in the spring of 1965.	Analysis of reports by seniors of changes in occupational plans since coming to college.	53% of the male seniors reported a change in occupational plans
Sparling (1933). Sampling of male and female seniors at Long Island University, 1931.	Analysis is of change in vocational choices as reported by 92 seniors.	42% of the male and female students reported a change in vocational choice after entering the university
Nichols and Astin (1965). Total sampling of all of the male and female students awarded National Merit Scholarships during the first four years of the Merit Program (1956-1959). Eight-year longitudinal.	Analysis is of changes in career choices during college (including graduate school) as reported by 3106 high-ability students.	66% of the male students and 76% of the female students reported major changes in career choices during college
Holland (1963). Sample of male and female high school senior finalists in the National Merit Scholarship program in 1956. Longitudinal, 1956-1960.	Comparison is between choice of vocation for each of 248 male and 98 female high-ability, high school seniors and his choice four years later (in college).	44% of the male students and 58% of the female students changed vocational choice
Newton (1962). Random sampling of male college seniors from each of 31 randomly selected degree-granting institutions in the southern region in the spring of 1960.	2,357 seniors are classified by category of occupational choice, as follows: "scientific and esthetic" occupations (N=1279); "general cultural" occupations (N=1038); "other" occupations (N=40). Each senior reported initial and current major field which was also classified as falling into "scientific and esthetic," "general cultural" and "other."	Of the 2,157 male seniors choosing either "scientific and esthetic" occupations or "general cultural" occupations, 23% reported a change in major field falling within the "scientific and esthetic," "general cultural" or "other" classification. Another 14% reported a change from one to another of these categories. In total, 37% reported a change in major field.
Jensen (1949). Total sampling of male and female students entering Brigham Young Univ. in the fall of 1946. Longitudinal, Fall 1946-May 1949.	Comparison is between vocational choice for each of 62 students when entering college and as juniors. Classification of vocational choices not given.	30% of the male and female students changed vocational choice
Rosenberg (1957). Representative sampling of male and female students at Cornell in 1950. Longitudinal, 1950-1952.	Comparison is between occupational choice for each of 940 students at Cornell in 1950 and in 1952. Classification of occupational choices: housewife, advertising-public relations, government service, social work, business, journalism-drama-art, secretarial work, personnel, social science, natural science, farming, teaching, law, medicine, architecture, hotel administration, engineering (17 categories)	60% of the male and female students changed occupational choice
Selvin (1963). Sampling of entering male freshmen at Univ. of California, Berkeley, Fall 1959. Longitudinal, Fall 1959-Spring 1961.	Comparison is between occupational choice for each of 730 students as freshmen and as sophomores. Classification of occupational choices: medicine or dentistry; law; ministry; college teaching; noncollege teaching; scientific research; art, music, etc.; engineering; other profession (9 categories)	31% of the male students changed occupational choice. In addition, 9% who had an original choice became undecided, and 13% who were undecided decided on an occupation. In total, 53% of the students changed.

Table 20.--Changes in occupational choice and choice of major field of study (CONTINUED)

REFERENCE, SAMPLE	DESCRIPTION OF ANALYSIS	RESULTS
Strong (1952). Sampling of male freshmen at Stanford in 1930. Longitudinal, 1930-1931.	Comparison is between occupational choice for each of 255 male students as freshmen and as sophomores. Classification of occupational choices: medicine, engineering, law, "business," specific business activity, miscellaneous, don't know (7 categories)	42% of the male students changed occupational choice
Holland and Lutz (1967). Sampling of male and female freshmen at six colleges in the fall of 1964 (Amherst, Baldwin-Wallace, Cuyahoga Community, California State at Hayward, Chico State, and the Univ. of Massachusetts). Longitudinal, Fall 1964-May 1965.	Comparison is between vocational choice for each of 1290 male and 1285 female students at the beginning and at the end of the freshman year. Classification of type of vocational choices for males: Realistic, Intellectual, Social, Conventional, Enterprising, Artistic, Undecided (7 categories) Classification of type of vocational choices for females: Intellectual, Social Intellectual, Social Conventional, Social Enterprising, Social Artistic, Conventional, Artistic, Undecided (8 categories)	33% of the male students and 29% of the female students changed vocational choice
MacIntosh (1953). Total sampling of entire student body (males) of Haverford College in September 1947. Longitudinal, September 1947-May 1948.	Comparison is between vocational goal for each of 493 students in 1947 and 1948. Classification of vocational goals: teaching, physical science, insurance, medicine, religion, dentistry, government service, engineering, biological science, social science, business, writing, fine arts, law, education, library, banking and investment, personnel administration, architecture, social service, accounting, agriculture, athletics, aviation, entertainer, humanities, transportation, merchandising (29 categories)	30% of the male students changed vocational goals
Sherry (1963). Sampling of male freshmen entering Swarthmore in the fall of 1958. Longitudinal, Fall 1958-Spring 1962. (Note: of the 87 students in the longitudinal sample, analysis was limited to the 75 students who had a choice of major field as freshmen.)	Comparison is between major field for each of 75 male students as freshmen and as seniors. Classification of major fields: physics, chemistry and mathematics; pre-medicine, biology and zoology; humanities, English, language, philosophy, and fine arts; psychology, sociology and anthropology; political science, international relations, pre-law, and history; economics, business administration and accounting; engineering; no choice of major (8 categories)	47% of the male students changed major field
Holland (1963). Sample of male and female high school senior finalists in the National Merit Scholarship Program in 1956. Longitudinal, 1956-1960.	Comparison is between choice of major field for each of 241 male and 74 female high-ability high school seniors and his choice four years later (in college). Classification of type of major fields: Realistic, Intellectual, Social, Conventional, Enterprising, and Artistic (6 categories)	37% of the male students and 43% of the female students changed to a different major field
McLaughlin (1965). Random sampling of male freshmen at Harvard in the fall of 1960. Longitudinal, 1960-1964.	Analysis is of students who changed major fields during the course of their four years of college. Classification of major fields not given.	64% of the male students changed major field
Bradley (1962). Total sampling of entering male and female freshmen, with a specified major, at Michigan State Univ. in the fall of 1958. Longitudinal, Fall 1958-Fall 1961.	Comparison is between major area of study for each of 792 male and 561 female students as freshmen and as seniors. Classification of major areas not given.	49% of the male students and 49% of the female students changed major area of study
Wightwick (1945). Sampling of female freshmen attending a small college "situated near New York City ... [attracting] a student body from the upper middle economic class" in the fall of 1933. Longitudinal, Fall 1933-Spring 1937.	Comparison is between choice of major for each of 115 female students as second-semester freshmen or sophomores and in later years of college. Classification of majors not given.	22% of the female students changed majors

Table 20.--Changes in occupational choice and choice of major field of study (CONTINUED)

REFERENCE, SAMPLE	DESCRIPTION OF ANALYSIS	RESULTS
Cole, Wilson, and Tiedeman (1964). Sampling of male freshmen admitted to the Univ. of Rochester during the period 1948-1951. Longitudinal (from entrance to graduation).	Field of concentration for each of 759 males as seniors is compared with the one at the time of initial choice. Classification of major fields: pure science, technical, general science, teaching, English, history, business, psychology (9 categories)	41% of the male students changed their field of concentration
Sampling of freshmen students (males) admitted to Harvard during the period 1946-1949. Longitudinal (from entrance to graduation).	Field of concentration for each of 774 male students as seniors is compared with the one at the time of initial choice. Classification of major fields: mathematics, physic , engineering, chemistry, biochemistry, biology, geology, social relations, economics, government, history, history of literature, English, Romance languages, philosophy, architecture (16 categories)	27% of the male students changed their field of concentration
Pierson (1962). Sampling of entire body of male and female candidates for bachelor degrees at Michigan State Univ. in June 1958. Longitudinal from time of entrance. (Note: students who entered the university with no declaration of major were not included in this study.)	Major for each of 2369 graduating seniors is compared with the one selected at entrance. Analysis excludes students who entered with no declaration of major. Classification of majors not given.	30% of the male and female students changed major field
Pemberton (1963). Sampling of Univ. of Delaware male and female seniors graduating in 1960, for whom complete background data were available. Longitudinal from time of entrance.	Major field for each of 334 students as seniors is compared with the one at the time of initial choice. Classification of major fields: commerce, humanities, biological science, physical science, social science, chemical engineering, electrical engineering, mechanical and civil engineering, education, home economics, and agriculture (11 categories)	25% of the male and female students changed to a completely different field of study after entering. More than 40% made some change, including changes within the same general field (e.g., from sociology to psychology).
Krulee, O'Keefe and Goldberg (1966). Sampling of senior male students at Northwestern Univ., Fall 1964 and Fall 1965.	Analysis is of changes in curricular program <u>within</u> a school as reported by 220 senior male students in the College of Liberal Arts and Sciences, by 108 senior male students in Business School, and by 115 senior male students in the Technological Institute at Northwestern Univ. (Note: these are the students who persisted within each school for their college years.)	34.2% of the male liberal arts seniors, 41% of the male business school seniors and 30.8% of the male engineering seniors reported a change of curricular program within their school
Iffert (1957). Sampling of enrolled male and female students and dropouts in 1953-1954 who had originally entered one of 149 institutions as freshmen in 1950.	Analysis is of the reported change of subject-field in college. For men, analysis is limited to the 3,435 students reporting that they initially chose one of the subject-fields having 100 initial adherents or more; viz., engineering, business administration, pre-medicine, chemistry, accounting, agriculture, mathematics, physical education, prelaw, history, education, physics, biology, English (14 categories) For women, analysis is limited to the 2,812 students reporting that they initially chose one of the subject-fields having 50 initial adherents or more; viz., education, home economics, English, music, business administration, languages, fine arts, nursing, physical education, journalism, speech and dramatic arts, psychology, mathematics, history, social work, premedicine (16 categories)	42.3% of the male students and 45.2% of the female students reported defecting from the initially chosen subject-fields under consideration
Adamek and Goudy (1966). Random sampling of male and female juniors at a "large midwestern university whose emphasis is primarily on scientific and technical fields." Year not given.	Analysis is of the change in major as reported by 372 juniors.	46% of the male and female juniors reported "switching majors"

Table 20.--Changes in occupational choice and choice of major field of study (CONTINUED)

REFERENCE, SAMPLE	DESCRIPTION OF ANALYSIS	RESULTS
Thistlethwaite (1960). Sampling of male and female college juniors in May 1959 who were Merit Scholar winners and Certificate of Merit finalists in high school.	Field of study for each of 1500 high-ability college juniors is compared with his recall of the field of study in which he planned to major when he entered college. Classification of fields of study: natural sciences, biological sciences, social sciences, arts and humanities, and unclassified (5 categories)	24.2% of the male students and 38.4% of the female students changed major field
Warrington (1958). Total sampling of entering student body (males and females) at Michigan State Univ. in the fall of 1953 (includes entering freshmen as well as transfer students). Longitudinal, Fall 1953-Fall 1955.	Comparison is between the curricular choice for each of a sample of students (both initially entering freshmen and transfer students) in the fall of 1953 and the fall of 1955. Classification of curricula: agriculture, business and public service, engineering, home economics, science ar arts, veterinary medicine, education, no preference (8 categories)	Nearly 40% of the male and female freshmen initially entering Michigan State Univ. and 25% of the transfer students changed curriculum
Warren (1961). Sampling of male National Merit Scholars and Certificate of Merit winners entering college as freshmen in 1956 in more than 200 colleges. Longitudinal, 1956-1958.	Comparison is between proposed field of study (before entering college) for each of 525 high-ability male students and the actual field of study as sophomores. Classification of fields of study not given. (Note: a change from a proposed choice to an actual choice, as well as from one actual choice to another, was classified as a change.)	20% of the male students made a minor change in field of study (a change between closely related fields of study) and another 26% made a major change (a change between unrelated fields of study). In total, 46% changed field of study.
Holland (1962). Sampling of male and female high school seniors (sampling of survivors of the National Merit Scholarship competition) in 1958. Longitudinal, 1958-1960.	Comparison is between choice of major field for each of 388 male and 179 female high-ability high school seniors and his choice two years later (in college). Classification of type of major fields: Realistic, Intellectual, Social, Conventional, Enterprising, and Artistic (6 categories)	53% of the male students and 53% of the female students changed their choice of major field
Gamble (1962). Sampling of male and female students entering Pennsylvania State Univ. in 1957 and who took part in the summer counseling program.	Comparison is between choice of curriculum or course of study for each of 2265 students at the time of admission, and his choice during the first, second and third semesters of school. Classification of curricula not given.	44% of the male and female students changed choice of curriculum at least once

OTHER STUDIES:

Along with changing vocational aspirations and major field plans, college students change their aspirations with respect to amount of higher education they plan to attain. Thistlethwaite (1963b) used the following four categories to classify the educational aspirations of some 4,000 high-ability students attending 140 colleges and universities in 1959: some college, bachelor's degree, master's degree, and doctorate or professional degree. During the first two years of college, 41% of the men and 40% of the women changed their educational aspirations. Although movement was in both directions, the net change was toward increased educational aspirations. In a four-year longitudinal study of students at seven colleges (Antioch, Reed, Swarthmore, Univ. of California at Berkeley, Univ. of the Pacific, St. Olaf, and the Univ. of Portland), the proportion of students who changed their plans about post-graduate training ranged from a low of 30% at Reed to a high of 67% at University of the Pacific and at University of Portland. Once again, although change was in both directions, the net result at each school was that a larger proportion of students were planning to attend graduate or professional schools when they were seniors than when they were freshmen (McConnell, Clark, Heist, Trow, and Yonge, forthcoming). Wallace (1966) reports that during the freshman year at "Midwest College," 37% of the men and 29% of the women changed their aspirations with respect to attending graduate or professional schools. Once again, although change was in both directions, on balance a larger proportion of freshmen at the end than at the beginning of their first year in college planned to go on to graduate or professional school after completing their undergraduate program of studies. Other investigations documenting that a higher percentage of seniors than freshmen plan to seek advanced training are the following: Thielens (1966); Thistlethwaite and Wheeler (1966); and Trent (1964a). The National Opinion Research Center surveyed plans of students graduating in 1964 from 50 predominantly Negro colleges. While about 60% of the students had as freshmen planned for graduate study, this percentage increased to 73% for senior men and decreased to 54% for senior women (Fichter, 1966).

Table 2P.--Net change in career choice and major fields

Davis (1965, taken from data in Table 2.5, p. 20):

Net change in various career choices (in percentages).

Comparison is between career choices of 49,817 male and female graduating seniors at 135 colleges and universities in 1961 and their recalled career aspirations when they were freshmen.

Career Choice	Net Change
Education:	+8.0%
Business:	+5.4%
Social Sciences:	+1.1%
Humanities and Fine Arts:	+0.7%
Law:	+0.5%
Biological Sciences:	+0.3%
Physical Sciences:	-0.9%
Other professional fields:	-1.0%
Medicine:	-2.2%*
Engineering:	-6.1%
None:	-6.2%

*Incorrectly given as -0.2% in Table 2.5 on p. 20. Correctly given as -2.2% in text, p. 21.

Nichols and Astin (1965, calculated from data presented in Table 9, p. 11):

Net change in various career choices (in percentages).

Comparison is between career choices of 3,106 National Merit Scholarship winners (in 1956-1959) as freshmen and their choices eight years later.

Males (N=2241)		Females (N=865)	
Career Choice	Net Change	Career Choice	Net Change
Other:	+18.6%	Other:	+22.8%
Law:	+ 4.8%	Law:	+ 3.1%
Teaching:	+ 4.0%	Ministry, Church work:	+ 0.9%
Business:	+ 3.7%	Business:	0.0%
Ministry, Church work:	+ 0.6%	Engineering:	- 0.6%
Writing, Journalism:	+ 0.2%	Social Work:	- 1.4%
Social Work:	+ 0.1%	Writing, Journalism:	- 2.3%
Medical Sciences:	- 0.1%	Teaching:	- 2.4%
Government Service:	- 0.2%	Government Service:	- 4.5%
Research:	-14.5%	Medical Sciences:	- 5.8%
Engineering:	-16.1%	Research:	- 9.6%

Birney, Coplin and Grose (1960, taken from data in Table 22, p. 73):

Net change in various vocational choices (in percentages).

Comparison is between vocational choices of 253 graduating male seniors at Amherst (1959) and the choices of these same men plus 54 others when applying for Amherst (1955).

Vocational Choice	Net Change
Business:	+17.3%
College Teaching:	+14.6%
Professional:	+ 2.7%
Law:	+ 2.3%
Public Official:	+ 1.5%
Medicine:	- 0.6%
News Media:	- 1.8%
Science and Engineering:	-17.5%
Don't know, No answer:	-17.6%

Darley (1962, calculated from data in Figure 1, p. 86):

Net change in various occupational choices (in percentages).

Comparison is between vocational choices of 446 male freshmen entering the College of Science, Literature and the Arts of the University of Minnesota in 1952 and their choices when graduating in 1956.

Occupational Choice	Net Change
Social Science/Service:	+11.4%
Business:	+10.7%
Law/Other verbal:	+ 5.4%
Semi-professional:	+ 1.5%
Biological Science/Medicine:	+ 0.2%
Physical Science/Engineering:	- 1.1%
None given:	-28.3%

Darley (1962, calculated from data in Figure 2, p. 87):

Net change in various occupational choices (in percentages).

Comparison is between vocational choices of 528 male freshmen entering seven private coeducational colleges in Minnesota in 1952 and their choices when graduating in 1956.

Occupational Choice	Net Change
Social Science/Service:	+14.6%
Law/Other verbal:	+ 4.8%
Physical Science/Engineering:	+ 1.1%
Biological Science/Medicine:	+ 0.6%
Semi-professional:	- 2.9%
Business:	- 6.5%
None given:	-11.7%

Krulee, O'Keefe and Goldberg (1966, calculated from data in Table 3-11, p. 31, and Table 5-11, p. 124):

Net change in various "realistic" career aspirations (in percentages).

Comparison is between career choices of 599 entering male freshmen in the College of Liberal Arts and Science at Northwestern in the fall of 1961 and fall of 1962 and the choices of these students who were still at Northwestern in the fall of 1964 and in the fall of 1965 and who returned the senior questionnaire (N=220).

Career Aspiration	Net Change
Teaching:	+15.0%
Lawyer:	+ 4.7%
Management:	+ 2.2%
Applied Research:	+ 1.3%
Basic Research:	+ 0.2%
Other:	- 2.3%
Undecided:	- 4.6%
Physician or dentist:	-18.5%

Table 2P.--Net change in career choice and major fields (CONTINUED)

Study	Choice	Net Change
Sisson (1937, calculated from data in Tables 1 and 3, pp. 766-767): Net change in various vocational choices (in percentages). Comparison is between vocational choices of 117 male junior students at Wesleyan University in the 1935-36 school year and the choices of these men when freshmen in 1933 plus entering freshmen in 1935.	Vocational Choice Business: Other: Teaching: Journalism: Engineering: Chemistry: Law: Medicine: No choice:	Net Change +14.3% + 8.8% + 6.4% + 1.1% 0.0% - 3.0% - 4.9% - 7.1% -15.6%
Werts (1967a, calculated from data in Table 1, p. 93):* Net change in various career choices (in absolute numbers). Comparison is between career choices of 30,000 male students of 248 colleges in the summer of 1962 and their choices in the fall of 1961 when they were freshmen. Analysis is limited to the 8,900 students initially choosing or recruited into one of the eight careers with the highest rate of defection. *Also see Werts (1966a).	Career Choice Businessman: Teacher: Lawyer: Physician: Accountant: Physicist: Chemist: Engineer:	Net Change +319 +254 +177 + 78 + 24 - 79 -110 -206
Akenson and Beecher (1967, calculated from data in Table 1, p. 177): Net change in various career choices (in percentages). Comparison is between career choices of 824 graduating seniors at Harvard in 1965 and their choices when they entered college.	Career Choice All education: Law: Business: Medicine: Engineering: Miscellaneous: Creative arts and journalism: Government: Scientific research:	Net Change + 7.7% + 6.6% + 4.9% + 2.9% + 0.5% - 0.5% - 0.8% - 2.6% -18.7%
Burgemeister (1940, calculated from data in Table 5, p. 30): Net change in various vocational choices (in percentages). Comparison is between vocational choices of 165 female freshmen at Barnard College in January-February 1939 and their choices as sophomores in November-December 1939.	Vocational Choice Other: Social Work: Psychology: Art: Music: Nursing: Home Economics: Undecided: Medicine, physician: Government service: Law: Writing: Research: Business: Teaching:	Net Change +3.7% +1.9% +1.3% +1.2% +1.2% +1.2% +0.6% +0.6% 0.0% 0.0% 0.0% -1.8% -1.9% -2.4% -5.5%
Krulee, O'Keefe and Goldberg (1966, calculated from data in Table 5-16, p. 130): Net change in various curricular choices (in percentages). Comparison is between curricular choices of 599 entering male freshmen in the College of Liberal Arts and Science at Northwestern in the fall of 1961 and in the fall of 1962 and the choices of these students who were still at Northwestern in the fall of 1964 and in the fall of 1965 who returned the senior questionnaire (N=220).	Curriculum Humanities: Social Sciences: Economics: Biology or Chemistry: Mathematics: Pre-Law: Physics: Pre-Dental: Undecided: Pre-Medical:	Net Change +16.5% + 9.3% + 2.8% + 1.3% + 0.3% - 0.9% - 1.8% - 2.3% - 5.9% -22.7%

Table 2P.--Net change in career choice and major fields (CONTINUED)

Pierson (1962, calculated from data in Table 1, p. 458):

Net change in various choices of major field (in absolute numbers).

Comparison is between the major fields of 403 male and female seniors at Michigan State University in the spring of 1958 and their choices of major field when entering the university.

Major Field	Net Change
Social Sciences:	+49
Business:	+21
Education:	+18
Language and Literature:	+12
Agriculture:	+ 4
Public Service:	+ 4
Fine Arts:	+ 2
Biological Sciences:	+ 1
Mathematics and Physical Sciences:	0
Commercial Arts	- 7
Home Economics:	-13
Veterinary Medicine:	-17
Engineering:	-13

Cole, Wilson and Tiedeman (1964, calculated from data in Table 1, p. 124):

Net change in various fields of concentration (in percentages).

Comparison is between initial choices of field of concentration of 759 male freshmen entering the University of Rochester (during the period 1948-51) and the fields of concentration in which they graduated.

Field of Concentration	Net Change
Psychology:	+8.4%
History:	+7.0%
English:	+5.4%
Business:	+1.4%
Teaching:	-1.1%
Pure Science:	-6.5%
General Science:	-7.1%
Technical:	-7.4%

Cole, Wilson,and Tiedeman (1964, calculated from data in Table 4, p. 127):

Net change in various fields of concentration (in percentages).

Comparison is between original choices of major field of 208 male freshmen entering Harvard (during the period 1946-49) and the fields of concentration in which they graduated.

Field of Concentration	Net Change
History:	+1.8%
Social Relations:	+1.1%
Biology:	+0.6%
English:	+0.6%
Geology:	+0.5%
Philosophy:	+0.5%
Architecture:	+0.4%
Government:	+0.2%
Economics:	-0.2%
Engineering:	-0.3%
Romance Languages:	-0.3%
History of Literature:	-0.5%
Biochemistry:	-0.9%
Mathematics:	-0.9%
Chemistry:	-1.1%
Physics:	-1.5%

Dole (1965, taken from data in Table 3, p. 31):

Net change in various curricular choices (in percentages).

Comparison is between initial curricular choices of 520 males and females entering the University of Hawaii in the fall of 1960 and their choices in the fall of 1963.

Curriculum	Net Change
Business Administration:	+5%
Humanities:	+4%
Social Sciences:	+3%
Agriculture:	+2%
Nursing:	0%
Natural Sciences:	-1%
Education:	-2%
Engineering:	-3%
Undecided ("Cannot say"):	-8%

U. S. Department of Commerce (1960, calculated from data in Table 1, p. 5):

Net change in various major fields of study (in percentages).

Comparison is between major field choices of approximately 1,847,000 first- and second-year male and female college students and the choices of approximately 997,000 third- and fourth-year college students (October 1959).

Total Sample		Males*		Females*	
Major Field of Study	Net Change	Major Field of Study	Net Change	Major Field of Study	Net Change
Social Sciences:	+3.2%	Social Sciences:	+4.8%	Education:	+6.1%
Business:	+2.6%	Business:	+4.8%	Humanities:	+4.8%
Education:	+2.1%	Education:	+3.8%	Not reported:	+4.5%
Biological Sciences:	+1.7%	Biological Sciences:	+2.8%	Physical Sciences:	+2.0%
Physical Sciences:	+1.6%	Physical Sciences:	+2.1%	Biological Sciences:	+0.4%
Not reported:	+1.2%	Not reported:	-0.4%	Engineering:	+0.3%
Humanities:	+0.6%	Humanities:	-0.6%	Business:	-4.9%
Agriculture	-0.4%	Agriculture:	-0.6%	Other:	-5.8%
Engineering:	-2.3%	Other:	-4.3%		
Other:	-4.4%	Undecided:	-5.5%		
Undecided:	-6.6%	Engineering:	-6.8%		

*For males, percentages are based on approximately 1,103,000 first- and second-year students and approximately 689,000 third- and fourth-year students. For females, percentages are based on approximately 744,000 first- and second-year students and approximately 308,000 third- and fourth-year students.

Table 2P.--Net change in career choice and major fields (CONTINUED)

Thistlethwaite (1960, calculated from data in Table 2, p. 225):

Net change in various major fields of study (in percentages).

Comparison is between major fields of study of 1,500 male and female National Merit Scholar winners and near-winners as juniors in high school (1959) and their choices when entering college in 1956.

Males (N=987)		Females (N=513)	
Field of Study	Net Change	Field of Study	Net Change
Social Sciences:	+5.5%	Arts and Humanities:	+8.0%
Arts and Humanities:	+3.1%	Social Sciences:	+2.3%
Unclassified fields:*	+1.7%	Biological Sciences:	-1.2%
Biological Sciences:	-2.1%	Unclassified fields:*	-3.3%
Natural Sciences:	-7.6%	Natural Sciences:	-5.8%

*Unclassified fields are accounting, business administration, home economics, journalism, prelaw, religious education, and other specialities not elsewhere classified.

Warrington (1958, calculated from data in Table 13, p. 59):

Net change in various curricular choices (in percentages).

Comparison is between various curricular choices of male and female juniors at Michigan State University in the fall of 1955 and their choices when entering in the fall of 1953.

Males (N=1188)		Females (N=792)	
Curriculum	Net Change	Curriculum	Net Change
Business and Public Service:	+11.0%	Science and Arts:*	+11.5%
Science and Arts:*	+ 7.1%	Education:	+ 9.0%
Education:	+ 2.4%	Home Economics:	+ 2.5%
Agriculture:	+ 1.7%	Veterinary Medicine:	+ 1.0%
Home Economics:	- 0.1%	Engineers:	+ 0.1%
Veterinary Medicine:	- 2.5%	Agriculture:	- 0.1%
Engineers:	- 4.3%	No Preference:	-24.0%
No Preference:	-15.3%		

*Includes Biological Sciences, Fine Arts, Language and Literature, Mathematics and Physical Sciences, and Social Sciences.

Table 2Q.--Percent defection from various career choices and major fields

Note: Numbers in parentheses following percentages are N's on which the percentages are based.

Darley (1962, calculated from data in Figure 1, p. 86):

Percentage defecting from freshman occupational choice.

Comparison is between occupational choices of 446 male seniors graduating from the College of Science, Literature, and the Arts of the University of Minnesota (in 1956) and their choices when they entered the college in the fall of 1952.

Freshman Occupational Choice	Percentage Defecting
Biological Science/Medicine:	29.7% (91)
Social Science/Service:	46.9% (32)
Semi-professional:	47.4% (19)
Law/Other verbal:	47.8% (67)
Business:	61.5% (52)
Physical Science/Engineering:	76.7% (91)
None given:	87.1% (155)

Darley (1962, calculated from data in Figure 2, p. 87):

Percentage defecting from freshman occupational choice.

Comparison is between occupational choices of 528 male seniors graduating from seven private coeducational colleges in Minnesota (in 1956) and their choices when they entered these colleges in the fall of 1952.

Freshman Occupational Choice	Percentage Defecting
Physical Science/Engineering:	37.8% (74)
Social Science/Service:	52.3% (130)
Biological Science/Medicine:	54.4% (68)
Semi-professional:	57.6% (59)
Business:	77.1% (70)
Law/Other verbal:	84.4% (45)
None given:	96.3% (82)

Darley (1962, taken from data in Table 42, p. 89):

Percentage defecting from freshman occupational choice.

Comparison is between occupational choices of 1856 male seniors graduating from 29 colleges in Minnesota (in 1956) and their choices when they entered these colleges in the fall of 1952.

Freshman Occupational Choice	Percentage Defecting
Physical Sciences and Engineering:	31% (501)
Biological Sciences and Medicine:	40% (249)
Social Sciences:	41% (220)
Semi-professional:	44% (208)
Verbal:	61% (202)
Business:	62% (330)
High-school teaching:	65% (146)

Darley (1962, taken from data in Table 43, p. 89):

Percentage defecting from freshman occupational choice.

Comparison is between occupational choices of 1470 female seniors graduating from 29 colleges in Minnesota (in 1956) and their choices when they entered these colleges in the fall of 1952.

Freshman Occupational Choice	Percentage Defecting
Semi-professional:	30% (266)
Literary:	36% (56)
Business:	36% (556)
Artistic:	45% (113)
Medical and scientific:	50% (110)
Social Science:	55% (303)
Social Service:	79% (66)

Akenson and Beecher (1967, calculated from data in Table 1 on p. 177):

Percentage defecting from freshman career choice.

Comparison is between career choices of 824 graduating seniors at Harvard in 1965 and their choices when they entered college.

Freshman career choice	Percentage Defecting
Law:	37.8% (119)
Medicine:	40.0% (120)
All education:	51.7% (149)
Business:	51.7% (87)
Engineering and technical:	69.0% (42)
Miscellaneous:	71.4% (14)
Government:	84.9% (53)
Scientific research:	85.0% (200)
Creative arts and journalism:	85.0% (40)

Davis (1965, taken from Table 20, p. 4):

Percentage defecting from freshman career aspiration.

Comparison is between career choices of 49,817 graduating male and female seniors at 135 colleges and universities in 1961 and their recalled career aspirations when they were freshmen.

Freshman Career Aspiration	Percentage Defecting
Education:	15.2% (12,619)
Business:	27.4% (5,763)
Other professional fields:	42.7% (8,411)
Law:	43.7% (1,708)
Engineering:	48.7% (7,398)
Physical Sciences:	49.3% (3,231)
Humanities and Fine Arts:	50.3% (2,953)
Medicine:	56.5% (2,643)
Biological Sciences:	58.4% (833)
Social Sciences:	64.2% (1,135)
None:	100.0% (3,123)

Werts (1967a, calculated from data in Table 1, p. 93):*

Percentage defecting from career plan made as freshman.

Comparison is between career plans of 8483 male students at 248 colleges (in the summer of 1962) choosing one of eight careers and their plans when they entered college in the fall of 1961. Analysis limited by Werts to the eight career categories showing the highest rate of defection.

*Also see Werts (1966a).

Freshman Career Plan	Percentage Defecting
Physician:	26.9% (1,576)
Teacher:	34.7% (1,816)
Engineer:	35.9% (1,999)
Lawyer:	36.0% (869)
Accountant:	42.9% (420)
Businessman:	49.7% (928)
Chemist:	58.9% (484)
Physicist:	59.3% (391)

Table 2Q.--Percent defection from various career choices and major fields (CONTINUED)

Strong (1952, taken from data in Table 2, p. 681):

Percentage defecting from freshman occupational choice.

Comparison is between occupational choices of 255 male sophomores at Stanford University in 1931 and their choices when they were freshmen in 1930.

Freshman Occupational Plan	Percentage Defecting
Medicine:	17.1% (26.5)*
Law:	27.9% (40.0)
Engineering:	29.2% (47.0)
Business (general):	34.8% (36.0)
Miscellaneous:	51.6% (44.0)
Specific business activity:	61.5% (39.5)

*N's are fractionalized because of some subjects giving two choices as freshmen. When this happened, each classification received a count of 1/2.

MacIntosh (1953, taken from data in Table 2, p. 16):

Percentage defecting from vocational choice.

Comparison is between the vocational choices of 493 male students at Haverford (at all class levels) at the beginning and end of the 1947-48 academic year.

Vocational Choice	Percentage Defecting
Religion:	11% (18)
Medicine:	13% (102)
Physical Science:	21% (28)
Teaching:	22% (45)
Law:	26% (41)
Writing:	32% (40)
Business:	32% (73)
Engineering:	37% (29)
Government Service:	40% (30)
Social Service:	60% (10)
Personnel Administration:	70% (10)

Iffert (1957, taken from data in Tables 26-29, pp. 53, 56, 58):

Percentage defecting from initial subject-field choice.

Comparison is between the latest subject-fields of 3435 male and 2812 female students and dropouts (in 1953-54) and the subject-fields they reported as being their original interest when entering college in 1950. Analysis is limited by Iffert to most frequently chosen initial subject-fields.

Males: Initial Subject-Field Choice	Percentage Defecting	Females: Initial Subject-Field Choice	Percentage Defecting
Engineering:	39.5% (830)	Education:	38.0% (639)
Physical Education:	46.6% (161)	Nursing:	39.4% (142)
Business Administration:	54.2% (487)	Home Economics:	40.4% (329)
Agriculture:	55.0% (200)	Physical Education:	45.4% (130)
Premedicine:	63.1% (344)	Music:	48.4% (217)
Accounting:	63.6% (217)	Business Administration:	56.6% (212)
Education:	66.7% (126)	Speech and Dramatic Arts:	62.4% (101)
Physics:	71.5% (116)	Fine Arts:	64.6% (158)
Prelaw:	72.4% (156)	Language:	66.4% (122)
History:	73.5% (143)	Journalism:	73.3% (101)
English:	75.2% (113)	English:	74.9% (283)
Chemistry:	78.8% (245)	History:	76.0% (75)
Biology:	79.6% (113)	Mathematics:	78.2% (87)
Mathematics:	80.4% (184)	Psychology:	79.5% (88)
		Premedicine:	79.6% (54)
		Social Work:	79.7% (74)

Cole, Wilson and Tiedeman (1964, calculated from data in Table 1, p. 124):

Percentage defecting from initial choice of field of concentration.

Comparison is between initial choices of field of concentration of 759 male freshmen entering the University of Rochester (during the period of 1948-51) and the fields of concentration in which they graduated.

Initial Choice of Field of Concentration	Percentage Defecting
History:	13.9% (36)
Psychology:	22.2% (9)
Business:	31.9% (119)
English:	35.0% (20)
Technical:	39.5% (185)
General Science:	46.7% (197)
Pure Science:	48.1% (154)
Teaching:	51.3% (39)

Cole, Wilson and Tiedeman (1964, calculated from data in Table 4, p. 127):

Percentage defecting from original choice of field of concentration.

Comparison is between original choices of field of concentration of 208 male freshmen entering Harvard (during the period 1946-1949) and the fields of concentration in which they graduated.

Original Choice of Field of Concentration	Percentage Defecting
Architecture:	9.5% (21)
English:	16.1% (62)
Government:	19.8% (116)
Social Relations:	23.1% (108)
Biology:	23.9% (46)
Biochemistry:	24.1% (54)
History:	24.2% (62)
Economics:	25.7% (101)
History of Literature:	27.8% (36)
Geology:	29.4% (17)
Romance Languages:	31.6% (19)
Engineering:	36.8% (19)
Philosophy:	42.9% (14)
Chemistry:	43.3% (30)
Physics:	51.3% (39)
Mathematics:	53.3% (30)

Thistlethwaite (1960), calculated from data in Table 2, p. 225):

Percentage defecting from choice of major field of study before entering college.

Comparison is between major fields of study of 987 male and 513 female Merit Scholar winners and near-winners as college juniors (1959) and their choices of major field when entering college in 1956.

Males: Choice of Major Field of Study Before Entering College	Percentage Defecting	Females: Choice of Major Field of Study Before Entering College	Percentage Defecting
Natural Sciences:	19.4%	Arts and Humanities:	24.8%
Social Sciences:	24.5%	Natural Sciences:	40.0%
Arts and Humanities:	31.4%	Social Sciences:	40.2%
Biological Sciences:	35.9%	Biological Sciences:	49.2%
Unclassified fields:*	40.3%	Unclassified fields:*	50.0%

*Unclassified fields are accounting, business administration, home economics, journalism, prelaw, religious education, and other specialities not elsewhere classified

Table 4A.--Summaries of studies comparing the expected college environment and the "actual" college environment

Note: E.E. = expected environment--as described by students entering the college
A.E. = "actual" environment--as described by students already attending the college
$\bar{X}$ = mean score

SS = statistically significant NSS = not statistically significant PNG = probability level of result(s) not given

CCI SCALE	Stern (1961). A "major Eastern university"	Weiss (1964). St. Louis Univ.	Becker and Mittman (1962a). State University of Iowa.	Pervin (1966b). Princeton Univ.	Standing (1962). Brigham Young Univ.	Chickering (nd[b]). Goddard College	COMMENTS
Abasement-Assurance	E.E.: $\bar{X}$=5.95 A.E.: $\bar{X}$=7.22 (PNG)	E.E.: $\bar{X}$=5.86 A.E.: $\bar{X}$=6.14 (PNG)	E.E.: $\bar{X}$=5.44 A.E.: $\bar{X}$=5.38 (PNG)	E.E.: $\bar{X}$=2.52 A.E.: $\bar{X}$=1.81 (SS)	Male: E.E.: $\bar{X}$=3.22 A.E.: $\bar{X}$=3.01 (NSS) Female: E.E.: $\bar{X}$=3.13 A.E.: $\bar{X}$=2.95 (NSS)	E.E.: $\bar{X}$=1.1 A.E.: $\bar{X}$=0.6 (PNG)	In 5 out of 7 comparisons, the expected environmental press in this area is higher than the actual environmental press.
Achievement	E.E.: $\bar{X}$=6.95 A.E.: $\bar{X}$=3.34 (PNG)	E.E.: $\bar{X}$=6.49 A.E.: $\bar{X}$=5.00 (PNG)	E.E.: $\bar{X}$=6.76 A.E.: $\bar{X}$=5.34 (PNG)	E.E.: $\bar{X}$=8.22 A.E.: $\bar{X}$=6.22 (SS)	Male: E.E.: $\bar{X}$=8.27 A.E.: $\bar{X}$=6.91 (SS) Female: E.E.: $\bar{X}$=8.70 A.E.: $\bar{X}$=7.08 (SS)	E.E.: $\bar{X}$=7.8 A.E.: $\bar{X}$=6.3 (PNG)	In all 7 comparisons, the expected environmental press in this area is higher than the actual environmental press.
Adaptability-Defensiveness	E.E.: $\bar{X}$=6.14 A.E.: $\bar{X}$=5.91 (PNG)	E.E.: $\bar{X}$=6.18 A.E.: $\bar{X}$=5.18 (PNG)	E.E.: $\bar{X}$=6.53 A.E.: $\bar{X}$=6.64 (PNG)	E.E.: $\bar{X}$=4.46 A.E.: $\bar{X}$=3.47 (SS)	Male: E.E.: $\bar{X}$=6.08 A.E.: $\bar{X}$=5.74 (SS) Female: A.E.: $\bar{X}$=5.96 A.E.: $\bar{X}$=6.06 (NSS)	E.E.: $\bar{X}$=3.4 A.E.: $\bar{X}$=3.1 (PNG)	In 5 out of 7 comparisons, the expected environmental press in this area is higher than the actual environmental press.
Affiliation-Rejection	E.E.: $\bar{X}$=6.33 A.E.: $\bar{X}$=4.61 (PNG)	E.E.: $\bar{X}$=5.97 A.E.: $\bar{X}$=4.03 (PNG)	E.E.: $\bar{X}$=5.86 A.E.: $\bar{X}$=4.57 (PNG)	E.E.: $\bar{X}$=7.28 A.E.: $\bar{X}$=5.52 (SS)	Male: E.E.: $\bar{X}$=7.72 A.E.: $\bar{X}$=7.19 (SS) Female: E.E.: $\bar{X}$=7.67 A.E.: $\bar{X}$=7.22 (SS)	E.E.: $\bar{X}$=8.2 A.E.: $\bar{X}$=7.1 (PNG)	In all 7 comparisons, the expected environmental press in this area is higher than the actual environmental press.
Aggression-Blame Avoidance	E.E.: $\bar{X}$=3.81 A.E.: $\bar{X}$=6.24 (PNG)	E.E.: $\bar{X}$=4.01 A.E.: $\bar{X}$=5.30 (PNG)	E.E.: $\bar{X}$=4.50 A.E.: $\bar{X}$=5.39 (PNG)	E.E.: $\bar{X}$=4.00 A.E.: $\bar{X}$=5.95 (SS)	Male: E.E.: $\bar{X}$=2.08 A.E.: $\bar{X}$=2.67 (SS) Female: E.E.: $\bar{X}$=1.47 A.E.: $\bar{X}$=2.60 (SS)	E.E.: $\bar{X}$=3.3 A.E.: $\bar{X}$=6.1 (PNG)	In all 7 comparisons, the expected environmental press in this area is lower than the actual environmental press.
Change-Sameness	E.E.: $\bar{X}$=5.66 A.E.: $\bar{X}$=5.51 (PNG)	E.E.: $\bar{X}$=5.58 A.E.: $\bar{X}$=5.57 (PNG)	E.E.: $\bar{X}$=5.88 A.E.: $\bar{X}$=6.13 (PNG)	E.E.: $\bar{X}$=7.51 A.E.: $\bar{X}$=7.63 (NSS)	Male: E.E.: $\bar{X}$=6.14 A.E.: $\bar{X}$=6.74 (SS) Female: E.E.: $\bar{X}$=6.21 A.E.: $\bar{X}$=6.81 (SS)	E.E.: $\bar{X}$=8.0 A.E.: $\bar{X}$=6.9 (PNG)	In 4 out of 7 comparisons, the expected environmental press in this area is lower than the actual environmental press.
Conjunctivity-Disjunctivity	E.E.: $\bar{X}$=6.25 A.E.: $\bar{X}$=4.15 (PNG)	E.E.: $\bar{X}$=6.03 A.E.: $\bar{X}$=4.73 (PNG)	E.E.: $\bar{X}$=5.81 A.E.: $\bar{X}$=4.85 (PNG)	E.E.: $\bar{X}$=7.92 A.E.: $\bar{X}$=7.72 (NSS)	Male: E.E.: $\bar{X}$=8.73 A.E.: $\bar{X}$=7.96 (SS) Female: E.E.: $\bar{X}$=8.90 A.E.: $\bar{X}$=8.26 (SS)	E.E.: $\bar{X}$=6.3 A.E.: $\bar{X}$=5.9 (PNG)	In all 7 comparisons, the expected environmental press in this area is higher than the actual environmental press.
Counteraction-Inferiority-Avoidance	E.E.: $\bar{X}$=6.25 A.E.: $\bar{X}$=4.15 (PNG)	E.E.: $\bar{X}$=6.03 A.E.: $\bar{X}$=4.73 (PNG)	E.E.: $\bar{X}$=5.81 A.E.: $\bar{X}$=4.85 (PNG)	E.E.: $\bar{X}$=6.41 A.E.: $\bar{X}$=5.47 (SS)	Male: E.E.: $\bar{X}$=5.54 A.E.: $\bar{X}$=5.21 (SS) Female: E.E.: $\bar{X}$=5.31 A.E.: $\bar{X}$=5.02 (NSS)	E.E.: $\bar{X}$=6.4 A.E.: $\bar{X}$=3.9 (PNG)	In all 7 comparisons, the expected environmental press in this area is higher than the actual environmental press.
Deference-Restiveness	E.E.: $\bar{X}$=6.26 A.E.: $\bar{X}$=5.50 (PNG)	E.E.: $\bar{X}$=5.84 A.E.: $\bar{X}$=6.12 (PNG)	E.E.: $\bar{X}$=5.93 A.E.: $\bar{X}$=5.28 (PNG)	E.E.: $\bar{X}$=4.01 A.E.: $\bar{X}$=3.55 (SS)	Male: E.E.: $\bar{X}$=6.19 A.E.: $\bar{X}$=5.86 (SS) Female: E.E.: $\bar{X}$=6.47 A.E.: $\bar{X}$=6.05 (SS)	E.E.: $\bar{X}$=1.8 A.E.: $\bar{X}$=1.1 (PNG)	In 6 out of 7 comparisons, the expected environmental press in this area is higher than the actual environmental press.

Table 4A.--Summaries of studies comparing the expected college environment and the "actual" college environment (CONTINUED)

CCI SCALE	Stern (1961). A "major Eastern university"	Weiss (1964). St. Louis Univ.	Becker and Mittman (1962a). State University of Iowa	Pervin (1966b). Princeton Univ.	Standing (1962). Brigham Young Univ.	Chickering (nd[b]). Goddard College	COMMENTS
Dominance-Tolerance	E.E.: $\bar{X}$=6.31 A.E.: $\bar{X}$=5.40 (PNG)	E.E.: $\bar{X}$=5.80 A.E.: $\bar{X}$=5.14 (PNG)	E.E.: $\bar{X}$=6.02 A.E.: $\bar{X}$=5.87 (PNG)	E.E.: $\bar{X}$=5.54 A.E.: $\bar{X}$=3.70 (SS)	Male: E.E.: $\bar{X}$=5.74 A.E.: $\bar{X}$=6.04 (SS) Female: E.E.: $\bar{X}$=5.40 A.E.: $\bar{X}$=5.94 (SS)	E.E.: $\bar{X}$=2.8 A.E.: $\bar{X}$=3.2 (PNG)	In 4 out of 7 comparisons, the expected environmental press in this area is higher than the actual environmental press.
Ego Achievement	E.E.: $\bar{X}$=7.64 A.E.: $\bar{X}$=6.00 (PNG)	E.E.: $\bar{X}$=6.04 A.E.: $\bar{X}$=4.51 (PNG)	E.E.: $\bar{X}$=7.42 A.E.: $\bar{X}$=6.73 (PNG)	E.E.: $\bar{X}$=8.22 A.E.: $\bar{X}$=6.97 (SS)	Male: E.E.: $\bar{X}$=8.13 A.E.: $\bar{X}$=7.88 (NSS) Female: E.E.: $\bar{X}$=8.42 A.E.: $\bar{X}$=8.24 (NSS)	E.E.: $\bar{X}$=7.3 A.E.: $\bar{X}$=7.7 (PNG)	In 6 out of 7 comparisons, the expected environmental press in this area is higher than the actual environmental press.
Emotionality-Placidity	E.E.: $\bar{X}$=6.39 A.E.: $\bar{X}$=4.59 (PNG)	E.E.: $\bar{X}$=5.99 A.E.: $\bar{X}$=4.96 (PNG)	E.E.: $\bar{X}$=6.37 A.E.: $\bar{X}$=5.65 (PNG)	E.E.: $\bar{X}$=7.26 A.E.: $\bar{X}$=5.76 (SS)	Male: E.E.: $\bar{X}$=7.30 A.E.: $\bar{X}$=6.76 (SS) Female: E.E.: $\bar{X}$=7.98 A.E.: $\bar{X}$=7.33 (SS)	E.E.: $\bar{X}$=7.3 A.E.: $\bar{X}$=7.6 (PNG)	In 6 out of 7 comparisons, the expected environmental press in this area is higher than the actual environmental press.
Energy-Passivity	E.E.: $\bar{X}$=6.71 A.E.: $\bar{X}$=4.08 (PNG)	E.E.: $\bar{X}$=6.16 A.E.: $\bar{X}$=4.38 (PNG)	E.E.: $\bar{X}$=6.36 A.E.: $\bar{X}$=5.04 (PNG)	E.E.: $\bar{X}$=7.94 A.E.: $\bar{X}$=6.50 (SS)	Male: E.E.: $\bar{X}$=7.12 A.E.: $\bar{X}$=6.01 (SS) Female: E.E.: $\bar{X}$=7.27 A.E.: $\bar{X}$=6.35 (SS)	E.E.: $\bar{X}$=8.3 A.E.: $\bar{X}$=7.0 (PNG)	In all 7 comparisons, the expected environmental press in this area is higher than the actual environmental press.
Exhibitionism-Inferiority Avoidance	E.E.: $\bar{X}$=7.95 A.E.: $\bar{X}$=5.42 (PNG)	E.E.: $\bar{X}$=6.02 A.E.: $\bar{X}$=4.07 (PNG)	E.E.: $\bar{X}$=7.01 A.E.: $\bar{X}$=6.05 (PNG)	E.E.: $\bar{X}$=7.53 A.E.: $\bar{X}$=5.73 (SS)	Male: E.E.: $\bar{X}$=7.90 A.E.: $\bar{X}$=6.88 (SS) Female: E.E.: $\bar{X}$=8.28 A.E.: $\bar{X}$=7.09 (SS)	E.E.: $\bar{X}$=6.5 A.E.: $\bar{X}$=5.8 (PNG)	In all 7 comparisons, the expected environmental press in this area is higher than the actual environmental press.
Fantasied Achievement	E.E.: $\bar{X}$=6.43 A.E.: $\bar{X}$=4.86 (PNG)	E.E.: $\bar{X}$=5.73 A.E.: $\bar{X}$=4.69 (PNG)	E.E.: $\bar{X}$=6.05 A.E.: $\bar{X}$=5.24 (PNG)	E.E.: $\bar{X}$=6.47 A.E.: $\bar{X}$=6.29 (NSS)	Male: E.E.: $\bar{X}$=5.87 A.E.: $\bar{X}$=5.64 (SS) Female: E.E.: $\bar{X}$=5.99 A.E.: $\bar{X}$=5.68 (SS)	E.E.: $\bar{X}$=6.5 A.E.: $\bar{X}$=5.6 (PNG)	In all 7 comparisons, the expected environmental press in this area is higher than the actual environmental press.
Harm Avoidance-Risktaking	E.E.: $\bar{X}$=4.29 A.E.: $\bar{X}$=3.57 (PNG)	E.E.: $\bar{X}$=4.77 A.E.: $\bar{X}$=4.17 (PNG)	E.E.: $\bar{X}$=4.52 A.E.: $\bar{X}$=3.88 (PNG)	E.E.: $\bar{X}$=4.82 A.E.: $\bar{X}$=4.20 (SS)	Male: E.E.: $\bar{X}$=6.51 A.E.: $\bar{X}$=6.01 (SS) Female: E.E.: $\bar{X}$=6.89 A.E.: $\bar{X}$=6.28 (SS)	Not given	In 6 out of 6 comparisons, the expected environmental press in this area is higher than the actual environmental press.
Humanities, Social Science (Humanism)	E.E.: $\bar{X}$=6.76 A.E.: $\bar{X}$=5.01 (PNG)	E.E.: $\bar{X}$=5.42 A.E.: $\bar{X}$=4.33 (PNG)	E.E.: $\bar{X}$=6.15 A.E.: $\bar{X}$=5.35 (PNG)	E.E.: $\bar{X}$=8.86 A.E.: $\bar{X}$=8.15 (SS)	Male: E.E.: $\bar{X}$=7.68 A.E.: $\bar{X}$=7.37 (SS) Female: E.E.: $\bar{X}$=8.41 A.E.: $\bar{X}$=7.96 (SS)	E.E.: $\bar{X}$=8.7 A.E.: $\bar{X}$=7.6 (PNG)	In all 7 comparisons, the expected environmental press in this area is higher than the actual environmental press.
Impulsiveness-Deliberation	E.E.: $\bar{X}$=5.73 A.E.: $\bar{X}$=6.22 (PNG)	E.E.: $\bar{X}$=4.53 A.E.: $\bar{X}$=4.38 (PNG)	E.E.: $\bar{X}$=6.21 A.E.: $\bar{X}$=6.05 (PNG)	E.E.: $\bar{X}$=6.53 A.E.: $\bar{X}$=6.39 (NSS)	Male: E.E.: $\bar{X}$=5.36 A.E.: $\bar{X}$=5.50 (NSS) Female: E.E.: $\bar{X}$=5.48 A.E.: $\bar{X}$=5.96 (SS)	E.E.: $\bar{X}$=7.1 A.E.: $\bar{X}$=6.4 (PNG)	In 4 out of 7 comparisons, the expected environmental press in this area is higher than the actual environmental press.

Table 4A.--Summaries of studies comparing the expected college environment and the "actual" college environment (CONTINUED)

CCI SCALE	Stern (1961). A "major Eastern university"	Weiss (1964). St. Louis Univ.	Becker and Mittman (1962a). State University of Iowa	Pervin (1966b). Princeton Univ.	Standing (1962). Brigham Young Univ.	Chickering (nd[b]). Goddard College	COMMENTS
Narcissism	E.E.: $\bar{X}$=7.04 A.E.: $\bar{X}$=5.56 (PNG)	E.E.: $\bar{X}$=6.47 A.E.: $\bar{X}$=4.98 (PNG)	E.E.: $\bar{X}$=7.01 A.E.: $\bar{X}$=6.10 (PNG)	E.E.: $\bar{X}$=5.43 A.E.: $\bar{X}$=2.95 (SS)	Male: E.E.: $\bar{X}$=7.45 A.E.: $\bar{X}$=6.29 (SS) Female: E.E.: $\bar{X}$=7.65 A.E.: $\bar{X}$=6.52 (SS)	E.E.: $\bar{X}$=2.9 A.E.: $\bar{X}$=1.9 (PNG)	In all 7 comparisons, the expected environmental press in this area is higher than the actual environmental press.
Nurturance-Rejection	E.E.: $\bar{X}$=6.89 A.E.: $\bar{X}$=5.55 (PNG)	E.E.: $\bar{X}$=6.14 A.E.: $\bar{X}$=4.63 (PNG)	E.E.: $\bar{X}$=6.35 A.E.: $\bar{X}$=4.66 (PNG)	E.E.: $\bar{X}$=6.03 S.E.E $\bar{X}$=4.70 (SS)	Male: E.E.: $\bar{X}$=7.68 A.E.: $\bar{X}$=7.19 (SS) Female: E.E.: $\bar{X}$=7.98 A.E.: $\bar{X}$=7.51 (SS)	E.E.: $\bar{X}$=6.5 A.E.: $\bar{X}$=5.2 (PNG)	In all 7 comparisons, the expected environmental press in this area is higher than the actual environmental press.
Objectivity-Projectivity	E.E.: $\bar{X}$=5.54 A.E.: $\bar{X}$=3.94 (PNG)	E.E.: $\bar{X}$=5.02 A.E.: $\bar{X}$=4.17 (PNG)	E.E.: $\bar{X}$=4.94 A.E.: $\bar{X}$=4.46 (PNG)	E.E.: $\bar{X}$=8.03 A.E.: $\bar{X}$=8.36 (SS)	Male: E.E.: $\bar{X}$=8.10 A.E.: $\bar{X}$=7.52 (SS) Female: E.E.: $\bar{X}$=8.26 A.E.: $\bar{X}$=7.90 (SS)	E.E.: $\bar{X}$=9.3 A.E.: $\bar{X}$=8.1 (PNG)	In 6 out of 7 comparisons, the expected environmental press in this area is higher than the actual environmental press.
Order-Disorder	E.E.: $\bar{X}$=5.67 A.E.: $\bar{X}$=4.22 (PNG)	E.E.: $\bar{X}$=5.86 A.E.: $\bar{X}$=5.02 (PNG)	E.E.: $\bar{X}$=5.41 A.E.: $\bar{X}$=5.12 (PNG)	E.E.: $\bar{X}$=5.94 A.E.: $\bar{X}$=4.62 (SS)	Male: E.E.: $\bar{X}$=7.58 A.E.: $\bar{X}$=8.14 (SS) Female: E.E.: $\bar{X}$=7.64 A.E.: $\bar{X}$=8.35 (SS)	E.E.: $\bar{X}$=4.2 A.E.: $\bar{X}$=4.3 (PNG)	In 4 out of 7 comparisons, the expected environmental press in this area is higher than the actual environmental press.
Play-Work	E.E.: $\bar{X}$=7.05 A.E.: $\bar{X}$=7.00 (PNG)	E.E.: $\bar{X}$=6.30 A.E.: $\bar{X}$=5.44 (PNG)	E.E.: $\bar{X}$=6.94 A.E.: $\bar{X}$=6.52 (PNG)	E.E.: $\bar{X}$=6.44 A.E.: $\bar{X}$=5.64 (SS)	Male: E.E.: $\bar{X}$=7.05 A.E.: $\bar{X}$=7.04 (NSS) Female: E.E.: $\bar{X}$=7.26 A.E.: $\bar{X}$=7.26 (NSS)	E.E.: $\bar{X}$=5.6 A.E.: $\bar{X}$=2.0 (PNG)	In 6 out of 7 comparisons, the expected environmental press in this area is higher than the actual environmental press.
Practicalness-Impracticalness	E.E.: $\bar{X}$=6.63 A.E.: $\bar{X}$=6.06 (PNG)	E.E.: $\bar{X}$=6.64 A.E.: $\bar{X}$=5.58 (PNG)	E.E.: $\bar{X}$=6.57 A.E.: $\bar{X}$=5.99 (PNG)	E.E.: $\bar{X}$=5.33 A.E.: $\bar{X}$=4.44 (SS)	Male: E.E.: $\bar{X}$=7.20 A.E.: $\bar{X}$=7.32 (NSS) Female: E.E.: $\bar{X}$=7.15 A.E.: $\bar{X}$=7.25 (NSS)	E.E.: $\bar{X}$=3.9 A.E.: $\bar{X}$=3.4 (PNG)	In 5 out of 7 comparisons, the expected environmental press in this area is higher than the actual environmental press.
Reflectiveness	E.E.: $\bar{X}$=7.02 A.E.: $\bar{X}$=5.28 (PNG)	E.E.: $\bar{X}$=5.68 A.E.: $\bar{X}$=4.27 (PNG)	E.E.: $\bar{X}$=6.44 A.E.: $\bar{X}$=5.93 (PNG)	E.E.: $\bar{X}$=9.01 A.E.: $\bar{X}$=7.34 (SS)	Male: E.E.: $\bar{X}$=7.95 A.E.: $\bar{X}$=7.57 (SS) Female: E.E.: $\bar{X}$=8.39 A.E.: $\bar{X}$=7.81 (SS)	E.E.: $\bar{X}$=8.4 A.E.: $\bar{X}$=7.2 (PNG)	In all 7 comparisons, the expected environmental press in this area is higher than the actual environmental press.
Science (Scientism)	E.E.: $\bar{X}$=6.50 A.E.: $\bar{X}$=4.12 (PNG)	E.E.: $\bar{X}$=6.23 A.E.: $\bar{X}$=5.11 (PNG)	E.E.: $\bar{X}$=6.63 A.E.: $\bar{X}$=5.88 (PNG)	E.E.: $\bar{X}$=9.04 A.E.: $\bar{X}$=7.98 (SS)	Male: E.E.: $\bar{X}$=8.13 A.E.: $\bar{X}$=7.85 (SS) Female: E.E.: $\bar{X}$=8.21 A.E.: $\bar{X}$=7.50 (SS)	E.E.: $\bar{X}$=5.9 A.E.: $\bar{X}$=4.0 (PNG)	In all 7 comparisons, the expected environmental press in this area is higher than the actual environmental press.
Sensuality (Sentience)-Puritanism	E.E.: $\bar{X}$=6.14 A.E.: $\bar{X}$=5.15 (PNG)	E.E.: $\bar{X}$=4.70 A.E.: $\bar{X}$=4.00 (PNG)	E.E.: $\bar{X}$=5.39 A.E.: $\bar{X}$=4.89 (PNG)	E.E.: $\bar{X}$=6.64 A.E.: $\bar{X}$=6.07 (SS)	Male: E.E.: $\bar{X}$=5.44 A.E.: $\bar{X}$=5.00 (SS) Female: E.E.: $\bar{X}$=5.80 A.E.: $\bar{X}$=5.72 (NSS)	E.E.: $\bar{X}$=7.8 A.E.: $\bar{X}$=7.2 (PNG)	In all 7 comparisons, the expected environmental press in this area is higher than the actual environmental press.

Table 4A.--Summaries of studies comparing the expected college environment and the "actual" college environment (CONTINUED)

CCI SCALE	Stern (1961). A "major Eastern university"	Weiss (1964). St. Louis Univ.	Becker and Mittman (1962a). State University of Iowa	Pervin (1966b). Princeton Univ.	Standing (1962). Brigham Young Univ.	Chickering (nd[b]). Goddard College	COMMENTS
Sexuality-Prudishness	E.E.: $\bar{X}$=6.46 A.E.: $\bar{X}$=7.06 (PNG)	E.E.: $\bar{X}$=4.56 A.E.: $\bar{X}$=4.50 (PNG)	E.E.: $\bar{X}$=6.45 A.E.: $\bar{X}$=6.63 (PNG)	E.E.: $\bar{X}$=5.25 A.E.: $\bar{X}$=5.07 (NSS)	Male: E.E.: $\bar{X}$=6.60 A.E.: $\bar{X}$=6.79 (NSS) Female: E.E.: $\bar{X}$=6.63 A.E.: $\bar{X}$=6.75 (NSS)	Not given	In 4 out of 6 cases, the expected environmental press in this area is lower than the actual environmental press.
Supplication (Succorance)-Autonomy	E.E.: $\bar{X}$=5.15 A.E.: $\bar{X}$=4.63 (PNG)	E.E.: $\bar{X}$=5.12 A.E.: $\bar{X}$=4.63 (PNG)	E.E.: $\bar{X}$=4.79 A.E.: $\bar{X}$=4.48 (PNG)	E.E.: $\bar{X}$=5.42 A.E.: $\bar{X}$=4.69 (SS)	Male: E.E.: $\bar{X}$=7.10 A.E.: $\bar{X}$=6.88 (NSS) Female: E.E.: $\bar{X}$=7.14 A.E.: $\bar{X}$=7.24 (NSS)	E.E.: $\bar{X}$=6.1 A.E.: $\bar{X}$=5.4 (PNG)	In 6 out of 7 cases, the expected environmental press in this area is higher than the actual environmental press.
Understanding	E.E.: $\bar{X}$=6.50 A.E.: $\bar{X}$=4.12 (PNG)	E.E.: $\bar{X}$=5.96 A.E.: $\bar{X}$=4.71 (PNG)	E.E.: $\bar{X}$=5.95 A.E.: $\bar{X}$=4.82 (PNG)	E.E.: $\bar{X}$=8.88 A.E.: $\bar{X}$=7.76 (SS)	Male: E.E.: $\bar{X}$=7.99 A.E.: $\bar{X}$=7.09 (SS) Female: E.E.: $\bar{X}$=8.31 A.E.: $\bar{X}$=7.39 (SS)	E.E.: $\bar{X}$=8.3 A.E.: $\bar{X}$=7.6 (PNG)	In all 7 comparisons, the expected environmental press in this area is higher than the actual environmental press.

Table 4B.--Summaries of studies comparing mean scores for different class levels on the College Characteristics Index (CCI)

Note: Fr = freshmen, So = sophomores, Jr = juniors, Sr = seniors. Fr > So is read as follows: The mean CCI scale score for freshmen is larger than the mean score for sophomores

CCI SCALE	Becker and Mittman (1962a). State Univ. of Iowa. Cross-sectional, Fall 1960. (Males and females)	Rowe (1964). Three women's colleges. Cross-sectional, 1961-62. (Females)	Weiss (1964). St. Louis Univ. Cross-sectional, Fall 1963. (Males and females)	Brewer (1963). Huston-Tillotson College (Negro liberal arts college). Cross-sectional, Spring 1961. (Males and females)	Webb and Crowder (1961a). Emory Univ. Cross-sectional, Spring 1959. (Males and females	Chickering (nd[b]). Goddard College. Longitudinal, Spring 1961-Spring 1963. (Males)	COMMENTS
Abasement-Assurance	So > Sr > Jr > Fr	College No. 1: So > Jr > Sr > Fr College No. 2: Fr = Sr > So > Jr College No. 3: Jr > So > Sr > Fr	Sr > So > Fr	Fr > Sr	Lower division students > Upper division students	Sr > So	No clear-cut ordering is apparent.
Achievement	Fr > So > Jr > Sr	College No. 1: So > Fr > Sr > Jr College No. 2: Fr > So > Jr > Sr College No. 3: Fr > So > Jr > Sr	Fr > So > Sr	Fr > Sr	Lower division students > Upper division students	So > Sr	In all cases, Fr-So score press higher in this area than do Jr-Sr.
Adaptability-Defensiveness	Fr > So > Jr > Sr	College No. 1: So > Sr > Jr > Fr College No. 2: Sr > So > Fr > Jr College No. 3: Fr > So > Sr > Jr	Fr > So > Sr	Fr > Sr	Lower division students > Upper division students	So > Sr	In 6 out of 8 cases, Fr-So score press higher in this area than do Jr-Sr.
Affiliation-Rejection	Fr > So = Jr > Sr	College No. 1: Sr > Fr > Jr > So College No. 2: Jr > Sr > So > Fr College No. 3: Jr > Sr > So > Fr	Fr > Sr > So	Sr > Fr	Lower division students > Upper division students	So = Sr	No clear-cut ordering is apparent.
Aggression-Blame Avoidance	Sr > So > Jr > Fr	College No. 1: Jr > Sr > Fr > So College No. 2: Sr > So > Jr > Fr College No. 3: Sr = Jr > So > Fr	So > Sr > Fr	Fr > Sr	Upper division students > Lower division students	Sr > So	In 4 out of 8 cases, Fr-So score press lower in this area than do Jr-Sr. In 3 of the 4 remaining cases, Fr score press lower than do So-Jr-Sr.
Change-Sameness	Fr > So > Jr > Sr	College No. 1: Fr > Sr > So > Jr College No. 2: Fr > So > Sr > Jr College No. 3: Fr > So > Jr > Sr	Fr > So > Sr	Fr > Sr	Lower division students > Upper division students	Sr > So	In 6 out of 8 cases, Fr-So score press higher in this area than do Jr-Sr. In 1 of the 2 remaining cases, Fr score press higher than do So-Jr-Sr.
Conjunctivity-Disjunctivity	Fr > Jr > So > Sr	College No. 1: So > Fr > Sr > Jr College No. 2: Sr > Fr > Jr > So College No. 3: Fr > Jr > So > Sr	Fr > So > Sr	Sr > Fr	Lower division students > Upper division students	So > Sr	In 4 out of 8 cases, Fr-So score press higher in this area than do Jr-Sr. In 2 of the remaining 4 cases, Fr score press higher than do So-Jr-Sr.
Counteraction-Inferiority Avoidance	Fr > So > Jr > Sr	College No. 1: Fr > Jr > So > Sr College No. 2: Fr > Jr > So > Sr College No. 3: Fr > So > Sr > Jr	Fr > So > Sr	Fr > Sr	Lower division students > Upper division students	Sr > So	In 5 out of 8 cases, Fr-So score press higher in this area than do Jr-Sr. In 2 of the remaining 3 cases, Fr score press higher than do So-Jr-Sr.

Table 4B.--Saummaries of studies comparing mean scores for different class levels on the College Characteristics Index (CCI (CONTINUED)

CCI SCALE	Becker and Mittman (1962a). State Univ. of Iowa.	Rowe (1964). Three women's colleges.	Weiss (1964). St. Louis Univ.	Brewer (1963). Huston-Tillotson College	Webb and Crowder (1961a). Emory Univ.	Chickering (nd[b]). Goddard College.	COMMENTS
Deference-Restiveness	Fr > Jr > So > Sr	College No. 1: So > Fr > Jr > Sr College No. 2: Fr > Sr > So > Jr College No. 3: So > Fr > Jr > Sr	Sr > So > Fr	Fr > Sr	Lower division students > Upper division students	So > Sr	In 5 out of 8 cases, Fr-So score press higher in this area than do Jr-Sr. In 2 of the 3 remaining cases, Fr score press higher than do So-Jr-Sr.
Dominance-Tolerance	Fr > So > Jr > Sr	College No. 1: Jr > Sr > Fr > So College No. 2: Sr > Jr > Fr > So College No. 3: So > Jr > Sr > Fr	Fr > So > Sr	Fr > Sr	Upper division students > Lower division students	Sr > So	In 4 out of 8 cases, Fr-So score press lower in this area than do Jr-Sr. In 3 out of the remaining 4 cases, this is clearly reversed.
Ego Achievement	Fr > So > Jr > Sr	College No. 1: Fr > So > Jr > Sr College No. 2: Jr > Fr > So > Sr College No. 3: Fr > So > Jr > Sr	Fr > Sr > So	Sr > Fr	Lower division students > Upper division students	So > Sr	In 5 out of 8 cases, Fr-So score press higher in this area than do Jr-Sr. In 1 of the remaining 3 cases, Fr score press higher than do So-Jr-Sr.
Emotionality-Placidity	Fr > So > Jr > Sr	College No. 1: Fr > Sr > So = Jr College No. 2: Fr > Jr > So > Sr College No. 3: Fr > Jr > So > Sr	Fr > So > Sr	Fr > Sr	Lower division students > Upper division students	So > Sr	With the exception of the three women's colleges studied by Rowe, Fr-So score press higher in this area than do Jr-Sr. With respect to the three women's colleges, Fr score press higher than do So-Jr-Sr.
Energy-Passivity	Fr > So > Jr > Sr	College No. 1: Fr > Sr > So > Jr College No. 2: Fr > Jr > So > Sr College No. 3: Fr > So > Sr > Jr	Fr > So > Sr	Sr > Fr	Lower division students > Upper division students	So > Sr	In 5 out of 8 cases, Fr-So score press higher in this area than do Jr-Sr. In 2 of the remaining 3 cases, Fr score press higher than do So-Jr-Sr.
Exhibitionism-Inferiority Avoidance	Fr > So > Jr > Sr	College No. 1: Fr > Sr > So > Jr College No. 2: Fr > Sr > So > Jr College No. 3: Fr > Jr > Sr > So	Fr > So > Sr	Sr > Fr	Lower division students > Upper division students	So > Sr	With the exception of the three women's colleges studied by Rowe and Huston-Tillotson College, Fr-So score press higher in this area than do Jr-Sr. With respect to the three women's colleges, Fr score press higher than do So-Jr-Sr.
Fantasied Achievement	Fr > So = Jr > Sr	College No. 1: Fr > So > Jr > Sr College No. 2: Fr > Sr > So > Jr College No. 3: Fr > So > Jr > Sr	Fr > So > Sr	Sr > Fr	Lower division students > Upper division students	So > Sr	In 6 out of 8 cases, Fr-So score press higher in this area than do Jr-Sr. In 1 of the remaining 2 cases, Fr score press higher than do So-Jr-Sr.

Table 4B.--Summaries of studies comparing mean scores for different class levels on the College Characteristics Index (CCI) (CONTINUED)

CCI SCALE	Becker and Mittman (1962a). State Univ. of Iowa.	Rowe (1964). Three women's colleges.	Weiss (1964). St. Louis Univ.	Brewer (1963). Huston-Tillotson College	Webb and Crowder (1961a). Emory Univ.	Chickering (nd[b]). Goddard College	COMMENTS
Harm Avoidance-Risk-taking	Sr > Jr > Fr > So	College No. 1: Fr > So > Jr > Sr College No. 2: Fr > Jr > So > Sr College No. 3: So > Fr > Jr > Sr	Fr > So > Sr	Fr > Sr	Lower division students > Upper division students	Not given	In 5 out of 7 cases, Fr-So score press higher in this area than do Jr-Sr. In 1 of the remaining 2 cases, this is clearly reversed. In the other case, Fr score press higher than do So-Jr-Sr.
Humanities, Social Science (Humanism)	Fr > Jr > Sr > So	College No. 1: Fr > So > Sr > Jr College No. 2: Fr > Sr > Jr > So College No. 3: Fr > Sr > Jr > So	Fr > So > Sr	Sr > Fr	Upper division students > Lower division students	So > Sr	In 3 out of 8 cases, Fr-So score press higher in this area than do Jr-Sr. In 3 out of the remaining 5 cases, Fr score press higher than do So-Jr-Sr.
Impulsiveness-Deliberation	Fr > Jr > So > Sr	College No. 1: Fr > Sr > Jr > So College No. 2: Jr > So > Sr > Fr College No. 3: Jr > Sr > Fr > So	Fr > So > Sr	Sr > Fr	Upper division students > Lower division students	Sr > So	In 4 out of 8 cases, Fr-So score press lower in this area than do Jr-Sr. But in 3 of the remaining 4 cases, Fr score press higher than do So-Jr-Sr.
Narcissism	So > Jr > Fr > Sr	College No. 1: Fr > So > Sr > Jr College No. 2: Fr > Sr > So > Jr College No. 3: So > Sr > Fr > Jr	Fr > So > Sr	Sr > Fr	Lower division students > Upper division students	So = Sr	No clear-cut ordering is apparent.
Nurturance-Rejection	Fr > So > Jr > Sr	College No. 1: Fr > So > Sr > Jr College No. 2: Fr > Sr > So > Jr College No. 3: Fr > Sr > So > Jr	Fr > So > Sr	Sr > Fr	Lower division students > Upper division students	So > Sr	In 5 out of 8 cases, Fr-So score press higher in this area than do Jr-Sr. In 2 of the remaining 3 cases, Fr score press higher than do So-Jr-Sr.
Objectivity-Projectivity	Jr > Sr > Fr > So	College No. 1: Fr > So > Sr > Jr College No. 2: Fr > Jr > Sr > So College No. 3: Fr > So > Jr > Sr	Fr > So > Sr	Sr > Fr	Upper division students > Lower division students	So > Sr	In 4 out of 8 cases, Fr-So score press higher in this area than do Jr-Sr. But in 3 of the remaining 4 cases, Fr-So score press lower in this area than do Jr-Sr.
Order-Disorder	Fr > So > Jr > Sr	College No. 1: So > Fr > Sr > Jr College No. 2: Fr > Sr > So > Jr College No. 3: Fr > So > Jr > Sr	Fr > So > Sr	Fr > Sr	Lower division students > Upper division students	So > Sr	In 7 out of 8 cases, Fr-So score press higher in this area than do Jr-Sr. In the remaining case, Fr score press higher than do So-Jr-Sr.
Play-Work	Jr > So > Fr = Sr	College No. 1: Fr > Sr > Jr > So College No. 2: Jr > So > Fr > Sr College No. 3: Fr > Jr > Sr > So	Fr > Sr > So	Sr > Fr	Upper division students > Lower division students	So = Sr	No clear-cut ordering is apparent.
Practicalness-Impracticalness	Fr > So > Jr > Sr	College No. 1: Fr > So > Jr > Sr College No. 2: Sr > Jr > Fr > So College No. 3: So > Fr > Jr > Sr	Fr > So > Sr	Fr > Sr	Lower division students > Upper division students	So > Sr	In 7 out of 8 cases, Fr-So score press higher in this area than do Jr-Sr.

Table 4B.--Summaries of studies comparing mean scores for different class levels on the College Characteristics Index (CCI) (CONTINUED)

CCI SCALE	Becker and Mittman (1962a). State Univ. of Iowa	Rowe (1964). Three women's colleges.	Weiss (1964). St. Louis Univ.	Brewer (1963). Huston-Tillotson College	Webb and Crowder (1961a). Emory Univ.	Chickering (nd[b]). Goddard College.	COMMENTS
Reflectiveness	Fr > So > Jr > Sr	College No. 1: Fr > So > Sr > Jr College No. 2: Fr > Sr > Jr > So College No. 3: Fr > Sr > So > Jr	Fr > So > Sr	Sr > Fr	Lower division students > Upper division students	So > Sr	In 5 out of 8 cases, Fr-So score press higher in this area than do Jr-Sr. In 2 of the remaining 3 cases, Fr score press higher than do So-Jr-Sr.
Science (Scientism)	Fr > Jr > So > Sr	College No. 1: Fr > So > Sr > Jr College No. 2: Fr > So > Jr > Sr College No. 3: Fr > Jr > So > Sr	Fr > So > Sr	Fr > Sr	Lower division students > Upper division students	So > Sr	In 6 out of 8 cases, Fr-So score press higher in this area than do Jr-Sr. In the remaining 2 cases, Fr score press higher than do So-Jr-Sr.
Sensuality (Sentience)-Puritanism	Sr > Jr > Fr > So	College No. 1: Sr > Fr > So > Jr College No. 2: Fr > Sr > Jr > So College No. 3: Jr > Fr > So > Sr	Fr > So > Sr	Sr > Fr	Lower division students > Upper division students	Sr > So	No clear-cut ordering is apparent.
Sexuality-Prudishness	Fr > Jr > So > Sr	College No. 1: Fr > So > Sr > Jr College No. 2: Sr > Jr > So > Fr College No. 3: So > Jr > Fr > Sr	Fr > So > Sr	Sr > Fr	Upper division students > Lower division students	Not given	No clear-cut ordering is apparent.
Supplication (Succorance)-Autonomy	Sr > Jr > Fr > So	College No. 1: Jr > Sr > Fr > So College No. 2: So > Jr > Sr > Fr College No. 3: Fr > So > Jr > Sr	Fr > So > Sr	Sr > Fr	Upper division students > Lower division students	So > Sr	In 3 out of 8 cases, Fr-So score press higher in this area than do Jr-Sr. But in 4 of the remaining cases, Fr-So score press lower than do Jr-Sr.
Understanding	Fr > Jr > So > Sr	College No. 1: Fr > Sr > So = Jr College No. 2: Fr > Sr > Jr > So College No. 3: Fr > Sr > Jr > So	Fr > So > Sr	Fr > Sr	Lower division students > Upper division students	So > Sr	In 4 out of 8 cases, Fr-So score press higher in this area than do Jr-Sr. In the remaining 4 cases, Fr score press higher than do So-Jr-Sr.

Table 5A.--Summaries of selected studies showing diversity of student attributes among colleges

REFERENCE, SAMPLE	VARIABLE	Univ. of North Carolina	Univ. of Texas	Dart-mouth	Univ. of Michigan	Yale	Fisk	Wes-leyan	Cornell	Wayne State Univ.	UCLA	Harvard
Goldsen, Rosenberg, Williams, and Suchman (1960). Random sampling of male students (all class levels) in 11 colleges and universities in 1952.	Percent of students who "agree" to the following statements:											
	"If people are certain of a minimum wage they might lose their initiative"	51%	45%	38%	36%	36%	34%	34%	32%	31%	27%	23%
	"Democracy depends fundamentally on the existence of free business enterprise"	72%	70%	59%	67%	60%	53%	62%	62%	62%	61%	46%
	"It seems almost everything these days is a racket"	33%	33%	21%	21%	24%	49%	14%	20%	29%	25%	15%
	Percent of students expecting religion to be "a major source of satisfaction in life"	27%	29%	10%	17%	12%	36%	16%	13%	20%	13%	11%
	Percent of students expecting each of the following to give them "the most satisfaction":											
	"Your career or occupation"	24%	24%	25%	28%	27%	33%	31%	30%	33%	35%	31%
	"Family relations"	62%	55%	61%	60%	54%	43%	56%	58%	49%	48%	51%
	Percent of students who rank the goal of providing "a basic general education and appreciation of ideas" as a "highly important goal of the ideal college or university"	74%	65%	84%	69%	88%	59%	90%	73%	64%	70%	85%
	Percent ranking each of the following occupational requirements as "highly important":											
	"Permit me to be creative and original"	36%	39%	39%	47%	53%	51%	50%	49%	51%	52%	56%
	"Give me an opportunity to be helpful to others"	49%	38%	38%	42%	43%	72%	54%	35%	45%	38%	36%
	"Enable me to look forward to a stable, secure future"	75%	64%	64%	62%	51%	77%	56%	56%	60%	62%	46%

REFERENCE, SAMPLE	VARIABLE	A four-year college M	A four-year college F	A state university M	A state university F	A junior college M	A junior college F
Abe, Holland, Lutz, and Richards (1965). Sampling of second-semester freshman male ([illegible]) and female ([illegible]) students in 31 colleges and universities in the spring of 1964. Results for three of these colleges are shown here.	Percent of students saying "yes" to each of the following statements:						
	"I believe interracial dating is likely to lead to trouble"	30%	16%	75%	79%	62%	73%
	"This would be a better school if more students had more school spirit"	28%	20%	59%	58%	67%	70%
	"The thing I'll remember most about going to college is the fun and good times"	13%	8%	32%	36%	37%	63%
	"I choose electives mainly for their cultural and intellectual value"	77%	90%	54%	62%	43%	60%
	Percent of students saying that each of the following life goals is "essential ... something you must achieve":						
	"Developing a meaningful philosophy of life"	49%	68%	31%	56%	28%	56%
	"Doing something which will make my parents proud of me"	13%	12%	35%	50%	51%	56%
	"Following a formal religious code"	7%	6%	30%	37%	43%	65%
	"Being well liked"	6%	12%	31%	46%	37%	59%
	Percentile rank of average score on the following scales:						
	Leadership Potential Scale	44	52	55	58	29	36
	Interpersonal Competency Scale	38	44	45	48	47	50
	Range of Experience Scale	58	70	64	65	40	52
	Dogmatism Scale	22	19	41	51	51	56

Table 5A.--Summaries of selected studies showing diversity of student attributes among colleges (CONTINUED)

REFERENCE, SAMPLE	VARIABLE	RESULTS											
Rose (1964). Random sampling of male and female students (at all class levels) at each of eleven colleges and universities in the Connecticut Valley of Western Massachusetts in December 1962.		Northhampton Commercial College	Holyoke Junior College	Greenfield Community College	Westfield State College for Teachers	Springfield College	American International College	Univ. of Massachusetts	The College of Our Lady of the Elms	Amherst College	Mt. Holyoke College	Smith College	
	Percent of students giving "vocational training" as the most important goal of a college education	77%	57%	55%	50%	43%	42%	41%	35%	14%	6%	4%	
	Percent of students scoring "high" on a religiousness scale	74%	60%	38%	59%	27%	40%	35%	96%	6%	29%	19%	
	Percent of students who said they were opposed to dating a Negro	87%	77%	75%	85%	75%	74%	71%	86%	46%	48%	56%	
	Percent scoring "high" on a disarmament scale	56%	54%	49%	55%	44%	41%	46%	60%	22%	44%	34%	
Educational Reviewer (1963). Sampling of male and female sophomores, juniors and seniors at twelve colleges and universities during 1961-1963.		Univ. of South Carolina	Marquette Univ.	Davidson College	Yale Univ.	Indiana Univ.	Boston Univ.	Stanford Univ.	Williams College	Howard Univ.	Sarah Lawrence College	Brandeis Univ.	Reed College
	Percent of students who were either "definitely" or "somewhat" in favor of socialization of the medical profession	11%	13%	16%	17%	19%	20%	21%	26%	44%	54%	54%	59%
	Percent of students who were either "definitely" or "somewhat" in favor of marked increase in American economic and non-military aid to other countries (doubling it or more)	13%	22%	10%	41%	22%	33%	26%	51%	22%	58%	59%	57%
	Percent of students who said they were "in accord" with the following proposition: "I believe that God is all powerful"	89%	97%	81%	60%	82%	62%	67%	64%	79%	50%	41%	57%
	Percent of students answering "yes" to the following: "Do you think the concept of the national state has become so dangerously anachronistic that the U. S. should take the risks involved in surrendering some of her sovereignty in a serious attempt at achieving a strong international federation or world government?"	16%	14%	24%	39%	19%	27%	45%	44%	18%	40%	57%	65%
Gaff (1965). Sampling of male and female freshmen at 3 universities.	Percent of students saying that each of the following was one of the two most important goals of a college education for them:	University of California at Berkeley	University of the Pacific	Raymond College									
	"Develop vocational training"	43%	43%	12%									
	"Develop your ability to get along with different kinds of people"	23%	39%	14%									
	"Prepare you to serve mankind"	17%	13%	41%									
	"Provide a basic general education and appreciation of ideas"	49%	40%	50%									
	Percent of students saying that they were "basically opposed to religion"	13%	6%	32%									
	Percent of students saying that they did not "believe in God or higher power of any kind"	4%	1%	30%									

Table 5A.--Summaries of selected studies showing diversity of student attributes among colleges (CONTINUED)

REFERENCE, SAMPLE	VARIABLE	RESULTS									
		City College of New York		American International		University of Minnesota		George Peabody		Ohio State University	
		M	F	M	F	M	F	M	F	M	F
Allport, Vernon and Lindzey (1960).	Allport-Vernon-Lindzey Study of Values (Note: first figure is the mean score and the second in parentheses is the standard deviation.)										
Sampling of male (M) and female (F) students at five colleges and universities (year or years not given).	Theoretical Scale	44.57 (7.07)	41.63 (5.94)	42.49 (6.35)	37.94 (7.15)	42.44 (7.00)	36.50 (8.15)	42.22 (8.10)	34.69 (7.00)	39.92 (7.18)	32.71 (6.38)
	Economic Scale	39.53 (8.48)	39.28 (6.23)	43.15 (8.30)	38.69 (8.25)	42.69 (9.09)	35.82 (7.51)	41.92 (8.84)	38.64 (6.69)	45.15 (8.33)	41.14 (6.10)
	Aesthetic Scale	41.96 (9.76)	45.75 (9.09)	32.93 (7.65)	40.72 (8.10)	35.84 (8.92)	43.20 (8.84)	35.89 (9.95)	41.76 (7.85)	34.48 (8.72)	40.03 (7.04)
	Social Scale	40.74 (7.26)	43.65 (6.45)	37.58 (6.65)	41.75 (7.40)	39.72 (7.09)	40.32 (7.40)	38.66 (6.09)	41.40 (6.53)	37.94 (6.62)	42.84 (6.54)
	Political Scale	43.10 (6.17)	38.65 (5.07)	42.96 (6.30)	38.41 (6.30)	39.66 (6.15)	37.36 (6.81)	40.31 (6.17)	36.94 (5.63)	43.30 (6.78)	39.26 (6.40)
	Religious Scale	30.10 (9.49)	31.04 (8.97)	40.89 (8.40)	42.49 (8.30)	39.74 (9.81)	46.64 (9.33)	41.00 (9.87)	46.58 (8.90)	39.21 (8.90)	44.02 (8.66)

REFERENCE, SAMPLE	VARIABLE	Males			Females		
		4 university-affiliated colleges	3 independent liberal arts colleges	3 denominational colleges	3 university-affiliated colleges	5 independent liberal arts colleges	5 denominational colleges
Stern (1963b).	Activities Index (Note: scale scores are given as standard scores.)						
Sampling of male and female students at three types of colleges.	Reflectiveness Scale: high score = high need for intraceptive activities	.14	.40	-.04	.21	.16	-.11
	Abasement Scale: high score = high need for self-depreciation and devaluation	-.43	.03	.37	-.10	-.29	.24
	Conjunctivity Scale: high score = high need for organization and planfulness	-.05	-.77	1.12	.07	-.61	.47
	Achievement Scale: high score = high need for striving for success through personal effort	.02	-.18	.17	.21	.30	-.19
	Affiliation Scale: high score = high need for close, friendly, reciprocal associations with others	-.11	.93	.78	.39	-1.38	.11

REFERENCE, SAMPLE	VARIABLE	Schools:	"C"	"A"	"B"	"D"	"O"	"J"	"G"	"H"	"I"	"E"	"K"	"L"	"F"	"N"
Chauncey (1952). Sampling of male freshmen, sophomores and juniors at fourteen colleges and universities who were in a liberal arts curriculum during 1951.	Percent of students achieving a score of at least 70 (a passing score) on the Selective Service Qualification Test		98%	95%	93%	92%	86%	77%	76%	73%	70%	69%	64%	49%	46%	35%

OTHER STUDIES:

For some other references in which colleges are compared and contrasted with respect to the attributes of their students, see the following: Abe, Holland, Lutz, and Richards (1965); Beardslee and O'Dowd (1962); Roberta Brown (1967); Brown and Bystryn (1956); Cantril and Allport (1933); Chickering (1966b, 1966c); Chickering et al. (1968); Claster (1966); Coker (1966, 1967); Cooley (1966a); Dressel and Mayhew (1954); Educational Testing Service (1955); Flacks (1963); Fox (1965); Fredericksen and Schrader (1951); Gurin and Katz (1966); Jacob (1957); Katz (1967a); Korn (1967a); Learned and Wood (1938); McCarthy and Johnson (1962); McConnell (1961b, 1962a, 1962b); McConnell et al. (forthcoming); McConnell and Heist (1959, 1962); McNamara (1963); Norman Miller (1958, 1959); Moore and Garrison (1932); Nelson (1938, 1940); Newcomb (1943, 1946); O'Dowd and Beardslee (1960); Peterson (1965b); Rowe (1964); William Scott (1959); Stern (1966b); Tisdale (1965 in press); Trent (1965b, 1967); Warren (1966); Warren and Heist (1960); Webb and Crowder (1961b, 1965); Webster, Freedman and Heist (1962); Wickenden (1932); Wilson and Lyons (1961); and Wolfle (1954).

Table 5B.--Summaries of studies comparing the scores of male and female students on the scales of the College Characteristics Index

REFERENCE, SCALES USED	SAMPLE	Rank-order correlation between scores of males and females	Scales on which females were significantly higher than males	Scales on which males were significantly higher than females
Webb and Crowder (1961a). All 30 scales of the CCI, used individually (see Figure 5A in this appendix for listing).	Students at all class levels at Emory University, Spring 1963. (N=244)	rho = +.90 ($p < .01$; 2-tailed test)	Affiliation (vs. Rejection) Conjunctivity (vs. Disjunctivity) Ego Achievement Energy (vs. Passivity) Exhibitionism (vs. Inferiority Avoidance) Harm Avoidance (vs. Risktaking) Humanities, Social Science Nurturance (vs. Rejection) Objectivity (vs. Projectivity) Play (vs. Work) Reflectiveness Sexuality (vs. Prudishness) Supplication (vs. Autonomy)	Abasement (vs. Assurance) Aggression (vs. Blame Avoidance Deference (vs. Re - tiveness)
Stern (1962b). All 30 scales of the CCI, used individually (see Figure 5A in this appendix for listing).	Seniors at a "large eastern university with a graduating class of approximately 1,000 students," year not given. (Males, N=573; Females, N=463)	rho = +.96 ($p< .01$; 2-tailed test)	Abasement (vs. Assurance) Dominance (vs. Tolerance) Ego Achievement Emotionality (vs. Placidity Humanities, Social Science Impulsiveness (vs. Deliberation) Narcissism Nurturance (vs. Rejection) Play (vs. Work) Sensuality (vs. Puritanism)	Adaptiveness (vs. Defensiveness) Counteraction (vs. Inferiority Avoidance) Fantasied Achievement Reflectiveness Sexuality (vs. Prudishness)
Brewer (1963). All 30 scales of the CCI, used individually (see Figure 5A in this appendix for listing).	Students at all class levels at Huston-Tillotson College (a Negro liberal arts college), Spring 1961. (Males, N=80; Females, N=80)	rho = +.92 ($p< .01$; 2-tailed test)	Harm Avoidance (vs. Risktaking)	(None)
Standing (1962). All 30 scales of the CCI, used individually (see Figure 5A in this appendix for listing).	Students enrolled in a lower-division English literature class, Spring 1962. (Males, N=139; Females, N=139)	rho = +.96 ($p < .05$; 2-tailed test)	Emotionality (vs. Placidity) Humanities, Social Science	(None)
McFee (1959). All 30 scales of the CCI, used individually (see Figure 5A in this appendix for listing).	Students (mostly sophomores) in a psychology class at Syracuse Univ., year not given. (Males, N=51; Females, N=49)	(Data in original reference insufficiently complete for calculation of rho)	Adaptiveness (vs. Defensiveness) Emotionality (vs. Placidity) Harm Avoidance (vs. Risktaking) Humanities, Social Science Impulsiveness (vs. Deliberation) Nurturance (vs. Rejection) Reflectiveness Sensuality (vs. Puritanism)	(None)
Fisher (1961). All 30 scales of the CCI, used individually (see Figure 5A in this appendix for listing).	Freshman and sophomore students in four classes at Brigham Young Univ., Spring 1961. (N=365)	(Data in original reference insufficiently complete for calculation of rho)	Freshmen Abasement (vs. Assurance) Harm Avoidance (vs. Risktaking) Impulsiveness (vs. Deliberation) Sophomores Emotionality (vs. Placidity) Humanities, Social Science Reflectiveness	Freshmen Achievement Dominance (vs. Tolerance) Sophomores Aggression (vs. Blame Avoidance Science

Table 5B.--Summaries of studies comparing the scores of male and female students on the scales of the College Characteristics Index (CONTINUED)

REFERENCE, SCALE USED	SAMPLE	Rank-order correlation between scores of males and females	Scales on which females were significantly higher than males	Scales on which males were significantly higher than females
Weiss (1964). The 30 scales of the CCI clustered into 11 first-order factors: Aspiration Level, Intellectual Climate, Student Dignity, Academic Climate, Academic Achievement, Self-expression, Group Life, Academic Organization, Social Form, Play-Work, and Vocational Climate (see Stern, 1963b).	Freshman, sophomore and senior students at St. Louis Univ., Fall 1963.	(Data in original reference insufficiently complete for calculation of rho)	Aspiration Level Intellectual Climate Student Dignity Academic Climate Academic Achievement Self-expression	(None)
Stricker (1964). The 30 scales of the CCI clustered into 2 second-order factors: Intellectual Climate and Non-Intellectual Climate (see Stern, 1963b).	Students at all class levels, Fall 1963. (N=855)	rho = +1.00 (test of significance not meaningful for N of 2)	Intellectual Climate Non-intellectual Climate	(None)
Becker and Mittman (1962b). The 30 scales of the CCI clustered into five factors: Intellectual-Humanistic, Group Welfare, Social Press, Excitement, and Individuality.	Students at all class levels at State Univ. of Iowa, Fall 1960. (Males, N=910; Females, N=895)	rho = +1.00 ($p < .05$; 2-tailed test)	Intellectual-Humanistic Group Welfare Social Press Excitement	(None)
Bruning (1965). 21 of the 30 CCI scales clustered into four factors: Intellectual-Humanistic-Esthetic, Independent-Scientific, Status Oriented-Practical, and Group Welfare.	Freshmen and juniors at Dr. Martin Luther College in Minnesota, Spring 1962. (Males, N=34; Females, N=143)	rho = +1.00 ($p < .05$; for 1-tailed test only)	Intellectual-Humanistic-Esthetic Group Welfare	Independent-Scientific
White (1965). 21 of the 30 CCI scales clustered into four factors: Intellectual-Humanistic-Esthetic, Independent-Scientific, Status Oriented-Practical, and Group Welfare.	Freshmen and sophomores at 12 junior colleges in Minnesota (Austin, Brainerd, Ely, Evelth, Fergus Falls, Hibbing, Itasca, Rochester, Virginia, Worthington, Bethany, and Concordia), Spring 1962. (Males, N=1,759; Females, N=1,072)	rho = +.80 ($p > .05$; 1- and 2-tailed tests)	Group Welfare	Independent-Scientific

Table 6A.--Summaries of studies showing relative importance of the Spranger Values by curriculum

Note: Ranking of fields is from high to low in relative importance of a particular value. The standardization of the rank is accomplished by dividing the rank of the curriculum by the number of curricula in the study. Information about the samples is given at the end of the table.

REFERENCE, VARIABLE	CURRICULUM	N	RANK	STANDARDIZATION OF RANK
	Theoretical			
Whitely (1933). A-V	Natural Science	26	1	.25
	Social Science	15	2	.50
	Arts and Literature	23	3	.75
	Business	20	4	1.00
Harris (1934). A-V	Arts	87	1	.33
	Engineering	145	2	.67
	Business	106	3	1.00
Schaefer (1936). A-V	Psychology	15	1	.20
	Natural Science	39	2	.40
	Political Science and Economics	22	3	.60
	History	17	4	.80
	Literature and Languages	43	5	1.00
Newcomb (1943). A-V	Science	4	1	.17
	Social Studies	13	2	.33
	Art	9	3	.50
	Music	7	4	.67
	Literature	3	5	.83
	Drama and Dance	4	6	1.00
Thompson (1960). A-V	Philosophy	4	1	.11
	Natural Science	20	2	.22
	Medicine and Medical Technology	4	3	.33
	Business	21	4	.44
	Social Science	22	5.5	.61
	English	13	5.5	.61
	Education	17	7	.78
	Foreign Languages	8	8	.89
	Arts	14	9	1.00
Sternberg (1953). A-V	Bio-Chemistry	30	1	.11
	Psychology	30	2	.22
	Chemistry	30	3	.33
	Mathematics	30	4	.44
	History	30	5	.56
	Music	30	6	.67
	Economics	30	7	.78
	Political Science	30	8	.89
	English	30	9	1.00
Twomey (1962). A-V-L	Science	--	1	.14
	Health and Physical Education	--	2	.29
	Industrial Arts	--	3	.43
	Social Studies	--	4	.57
	Humanities	--	5	.71
	Education	--	6	.86
	Music	--	7	1.00
Huntley (1965). A-V-L	Physics	41	1	.11
	Pre-medical (Science)	136	2	.22
	Pre-medical (Arts)	27	3	.33
	Chemistry	26	4	.44
	Science	124	5	.56
	Engineering	257	6	.67
	Industrial Administration	55	7	.78
	Social Studies	296	8	.89
	Humanities	65	9	1.00
Pace (1964). Sample A. A-V-L	Physical Science	14	1	.11
	Industrial Arts	9	2	.22
	Commerce	14	3	.33
	Social Science	17	4	.44
	Health and Physical Education	16	5	.55
	Education (Academic)	15	6	.67
	Education (General)	11	7	.78
	English and Languages	13	8	.89
	Education (Elementary)	11	9	1.00

Table 6A.--Summaries of studies showing relative importance of the Spranger Values (CONTINUED)

REFERENCE, VARIABLE	CURRICULUM	N	RANK	STANDARDIZATION OF RANK
	Theoretical (continued)			
Pace (1964).	Natural Science	39	1	.14
Sample B.	Social Science	30	2	.29
A-V-L	Business Administration	36	3	.43
	Language Arts	19	4	.57
	Journalism	9	5	.71
	Education	38	6	.86
	Nursing	38	7	1.00
	Economic			
Whitely (1933).	Business	20	1	.25
A-V	Natural Science	26	2	.50
	Arts and Literature	23	3	.75
	Social Science	15	4	1.00
Schaefer (1936).	Political Science and Economics	22	1	.20
A-V	Natural Science	39	2	.40
	Psychology	15	3	.60
	Literature and Languages	43	4	.80
	History	17	5	1.00
Newcomb (1943).	Social Studies	13	1	.17
A-V	Literature	3	2	.33
	Science	4	3	.50
	Art	9	4	.67
	Drama and Dance	4	5	.83
	Music	7	6	1.00
Thompson (1960).	Business	21	1	.11
A-V	Medicine and Medical Technology	4	2	.22
	English	13	3	.33
	Philosophy	4	4	.44
	Education	17	5	.56
	Natural Science	20	6	.67
	Foreign Languages	8	7	.78
	Social Science	22	8.5	.94
	Arts	22	8.5	.94
Sternberg (1953).	Economics	30	1	.11
A-V	Mathematics	30	2	.22
	Political Science	30	3	.33
	Psychology	30	4	.44
	Bio-Chemistry	30	5	.56
	Chemistry	30	6	.67
	History	30	7	.78
	Music	30	8	.89
	English	30	9	1.00
Twomey (1962).	Industrial Arts	--	1	.14
A-V-L	Education	--	2	.29
	Science	--	3	.43
	Health and Physical Education	--	4	.57
	Music	--	5	.71
	Social Studies	--	6	.86
	Humanities	--	7	1.00
Huntley (1965).	Industrial Administration	55	1	.11
A-V-L	Social Studies	296	2	.22
	Engineering	257	3	.33
	Science	124	4	.44
	Chemistry	26	5	.56
	Premedical (Science)	136	6	.67
	Humanities	65	7	.78
	Physics	41	8	[illegible]
	Premedical (Arts)	27	9	1.00
Pace (1964).	Commerce	14	1	.11
Sample A.	Industrial Arts	9	2	.22
A-V-L	Social Science	17	3	.33
	Physical Science	14	4	.44
	Health and Physical Education	16	5	.56
	Education (General)	11	6	.67
	English and Languages	13	7	.78
	Education (Academic)	15	8	.89
	Education (Elementary)	11	9	1.00

Table 6A.--Summaries of studies showing relative importance of the Spranger Values (CONTINUED)

REFERENCE, VARIABLE	CURRICULUM	N	RANK	STANDARDIZATION OF RANK
	Economic (continued)			
Pace (1964). Sample B. A-V-L	Journalism	9	1	.14
	Business Administration	36	2	.29
	Natural Science	39	3	.43
	Education	38	4	.57
	Social Science	30	5	.71
	Language Arts	19	6	.86
	Nursing	38	7	1.00
	Aesthetic			
Whitely (1933). A-V	Arts and Literature	23	1	.25
	Social Science	15	2	.50
	Natural Science	26	3	.75
	Business	20	4	1.00
Harris (1934). A-V	Arts	87	1	.33
	Engineering	145	2	.67
	Business	106	3	1.00
Schaefer (1936). A-V	Literature and Languages	43	1	.20
	History	17	2	.40
	Psychology	15	3	.60
	Political Science and Economics	22	4	.80
	Natural Science	39	5	1.00
Newcomb (1943). A-V	Drama and Dance	4	1	.14
	Literature	3	2	.29
	Art	9	3	.43
	Music	7	4	.51
	Social Studies	13	5	.86
	Science	4	6	1.00
Thompson (1960). A-V	Arts	14	1	.11
	English	13	2	.22
	Foreign Languages	8	3	.33
	Education	17	4	.44
	Social Science	22	5	.56
	Philosophy	4	6	.67
	Natural Science	20	7	.78
	Medicine and Medical Technology	4	8	.89
	Business	21	9	1.00
Sternberg (1953). A-V	Music	30	1	.11
	English	30	2	.22
	Political Science	30	3	.33
	History	30	4	.44
	Psychology	30	5	.56
	Economics	30	6	.67
	Chemistry	30	7	.78
	Mathematics	30	8	.89
	Bio-Chemistry	30	9	1.00
Twomey (1962). A-V-L	Music	--	1	.14
	Humanities	--	2	.29
	Social Studies	--	3	.43
	Education	--	4	.57
	Industrial Arts	--	5	.71
	Science	--	6	.86
	Health and Physical Education	--	7	1.00
Huntley (1965). A-V-L	Premedical (Arts)	--	1	.11
	Humanities	--	2	.22
	Physics	--	3	.33
	Premedical (Science)	--	4	.44
	Science	--	5	.56
	Social Studies	--	6	.67
	Chemistry	--	7	.78
	Engineering	--	8	.89
	Industrial Administration	--	9	1.00

Table 6A.--Summaries of studies showing relative importance of the Spranger Values (CONTINUED)

REFERENCE, VARIABLE	CURRICULUM	N	RANK	STANDARDIZATION OF RANK
	Aesthetic (continued)			
Pace (1964).	English and Languages	13	1	.11
Sample A.	Education (Elementary)	11	2	.22
A-V-L	Education (Academic)	15	3	.33
	Education (General)	11	4	.44
	Social Science	17	5	.56
	Health and Physical Education	16	6	.67
	Physical Science	14	7	.78
	Commerce	14	8	.89
	Industrial Arts	9	9	1.00
Pace (1964).	Language Arts	19	1	.14
Sample B.	Nursing	38	2	.29
A-V-L	Social Science	30	3	.43
	Education	38	4	.57
	Natural Science	39	5	.71
	Journalism	9	6	.86
	Business Administration	36	7	1.00
	Social			
Whitely (1933).	Business	20	1	.25
A-V	Social Science	15	2	.50
	Natural Science	26	3	.75
	Arts and Literature	23	4	1.00
Schaefer (1936).	Political Science and Economics	22	1	.20
A-V	Natural Science	39	2	.40
	Psychology	15	3	.60
	Literature and Languages	43	4	.80
	History	17	5	1.00
Newcomb (1943).	Science	4	1	.17
A-V	Drama and Dance	4	2	.33
	Social Studies	13	3	.50
	Literature	3	4	.67
	Art	9	5.5	.92
	Music	7	5.5	.92
Thompson (1960).	Social Science	22	1	.11
A-V	Education	17	2.5	.28
	Foreign Languages	8	2.5	.28
	Philosophy	4	4	.44
	Arts	14	5	.56
	English	13	7	.78
	Natural Science	20	7	.78
	Medicine and Medical Technology	4	7	.78
	Business	21	9	1.00
Sternberg (1953).	History	30	1	.11
A-V	Psychology	30	2	.22
	Bio-Chemistry	30	3	.33
	English	30	4	.44
	Music	30	5	.56
	Political Science	30	6	.67
	Economics	30	7	.78
	Mathematics	30	8	.89
	Chemistry	30	9	1.00
Twomey (1962).	Health and Physical Education	--	1	.14
A-V-L	Education	--	2	.29
	Social Studies	--	3	.43
	Humanities	--	4	.57
	Music	--	5	.71
	Science	--	6	.86
	Industrial Arts	--	7	1.00
Huntley (1965).	Premedical (Science)	136	1	.11
A-V-L	Premedical (Arts)	27	2	.22
	Social Studies	296	3	.33
	Engineering	257	4	.44
	Chemistry	26	5.5	.61
	Industrial Administration	55	5.5	.61
	Science	124	7	.78
	Humanities	65	8	.89
	Physics	41	9	1.00

Table 6A.--Summaries of studies showing relative importance of the Spranger Values (CONTINUED)

REFERENCE, VARIABLE	CURRICULUM	N	RANK	STANDARDIZATION OF RANK
	Social (continued)			
Pace (1964). Sample A. A-V-L	Social Science	17	1	.11
	Health and Physical Education	16	2	.22
	Education (General)	11	3.5	.39
	Education (Elementary)	11	3.5	.39
	Education (Academic)	15	5	.56
	English and Languages	13	6	.67
	Physical Science	14	7	.78
	Commerce	14	8	.89
	Industrial Arts	9	9	1.00
Pace (1964). Sample B. A-V-L	Nursing	38	1	.14
	Education	38	2	.29
	Social Science	30	3	.43
	Journalism	9	4	.57
	Language Arts	19	5	.71
	Business Administration	36	6	.86
	Natural Science	39	7	1.00
	Political			
Whiteley (1933). A-V	Business	20	1	.25
	Social Science	15	2	.50
	Natural Science	26	3	.75
	Arts and Literature	23	4	1.00
Harris (1934). A-V	Business	106	1	.33
	Engineering	145	2	.67
	Arts	87	3	1.00
Schaefer (1936). A-V	Political Science and Economics	22	1	.20
	Literature and Languages	43	2	.40
	Natural Science	39	3	.60
	History	17	4	.80
	Psychology	15	5	1.00
Newcomb (1943). A-V	Science	4	1	.17
	Social Studies	13	2	.33
	Music	7	3	.50
	Literature	3	4	.67
	Art	9	5	.83
	Drama and Dance	4	6	1.00
Thompson (1960). A-V	Foreign Languages	8	1	.11
	Medicine and Medical Technology	4	2	.22
	Natural Science	20	3.5	.39
	English	13	3.5	.39
	Social Science	22	7	.78
	Business	21	7	.78
	Education	17	7	.78
	Philosophy	4	7	.78
	Arts	14	7	.78
Sternberg (1953). A-V	Political Science	30	1	.11
	Economics	30	2	.22
	History	30	3	.33
	Chemistry	30	4	.44
	Mathematics	30	5	.56
	Bio-Chemistry	30	6	.67
	Psychology	30	7	.78
	English	30	8	.89
	Music	30	9	1.00
Twomey (1962). A-V-L	Industrial Arts	--	1	.14
	Social Studies	--	2	.29
	Health and Physical Education	--	3	.43
	Science	--	4	.57
	Humanities	--	5	.71
	Education	--	6	.86
	Music	--	7	1.00

Table 6A.--Summaries of studies showing relative importance of the Spranger Values (CONTINUED)

REFERENCE, VARIABLE	CURRICULUM	N	RANK	STANDARDIZATION OF RANK
	Political (continued)			
Huntley (1965). A-V-L	Social Studies	296	1	.11
	Industrial Administration	55	2	.22
	Humanities	65	3	.33
	Engineering	257	4	.44
	Science	124	5	.56
	Chemistry	26	6	.67
	Premedical (Arts)	27	7	.78
	Premedical (Science)	136	8	.89
	Physics	41	9	1.00
Pace (1964). Sample A. A-V-L	Commerce	14	1	.11
	Health and Physical Education	16	2	.22
	Industrial Arts	9	3	.33
	Social Science	17	4	.44
	Education (Academic)	15	5	.56
	Physical Science	14	6	.67
	English and Languages	13	7	.78
	Education (Elementary)	11	8	.89
	Education (General)	11	9	1.00
Pace (1964). Sample B. A-V-L	Journalism	9	1	.14
	Business Administration	36	2	.29
	Social Science	30	3	.43
	Natural Science	39	4	.57
	Language Arts	19	5	.71
	Education	38	6	.86
	Nursing	38	7	1.00
	Religious			
Whiteley (1933). A-V	Arts and Literature	23	1	.25
	Social Science	15	2	.50
	Natural Science	26	3	.75
	Business	20	4	1.00
Harris (1934). A-V	Engineering	145	1	.33
	Arts	87	2	.67
	Business	106	3	1.00
Schaefer (1936). A-V	Literature and Langauges	43	1	.20
	History	17	2	.40
	Natural Science	39	3	.60
	Psychology	15	4	.80
	Political Science and Economics	22	5	1.00
Newcomb (1943). A-V	Music	7	1	.17
	Drama and Dance	4	2	.33
	Art	9	3	.50
	Literature	3	4	.67
	Social Studies	13	5	.84
	Science	4	6	1.00
Thompson (1960). A-V	Education	17	1	.11
	Foreign Languages	8	3.5	.39
	Social Science	22	3.5	.39
	Philosophy	4	3.5	.39
	Arts	14	3.5	.39
	English	13	6	.67
	Medicine and Medical Technology	4	8	.89
	Business	21	8	.89
	Natural Science	20	8	.89
Bender (1958). A-V	Humanities	21	1	.33
	Science	11	2	.67
	Social Science	[illegible]	3	1.00

Table 6A.--Summaries of studies showing relative importance of the Spranger Values (CONTINUED)

REFERENCE, VARIABLE	CURRICULUM	N	RANK	STANDARDIZATION OF RANK
	Religious (continued)			
Sternberg (1953).	Chemistry	30	1	.11
	Mathematics	30	2	.22
A-V	Bio-Chemistry	30	3	.33
	Political Science	30	4	.44
	English	30	5	.56
	History	30	6	.67
	Economics	30	7	.78
	Music	30	8	.89
	Psychology	30	9	1.00
Twomey (1962).	Music	--	1	.14
	Education	--	2	.29
A-V-L	Science	--	3	.43
	Industrial Arts	--	4	.57
	Humanities	--	5	.71
	Health and Physical Education	--	6	.86
	Social Studies	--	7	1.00
Huntley (1965).	Chemistry	26	1	.11
	Physics	41	2	.22
A-V-L	Engineering	257	3	.33
	Science	124	4	.44
	Industrial Administration	55	5	.56
	Social Studies	296	6	.67
	Humanities	65	7	.78
	Premedical (Science)	136	8	.89
	Premedical (Arts)	27	9	1.00
Pace (1964).	Education (Elementary)	11	1	.11
Sample A.	Education (General)	11	2	.22
A-V-L	Education (Academic)	15	3	.33
	English and Languages	13	4	.44
	Industrial Arts	9	5	.56
	Health and Physical Education	16	6	.67
	Physical Science	14	7	.78
	Social Science	17	8	.87
	Commerce	14	9	1.00
Pace (1964).	Nursing	38	1	.14
Sample B.	Education	38	2	.29
A-V-L	Language Arts	19	3	.43
	Natural Science	39	4	.57
	Business Administration	36	5	.71
	Social Science	30	6	.86
	Journalism	9	7	1.00

SAMPLES USED IN THE TABLE ABOVE:

Bender (1958). Male seniors at Dartmouth.

Harris (1934). Male students at Lehigh Univ.

Huntley (1965). Male seniors at Union College.

Newcomb (1943). Female seniors at Bennington College.

Pace (1964). Sample A: Male and female juniors and seniors at Eastern Washington; Sample B: Male and female upperclassmen at the Univ. of Florida.

Schaefer (1936). Male and female sophomores and seniors at Reed College.

Sternberg (1953). Male juniors at Queens College.

Thompson (1960). Male and female seniors at Macalester College.

Twomey (1962). Male and female freshmen, sophomores, juniors, and seniors at Colorado State College.

Whitely (1933). Students at Franklin and Marshall College.

Table 6B.--Summaries of studies showing degree of politico-economic and social liberalism by curriculum

Note: Ranking of fields is from high to low in degree of politico-economic and social liberalism. The standardization of the rank is accomplished by dividing the rank of the curriculum by the number of curricula in the study.

REFERENCE, SAMPLE	VARIABLE	CURRICULUM	N	RANK	STANDARDIZATION OF RANK
Newcomb (1943). Female juniors and seniors at Bennington College.	Political and Economic Progressivism (P.E.P.) Scale (low score = political and economic progressivism or liberalism)	Social Studies	100	1	.17
		Literature	54	2	.33
		Drama-Dance	48	3	.50
		Art	75	4	.67
		Music	38	5	.83
		Science	37	6	1.00
Noble and Noble (1954). Male and female students at a "professional and technical school in the New York metropolitan area."	20-item questionnaire concerning civil rights (high score = support of civil rights)	Art for Commerce and Industry	91	1	.25
		Architecture	38	3	.50
		Home Economics	32	3	.75
		Engineering	34	4	1.00
Boldt and Stroud (1934). Students at the Kansas State Teachers College of Emporia.	Harper's Test of Social Beliefs and Attitudes (high score = liberalism with respect to politico-economic, social and religious matters)	Social Science	29	1	.33
		Physical Science	37	2	.67
		Humanities	46	3	1.00
Bugelski and Lester (1940). Male and female seniors at the Univ. of Buffalo.	Opinion Test (high score = liberalism with respect to politico-economic, social and religious matters)	Social Science	59	1	.25
		Languages	44	2	.50
		Biological Science	34	3	.75
		Physical Science	18	4	1.00
Phillips and Erickson (1964). Male and female freshmen, sophomores, juniors, and seniors at Washington State Univ.	Conservative Scale from Phillips and Ericksons' Conceived Value Inventory (low score = low conservatism in the sense of not favoring the old, not looking to the past, rejecting the status quo)	Social Science	--	1	.14
		Humanities	--	2	.29
		Business Administration	--	3	.43
		Science	--	4	.57
		Physical Education	--	5	.71
		Engineering	--	6	.86
		Agriculture	--	7	1.00
Droba (1931a). Male and female freshmen, sophomores, juniors, and seniors (and a small proportion of graduate students) at the Univ. of Chicago.	Droba's Militarism-Pacifism Scale (high score = pacifism; interpreted as liberalism)	Social Science	304	1	.33
		Languages and Literature	188	2	.67
		Exact Sciences	134	3	1.00
Peterson (1965b). Male and female students at sixteen colleges: Applachian State Teachers College, Bellarmine College, Brown Univ., Pembroke College, C.I.T., Clarkson College, East Carolina College, Flint Junior College, Fordham Univ., Georgia Southern College, Kutztown State College, Orange Coast College, Pomona College, Univ. of Connecticut, Univ. of Delaware, and Whitman College.	Liberalism Scale from ETS College Student Questionnaire (high score = high political-economic-social liberalism)	Social Science	--	1	.17
		Humanities-Fine Arts	--	2	.33
		Natural Science	--	3	.50
		Education	--	4	.67
		Engineering	--	5	.83
		Business	--	6	1.00
Jones (1938b). Male seniors at a "rather small New England liberal arts college for men."	Droba's Attitude toward War Scale (high score = unfavorable attitude toward war; interpreted as liberalism)	English, Languages	41	1	.25
		Natural Science	62	2	.50
		Economics and Sociology	19	3	.75
		History and Geography	27	4	1.00

Table 6B.--Summaries of studies showing degree of politico-economic and social liberalism (CONTINUED)

REFERENCE, SAMPLE	VARIABLE	CURRICULUM	N	RANK	STANDARDIZATION OF RANK
Ferguson (1944). Male and female students at eighteen universities and colleges: Brown Univ., Chico State College, Connecticut College, Dartmouth, George Washington Univ., Northwestern Univ., Ohio State Univ., Pembroke College, Sacramento Junior College, Springfield College, Stanford Univ., Stephens College, Univ. of Connecticut, Univ. of Maine, Univ. of Washington, Univ. of Wisconsin, Wesleyan Univ. and Wheaton College.	Humanitarianism Factor--composed of three scales measuring attitudes toward war, capital punishment and treatment of criminals (high negative score = high humanitarianism, including pacifism and social liberalism)	Males*			
		Arts	167	1	.17
		Science	88	2	.33
		Physical Education	32	3	.50
		Business	73	4	.67
		Mathematics	14	5	.83
		Engineering	21	6	1.00
		*Major fields of Home Economics and Agriculture not included because of small N's			
		Females*			
		Arts	317	1	.20
		Business	40	2	.40
		Mathematics	10	3	.60
		Science	71	4	.80
		Home Economics	52	5	1.00
		*Major fields of Agriculture and Physical Education not included because of small N's			
Selvin and Hagstrom (1960). Male and female freshmen, sophomores, juniors, and seniors at the Univ. of California, Berkeley.	Libertarianism Index (high score = favorable attitude toward the principles of the Bill of Rights) Note: Ranking is of the percentages of students in each curriculum who are "highly libertarian" (i.e., those who score from 12 to 15 on the 15-item scale).	Males			
		Social Science	30	1	.14
		Humanities	45	2	.29
		Life Science (Medical and Biological Science, Pure and Applied)	37	3	.43
		Physical Science and Mathematics	31	4	.57
		Engineering (and other applied Physical Sciences)	245	5	.71
		Education	24	6	.86
		Business Administration	33	7	1.00
		Females			
		Applied Social Science (Social Welfare, Criminology, etc.)	20	1	.20
		Life Science (Medical and Biological Science, Pure and Applied)	60	2	.40
		Social Science	32	3.5	.70
		Humanities	112	3.5	.70
		Education	73	5	1.00
Norman Miller (1958). Male freshmen, sophomores, juniors, and seniors at four Ivy League universities (Dartmouth, Harvard, Wesleyan, and Yale) and at five state-supported universities (Univ. of N. Carolina, Univ. of Michigan, Univ. of Texas, UCLA, and Wayne State Univ.).	4-item Civil Rights Index (high score = pro civil rights, interpreted as political and social liberalism) Note: Ranking is of the percentage of students in each curriculum who score in the highest two positions on the index. (Based on data in Table 66.)	Ivy League			
		Social Science	--	1	.14
		Natural Science	--	2	.29
		Humanities	--	3	.43
		Pre-medical	--	4	.57
		Business	--	5	.71
		Engineering	--	6	.86
		Education	--	7	1.00
		State-supported			
		Business	--	1	.14
		Engineering	--	2	.29
		Pre-medical	--	3	.43
		Natural Science	--	4	.57
		Humanities	--	5	.71
		Social Science	--	6	.86
		Education	--	7	1.00
Norman Miller (1958). Male freshmen, sophomores, juniors, and seniors at Dartmouth, Harvard, Wesleyan, Yale, Cornell, Fisk, Univ. of N. Carolina, Univ. of Michigan, Univ. of Texas, UCLA, and Wayne State Univ.	4-item Labor Index (high score = pro labor; interpreted as politico-economic liberalism) Note: Ranking is of the percentage of students in each curriculum who score in the highest two positions on the index.	Education	--	1	.13
		Social Science	--	2	.25
		Natural Science	--	3	.38
		Business	--	4	.50
		Humanities	--	5	.63
		Pre-medical	--	6	.75
		Engineering	--	7	.88
		Agriculture	--	8	1.00

Table 6B.--Summaries of studies showing degree of politico-economic and social liberalism (CONTINUED)

REFERENCE, SAMPLE	VARIABLE	CURRICULUM	N	RANK	STANDARDIZATION OF RANK
Carlson (1934). Male and female seniors at the Univ. of Chicago.	Attitude toward Prohitibion Scale (low score = unfavorable attitude; interpreted as liberalism)	Biological Science	--	1	.25
		Physical Science	--	2	.50
		Social Science	--	3.5	.88
		Humanities	--	3.5	.88
	Attitude toward Pacifism Scale (high score = favorable attitude; interpreted as liberalism)	Social Science	--	1	.25
		Biological Science	--	2	.50
		Humanities	--	3	.75
		Physical Science	--	4	1.00
	Attitude toward Communism Scale (high score = favorable attitude; interpreted as liberalism)	Humanities	--	1	.25
		Social Science	--	2	.50
		Biological Science	--	3	.75
		Physical Science	--	4	1.00
	Attitude toward Birth Control Scale (high score = favorable attitude; interpreted as liberalism)	Social Science	--	1	.25
		Biological Science	--	2	.50
		Humanities	--	3	.75
		Physical Science	--	4	1.00
	Degree of liberalism when combining the above four scales: rank of the average rank of students in each curriculum across the four scales	Social Science	--	1	.25
		Biological Science	--	2	.50
		Humanities	--	3	.75
		Physical Science	--	4	1.00
Pace (1964). Female juniors at Bennington College.	Liberalism Scale (derived from earlier measures by McCloskey) from an early form of the Omnibus Personality Inventory (high score = liberalism, favorability to change)	Social Science	--	1	.33
		Literature	--	2	.67
		Art, Music, Dance	--	3	1.00
	Political Liberalism Scale (high score = political liberalism)	Social Science	--	1.5	.50
		Art, Music, Dance	--	1.5	.50
		Literature	--	3	1.00
	Radicalism Scale (high score = high radicalism)	Social Science	--	1	.33
		Art, Music, Dance	--	2	.67
		Literature	--	3	1.00
	Degree of liberalism when combining the above three scales: rank of the average rank of students in each curriculum across the three scales	Social Science	--	1	.33
		Art, Music, Dance	--	2	.67
		Literature	--	3	1.00
Fay and Middleton (1939). Male and female freshmen, sophomores, juniors, and seniors at De Pauw Univ.	Attitude toward Communism Scale (high score = favorable attitude toward communism; interpreted as liberalism)	Philosophy and Bible	10	1	.09
		Political Science	34	2	.18
		Sociology	43	3	.27
		Biological and Physical Science	106	4	.36
		English	97	5	.45
		History	38	6	.55
		Foreign Languages	39	7	.64
		Economics	94	8	.73
		Psychology	25	9	.82
		Home Economics	50	10	.91
		Art and Music	50	11	1.00
	Attitude toward Patriotism Scale (low score = unfavorable attitude toward patriotism; interpreted as liberalism)	Philosophy and Bible	10	1	.09
		Foreign Languages	39	2	.18
		History	38	3	.27
		Sociology	43	4	.36
		Biological and Physical Science	106	5.5	.50
		English	97	5.5	.50
		History	38	7	.64
		Art and Music	50	8	.73
		Economics	94	9	.82
		Political Science	34	10	.91
		Home Economics	50	11	1.00
	Attitude toward the United States Constitution (low score = unfavorable attitude toward the constitution; interpreted as liberalism)	Sociology	43	1	.09
		Philosophy and Bible	10	2	.18
		Biological and Physical Science	106	3	.27
		Economics	94	4	.36
		English	97	5	.45
		Foreign Languages	39	6	.55
		Political Science	34	7	.64
		History	38	8	.73
		Psychology	25	9	.82
		Home Economics	50	10	.91
		Art and Music	50	11	1.00

Table 6B.--Summaries of studies showing degree of politico-economic and social liberalism (CONTINUED)

REFERENCE, SAMPLE	VARIABLE	CURRICULUM	N	RANK	STANDARDIZATION OF RANK
Fay and Middleton (continued).	Attitude toward Law Scale (low score = unfavorable attitude toward law; interpreted as liberalism)	Philosophy and Bible	10	1	.09
		Biological and Physical Science	106	2	.18
		Sociology	43	3	.27
		Psychology	25	4	.36
		Foreign Languages	39	5.5	.50
		Economics	94	5.5	.50
		English	97	7	.64
		Political Science	34	8	.73
		Art and Music	50	9	.82
		History	38	10	.91
		Home Economics	50	11	1.00
	Attitude toward Censorship Scale (low score = unfavorable attitude toward censorship; interpreted as liberalism)	Philosophy and Bible	10	1	.09
		Political Science	34	2	.18
		Biological and Physical Science	106	3	.27
		Economics	94	4	.36
		Foreign Languages	39	5	.45
		History	38	6	.55
		English	97	7	.64
		Sociology	43	8.5	.77
		Home Economics	50	8.5	.77
		Psychology	25	10	.91
		Art and Music	50	11	1.00
	Degree of liberalism when combining the above five scales: rank of the average rank of students in each curriculum across the five scales	Philosophy and Bible	10	1	.09
		Biological and Physical Science	106	2	.18
		Sociology	43	3	.27
		Foreign Languages	39	4	.36
		Political Science	34	5	.45
		English	97	6	.55
		Economics	94	7	.64
		History	38	8	.73
		Psychology	25	9	.82
		Art and Music	50	10	.91
		Home Economics	50	11	1.00
Goldsen (1951). Male and female freshmen, sophomores, juniors, and seniors at Cornell Univ.	5-item Ideology of Government Planning Index (low score = favorable attitude toward government planning; interpreted as politico-economic liberalism) Note: Ranking is of the percentage of students in each curriculum who score in the two lowest positions on this index	Industrial and Labor Relations	107	1	.14
		Arts and Sciences	955	2	.29
		Home Economics	315	3	.43
		Architecture	69	4	.57
		Agriculture	567	5	.71
		Engineering	607	6	.86
		Hotel Administration	121	7	1.00
	6-item Ideology of Big Business Index (low score = anti-big business ideology; interpreted as economic liberalism) Note: Ranking is of the percentage of students in each curriculum who score in the three lowest positions on this index	Industrial and Labor Relations	107	1	.14
		Arts and Sciences	955	2.5	.36
		Architecture	69	2.5	.36
		Home Economics	315	4	.57
		Engineering	607	5	.71
		Agriculture	567	6	.86
		Hotel Administration	121	7	1.00
	6-item Opinion on Civil Liberties Cases Scale (high score = support of those accused of subversiveness; interpreted as political and social liberalism) Note: Ranking is of the percentage of students in each curriculum who support those accused of subversiveness in more than half of the six cases	Industrial and Labor Relations	107	1	.14
		Architecture	68	2	.29
		Arts and Sciences	952	3	.43
		Engineering	604	4	.57
		Home Economics	310	5	.71
		Agriculture	557	6	.86
		Hotel Administration	119	7	1.00
	Degree of liberalism when combining the above three indices: rank of the average rank of students in each curriculum across the three indices	Industrial and Labor Relations	107	1	.14
		Arts and Sciences	952	2	.29
		Architecture	68	3	.43
		Home Economics	310	4	.57
		Engineering	604	5	.71
		Agriculture	557	6	.86
		Hotel Administration	119	7	1.00

Table 6C.--Summaries of studies showing degree of religious orthodoxy or religious conventionality by curriculum

Note: Ranking of fields is from low to high in degree of religious orthodoxy or conventionality (i.e., from high to low in degree of religious "liberalism"). The standardization of the rank is accomplished by dividing the rank of the curriculum by the number of curricula in the study.

REFERENCE, SAMPLE	VARIABLE	CURRICULUM	N	RANK	STANDARDIZATION OF RANK
Hall (1951). Male and female seniors at Syracuse Univ.	Hall's You and the Universe Inventory (low score = rejection or skepticism about the existence of God; anti-religious tendency)	Males			
		Science	90	1	.14
		Sociology	47	2	.29
		Education	63	3	.43
		Business Administration	195	4	.57
		Fine Arts	35	5	.71
		Forestry	105	6.5	.93
		Applied Science	197	6.5	.93
		Females			
		Science	11	1	.20
		Sociology	57	2	.40
		Business Administration	14	3	.60
		Fine Arts	51	4	.80
		Education	36	5	1.00
Ferguson (1944). Male and female students at eighteen universities and colleges: Brown Univ., Chico State College, Connecticut College, Dartmouth, George Washington Univ., Northwestern Univ., Ohio State Univ., Pembroke College, Sacramento Junior College, Springfield College, Stanford Univ., Stephens College, Univ. of Connecticut, Univ. of Maine, Univ. of Washington, Univ. of Wisconsin, Wesleyan Univ., and Wheaton College.	Religionism Factor--composed of three scales measuring attitudes toward God, evolution and birth control (high positive score = high "anti-religionism")	Males*			
		Science	88	1	.17
		Arts	167	2	.33
		Physical Education	32	3	.50
		Engineering	21	4	.67
		Business	73	5	.83
		Mathematics	14	6	1.00
		*Major fields of Home Economics and Agriculture not included because of small N's			
		Females*			
		Mathematics	10	1	.20
		Science	71	2	.40
		Arts	317	3	.60
		Home Economics	52	4	.80
		Business	40	5	1.00
		*Major fields of Agriculture and Physical Education were not included because of small N's			
Wickenden (1932). Students at fifteen church colleges and five non-church colleges in Ohio, Indiana, Michigan, Illinois, and Minnesota.	35-item scale to measure student's concept of God	Church colleges			
		Business Administration	--	1	.14
		Physical Science	--	2	.29
		History	--	3	.43
		Fine Arts	--	4	.57
		Sociology	--	5	.71
		Language	--	6	.86
		Biological Science	--	7	1.00
		Non-church colleges			
		Language	--	1	.25
		Science (Biological and Physical)	--	2	.50
		Engineering	--	3	.75
		Business Administration	--	4	1.00
Carlson (1934). Male and female seniors at the Univ. of Chicago.	Attitude toward Reality of God Scale (low score = unfavorable attitude toward the reality of God)	Biological Science	--	1	.25
		Social Science	--	2.5	.63
		Humanities	--	2.5	.63
		Physical Science	--	4	1.00
Jones (1938b). Male seniors at a "rather small New England liberal arts college for men."	Favorableness toward the church and belief in God as measured by Thurstone and Chave's Attitude toward the Church Scale, Attitude toward God as an Influence on Conduct Scale, and Attitude toward the Reality of God Scale (high score = low favorableness toward the church and disbelief in God) Note: Ranking is of the average of the means in these three scales	Natural Science	62	1	.25
		English, Languages	41	2	.50
		Economics and Sociology	19	3	.75
		History and Geography	27	4	1.00

Table 6C.--Summaries of studies showing degree of religious orthodoxy (CONTINUED)

REFERENCE, SAMPLE	VARIABLE	CURRICULUM	N	RANK	STANDARDIZATION OF RANK
Pace (1964). Male and female upperclassmen at Swarthmore.	Religious Liberalism Scale from Omnibus Personality Inventory (high score = skepticism of conventional religious beliefs and practices)	English	--	1	.20
		History	--	2	.40
		Physics, Mathematics	--	3	.60
		Biological Science	--	4	.80
		Political Science, Economics	--	5	1.00
Pace (1964). Female juniors at Bennington College.	Atheism-Agnositcism Scale from an early form of the Omnibus Personality Inventory (high score = skepticism of conventional religious beliefs and practices)	Literature	--	1	.33
		Social Science	--	2	.67
		Art, Music, Dance	--	3	1.00
Young, Dustin and Holtzman (1966). Male and female freshmen, sophomores, juniors, and seniors at the Univ. of Texas.	R Scale (low score = negative attitude toward organized religion)	Social Science	--	1	.13
		Fine Arts	--	2	.25
		Pharmacy	--	3	.38
		Engineering	--	4	.50
		Natural Science	--	5	.63
		Business Administration	--	6	.75
		Humanities	--	7	.88
		Education	--	8	1.00
Hessel (nd). Male and female entrants into the College of Letters and Science at UCLA.	Religious Liberalism Scale from the Omnibus Personality Inventory (high score = skepticism or rejection of religious beliefs and practices) Note: Analysis gives only distinctively high and low groups	Political Science	--	Distinctively high on scale	
		Education	--	Distinctively low on scale	

Table 6D.--Summaries of studies showing degree of intellectual ability by curriculum

Note: Ranking of fields is from high to low in degree of intellectual ability. The standardization of the rank is accomplished by dividing the rank by the number of curricula in the study.

REFERENCE, SAMPLE	VARIABLE	CURRICULUM	N	RANK	STANDARDIZATION OF RANK
Pace (1964). Seniors at De Pauw Univ.	ACE Psychological Examination-Linguistic (L)	Biological Science	11	1	.11
		Languages	19	2	.22
		Psychology	30	3	.33
		Physical Science	12	4	.44
		English	8	5	.56
		Education	20	6	.67
		History, Philosophy	17	7	.78
		Social Science	12	8	.89
		Speech, Art, Music	10	9	1.00
	ACE Psychological Examination-Quantitative (Q)	Physical Science	12	1	.11
		Biological Science	11	2	.22
		Social Science	12	3	.33
		Speech, Art, Music	10	4	.44
		Psychology	12	5	.56
		Education	20	6	.67
		History, Philosophy	17	7	.78
		Languages	19	8	.89
		English	8	9	1.00
	ACE Psychological Examination-Total	Biological Science	11	1	.11
		Physical Science	12	2	.22
		Languages	19	3	.33
		Psychology	12	4	.44
		English	8	5	.56
		Education	20	6	.67
		History, Philosophy	17	7	.78
		Speech, Art, Music	10	8	.89
		Social Science	12	9	1.00
Hartson (1936). Male and female seniors at Oberlin.	Ohio State Univ. Psychological Examination consisting of five subtests: (1) Arithmetic; (2) Synonyms-Antonyms Vocabulary; (3) Verbal Analogies; (4) Number Series; (5) Reading Comprehension (scored for number of "rights")	Rank of the average rank for students in each curriculum across the three tests of verbal or linguistic ability (Subtests 2, 3 and 5)			
		Languages	57	1	.08
		English	72	2	.17
		Philosophy and Bible	8	3	.25
		Political Science	29	4	.33
		Economics	29	5	.42
		Physical Science	35	6	.50
		Biological Science	34	7	.58
		History	30	8	.67
		Mathematics	26	9	.75
		Music and Fine Arts	33	10.5	.88
		Sociology	27	10.5	.88
		Physical Education	36	12	1.00
		Rank of the average rank for students in each curriculum across the two tests of mathematical or quantitative ability (Subtests 1 and 4)			
		Mathematics	26	1	.08
		Physical Science	35	2	.17
		Economics	29	3	.25
		Biological Science	34	4.5	.38
		Political Science	29	4.5	.38
		English	14	6.5	.54
		Philosophy and Bible	8	6.5	.54
		Languages	57	8	.67
		History	30	9	.75
		Music and Fine Arts	33	10	.83
		Sociology	27	11.5	.96
		Physical Education	36	11.5	.96
		Rank of total score			
		Languages	57	1	.08
		Political Science	29	2	.17
		English	72	3	.25
		Philosophy and Bible	8	4	.33
		Economics	29	5	.42
		Physical Science	35	6	.50
		Biological Science	34	7	.58
		Mathematics	26	8	.67
		History	30	9	.75
		Music and Fine Arts	33	10	[illegible]
		Sociology	27	11	.92
		Physical Education	36	12	1.00

Table 6D.--Summaries of studies showing degree of intellectual ability by curriculum (CONTINUED)

REFERENCE, SAMPLE	VARIABLE	CURRICULUM	N	RANK	STANDARDIZATION OF RANK
Stern (1962b). Male and female students at a "large eastern university."	College Entrance Examination Board Test—Verbal	Nursing	47	1	.14
		Speech and Dramatic Arts	101	2	.29
		Liberal Arts	1367	3	.43
		Engineering	186	4	.57
		Fine Arts	270	5	.71
		Business Administration	251	6	.86
		Home Economics	63	7	1.00
	College Entrance Examination Board Test—Mathematical	Engineering	186	1	.14
		Business Administration	251	2	.29
		Liberal Arts	1367	3	.43
		Nursing	47	4	.57
		Speech and Dramatic Arts	101	5	.71
		Fine Arts	270	6	.86
		Home Economics	63	7	1.00
	Intellectual Ability: rank of the average rank of students in each curriculum across the above two tests	Engineering	186	1.5	.21
		Nursing	47	1.5	.21
		Liberal Arts	1367	3	.43
		Speech and Dramatic Arts	101	4	.57
		Business Administration	251	5	.71
		Fine Arts	270	6	.86
		Home Economics	63	7	1.00
Pemberton (1963). Graduating male and female seniors at the Univ. of Delaware.	Otis IQ Test	Physical Science	23	1	.11
		Humanities	29	2	.22
		Engineering	70	3	.33
		Biological Science	34	4	.44
		Social Science	52	5	.56
		Home Economics	22	6	.67
		Commerce	32	7.5	.83
		Education	54	7.5	.83
		Agriculture	18	9	1.00
	School and College Ability Test	Engineering	70	1	.11
		Physical Science	23	3	.33
		Social Science	52	3	.33
		Commerce	32	3	.33
		Humanities	29	5.5	.61
		Biological Science	34	5.5	.61
		Home Economics	22	7	.78
		Education	54	8	.89
		Agriculture	18	9	1.00
	Intellectual Ability: rank of the average rank of students in each curriculum across the above two tests	Physical Science	23	1.5	.17
		Engineering	70	1.5	.17
		Humanities	29	3	.33
		Social Science	52	4	.44
		Commerce	32	5	.56
		Biological Science	34	6	.67
		Home Economics	22	7	.78
		Education	54	8	.89
		Agriculture	18	9	1.00
Stricker (1964). Male and female freshmen, sophomores, juniors, and seniors at Adelphi Univ.	Scholastic Aptitude Test-Verbal	Humanities	--	1	.20
		Science and Mathematics	--	2	.40
		Creative and Performing Arts	--	3	.60
		Behavioral and Social Sciences	--	4	.80
		Business Studies	--	5	1.00
	Scholastic Aptitude Test-Qualitative	Science and Mathematics	--	1	.20
		Business Studies	--	2	.40
		Behavioral and Social Sciences	--	3	.60
		Humanities	--	4	.80
		Creative and Performing Arts	--	5	1.00
	Intellectual Ability: rank of the average rank of students in each curriculum across the above two tests	Science and Mathematics	--	1	.20
		Humanities	--	2	.40
		Behavioral and Social Sciences	--	3.5	.70
		Business Studies	--	3.5	.70
		Creative and Performing Arts	--	5	1.00

Table 6D.--Summaries of studies showing degree of intellectual ability by curriculum (CONTINUED)

REFERENCE, SAMPLE	VARIABLE	CURRICULUM	N	RANK	STANDARDIZATION OF RANK
Pace (1964). Male and female seniors at Swarthmore.	Scholastic Aptitude Test-Verbal	Mathematics, Physics	--	1	.20
		History	--	2	.40
		Biological Science	--	3	.60
		English	--	4	.80
		Political Science, Economics	--	5	1.00
	Scholastic Aptitude Test-Mathematical	Mathematics, Physics	--	1	.20
		Political Science, Economics	--	2	.40
		Biological Science	--	3	.60
		History	--	4	.80
		English	--	5	1.00
	Intellectual Ability: rank of the average rank of students in each curriculum across the above two tests	Mathematics, Physics	--	1	.20
		Biological Science	--	2.5	.50
		History	--	2.5	.50
		Political Science, Economics	--	4	.80
		English	--	5	1.00
Pace (1964). Female juniors at Bennington College.	Scholastic Aptitude Test-Verbal	Literature	--	1	.33
		Art, Music, Dance	--	2	.67
		Social Science	--	3	1.00
	Scholastic Aptitude Test-Mathematical	Art, Music, Dance	--	1	.33
		Literature	--	2	.67
		Social Science	--	3	1.00
	Intellectual Ability: rank of the average rank of students in each field across the above two tests	Literature	--	1.5	.50
		Art, Music, Dance	--	1.5	.50
		Social Science	--	3	1.00
Wilson and Lyons (1961). Male and female freshmen at a variety of cooperative institutions (with work-study programs) and noncooperative institutions (without work-study programs).	College Entrance Examination Board Test-Verbal	Liberal Arts	160	1	.33
		Engineering	216	2	.67
		Business	71	3	1.00
	College Entrance Examination Board Test-Mathematical	Engineering	160	1	.33
		Liberal Arts	216	2	.67
		Business	71	3	1.00
	Intellectual Ability: rank of the average rank of students in each curriculum across the above two tests	Engineering	160	1.5	.50
		Liberal Arts	216	1.5	.50
		Business	71	3	1.00
Krulee, O'Keefe and Goldberg (1966). Entering male and female freshmen at Northwestern Univ. Note: Ranking is based on total scores for freshmen entering in 1961, 1962, 1963, 1964, and 1965.	College Entrance Examination Board Test-Verbal	Engineering	--	1	.33
		Liberal Arts	--	2	.67
		Business	--	3	1.00
	College Entrance Examination Board Test-Mathematical	Engineering	--	1	.33
		Business	--	2	.67
		Liberal Arts	--	3	1.00
	Intellectual Ability: rank of the average rank of students in each curriculum across the above two tests	Engineering	--	1	.33
		Liberal Arts	--	2.5	.83
		Business	--	2.5	.83
Educational Testing Service (1955); also see Chauncey (1952). Males at all class levels in colleges and universities throughout the United States.	Selective Service College Qualification Test: rank of the average rank for students in each curriculum for each class level (using combined data for three calendar years, 1951, 1952 and 1953)	Engineering	82600	1	.11
		Physical Science and Mathematics	50710	2	.22
		Social Science	73200	3	.33
		Biological Science	63570	4	.44
		Humanities	41160	5.5	.61
		General Arts	5990	5.5	.61
		Business and Commerce	80710	7	.78
		Agriculture	16660	8	.89
		Education	35890	9	1.00

Table 6D.--Summaries of studies showing degree of intellectual ability by curriculum (CONTINUED)

REFERENCE, SAMPLE	VARIABLE	CURRICULUM	N	RANK	STANDARDIZATION OF RANK
Darley (1962). Male and female entrants to Ohio State Univ.	Ohio State Univ. Psychological Examination	Males			
		Engineering	517	1	.20
		Arts and Science	554	2	.40
		Commerce	431	3.5	.70
		Agriculture	394	3.5	.70
		Education	117	5	1.00
		Females			
		Engineering	9	1	.14
		Arts and Science	278	2	.29
		Nursing	131	3	.43
		Education	382	4	.57
		Agriculture	9	5	.71
		Home Economics	150	6	.86
		Commerce	190	7	1.00
Darley (1962). Male and female entrants to the Univ. of Minnesota.	ACE Psychological Examination	Males			
		Engineering	474	1	.20
		Pharmacy	39	2	.40
		Science, Literature and the Arts	770	3	.60
		Agriculture	154	4	.80
		Education	32	5	1.00
		Females			
		Science, Literature and the Arts	609	1	.25
		Agriculture	110	2	.50
		Dental Hygiene	33	3	.75
		Education	123	4	1.00
Lehmann (1965b). Male and female freshmen at Michigan State Univ.	College Qualification Test	Males			
		Science and Arts	212	1	.17
		Engineering	419	2	.33
		Veterinary Medicine	55	3	.50
		Communication Arts	43	4	.67
		Business and Public Service	315	5	.83
		Agriculture	177	6	1.00
		Females			
		Veterinary Medicine	50	1	.17
		Science and Arts	317	2	.33
		Communication Arts	102	3	.50
		Home Economics	174	4	.67
		Education	272	5	.83
		Business and Public Service	184	6	1.00
Wolfle (1954); Wolfle and Oxtoby (1952). Graduating male seniors at 41 colleges and universities.	Army General Qualification Test	Physical Science	--	1	.05
		Chemistry	--	2	.10
		Engineering	--	3.5	.18
		Law	--	3.5	.18
		English	--	6	.30
		Foreign Languages	--	6	.30
		Psychology	--	6	.30
		Economics	--	8	.40
		Earth Science (includes Astronomy, Geography and Geology)	--	10	.50
		Biological Science	--	10	.50
		Fine Arts	--	10	.50
		Nursing	--	12.5	.63
		History	--	12.5	.63
		Agriculture	--	15	.75
		Business and Commerce	--	15	.75
		Humanities	--	15	.75
		Education	--	17.5	.88
		Social Science	--	17.5	.88
		Home Economics	--	19	.95
		Physical Education	--	20	1.00

Table 6D.--Summaries of studies showing degree of intellectual ability by curriculum (CONTINUED)

REFERENCE, SAMPLE	VARIABLE	CURRICULUM	N	RANK	STANDARDIZATION OF RANK
Centra (1965). Male and female juniors and seniors at Michigan State Univ.	College Qualifying Test. Note: Test was given to students at entrance to college.	Natural Science	67	1	.10
		Engineering	42	2	.20
		Arts and Letters	79	3	.30
		Social Science	77	4	.40
		Business	83	5	.50
		Veterinary Medicine	18	6	.60
		Communication Arts	25	7	.70
		Agriculture	37	8	.80
		Education	52	9	.90
		Home Economics	33	10	1.00
Coffelt and Hobbs (1964). Freshmen males and females in 32 Oklahoma colleges.	American College Testing Battery	Geology	21	1	.05
		Physical Science	200	2	.10
		Mathematics	433	3	.14
		Engineering	1340	4	.19
		Medicine	424	5	.24
		Law	358	6	.29
		Language Arts	324	7	.33
		Psychology	241	8	.38
		Biological Science	159	9	.43
		Pharmacy	174	10	.48
		Dentistry	170	11	.52
		Medical Technology	146	12	.57
		Fine Arts	626	13	.62
		Social Science	286	14	.67
		Veterinary Medicine	159	15	.71
		Religion	394	16	.76
		Nursing	181	17	.81
		Home Economics	415	18	.86
		Business	1689	19	.90
		Elementary Education	173	20	.95
		Agriculture	353	21	1.00
Thistlethwaite (1963b). Male and female college entrants who had participated in the National Merit Scholarship Qualifying Examination (in 1958).	National Merit Scholarship Qualifying Test scores. Note: Curriculum is the probable major field of students	Physics	588	1	.04
		Mathematics	1191	2	.08
		Chemistry	1050	3	.12
		Political Science and Government	278	4	.16
		English	1015	5	.20
		Modern Foreign Languages	543	6	.24
		Pre-medical	1089	7	.28
		Engineering	3473	8	.32
		History	552	9	.36
		Psychology	487	10	.40
		Biological Science	926	11	.44
		Pre-law	510	12	.48
		Architecture	214	13	.52
		Economics	440	14	.56
		Health Professions (includes Nursing or Medical Technology)	706	15	.60
		Sociology	263	16	.64
		Music	420	17	.68
		Journalism and Advertising	279	18	.72
		Religion	192	19	.76
		Pre-dental	217	20	.80
		Home Economics	433	21	.84
		Elementary and Secondary Education	2705	22	.88
		Business and Commerce	1189	23	.92
		Agriculture	104	24	.96
		Physical Education	189	25	1.00
Sternberg (1955). Male juniors at Queens College	ACE Psychological Examination	English	30	1	.11
		Psychology	30	2	.22
		Bio-Chemistry	30	3	.33
		Mathematics	30	4	.44
		History	30	5	.56
		Chemistry	30	6	.67
		Political Science	30	7	.78
		Economics	30	8	.89
		Music	30	9	1.00

Table 6D.--Summaries of studies showing degree of intellectual ability by curriculum (CONTINUED)

REFERENCE, SAMPLE	VARIABLE	CURRICULUM	N	RANK	STANDARDIZATION OF RANK
Warner (1957). Graduating male and female seniors at Brigham Young Univ.	ACE Psychological Examination	Physical and Engineering Science	--	1	.13
		Humanities and Social Science	--	2	.25
		Fine Arts	--	3	.38
		Family Living	--	4	.50
		Education	--	5	.63
		Commerce	--	6	.75
		Biological and Agricultural Science	--	7	.88
		Recreation, Physical and Health Education and Athletics	--	8	1.00
Smith (1956). Male and female graduating seniors at the Univ. of Kansas.	ACE Psychological Examination. Note: Ranking is of the percentage of students in each curriculum whose score was below the 75th percentile upon entrance to the university	Medicine	61	1	.11
		Engineering	138	2	.22
		Law	34	3	.33
		Arts and Science	339	4	.44
		Business	153	5	.56
		Pharmacy	23	6	.67
		Journalism	28	7	.78
		Education	161	8	.89
		Fine Arts	69	9	1.00
Shuey (1950). Female freshmen at Randolph-Macon Woman's College.	ACE Psychological Examination. Note: Results are for freshmen tested from 1939 to 1947 and grouped according to subsequent choice of major	French	54	1	.08
		Mathematics	104	2	.15
		Chemistry	119	3	.23
		Spanish	61	4	.31
		Art	31	5	.39
		Psychology	84	6	.46
		Latin	58	7	.54
		Music	33	8	.62
		History	100	9	.69
		English and English Literature	299	10	.77
		Economics and Sociology	151	11	.85
		Political Science	57	12	.92
		Biology	101	13	1.00
Weiss (1964). Male and female freshmen at St. Louis Univ.	American College Testing Battery	Engineering	97	1	.20
		Arts and Sciences	513	2	.40
		Aeronautical Technology	143	3	.60
		Nursing and Health Services	81	4	.80
		Commerce and Finance	162	5	1.00
Flory (1940). Male and female seniors At Lawrence College.	ACE Psychological Examination	Language Arts	25	1	.25
		Science	14	2	.50
		Fine Arts	8	3	.75
		Social Science	27	4	1.00
Stoddard, Davidson and Stratton (1956). Male and female entrants to the New York Univ.		Arts, Science and Literautre (Univ. College and Washington Square College)	570	1	.25
		Engineering	265	2	.50
		Education	211	3	.75
		Commerce	443	4	1.00

Table 6E.--Summaries of studies showing degree of intellectual disposition by curriculum

Note: Number in parentheses following curriculum classification is the rank of the curriculum (from high to low in degree of intellectual disposition). In some instances, the original investigator has noted only the distinctively high (or low) fields; when this is the case, the exact rank is not given. Information about samples is given at the end of the table.

VARIABLE	SAMPLE	RANKING BY HIGH, MEDIUM AND LOW THIRDS		
Ranking of students in various curricula from high to low on scales of intellectual disposition				
Thinking Introversion Scale (from the Omnibus Personality Inventory): high score = liking for reflective thought, particularly of an abstract nature, interested in a variety of areas, such as literature, art and philosophy	Farwell, Warren and McConnell (1962).	Social Science (1) Humanities (2)	Physics and Mathematics (3) Biological Science (4)	Other Physical Science (5) Engineering (6)
	Pace (1964). Sample B.	English (1)	History (2) Biological Science (3)	Mathematics and Physics (4) Political Science, Economics (5)
	Warren (1964).	Engineering (nonfarm background) (1) Arts and Sciences (nonprofessional) (2)	Arts and Sciences (professional) (3) Engineering (farm background) (4)	Agriculture (5) Education (6) Business Administration (7)
	Hessel (nd).	Political Science (distinctively high)		Business Administration (distinctively low)
Analytical Thinking Scale (from the Heston Personal Adjustment Inventory): intellectually independent, analyzing and theorizing a great deal, enjoying solving problems, liking carefully planned and detailed work	Pace (1964). Sample C.	Biological Science (1) History and Philosophy (2) Physical Science (3)	Psychology (4) Languages (5) Social Science (6)	English (7) Education (8) Dance, Art and Music (9)
Understanding Scale (from Stern's Activities Index): "intellectuality," need for detached intellectualization, problem-solving, analysis or abstraction as an end in itself	Stern (1960, 1962b).	Journalism (1) Education (2) Fine Arts (3) Biological Science (4) Social Science (5)	History, Economics and Government (6) Speech and Dramatic Arts (7) Nursing (8) Home Economics (9) Architecture (10)	Classics and Humanities (11) Natural Science (12) Forestry (13) Business Administration (14) Engineering (15)
	Morrill (1966). Sample A.	Psychology and Sociology (1)	Biological Science (2)	English and Languages (3)
	Morrill (1966). Sample B.	Biological Science (1)	English and Languages (2)	Psychology and Sociology (3)
	Wilson and Lyons (1961). Sample A.	Liberal Arts (1)	Engineering (2)	Business Administration (3)
	Wilson and Lyons (1961). Sample B.	Engineering (1)	Liberal Arts (2)	Business Administration (3)
Complexity Scale (from the Omnibus Personality Inventory): high score = experimental orientation rather than a fixed way of viewing and organizaing phenomena, tolerance of ambiguities and uncertainties, fondness for novel situations and ideas	Farwell, Warren and McConnell (1962).	Humanities (1) Other Physical Science (2)	Physics and Mathematics (3) Social Science (4)	Biological Science (5) Engineering (6)
	Pace (1964). Sample B.	English (1)	Mathematics and Physics (2.5) History (2.5)	Biological Science (4.5) Political Science and Economics (4.5)
	Warren (1964).	Arts and Sciences (nonprofessional) (1) Engineering (nonfarm background) (2)	Agriculture (3) Arts and Sciences (professional) (4)	Education (5) Engineering (farm background) (6) Business Administration (7)
	Hessel (nd).	Psychology (distinctively high)		Business Administration, Education (both distinctively low)
Originality Scale (from an early form of the Omnibus Personality Inventory): high score = high independence of thought, freedom of expression and novelty of insight	Farwell, Warren and McConnell (1962).	Physics and Mathematics (1) Social Science (2)	Humanities (3) Other Physical Science (4)	Biological Science (5) Engineering (6)
	Pace (1964). Sample A.		Literature (1.5) Social Science (1.5)	Art, Music and Dance (3)

Table 6E.--Summaries of studies showing degree of intellectual disposition by curriculum (CONTINUED)

VARIABLE	SAMPLE	RANKING BY HIGH, MEDIUM AND LOW THIRDS		
Ranking of students in various curricula from high to low on scales of intellectual disposition (continued)				
Reflectiveness Scale (from Stern's Activities Index): high score = need for intraceptive activities, introspective contemplation about private psychological, spiritual, esthetic, or metaphysical experience	Stern (1960, 1962b).	Natural Science (1) Biological Science (2) Engineering (3) Nursing (4) Classics and Humanities (5)	Journalism (6) Education (7) Architecture (8) History, Economics and Government (9) Social Science (10)	Fine Arts (11) Forestry (12) Business Administration (13) Speech and Dramatic Arts (14) Home Economics (15)
	Morrill (1966). Sample A.	Psychology and Sociology (1)	Biological Science (2)	English and Languages (3)
	Morrill (1966). Sample B.	Biological Science (1)	English and Languages (2)	Psychology and Sociology (3)
	Wilson and Lyons (1961). Sample A.	Liberal Arts (1)	Business Administration (2)	Engineering (3)
	Wilson and Lyons (1961). Sample B.	Liberal Arts (1)	Business Administration (2)	Engineering (3)
Intellectualism Scale (constructed by Yuker and Block, 1967): high score = favorable attitude toward intellectual activities	Yuker and Block (1967).	Humanities (1)	Social Science (2) Education (3)	Natural Science (4) Business (5)
Thinking Orientation Scale (from the Omnibus Personality Inventory): high score = high interest in science and in scientific activities; high scorers are generally logical, rational and critical in their approach to problems	Pace (1964). Sample B.	Mathematics and Physics (1)	Biological Science (2) English (3)	History (4) Political Science and Economics (5)
	Warren (1964).	Engineering (nonfarm background) (1) Engineering (farm background) (2)	Arts and Sciences (nonprofessional) (3) Arts and Sciences (professional) (4)	Agriculture (5) Education (6) Business Administration (7)
	Kirk (1965).	Physics (1) Chemistry (2) Painting, Design and Sculpture (3) Architecture (4) Graphic Arts (5) Industrial Management (6)	Humanities (7) Chemical Engineering (8) Drama (9) Natural Science (10) Mechanical Engineering (11) Mathematics (12)	Electrical Engineering (13) Civil Engineering (14) Business and Social Studies (15) Home Economics (16) Music (17) Metallurgical Engineering (18)
	Center for the Study of Higher Education (1962).	Physics and Mathematics (1) Social Science (2)	Engineering (3.5) Humanities (3.5)	Creative Arts (5) Business Administration (6)
	Hessel (nd).	Physics and Chemistry (distinctively high)		Business Administration; Education (distinctively low)
Science Scale (from Stern's Activities Index): high score = high interest in science (manipulating external physical objects through empirical analysis, reflection and discussion)	Stern (1960, 1962b).	Biological Science (1) Engineering (2) Natural Science (3) Forestry (4) Architecture (5)	Classics and Humanities (6) Fine Arts (7) Education (8) History, Economics and Government (9) Social Science (10)	Nursing (11) Business Administration (12) Home Economics (13) Speech and Dramatic Arts (14) Journalism (15)
	Morrill (1966). Sample A.	Biology (1)	Psychology and Sociology (2)	English and Languages (3)
	Morrill (1966). Sample B.	Biology (1)	Psychology and Sociology (2)	English and Languages (3)
	Wilson and Lyons (1961). Sample A.	Engineering (1)	Liberal Arts (2)	Business Administration (3)
	Wilson and Lyons (1961). Sample B.	Engineering (1)	Business Administration (2)	Liberal Arts (3)

Table 63.--Summaries of studies showing degree of intellectual disposition by curriculum (CONTINUED)

VARIABLE	SAMPLE	RANKING BY HIGH, MEDIUM AND LOW THIRDS		
Ranking of students in various curricula from high to low on scales of intellectual disposition (continued)				
Humanities, Social Science Scale (from Stern's Activities Index): high score = high interest in the Humanities and the Social Sciences (manipulating of external social objects or artifacts through empirical analysis, reflection and discussion)	Stern (1960, 1962b).	Journalism (1) Education (2) Fine Arts (3) Biological Science (4) Social Science (5)	History, Economics and Government (6) Speech and Dramatic Arts (7) Nursing (8) Home Economics (9) Architecture (10)	Classics and Humanities (11) Natural Sciences (12) Forestry (13) Business Administration (14) Engineering (15)
	Morrill (1966). Sample A.	Psychology and Sociology (1)	English, Languages (2)	Biological Science (3)
	Morrill (1966). Sample B.	English, Languages (1)	Psychology and Sociology (2)	Biological Science (3)
	Wilson and Lyons (1961). Sample A.	Liberal Arts (1)	Business Administration (2)	Engineering (3)
	Wilson and Lyons (1961). Sample B.	Liberal Arts (1)	Business Administration (2)	Engineering (3)
Estheticism Scale (from the Omnibus Personality Inventory): high score = high interest in artistic matters and activities	Pace (1964). Sample A.	Art, Music and Drama (1)	Literature (2)	Social Science (3)
	Pace (1964). Sample B.	English (1)	History (2.5) Biological Science (2.5)	Political Science and Economics (4) Mathematics and Physics (5)
	Center for the Study of Higher Education (1962).	Creative Arts (1)	Social Science (2.5) Humanities (2.5) Physics and Mathematics (4)	Business Administration (5) Engineering (6)
	Warren (1964).	Education (1) Arts and Science (non-professional) (2)	Engineering (nonfarm background) (3) Arts and Sciences (professional) (4)	Engineering (farm background) (5) Agriculture (6) Business Administration (7)
	Hessel (nd).	English (distinctively high)		Mathematics; Business Administration (both distinctively low)
The following are various indicators of "intellectuality" gained by combining two or more scales:				
Intellectual Interests (based on scores on the Reflectiveness, Humanities-Social Science, Understanding, and Science Scales of Stern's Activities Index)	Stern (1966b). Sample A.	Liberal Arts Education (1) Engineering (2)	Liberal Arts (3) Architecture (4)	Forestry (5) Art (6) Business Administration (7)
	Stern (1966b). Sample B.	Liberal Arts Education (1) Art (2)	Liberal Arts (3) Education (4)	Nursing (5) Home Economics (6) Business Administration (7)
	Morrill (1966). Sample A.	Psychology and Sociology (1)	Biology (2)	English and Languages (3)
	Morrill (1966). Sample B.	Biology (1)	English and Languages (2)	Psychology and Sociology (3)
Reflectiveness (based on scores on the Reflectiveness, Humanities-Social Sciences, Understanding and Ego Achievement Scales of Stern's Activities Index)	Pace (1964). Sample D.	Humanities (1) Education (2)	Mathematics and Chemistry (3) Engineering (4)	Commerce (5) Pharmacy (6)

Table 6E.--Summaries of studies showing degree of intellectual disposition by curriculum (CONTINUED)

VARIABLE	SAMPLE	RANKING BY HIGH, MEDIUM AND LOW THIRDS		
Various indicators of "intellectuality" gained by combining two or more scales (continued)				
Intellectual Disposition (based on scores on the Thinking Introversion, Complexity and Estheticism Scales of the Omnibus Personality Inventory)	Trent, Athey and Craise (1964); Trent and Craise (1967).	Liberal Arts (1)	Education (2)	Technology and Business (3)
Intellectual Orientation (based on scores on the Thinking Introversion, Theoretical Orientation, Estheticism, Complexity, Autonomy and Religious Liberalism Scales of the Omnibus Personality Inventory; on the Sensory-Intuitive Scale of the Myers-Briggs Type Indicator; and on a 4-item "Intellectual Orientation" Scale)	Warren (1964).	Arts and Sciences (nonprofessional) (1) Engineering (farm background) (2)	Engineering (nonfarm background) (3) Agriculture (4)	Arts and Sciences (professional) (5) Education (6) Business Administration (7)

SAMPLES USED IN THE ABOVE TABLE:

Center for the Study of Higher Education, Omnibus Personality Inventory--Research Manual (1962). "A sample of liberal arts college seniors."

Farwell, Warren and McConnell (1962). Male winners and near-winners of National Merit Scholarships (in 1956) entering a variety of colleges and universities.

Hessel (nd). Male and female freshman entrants in the College of Letters and Science at UCLA.

Kirk (1965). Male and female sophomores, juniors and seniors at Carnegie Institute of Technology. (Note that Painting, Design and Sculpture, Humanities, Natural Science, Business and Social Studies, and Home Economics are all curricula in the Margaret Carnegie College for women only.)

Morrill (1966). Sample A: Male juniors and seniors at the Univ. of Missouri at Columbia; Sample B: Male juniors and seniors at the Univ. of Missouri at Kansas City.

Pace (1964). Sample A: Female juniors at Bennington College; Sample B: Male and female seniors at Swarthmore; Sample C: Male and female seniors at De Pauw; Sample D: Male and female sophomores, juniors and seniors at the Univ. of Mississippi.

Stern (1960, 1962b). Male and female seniors at a "large eastern university."

Stern (1966). Sample A: Male graduating seniors at Syracuse Univ.; Sample B: Female graduating seniors at Syracuse Univ.

Trent, Athey and Craise (1964); Trent and Craise (1967). Male and female seniors at various colleges and universities (high school graduates from sixteen communities in the United States who entered and completed college).

Warren (1964). Male entrants to the Univ. of Nebraska.

Wilson and Lyons (1961). Sample A: Senior students at a variety of cooperative institutions (with work-study programs); Sample B: Senior students at a variety of noncooperative institutions (without work-study programs).

Yuker and Block (1967). Male and female students at Hofstra Univ.

Table 6F.--Summaries of studies showing degree of authoritarianism and related characteristics by curriculum

Note: Ranking of fields is from low to high in authoritarianism, dogmatism, prejudice, and related variables. The standardization of the rank is accomplished by dividing the rank of the curriculum by the number of curricula in the study.

REFERENCE, SAMPLE	VARIABLE	CURRICULUM	N	RANK	STANDARDIZATION OF RANK
Pace (1964). Male and female seniors at Swarthmore.	Social Maturity Scale from the Omnibus Personality Inventory (high score = nonauthoritarianism)	English	--	1	.20
		History	--	2	.40
		Biological Science	--	3	.60
		Mathematics, Physics	--	4	.80
		Political Science, Economics	--	5	1.00
Kirk (1965). Male and female sophomores, juniors and seniors at Carnegie Institue of Technology. Analysis is based on data in Table 12.	Social Maturity Scale (Kirk's modification of the Omnibus Personality Inventory Scale of the same name; high score = nonauthoritarianism)	Painting, Design and Sculpture, Drama	97*	1	.08
		Architecture	18	2	.15
		Humanities**	19	3	.23
		Graphic Arts	30	4	.31
		Physics	53	5	.38
		Industrial Management	10	6	.46
		Music	30	7	.54
		Natural Science**	36	8	.62
		Business and Social Studies**	21	9	.69
		Chemistry	22	10	.77
		Mathematics	60	11	.85
		Home Economics**	29	12	.92
		Engineering (Chemical, Civil, Electrical, Mechanical, Metallurgical)	159	13	1.00
		*N's supplied by Kirk in personal communication to authors. **Curriculum in the Margaret Morrison Carnegie College for women only.			
Pace (1964). Female juniors and seniors at Bennington College.	Nonauthoritarian Scale from an early form of the Omnibus Personality Inventory (high score = nonauthoritarianism)	Literature	--	1	.33
		Social Science	--	2	.67
		Art-Music-Dance	--	3	1.00
Farwell, Warren and McConnell (1962). Male National Merit Scholarship winners and near-winners entering a variety of colleges and universities. Note: For authoritarianism of students in this sample in a three-fold classification of curricula--mathematics, physics and engineering--rather than the six-fold classification presented here, see Heist and Webster, 1959, and Webster, Trow and McConnell, 1962.	Authoritarianism Scale from an early form of the Omnibus Personality Inventory (low score = low authoritarianism)	Humanities	42	1	.17
		Other Physical Sciences	85	2	.33
		Social Science	59	3	.50
		Physics and Mathematics	120	4	.50
		Biological Science	52	5	.83
		Engineering	188	6	1.00
Heist and Webster (1959). Male freshman entrants to the California Institute of Technology.	Social Maturity Scale from the Omnibus Personality Inventory (high score = nonauthoritarianism)	Mathematics	20	1	.33
		Physics	64	2	.67
		Engineering	30	3	1.00
	Authoritarianism Scale from an early form of the Omnibus Personality Inventory (low score = low authoritarianism)	Physics	64	1	.33
		Mathematics	20	2	.67
		Engineering	30	3	1.00
	Degree of authoritarianism: rank of the average rank of students in each curriculum across the above two scales	Physics	64	1.5	.50
		Mathematics	20	1.5	.50
		Engineering	30	3	1.00

Table 6F.--Summaries of studies showing degree of authoritarianism and related characteristics by curriculum (CONTINUED)

REFERENCE, SAMPLE	VARIABLE	CURRICULUM	N	RANK	STANDARDIZATION OF RANK
Lehmann (1965b). Male freshmen at Michigan State Univ.	Rokeach's Dogmatism Scale (low score = low dogmatism)	Communication Arts	43	1	.14
		Science and Arts	212	2	.29
		Engineering	419	3	.43
		Business and Public Service	315	4	.57
		Agriculture	177	5	.71
		Veterinary Medicine	55	6	.86
		Education	27	7	1.00
	Inventory of Beliefs (high score = low stereotypic thinking)	Science and Arts	212	1	.14
		Communication Arts	43	2	.29
		Veterinary Medicine	55	3	.43
		Engineering	419	4	.57
		Business and Public Service	315	5	.71
		Agriculture	177	6	.86
		Education	27	7	1.00
	Degree of dogmatism and stereotypic thinking when combining the above two scales: rank of the average rank of students in each curriculum across the two scales	Communication Arts	43	1.5	.21
		Science and Arts	212	1.5	.21
		Engineering	419	3	.43
		Business and Public Service	315	4.5	.64
		Veterinary Medicine	55	4.5	.64
		Agriculture	177	6	.86
		Education	27	7	1.00
Lehmann (1965b). Female freshmen at Michigan State Univ.	Rokeach's Dogmatism Scale (low score = low dogmatism)	Communication Arts	102	1	.17
		Science and Arts	317	2	.33
		Business and Public Service	184	3	.50
		Home Economics	174	4	.67
		Education	272	5	.83
		Veterinary Medicine	50	6	1.00
	Inventory of Beliefs (high score = low stereotypic thinking)	Science and Arts	317	1	.17
		Communication Arts	102	2	.33
		Business and Public Service	184	3	.50
		Education	272	4	.67
		Home Economics	174	5	.83
		Veterinary Medicine	50	6	1.00
	Degree of dogmatism and stereotypic thinking when combining the above two scales: rank of the average rank of students in each curriculum across the two scales	Communication Arts	102	1.5	.25
		Science and Arts	317	1.5	.25
		Business and Public Service	184	3	.50
		Home Economics	174	4.5	.75
		Education	272	4.5	.75
		Veterinary Medicine	50	6	1.00
William D'Antonio (personal communication to authors). Male freshmen, sophomores, juniors, and seniors at Notre Dame.	Rokeach's Dogmatism Scale (low score = low dogmatism)	Commerce	67	1	.25
		Science	39	2	.50
		Arts and Letters	88	3	.75
		Engineering	68	4	1.00
Fox (1965). Male freshmen, sophomores, juniors, and seniors at St. Ambrose College.	Fox's Omnibus Opinion Survey (high score = low authoritarianism, high equalitarianism)	Seminary	23	1	.11
		Political Science	42	2	.22
		Business Administration	36	3	.33
		History-Geography	20	4	.44
		Fine Arts	24	5	.56
		Science	31	6	.67
		Accounting	28	7	.78
		English	14	8	.89
		Sociology	17	9	1.00
Gordon and Lindeman (1966). Male and female freshmen at Wagner College.	Christie Machiavellian Scale scored for authoritarisnism (low score = low authoritarianism)	Males			
		Social Science	11	1	.20
		Biological Science	31	2	.40
		Humanities	36	3	.60
		Physical Science, Math.	29	4	.80
		Business Administration	18	5	1.00
		Females			
		Humanities	28	1	.17
		Biological Science	20	2	.33
		Social Science	25	3	.50
		Nursing	30	4	.67
		Education	40	5	.83
		Physical Science, Math.	8	6	1.00

Table 6F.--Summaries of studies showing degree of authoritarianism and related characteristics by curriculum (CONTINUED)

REFERENCE, SAMPLE	VARIABLE	CURRICULUM	N	RANK	STANDARDIZATION OF RANK
Holtzman (1956). Male and female freshman, sophomores, juniors, and seniors at the Univ. of Texas.	Tolerance of Non-Segregation (low score = high tolerance of non-segregation)	Social Science, Humanities	--	1.5	.19
		Architecture	--	1.5	.19
		Education	--	3	.38
		Fine Arts	--	4	.50
		Natural Science	--	5	.63
		Engineering	--	6	.75
		Business	--	7	.88
		Pharmacy	--	8	1.00
Kelly, Ferson and Holtzman (1958); Young, Benson and Holtzman (1960); and Young, Clore and Holtzman (1966). Three samples of freshmen, sophomores, juniors, and seniors at the Univ. of Texas: 1955, 1958 and 1964.	Desegregation Scale (high score = intolerance of the Negro; low score = acceptance of the Negro)	1955 sample			
		Social Science	36	1	.13
		Natural Science	68	2	.25
		Fine Arts	25	3	.38
		Humanities	26	4	.50
		Engineering	116	5	.63
		Education	63	6	.75
		Pharmacy	18	7	.88
		Business	126	8	1.00
		1958 sample			
		Social Science	26	1	.13
		Fine Arts	29	2	.25
		Humanities	42	3	.38
		Education	51	4	.50
		Natural Science	73	5	.63
		Engineering	104	6	.75
		Business	80	7	.88
		Pharmacy	11	8	1.00
		1964 sample			
		Social Science	54	1	.13
		Fine Arts	21	2.5	.31
		Humanities	110	2.5	.31
		Natural Science	96	4.5	.56
		Engineering	61	4.5	.56
		Pharmacy	23	6	.75
		Education	62	7	.88
		Business	108	8	1.00
	Degree of intolerance or acceptance of the Negro when combining the above three samples: rank of the average rank of students in each curriculum across the three samples	Social Science	118	1	.13
		Fine Arts	75	2	.25
		Humanities	178	3	.38
		Natural Science	237	4	.50
		Engineering	281	5	.63
		Education	176	6	.75
		Pharmacy	52	7	.88
		Business	314	8	1.00
Stephenson (1952). Male and female freshmen and seniors at Miami Univ.	Hinckley's Attitude toward the Negro Scale (high score = high favorableness toward the Negro)	Males			
		Education	105	1	.33
		Arts and Science	57	2	.67
		Business Administration	55	3	1.00
		Females			
		Business Administration	7	1	.33
		Education	95	3	.67
		Arts and Science	34	3	1.00
Stephenson (1955). Male and female senior students in the Miami Univ. School of Education.	Hinckley's Attitude toward the Negro Scale (high score = high favorable attitude toward the Negro)	Social Science	15	1	.09
		Art Education	5	2	.18
		Mathematics, Science	20	3	.27
		Languages	11	4	.36
		Music Education	16	5	.45
		Business Education	11	6	.55
		Health and Physical Education, Women	7	7	.64
		Industrial Arts	17	8	.73
		Four-year Elementary Education	34	9	.82
		Health and Physical Education, Men	33	10	.91
		Home Economics	10	11	1.00
Jones (1938b). Male seniors at a "rather small New England liberal arts college for men."	Hinckley's Attitude toward the Negro Scale (high score = high favorable attitude toward the Negro)	Natural Science	62	1	.25
		English, Languages	41	2	.50
		Economics, Sociology	19	3	.75
		History-Geography	37	4	1.00

Table 6G.--Summaries of studies showing degree of masculinity (or femininity) of interests and attitudes by curriculum

Note: Numbers in parentheses following curriculum classification are the rank of the curriculum. In some instances, the original investigator has noted only the distinctively high (or low) fields; when this is the case, the exact rank is not given. Information about samples is given at the end of the table.

VARIABLE	SAMPLE	RANKING BY HIGH, MEDIUM AND LOW THIRDS		
Ranking of male students in various curricula from high to low in masculinity of interests				
Masculinity-Femininity (Interest) Scale from the Minnesota Multiphasic Personality Inventory	Sternberg (1953).	Mathematics (1) Chemistry (2) Economics (3)	Psychology (4.5) Bio-Chemistry (4.5) Political Science (6)	History (7) Music (8) English (9)
	Norman and Redlo (1952).	Engineering (1) Business Administration (2)	Psychology and Sociology (3) Mathematics, Chemistry and Physics (4)	Geology (5) Anthropology (6) Art and Music (7)
	Blum (1947).	Mechanical Engineering (1)	Journalism (2)	Education (3)
	Harder (1959).	Engineering (1)	Business (2)	Education (3)
	Clark (1953). Sample A.	Mathematics and Physical Science; Physical Education (distinctively high)		English and Foreign Languages (distinctively low)
Masculinity-Femininity Scale from the Strong Vocational Interest Blank	Sherry (1963).	Engineering (1) Physics, Chemistry and Mathematics (2)	Psychology, Sociology and Anthropology (3) Economics, Business Administration and Accounting (4)	Pre-Medicine, Biology and Zoology (6) Political Science, International Relations, Pre-Law, and History (6) Humanities, English, Languages, Philosophy, and Fine Arts (6)
	Blum (1947).	Mechanical Engineering (1)	Education (2)	Journalism (3)
Masculinity-Femininity Scale from the Omnibus Personality Inventory	Warren (1964).	Engineering (farm background) (1) Business Administration (2)	Agriculture (3) Engineering (nonfarm background) (4)	Arts and Sciences (nonprofessional) (5) Arts and Sciences (professional) (6) Education (7)
Ranking of female students in various curricula from high to low in femininity of interests				
Masculinity-Femininity (Interest) Scale from the Minnesota Multiphasic Personality Inventory	Lough (1947, 1951).	Music (1)	Education (2)	Liberal Arts (3) Nursing (4)
	Clark (1953). Sample B.	English and Foreign Languages (distinctively high)		Physical Education (distinctively low)

SAMPLES USED IN THE ABOVE TABLE:

Blum (1947). Male students at the Univ. of Wisconsin.

Clark (1953). Sample A: Male students entering the Univ. of California, Santa Barbara; Sample B: Female students entering the Univ. of California, Santa Barbara.

Harder (1959). Male juniors and seniors at the Univ. of Kansas.

Lough (1947, 1951). Female students in a New York "liberal arts college" and a New York "state teachers college."

Norman and Redlo (1952). Male seniors and graduate students at the Univ. of New Mexico.

Sherry (1963). Male seniors at Swarthmore.

Sternberg (1953). Male juniors at Queens College.

Warren (1964). Male freshman entrants to the Univ. of Nebraska.

Table 6H.--Summaries of studies showing degree of psychological well-being by curriculum

Note: Number in parentheses following curriculum classification is the rank of the curriculum (from high to low in psychological well-being). In some instances, the original investigator has noted only the distinctively high (or low) fields; when this is the case, the exact rank is not given. Information about samples is given at the end of the table.

VARIABLE	SAMPLE	RANKING BY HIGH, MEDIUM AND LOW THIRDS		
Ranking of students in various curricula from high to low on psychological well-being or from low to high on emotional distress				
Minnesota Multiphasic Personality Inventory--Total Score; Combined score for the following eight scales: Hypochondriasis, Depression, Hysteria, Psychopathic Deviate, Paranoia, Psychothenia, Schizophrenia, and Hypomania. Note: Total scores calculated from scale scores given in original article.	Sternberg (1953).	Bio-Chemistry (1) Mathematics (2) Psychology (3)	Chemistry (4) Economics (5) History (6)	Music (7) Political Science (8) English (9)
	Norman and Redlo (1952).	Mathematics, Chemistry and Physics (1) Engineering (2)	Anthropology (3) Psychology and Sociology (4)	Business Administration (5) Geology (6) Art and Music (7)
	Lough (1947, 1951).	Nursing (1)	Liberal Arts (2)	Education (3) Music (4)
	Blum (1947).	Education (1)	Journalism (2)	Mechanical Engineering (3)
	Harder (1959).	Education (1)	Business Administration (2)	Engineering (3)
	Hancock and Carter (1954).	Engineering (1)	Liberal Arts and Sciences (2)	Commerce (3)
Schizoid Functioning Scale from the Omnibus Personality Inventory	Pace (1964). Sample A.	Biological Science (1)	Political Science and Economics (2)	Mathematics and Physics (3.5) English (3.5) History (5)
Emotional Stability Scale from the Heston Personal Adjustment Inventory	Pace (1964). Sample B.	History and Philosophy (1) Biological Science (2) English (3)	Physical Science (4) Speech, Art and Music (5) Psychology (6)	Education (7) Languages (8) Social Science (9)
Lack of Anxiety Scale from an early form of the Omnibus Personality Inventory	Warren (1964).	Business Administration (1)	Arts and Sciences (professional) (2.5) Engineering (nonfarm background) (2.5) Arts and Sciences (nonprofessional) (2.5)	Engineering (farm background) (5) Agriculture (6) Education (7)
	Hessel (nd).	Mathematics (distinctively high)		
Blacky Pictures. The ranking given is the average rank of the ranks of students in different curricula with respect to disturbance along five of the Blacky dimensions (oral eroticism, Oedipal intensity, oral sadism, guilt feelings, and anaclitic love object).	Teevan (1954).	Natural Science (1)	Art, Music, English, and Languages (2)	Economics, Government and History (3)

SAMPLES USED IN THE ABOVE TABLE:

Blum (1947). Male students at the Univ. of Wisconsin.

Hancock and Carter (1954). Students enrolled at the Galesburg Undergraduate Division of the Univ. of Illinois.

Harder (1959). Male juniors and seniors at the Univ. of Kansas.

Hessel (nd). Male and female freshman entrants to the College of Letters and Science at UCLA.

Lough (1947, 1951). Female students in a New York "liberal arts college" and a New York "state teachers college."

Norman and Redlo (1952). Male seniors and graduate students at the Univ. of New Mexico.

Pace (1964). Sample A: Male and female seniors at Swarthmore; Sample B: Male and female seniors at De Pauw.

Sternberg (1953). Male juniors at Queens College.

Teevan (1954). Male students at Wesleyan Univ.

Warren (1964). Male freshman entrants to the Univ. of Nebraska.

Table 6I.--Summaries of studies showing degree of dominance and confidence, degree of impulse expression, degree of sociability, and degree of achievement motivation by curriculum

Note: Number in parentheses following curriculum classification is the rank of the curriculum. In some instances, the original investigator has noted only the distinctively high (or low) fields; when this is the case, the exact rank is not given. Information about samples is given at the end of the table. More than one of the scales from Stern's Activities Index is appropriate for each of the four personality areas; we have selected for inclusion in each area the one scale that we felt was most relevant.

VARIABLE	SAMPLE	RANKING BY HIGH, MEDIUM AND LOW THIRDS		
Dominance and confidence: ranking of students in various curricula from high to low in dominance and confidence				
Dominance-Tolerance Scale from Stern's Activities Index	Stern (1960, 1962b).	History, Economics and Government (1) Biological Science (2) Business Administration (3) Architecture (4) Engineering (5)	Forestry (6) Social Science (7) Journalism (8) Speech and Dramatic Arts (9) Education (10)	Classics and Humanities (11) Home Economics (12) Fine Arts (13) Natural Science (14) Nursing (15)
	Wilson and Lyons (1961). Sample A.	Business Administration (1)	Engineering (2)	Liberal Arts (3)
	Wilson and Lyons (1961). Sample B.	Business Administration (1)	Engineering (2)	Liberal Arts (3)
	Morrill (1966). Sample A.	Psychology and Sociology (1)	English and Languages (2)	Biology (3)
	Morrill (1966). Sample B.	Psychology and Sociology (1)	English and Languages (2)	Biology (3)
	Vacchiano and Adrian (1966).	Business (1)	Chemistry (2)	Mathematics (3)
Confidence Scale from Heston's Personal Adjustment Inventory	Pace (1964). Sample B.	English (1) Biological Science (2)	History and Philosophy (3) Psychology (4) Languages (5)	Physical Science (6) Speech, Art and Music (7) Social Science (8)
Social Confidence Factor (one of three factors accounting for most of the variations on the seven Vassar Attitude-Inventory scales)	Bereiter and Freedman (1962).	Economics (1) Political Science (2) Drama (3) Anthropology (4) Sociology (5) Child Study (6)	History (7.5) Art and Art History (7.5) Physiology (9) Mathematics (10) Religion (11) English (12)	Philosophy (14.5) Psychology (14.5) American Culture (14.5) Spanish (14.5) Music (17) French (18) Chemistry (19) Zoology (20) Classics (21)
Impulse Expression: ranking of students in various curricula from high to low in readiness to express impulses or from low to high in restraint and self-control				
Impulsiveness-Deliberation Scale from Stern's Activities Index	Stern (1960, 1962b).	Speech and Dramatic Arts (1) Classics and Humanities (2) Home Economics (3) Architecture (4) Journalism (5)	Fine Arts (6) Education (7) History, Economics and Government (8) Social Science (9) Business Administration (10)	Engineering (11) Nursing (12) Forestry (13) Natural Science (14) Biological Science (15)
	Wilson and Lyons (1961). Sample A.	Liberal Arts (1)	Business Administration (2)	Engineering (3)
	Wilson and Lyons (1961). Sample B.	Liberal Arts (1)	Engineering (2)	Business Administration (3)
	Morrill (1966). Sample A.	Psychology and Sociology (1)	English and Languages (2)	Biology (3)
	Morrill (1966). Sample B.	Psychology and Sociology (1)	English and Languages (2)	Biology (3)
	Vacchiano and Adrian (1966).	Business (1)	Mathematics (2)	Chemistry (3)

Table 6I.--Summaries of studies showing degree of dominance and confidence, impulse expression, sociability, and achievement motivation (CONTINUED)

VARIABLE	SAMPLE	RANKING BY HIGH, MEDIUM AND LOW THIRDS		
Impulse Expression: ranking of students in various curricula from high to low in readiness to express impulses or from low to high in restraint and self-control (continued)				
Impulse Expression Scale from the Omnibus Personality Inventory	Pace (1964). Sample A.	English (1)	History (2) Political Science and Economics (3)	Mathematics and Physics (4.5) Biological Science (4.5)
	Hessel (nd).			Education (distinctively low) Mathematics (distinctively low)
Self-control Scale from Gough's California Psychological Inventory	Pace (1964). Sample C.	Art (1) Business (2) Psychology (3)	Mathematics and Physics (4.5) Other Science (4.5) Elementary Education (6) Biological Science (7)	English (8) Engineering (9) Academic Education (10) Social Science (11)
Disciplined (Self-Control) Scale from Phillips and Erickson's Conceived Value Inventory	Phillips and Erickson (1964).	Humanities (1) Physical Education (2)	Science (3) Social Science (4)	Business Administration (5) Engineering (6.5) Agriculture (6.5)
Sociability: ranking of students in various curricula from high to low in sociability or from low to high in social introversion				
Affiliation-Rejection Scale from Stern's Activities Index	Stern (1960, 1962b).	Home Economics (1) Nursing (2) Education (3) Business Administration (4) Social Science (5)	History, Economics and Government (6) Journalism (7) Speech and Dramatic Arts (8) Architecture (9) Biological Science (10)	Fine Arts (11) Engineering (12) Classics and Humanities (13) Forestry (14) Natural Science (15)
	Wilson and Lyons (1961). Sample A.	Business Administration (1)	Liberal Arts (2)	Engineering (3)
	Wilson and Lyons (1961). Sample B.	Business Administration (1)	Engineering (2)	Liberal Arts (3)
	Morrill (1966). Sample A.	English and Languages (1)	Psychology and Sociology (2)	Biology (3)
	Morrill (1966). Sample B.	Psychology and Sociology (1)	Biology (2)	English and Languages (3)
	Vacchiano and Adrian (1966).	Business (1)	Mathematics (2)	Chemistry (3)
Sociability Scale from Gough's California Psychological Inventory	Pace (1964). Sample C.	Social Science (1) English (2) Psychology (3)	Academic Education (4) Engineering (5) Mathematics and Physics (6) Biological Science (7)	Art (8) Elementary Education (9) Business (10) Other Science (11)
Social Introversion Scale from the Omnibus Personality Inventory	Pace (1964). Sample A.	Biological Science (1.5) Political Science and Economics (1.5)		English (3.5) History (3.5) Mathematics and Physics (5)
	Hessel (nd).	Education (distinctively low in social introversion)		
Social Introversion Scale from the Minnesota Multiphasic Personality Inventory	Blum (1947).	Journalism (1)	Education (2)	Engineering (3)

Table 6I.--Summaries of studies showing degree of dominance and confidence, impulse expression, sociability, and achievement motivation (CONTINUED)

VARIABLE	SAMPLE	RANKING BY HIGH, MEDIUM AND LOW THIRDS		
Achievement motivation: ranking of students in various curricula from high to low in need for achievement				
Achievement Scale from Stern's Activities Index	Stern (1960, 1962b).	Journalism (1) Architecture (2) Fine Arts (3) Natural Science (4) History, Economics and Government (5)	Engineering (6) Nursing (7) Biological Science (8.5) Speech and Dramatic Arts (8.5) Forestry (10)	Business Administration (11) Classics and Humanities (12) Education (13) Social Science (14) Home Economics (15)
	Wilson and Lyons (1961). Sample A.		Engineering (1.5) Business Administration (1.5)	Liberal Arts (3)
	Wilson and Lyons (1961). Sample B.	Engineering (1)	Liberal Arts (2)	Business Administration (3)
	Morrill (1966). Sample A.	English and Languages (1)	Biology (2)	Psychology and Sociology (3)
	Morrill (1966). Sample B.	English and Languages (1)	Psychology and Sociology (2)	Biology (3)
	Vacchiano and Adrian (1966).	Business (1)	Chemistry (2)	Mathematics (3)

SAMPLES USED IN THE ABOVE TABLE:

Bereiter and Freedman (1962). Female freshmen (three successive classes) at Vassar.

Hessel (nd). Male and female freshman entrants into the College of Letters and Science at UCLA.

Morrill (1966). Sample A: Male juniors and seniors at the Univ. of Missouri at Columbia; Sample B: Male juniors and seniors at the Univ. of Missouri at Kansas City.

Pace (1964). Sample A: Male and female seniors at Swarthmore; Sample B: Male and female seniors at De Pauw; Sample C: Male and female seniors at San Jose State College.

Phillips and Erickson (1964). Male and female freshmen, sophomores, juniors, and seniors at Washington State Univ.

Stern (1960, 1962b). Male and female seniors at a "large eastern university."

Vacchiano and Adrian (1966). Male seniors attending a "large metropolitan university."

Wilson and Lyons (1961). Sample A: Senior students at a variety of cooperative institutions (with work-study programs); Sample B: Senior students at a variety of noncooperative institutions (without work-study programs).

Table 6J.--Summaries of studies showing student descriptions of the environment of their major field

Note: For each study, we have noted the fields that were particularly high and those that were particularly low on various environmental emphases. For Pace (1964) below, present analysis is limited to the four largest of the nine colleges in the original analysis.

REFERENCE, SAMPLE AND INSTRUMENT	MAJOR FIELD						
	Natural Science	Engineering	Social Science	Humanities and Fine Arts	Education	Business	Other
Thistlethwaite (1962a). High-ability, end-of-year sophomore students enrolled at 335 colleges and universities. Modified version of the College Characteristics Inventory (CCI). More or less parallel findings, using a different sample of high-ability students and combining the curricular into a four-way classification, are given in Thistlethwaite (1960).	Physics: High faculty and student pressure for scientism; low faculty pressure for humanism and independence; low faculty enthusiasm; low student pressure for estheticism and reflectiveness. Chemistry: High faculty pressure for scientism and compliance; low faculty pressure for humanism and independence; low faculty enthusiasm. Mathematics: High faculty and student pressure for scientism; low faculty pressure for humanism and independence. Biology: High faculty and student pressure for scientism.	Engineering: High faculty and student pressure for scientism; high faculty pressure for compliance and vocationalism; low faculty pressure for humanism and independence; low faculty enthusiasm; low student pressure for estheticism and reflectiveness.	Sociology: High faculty pressure for humanism and independence; low faculty pressure for compliance; high student pressure for estheticism and reflectiveness. Economics: High student pressure for reflectiveness. Political Science: High faculty pressure for independence; high faculty enthusiasm; low faculty pressure for scientism and compliance. History: High faculty pressure for humanism and independence; high faculty enthusiasm; low faculty and student pressure for scientism, compliance and vocationalism; high student pressure for estheticism and reflectiveness.	English: High faculty pressure for humanism; low faculty and student pressure for scientism; low faculty pressure for vocationalism; high student pressure for estheticism. Languages: High faculty pressure for humanism; low faculty pressure for vocationalism; low faculty and student pressure for scientism. Philosophy: High faculty pressure for humanism and independence; high faculty enthusiasm; low faculty pressure for compliance and vocationalism; high student pressure for estheticism.	Education: High faculty pressure for compliance; low faculty and student pressure for scientism; low student pressure for reflectiveness.	Business: High faculty pressure for compliance and vocationalism; low faculty pressure for humanism and independence; low faculty enthusiasm; low student pressure for estheticism and reflectiveness.	
Centra (1965). Male and female juniors and seniors at Michigan State Univ. Modified version of the College and University Environment Scales (CUES).	Natural Science: High environmental emphasis on (a) personal, poetic and political understanding and (b) competitive academic achievement and intellectual discipline.	Engineering: High environmental emphasis on competitive academic achievement and intellectual discipline; low emphasis on (a) personal status, practical benefits, and order and (b) personal, poetic and political understanding.	Social Science: Low environmental emphasis on (a) friendliness, cohesiveness and group-orientation; (b) politeness, protocol and consideration, and (c) competitive academic achievement and intellectual discipline.	Humanities and Fine Arts: High environmental emphasis on personal, poetic and political understanding; low emphasis on (a) personal status, practical benefits, and order, (b) friendliness, cohesiveness and group-orientation, (c) politeness, protocol and consideration.	Education: Low environmental emphasis on competitive academic achievement and intellectual discipline.	Business: Low environmental emphasis on (a) friendliness, cohesiveness and group-orientation and (b) politeness, protocol and consideration.	Agriculture: Low environmental emphasis on personal, poetic and political understanding. Home Economics: High environmental pressure on (a) personal status, practical benefits and order, (b) politeness, protocol and consideration and (c) personal, poetic and political understanding.

Table 6J.--Summaries of studies showing student descriptions of the environment of their major field (CONTINUED)

REFERENCE, SAMPLE AND INSTRUMENT	MAJOR FIELD						
	Natural Science	Engineering	Social Science	Humanities and Fine Arts	Education	Business	Other
Kirk (1965). Sophomore, junior and senior males and females at Carnegie Institute of Technology. Modification of Thistlethwaite's College Characteristics Index. Note: Business and Social Studies, Home Economics, Humanities, and Natural Science are curricula in the Margaret Morrison Carnegie College for Women.	Physics: Low on faculty organization; low on student mannerliness and reflectiveness. Chemistry. High on student competiveness. Mathematics: Low on faculty humanism and faculty warmth; high on student competiveness; low on student reflectiveness. Natural Science: High on faculty instrumentalism.	Mechanical and Chemical Engineering: Low on faculty humanism and warmth; low on student reflectivehess, high on student competitiveness. Electrical Engineering: Low on faculty humanism, warmth, instrumentalism and organization; low on student mannerliness and reflectiveness; high on student competitiveness. Metallurgical Engineering: Low on faculty warmth; low on student reflectiveness. Civil Engineering: Low on faculty warmth; high on faculty organization; low on student reflectiveness.	Business and Social Studies: High on faculty humanism; high on student mannerliness and reflectiveness.	Humanities: High on faculty organization; high on student mannerliness and reflectiveness. Painting, Design and Sculpture: High on faculty humanism; low on faculty organization; high on student reflectiveness; low on student competitiveness. Drama: High on faculty humanism and warmth; high on student reflectiveness; low on student competitiveness. Music: High on faculty humanism and warmth; high on faculty organization; high on student reflectiveness; low on student competitiveness. Graphic Arts: High on faculty humanism, warmth and instrumentalism; low on student reflectiveness. Architecture: Low on faculty organization; high on student reflectiveness; low on student competitiveness.		Industrial Management: Low on faculty organization; high on student competitiveness.	Home Economics: Low on faculty instrumentalism; high on student mannerliness, reflectiveness and competiness.

Table 6J.--Summaries of studies showing student descriptions of the environment of their major field (CONTINUED)

REFERENCE, SAMPLE AND INSTRUMENT	MAJOR FIELD						
	Natural Science	Engineering	Social Science	Humanities and Fine Arts	Education	Business	Other
Pace (1964). Male and female juniors and seniors at Eastern Washington State College. Academic Subarea of the College Characteristics Analysis (CCA).	Physical Science: High environmental emphasis on scientism and independence; low emphasis on (a) friendliness and group-welfare orientation and (b) practicality and status orientation.		Social Science: High environmental emphasis on (a) scientism and independence and (b) practicality and status orientation.	English-Languages: Low environmental emphasis on practicality and status orientation.	Academic Education: Low environmental emphasis on (a) intellectualism, humanism and aestheticism, (b) friendliness and group-welfare orientation and (c) scientism and independence. Elementary Education: High environmental emphasis on practicality and status orientation. General Education: High environmental emphasis on (a) friendliness and group-welfare orientation and (b) scientism and independence.	Business: Low environmental emphasis on (a) intellectualism, humanism and estheticism and (b) scientism and independence.	Physical and Health Education: High environmental emphasis on intellectualism, humanism and estheticism.
Pace (1964). Male and female seniors at the Univ. of Mississippi. Academic Subarea of the College Characteristics Analysis (CCA).	Math-Chemistry: High environmental emphasis on scientism and independence; low emphasis on practicality and status orientation.	Engineering: High environmental emphasis on friendliness and group-welfare orientation.		Humanities: High environmental emphasis on intellectualism, humanism and estheticism; low emphasis on friendliness and group-welfare orientation.	Education: High emphasis on practicality and status orientation; low mphasis on scientism and independence.	Business: High environmental emphasis on (a) friendliness and group-welfare orientation and (b) practicality and status orientation; low emphasis on (a) intellectualism, humanism and estheticism and (b) scientism and independence.	Pharmacy: High environmental emphasis on intellectualism, humanism and estheticism.
Pace (1964). Male and female upperclassmen at Univ. of Florida. Academic Subarea of the College Characteristics Analysis (CCA).	Natural Science: High environmental emphasis on scientism and independence; low emphasis on friendliness and group-welfare orientation.		Social Science: High environmental emphasis on (a) friendliness and group-welfare orientation and (b) practicality and status orientation; low emphasis on scientism and independence.	Language Arts: High environmental emphasis on (a) intellectualism, humanism and estheticism and (b) practicality and status orientation.	Education: High environmental emphasis on scientism and independence.	Business: Low environmental emphasis on intellectualism, humanism and estheticism.	Nursing: Low environmental emphasis on (a) intellectualism, humanism and estheticism, (b) friendliness and group-welfare orientation, and (c) scientism and independence. Journalism: High environmental emphasis on intellectualism, humanism and estheticism; low emphasis on (a) friendliness and group-welfare orientation and (b) practicality and status orientation.

Table 6J.--Summaries of studies showing student descriptions of the environment of their major field (CONTINUED)

REFERENCE, SAMPLE AND INSTRUMENT	MAJOR FIELD						
	Natural Science	Engineering	Social Science	Humanities and Fine Arts	Education	Business	Other
Pace (1964). Male and female sophomores, juniors and seniors at San Jose State College. Academic Subarea of the College Characteristics Analysis (CCA).	Math-Physics: Low environmental emphasis on friendliness and group-welfare orientation. Biological Science: High environmental emphasis on (a) intellectualism, humanism and estheticism and (b) friendliness and group-welfare orientation. Other Science: High environmental emphasis on practicality and status orientation; low emphasis on friendliness and group-welfare orientation.		Social Science: High environmental emphasis on friendliness and group-welfare orientation; low emphasis on intellectualism, humanism and estheticism. Psychology: High environmental emphasis on scientism and independence; low emphasis on practicality and status orientation.	English: High environmental emphasis on intellectualism, humanism and estheticism; low emphasis on (a) scientism and independence; (b) friendliness and group-welfare orientation; (c) practicality and status orientation. Art: High environmental emphasis on scientism and independence.	Elementary Education: High environmental emphasis on (a) friendliness and group-welfare orientation and (b) practicality and status orientation; low emphasis on intellectualism, humanism and estheticism. Academic Education: High environmental emphasis on intellectualism, humanism and estheticism; low emphasis on scientism and independence.	Business Administration: High environmental emphasis on practicality and status orientation.	

ANOTHER STUDY:

Astin (1965a) obtained ratings of introductory undergraduate courses in nineteen different fields from over 4,000 freshman students each of whom described the introductory course he had taken during the year which was most closely related to his primary field of interest. The two or three highest ranking and the two or three lowest ranking fields are given for each of 35 environmental characteristics associated with the classroom. To give some examples of the findings, students taking introductory work in sociology, fine arts and psychology were most likely to agree with the following statement: "If he had wanted, a student could have passed this course mainly on bluff." Students taking the introductory math or chemistry course were least likely to agree with this statement. Students taking introductory music and fine arts courses were most likely to have been in the instructor's home one or more times, while students in engineering or economics courses were the least likely. Students in English, German and French were the most likely, while students in biology and physics were the least likely, to feel that their "instructors encouraged a lot of class discussion."

Table 6K.--Summaries of studies showing differential change by major field

Note: We have included in the main portion of this table those studies that give data for four or more major fields, because the rho statistic is not really meaningful when N is less than four, since both the size and the magnitude of rho become increasingly less dependable as number of the ranked values become very small. Studies of changes by students in two or three major fields are reviewed at the end of the table under "other studies."

In the table, initial scores (usually freshman scores) are ranked from high to low in Column 3. In Column 4, the changes between lower and upperclassmen (usually freshmen and seniors) are ranked from the largest positive difference to the largest negative difference. $Rho_{(3)(4)}$ refers to the rank-order correlation (Spearman) between Column 3 and Column 4--i.e., the rank-order correlation between initial position and gain. A positive rho indicates an accentuation of initial major field differences. We have tested for significance levels of rhos, although because of the spurious negative element in the correlation between initial score and gain, the standard procedure of determining the statistical significance of a rank-order correlation coefficient is not fully appropriate. Since positive rank-order correlations between initial score and gain are artificially deflated, the standard statistical test is overly conservative, thus making it harder for these positive correlations to show statistical significance at the .05 level. (See Chapter 3.)

In this table, Fr = freshmen, So = sophomores, Jr = juniors, and Sr = seniors.

Table 6K.--Summaries of studies showing differential change by major field (CONTINUED)

Huntley (1965): longitudinal study of male students at Union College. Original analysis combines data for six successive classes of students who were given the Allport-Vernon-Lindzey Study of Values Test when entering college in 1956-1961 and again when graduating four years later (from 1960-1965). Students have been grouped by Huntley according to their major field of study at graduation. High mean score = high importance of value (relative to other values).

Importance of Theoretical Value

Curriculum	(1) Fr score	(2) Fr-Sr gain	(3) Rank of Fr score	(4) Rank of Fr-Sr gain
Physics	51.25	+1.24	1	3
Chemistry	49.08	+0.58	2	5
Premedical (Arts)	49.00	+0.89	3	4
Engineering	48.22	-1.03	4	9
Premedical (Science)	47.75	+2.91	5	1
Science	46.49	+2.23	6	2
Industrial Adminis.	45.80	-2.45	7	8
Humanities	44.00	-2.95	8	9
Social Studies	41.80	-0.36	9	6

$rho_{(3)(4)} = +.45$

$p > .05$ (1- and 2-tailed tests)

Importance of Economic Value

Curriculum	(1) Fr score	(2) Fr-Sr gain	(3) Rank of Fr score	(4) Rank of Fr-Sr gain
Industrial Adminis.	47.11	+1.96	1	1
Engineering	45.56	-1.08	2	3
Social Studies	43.99	-0.20	3	2
Chemistry	43.31	-3.92	4	6
Science	42.09	-1.79	5	4
Premedical (Science)	40.56	-3.68	6	5
Humanities	39.99	-4.22	7	7
Physics	38.95	-4.32	8	8
Premedical (Arts)	36.11	-4.89	9	9

$rho_{(3)(4)} = +.93$

$p < .01$ (1- and 2-tailed tests)

Importance of Aesthetic Value

Curriculum	(1) Fr score	(2) Fr-Sr gain	(3) Rank of Fr score	(4) Rank of Fr-Sr gain
Premedical (Arts)	41.22	+11.11	1	2
Humanities	39.71	+12.18	2	1
Science	34.76	+ 5.30	3	7
Physics	34.27	+ 8.49	4	3
Premedical (Science)	33.85	+ 7.59	5	4
Social Studies	33.08	+ 5.86	6	6
Chemistry	31.66	+ 6.69	7	5
Industrial Adminis.	31.13	+ 3.92	8	9
Engineering	30.69	+ 5.11	9	8

$rho_{(3)(4)} = +.78$

$p < .05$ (1- and 2-tailed tests)

Importance of Social Value

Curriculum	(1) Fr score	(2) Fr-Sr gain	(3) Rank of Fr score	(4) Rank of Fr-Sr gain
Premedical (Science)	37.08	+0.02	1	2
Premedical (Arts)	36.22	-0.22	2	4
Chemistry	35.35	-2.31	3	9
Social Studies	35.07	-0.20	4	3
Science	34.73	-1.93	5	8
Humanities	34.17	-1.89	6	7
Engineering	33.94	-0.63	7	6
Physics	32.59	-0.52	8	5
Industrial Adminis.	32.33	+0.71	9	1

$rho_{(3)(4)} = -.05$

$p > .05$ (1- and 2-tailed tests)

Importance of Political Value

Curriculum	(1) Fr score	(2) Fr-Sr gain	(3) Rank of Fr score	(4) Rank of Fr-Sr gain
Social Studies	45.98	+0.23	1	6
Industrial Adminis.	43.51	+1.20	2	2
Engineering	42.47	+1.06	3	3
Science	42.38	+0.23	4	5
Premedical (Arts)	42.00	-1.89	5	9
Humanities	41.88	+2.53	6	1
Premedical (Science)	41.57	-1.76	7	8
Physics	40.63	-1.61	8	7
Chemistry	40.31	+0.80	9	4

$rho_{(3)(4)} = +.22$

$p > .05$ (1- and 2-tailed tests)

Importance of Religious Value

Curriculum	(1) Fr score	(2) Fr-Sr gain	(3) Rank of Fr score	(4) Rank of Fr-Sr gain
Physics	41.44	-2.93	1	2
Chemistry	40.54	-1.73	2	1
Industrial Adminis.	40.07	-5.40	3	7
Humanities	40.03	-5.86	4	9
Social Studies	39.91	-5.63	5	8
Science	39.77	-4.55	6	5
Engineering	39.10	-3.76	7	3
Premedical (Science)	38.99	-5.18	8	6
Premedical (Arts)	34.56	-4.12	9	4

$rho_{(3)(4)} = +.18$

$p > .05$ (1- and 2-tailed tests)

Table 6K.--Summaries of studies showing differential change by major field (CONTINUED)

Jones (1938a, 1938b): longitudinal study of male students at a "rather small New England liberal arts college for men." Original analysis combines data for two successive classes of students who were given five attitudinal instruments when entering the college in 1930 and 1931 and again when graduating four years later (in 1934 and 1935). Students have been grouped by Jones into four curricula--presumably by the field in which they graduated. The measuring instruments used were five of the attitude scales edited by Thurstone: Droba's Attitude toward War and Attitude toward the Negro Scales; and Thurstone and Chave's Attitude toward God (Influence on Conduct), Attitude toward God (The Reality of God) and Attitude toward the Church Scales. Scores for the five scales are totalled by Jones producing an overall social, political and religious "liberalism" score; high mean score = high "liberalism."

Social, political and religious "liberalism"

Curriculum	(1) Fr score	(2) Fr-Sr gain	(3) Rank of Fr score	(4) Rank of Fr-Sr gain
Natural Science	5.17	+1.39	1	1
English and Languages	5.10	+0.86	2	3
Economics and Sociology	4.69	+1.09	3	2
History and Geography	4.33	+0.85	4	4

$rho_{(3)(4)} = +.80$

$p > .05$ (1- and 2-tailed tests)

Bugelski and Lester (1940): longitudinal study of male and female students at the University of Buffalo. Original analysis combines data for three graduating classes (1931, 1933 and 1934) for whom data were available upon entrance to the university. Students have been grouped by Bugelski and Lester according to the major field in which they graduated. The instrument used, called the Opinion Test, measures degree of politico-economic, social and religious "liberalism"; high mean score = high liberalism.

Politico-economic, social and religious "liberalism"

Curriculum	(1) Fr score	(2) Fr-Sr gain	(3) Rank of Fr score	(4) Rank of Fr-Sr gain
Social Science	66.91	+24.83	1	1
Languages	65.40	+21.48	2	3
Biological Science	61.70	+20.80	3	4
Physical Science	61.55	+21.97	4	2

$rho_{(3)(4)} = +.40$

$p > .05$ (1- and 2-tailed tests)

Newcomb (1943): longitudinal study of female students at Bennington. Original analysis combines scores for two classes of students who took the Political and Economic Progressivism Scale upon entrance to the college (in 1935 and 1936) and in the spring of 1939 (as juniors or seniors). High mean score = high politico-economic conservatism.

Politico-economic conservatism

Curriculum	(1) Fr score	(2) Fr-Jr/ Sr gain	(3) Rank of Fr score	(4) Rank of Fr-Jr/Sr gain
Science	79.0	- 5.0	1	2
Art	75.9	-11.6	2	6
Social Studies	74.4	-10.9	3	5
Music	73.5	- 2.7	4	1
Drama-Dance	71.0	-10.6	5	4
Literature	66.6	- 8.2	6	3

$rho_{(3)(4)} = -.14$

$p > .05$ (1- and 2-tailed tests)

Table 6K.--Summaries of studies showing differential change by major field (CONTINUED)

Learned and Wood (1938): longitudinal study of male and female students in forty-five colleges and universities in Pennsylvania. On two occasions, the same students--as sophomores in May, 1930, and as seniors in May, 1932--took an achievement test to measure their general knowledge in the areas of mathematics, history and social studies, general science, fine arts, foreign literature, literature, and vocabulary. High score = high total achievement in these seven areas of knowledge.

Total achievement in various areas of knowledge--Men

Curriculum	(1) So score*	(2) So-Sr gain*	(3) Rank of So score	(4) Rank of So-Sr gain
Engineering	58.3	+3.7	1	7
Foreign Languages	56.2	+7.3	2	1
English	54.1	+6.6	3	2
Natural Science	52.1	+5.7	4	3
Mathematics	51.2	+5.6	5	4
Social Studies	50.5	+4.7	6	5
Business	45.8	+3.0	7	8
Miscellaneous**	45.5	+3.9	8	6

rho = +.45

p > .05 (1- and 2-tailed tests)

Total achievement in various areas of knowledge--Women

Curriculum	(1) So score*	(2) So-Sr gain*	(3) Rank of So score	(4) Rank of So-Sr gain
Natural Science	51.2	+6.9	1	1
Mathematics	50.5	+4.7	2	4
English	49.8	+5.6	3	3
Foreign Languages	49.3	+5.8	4	2
Social Studies	48.2	+0.8	5	7
Business	44.0	+2.4	6	6
Miscellaneous**	43.0	+3.3	7	5

rho = +.71

p < .05 (1-tailed test)
p > .05 (2-tailed test)

*These scores are standard scores, as estimated from Chart 75, on p. 284.

**This includes health education, home economics, secretarial, and music.

Hall (1951): cross-sectional study of male and female freshmen and seniors at the University of Syracuse during the spring of 1950. The two instruments used were constructed by Hall. One, which Hall refers to as the scale of religious beliefs, measures the degree of orthodoxy of a person's religious belief (high mean score = high orthodoxy). The other, referred to as the scale of social values, measures the extent to which a person is primarily "socio-centric" (concerned for the welfare of others) rather than "egocentric" (putting welfare of self above welfare of others regardless of ethics)--high score = high socio-centrism.

Degree of religious orthodoxy

Curriculum	(1) Fr score	(2) Fr-Sr difference	(3) Rank of Fr score	(4) Rank of Fr-Sr difference
Fine Arts	172.0	- 0.6	1	4
Applied Science	170.6	+ 0.7	2	3
Education	168.4	- 0.9	3	5
Science	166.2	-15.2	4	6
Forestry	164.5	+ 6.8	5	1
Business Adminis.	161.5	+ 6.4	6	2

$rho_{(3)(4)} = -.43$

p > .05 (1- and 2-tailed tests)

Degree of socio-centrism rather than egocentrism

Curriculum	(1) Fr score	(2) Fr-Sr difference	(3) Rank of Fr score	(4) Rank of Fr-Sr difference
Education	160.2	+6.7	1	2
Fine Arts	158.3	+9.0	2	1
Science	157.4	-0.2	3	6
Forestry	150.0	+4.9	4	3
Business Adminis.	146.1	+4.5	5.5	4
Applied Science	146.1	+0.3	5.5	5

$rho_{(3)(4)} = +.41$

p > .05 (1- and 2-tailed tests)

OTHER STUDIES:

Barkley (1942a, 1942b) studied one-year changes of female students in a southern woman's college with respect to scores on seven attitudinal scales edited by Thurstone (measuring attitudes toward the Negro, the United States Constitution, evolution, law, God, and the church) and scores on Shield's Moral Judgment Examination. At the beginning of the freshman year, students in the liberal arts curriculum were significantly more liberal than students in the commercial curriculum on the scales measuring attitudes toward war and toward evolution, and also scored significantly higher on the moral judgment scale. In all three instances, the differences between the two groups at the end of the year were not only in the same direction but were larger--indicating an accentuation of the initial differences. Arsenian (1943) conducted longitudinal studies

Table 6K.--Summaries of studies showing differential change my major field (CONTINUED)

OTHER STUDIES: (continued)

of freshman-senior changes on the six scales of the Allport-Vernon Study of Values for three successive classes of students entering a "men's college in New England" in 1938-1940. In a combined analysis for all three classes, he grouped students into two curricula; social science and health and physical education. Although he did not test for statistical significance of the initial differences between curricula on each of the scales, by inspection only two would seem to be large enough to be (or to approach) such significance: those for the political and religious scales. In both cases, these initial differences were in the same direction and larger for seniors. In a cross-sectional study of freshmen and seniors at Miami University in Oxford, Ohio, Stephenson (1952) found that not only did male freshmen in the School of Education score as significantly less prejudiced on the Hinckley Attitude Toward the Negro Scale than did freshmen in Business Administration, but also that the difference between seniors in the two fields was larger. With respect to female students, freshmen in the College of Arts and Science as well as in the School of Education were significantly less prejudiced than freshmen in the School of Business Administration; here, differences were less rather than greater among seniors in these groups.

Four other studies discuss differential change by major fields, as measured by change on multi-item attitudinal or personality scales, although all present less detail than do the above studies. All four give some indication of accentuation of initial major field differences. Thus Trent (1965a), reporting results from a four-year longitudinal study of students in a number of colleges and universities, writes that the engineering, business and education students, who were lower in intellectual and autonomous dispositions than students in other curricula to begin with, also showed smaller increases in these dispositions than students in other curricula. In a four-year longitudinal study of high-ability students in a variety of colleges, Tyler (1963) reports the following: "In general, the students in engineering have less liking for ideas, less interest in reflective, abstract thought than have those in the physical sciences. Also, the engineers tend to be more conventional and dependent, and less likely to feel comfortable in dealing with ambiguity and uncertainty. <u>These conclusions apply to the students as freshmen and even more so to them as seniors</u>" (p. 4, emphasis added). In an analysis by Pemberton (1963) of sophomore-senior change by major field at the University of Delaware with respect to academic-theoretical orientation (in contrast to technical-vocational orientation), the author's discussion implies an accentuation effect--although exact data are not given. Finally, Palubinskas (1952) studied changes (on the scales of Darley and McNamara's Minnesota Personality Scale) of female freshmen entering the Home Economics Division of Iowa State College. Of changes by the different curricular divisions in the general Home Economics Division, she writes: "The group of subjects in the curricula other than technical home economics and home economics education showed ... high Family Relations ... scores [purportedly signifying friendly and healthy parent-child relations]. This group improved in Family Relations score over the four-year period significantly more than the other two groups" (p. 390).

In addition to the above, other studies were found that present differences in percentage of endorsement (by students in various curricular groups) of single questionnaire items not combined into overall indices. In the first (Webster, Freedman and Heist, 1962), although differences among high-ability male freshmen in engineering, mathematics and humanities were found to be small with respect to favorableness toward government provisions for "medical and dental care for citizens who cannot afford such services" (and may well be insignificant statistically), the same men as juniors did show large, probably significant differences. On the other hand, initial differences among these fields decreased between freshman and junior years for the variable of personal need for religious faith. In a study by Stember (1961), in which cross-sectional data on attitudes of freshmen and seniors toward Jews and Negroes are presented, no general accentuation of initial differences is evident. Likewise, we found no indication of such accentuation among male students at Northwestern University in three fields of study (liberal arts, engineering, and business) with respect to endorsement of various life-satisfactions and career requirements (Krulee, O'Keefe and Goldberg, 1966; compare Tables 5-8 and 5-9 with Tables 3-9 and 3-12, respectively). Finally, Thistlethwaite (1965)--in a four-year longitudinal study of high-ability students--found a minimization of initial major field differences with respect to the percent of students who said they were planning to attend graduate or professional school after completion of their undergraduate education.

We have not included a review of a study by Thompson (1960), in which median freshman and senior scores for the Allport-Vernon Study of Values are given for students in several curricula. Not enough information is presented to be able to determine the median change between freshman and senior year, and thus to determine the rank of the median gains in addition to the rank of the initial medians.

Table 7A.--Summaries of studies comparing academic achievement of students in various residence groupings

Reference, Sample	Comparison Variable	Rank of various groups on comparison variable (from high to low in academic achievement)	Is there a consideration of differences in intellectual ability between or among groups?	Are differences between or among groups statistically significant?
Eurich (1927). Freshman and sophomore students at the Univ. of Maine, 1909-1920.	Cumulative grade-point average for freshmen	Fraternity: 1 Nonfraternity: 2	No	Yes
	Cumulative grade-point average for sophomores in the College of Arts and Sciences	Nonfraternity: 1 Fraternity: 2	No	Yes
	Cumulative grade-point average for sophomores in the College of Technology	Fraternity: 1 Nonfraternity: 2	No	Yes
	Cumulative grade-point average for sophomores in the College of Agriculture	Fraternity: 1 Nonfraternity: 2	No	Yes
Mary Rose Prosser (cited in Griffeth, 1958). Female freshmen at the Univ. of Iowa, Fall 1927.	Grade-point average	Home: 1 Sorority: 2 Dormitory: 3 Approved room: 4 Private home (working for self-support): 5	No	Significance level not given
Constance (1929). Male and female freshmen at the Univ. of Oregon, 1927 and 1928.	First term grade-point average	Fraternity or sorority: 1 Dormitory: 2 "Outside": 3	Yes	Yes
Byrns (1930). Male and female students at the Univ. of Wisconsin, during 1925-1929 (males) and 1926-1929 (females).	Grade-point average of males for each of eight semesters (rank of the average rank across semesters)	Professional fraternity: 1 Dormitory: 2 Social fraternity: 3	No	Significance level not given
	Grade-point average of females for each of six semesters (rank of the average rank across semesters)	Professional sorority: 1 Social sorority: 2 Dormitory: 3	No	Significance level not given
Grote (1932). Female freshmen at the Western Illinois State Teachers College, during the school years 1926-27, 1927-28, 1928-29, and 1929-30.	Honor points	Students rooming in rooming houses, but eating elsewhere: 1 Students living in their own homes in the college town: 2 Students living in the college dormitory: 3 Students rooming and boarding in boarding houses: 4 Students doing light housekeeping: 5 Students working for their board and room with families or in boarding houses: 6 Students living at home, but not in the college town: 7	Yes	Yes
MacPhail (1933). Students at Brown Univ., during 1927-1930.	Grade-point average for freshman year	Nonfraternity: 1 Fraternity: 2	Yes	No
	Grade-point average for combined freshman and sophomore years	Nonfraternity: 1 Fraternity: 2	Yes	No
	Grade-point average for all four years of college combined	Nonfraternity: 1 Fraternity: 2	Yes	Yes
Walker (1934). Male and female students at the Univ. of Chicago, 1926-1933.	Grade-point average	Residence hall: 1 Home: 2 Chapter house: 3 Rooming house: 4	Yes	Yes
Ludeman (1940). Male and female students at Southern State Normal School in Springfield, South Dakota, in the spring of 1939.	Grade-point average for fall and winter quarters	Students in dormitories: 1 Students living outside in private homes: 2	No	Significance level not given

Table 7A.--Summaries of studies comparing academic achievement of various residence groupings (CONTINUED)

Reference, Sample	Comparison Variable	Rank of various groups on comparison variable (from high to low in academic achievement)	Is there a consideration of differences in intellectual ability between or among groups?	Are differences between or among groups statistically significant?
Peterson (1943). Male and female students enrolled in the four-year curricula of agriculture or home economics in the College of Agriculture, Univ. of California at Davis, during the school years 1939-40, 1940-41 and 1941-42.	Grade-point average	Dormitory: 1 Cooperative: 2 Rooming house: 3 Home: 4 Fraternity: 5	Yes (also simultaneous control for sex, major field of study, class level, and educational background)	Yes
Bergeron (1953). Male freshmen at the Univ Univ. of Arkansas, school year 1950-51 and 1951-52.	Cumulative grade-point average	Dormitory: 1.5 Private residence: 1.5 Commuter: 3 Fraternity: 4	No	No
Goldsen, Rosenberg, Williams, and Suchman (1960). Males at all class levels in eleven colleges in 1952.	Cumulative grade-point average	Independent students: 1 Fraternity members: 2	No	Significance level not given
Wellington (1954). Freshmen at a "coeducational liberal arts college located in Iowa" with an enrollment of approximately 700 students, school year 1952-53.	Percent of students whose grade-point average was between 1.50 and 3.00 (A=3.00, B=2.00 ... E= -1.00)	Nonfraternity: 1 Fraternity: 2	No	Yes
Patterson (1956). Male freshmen at Kansas State College, Fall 1953.	Grade-point average	Married students: 1 Organized independent houses: 2 Private housing (including parents' home): 3 Dormitory: 4 Fraternity: 5	Yes (also simultaneous control for difficulty of courses)	Yes (Primarily due to high grade-point average of married students. Results not replicated for a 1954 sample.)
	Grade-point average	Married students: 1 Organized independent houses: 2.5 Private housing (including parents' home): 2.5 Dormitory: 4 Fraternity: 5	Yes (also simultaneous control for number of credit hours)	Yes (Primarily due to high grade-point average of married students. Results not replicated for a 1954 sample.)
Shutt (1955). Male freshmen at Purdue Univ., school year 1953-1954.	Grade-point average for first and second semesters	Residence hall: 1 Fraternity pledges: 2	No	Significance level not given
Iffert (1957). Male and female students entering 149 institutions of higher education in [illegible] and who graduated in 1954.	Cumulative grade-point average for male students	Nonfraternity: 1 Fraternity: 2	No	No
	Cumulative grade-point average for female students	Sorority: 1 Nonsorority: 2	No	Yes

Table 7A.--Summaries of studies comparing academic achievement of various residence groupings (CONTINUED)

Reference, Sample	Comparison Variable	Rank of various groups on comparison variable (from high to low in academic achievement)	Is there a consideration of differences in intellectual ability between or among groups?	Are differences between or among groups statistically significant?
Gamble (1961). Female students at all class levels at the Univ. of California, Berkeley, Fall 1956.	Grade-point average	Cooperatives: 1 Dormitories: 2 Approved Boarding Houses: 3 Sororities: 4	No	Significance level not given
Diener (1960). Male and female sophomores, juniors and seniors at the Univ. of Arkansas, first semester of the 1956-57 school year.	Ratio of "overachievers" to "underachievers" (i.e., those students earning noticeably higher and lower cumulative grade-point average than predicted by their scores on the ACE Psychological Examination)* *Calculated from raw data in Table 4, p. 399.	Sorority house: 1 Dormitory: 2 Apartment shared with other students: 3 Own home: 4 Rooming house: 5 Fraternity house: 6	No	Significance level not given
Griffeth (1958). Male and female freshmen entering the State Univ. of Iowa in September 1953 and who were graduated in 1957.	Cumulative grade-point average of graduating male seniors (See original reference for results of each of the four college years considered separately.)	Residence Halls: 1 Fraternities: 2 Rooming houses: 3 Students who changed housing: 4 Homes: 5	Yes	No
	Grade-point average for senior year for females (See original reference for results of the other three college years.)	Students who changed housing: 1 Rooming houses: 2 Sororities: 3 Homes: 4 Residence Halls: 5	Yes	No
Crookston (1960). Freshmen at the Univ. of Utah, Fall 1958.	Grade-point average	Fraternity pledges: 1 Independents: 2	Yes (also simultaneous control for college of enrollment)	No
Matson (1963). Male students entering Indiana Univ. in 1954, who remained in the same residence grouping between 1954 and 1958.	Frequency with which categories of students (grouped by 4 ability categories and 5 types of residences) showed the highest cumulative grade-point average for each of the eight semesters of college	High prestige fraternities: 1 Middle prestige fraternities: 2.5 Residence halls: 2.5 Low prestige fraternities: 4.5 Off-campus students: 4.5	Yes	Yes
Collins and Whetstone (1965). Female freshmen at the Univ. of Colorado, Fall 1960.	Percent of students with a C average or better	Independents: 1 Sorority pledges: 2	Yes	No
Willingham (1962). Freshman and senior students at Georgia Tech, January 1961.	Grade-point average of freshmen	Fraternity pledges: 1 Independents: 2	Yes	Yes
	Cumulative grade-point average of seniors	Fraternity members: 1 Independents: 2	No	Yes
Warwick (1962, 1964). Male freshmen at Cornell, school year 1960-61.	First-term grade-point average	Fraternity pledges: 1 Independents: 2	Yes	Yes
	Second-term grade-point average	Fraternity pledges: 1 Independents: 2	Yes	Significance level not given

Table 7A.--Summaries of studies comparing academic achievement of various residence groupings (CONTINUED)

Reference, Sample	Comparison Variable	Rank of various groups on comparison variable (from high to low in academic achievement	Is there a consideration of differences in intellectual ability between or among groups?	Are differences between or among groups statistically significant?
Prusok and Walsh (1964). Male freshmen at the State Univ. of Iowa, Fall 1961.	First semester grade-point average	Fraternity: 1 Dormitory: 2 Off-campus: 3 Living at home: 4	Yes	No
Beal (1965). Male and female freshmen at the Univ. of Oregon, school year 1961-62.	Fall term grade-point average	Students living in cooperatives: 1 Students living in dormitories: 2 Students living at home: 3	No	Yes
	Grade-point average at the end of the school year	Students living in cooperatives: 1 Students living in dormitories: 2 Students living at home: 3	No	Yes
Dollar (1963). Sample of male students at Oklahoma State Univ., Spring 1963.	First semester grade-point average	Fraternity: 1 Dormitory: 2 Off-campus: 3	Yes	No
Kaludis and Zatkin (1966). Male freshmen at the Univ. of Maryland, Fall 1964.	First-semester grade-point average	Independents: 1 Fraternity pledges: 2	Yes	No
Rhatigan (1965). Male and female students at all class levels at the State Univ. of Iowa, December 1964.	Percent of students whose grade-point average is 2.6 or above (highest possible grade-point average = 4.0)	Off-campus: 1 Fraternity or Sorority: 2 Men's or women's residence hall: 3	No	Significance level not given
Butts (1937). Students at the Univ. of Wisconsin, year not given.	Grade-point average	Special interest houses: 1 Students in private homes: 2 University dormitories: 3 Fraternities: 4 Students in own homes: 5 Co-operative houses: 6 Private dormitories 7 Rooming houses 8 Rooming houses (fraternity members): 9 Apartments: 10	No	Significance level not given
Stickler (1958). Freshman men at Florida State Univ., year not given.	Grade-point average	Home: 1 Dormitory: 2 "Out-in-town": 3 Fraternity: 4	No	Significance level not given
Selvin (1966). Male students at the Univ. of California at Berkeley, year not given.	Grade-point average	University residence hall: 1 Co-operative: 2 Home: 3 Apartment: 4 Student club ("fraternity"): 5	No	Significance level not given
	Grade-point average	Home: 1 University residence hall: 2 Apartment: 3 Co-operative: 4 Student club ("fraternity"): 5	Yes (simultaneous control for a wide variety of background variables)	Significance level not given

Table 7A.--Summaries of studies comparing academic achievement of various residence groupings (CONTINUED)

OTHER STUDIES:

Gordon and Lindeman (1966) report that students at Wagner College "who lived on campus made significantly better grades than those with similar backgrounds who lived at home" (p. 2). DeWaal (1954) reports that at Brigham Young University during the winter of the 1953-54 school year, sophomores living in two dormitories earned a significantly higher grade-point average than sophomore girls living either in a "family life unit" or in off-campus housing. During this same quarter, the grade-point average for the female freshmen in these several types of residences were not significantly different. In the previous fall quarter, female sophomores living in the two dormitories earned significantly higher grades than those living off campus; also during that same quarter, female freshmen living in these two dormitories earned significantly higher grades than those living in the "family life unit."

Lindahl (1965) did not find a significant difference in the cumulative grade-point averages of resident and commuter students at the San Fernando Valley State College. MacDonald (1967), in his study at Adams State College of Colorado, did not find a significant difference in grade-point averages between sophomores living in residence halls and those living in off-campus accommodations.

For freshmen at a wide variety of colleges in the middle 1930s, Hale (1939) found that "there was no tendency for off-campus students to do better or worse work than those on the campus. There was a strong tendency, however, for those living in fraternity houses to make a poorer showing in scholarship than the rest. The rooming-house group averaged slightly higher than other groups" (p. 142). In a study of sophomores, juniors and seniors at Michigan State University, Hartnett (1963, nd) found that a larger percent of students in residence halls than fraternities, sororities or off-campus housing were likely to receive higher grades for that year than were predicted from their academic performances the year prior. In a study of male students at the University of Iowa, Frantz (nd) presents evidence that a higher percent of men do unsatisfactory academic work while living in dormitories and fraternities than when living in off-campus housing or commuting. Van Alstine, Douglas and Johnson (1942) compared the grade-point averages (adjusted for high school averages) of male students in the following six Colleges at the University of Minnesota: Medicine, Law, Pharmacy, Engineering, Business, and Education. A significant difference in the adjusted grade-point average of students, classified by type of residence (dormitory, fraternity, private home, own home), was found only in the College of Pharmacy. Here, the average of freshmen in the private-residence group was significantly greater than that of the freshmen in the dormitory group, and as sophomores the grades of the first group were significantly greater than those of the groups who lived at home, in fraternities, or in dormitories.

Comparing students pledging a "social unit" (in the winter quarter of the 1959-1960 school year at Brigham Young University) with a control group of students not so pledging, Dahl (1961) found that the latter earned significantly higher grades on the average than did the former. During the earlier autumn quarter and the later spring quarter, differences between the two groups were not statistically significant. Questionning a sample of undergraduate men at the University of Michigan, Forbes, Johri and Montague (1962) found that "fraternity men report lower grade-point averages than non-fraternity men. The freshmen who join fraternities report high school grade averages at least as high as those of men who do not join but in subsequent classes the fraternity averages are consistently below the non-fraternity" (p. 11). Faguy-Coté (cited in W. A. Scott, 1965) found that when academic aptitude scores and first-semester grades of fraternity members and nonmembers (at the University of Colorado) were equated, the Greeks showed some decrement in academic performance relative to Independents during their subsequent school years.

Comparing grade-point averages of sorority and nonsorority females at ten universities, Worchester (1923) found that in eight of the ten comparisons the first group was higher than the second; with respect to male, fraternity members earned a higher grade-point average than did the Independents in only four of the ten schools. (Probability levels of the results are not given for either males or females.) In a study of academic achievement at the University of Minnesota in 1921, Johnston (1924) concluded: "In scholarship the sorority pledges did a little better than other women. The fraternity pledges, on the contrary, did distinctly worse than other men" (p. 31). At the University of Vermont, "the cumulative averages of Greek and non-Greek students were more or less the same, though the sorority women did have slightly higher averages than the nonsorority women" (University of Vermont, 1965).

Lehman (1935) studied the grade-point averages of male students at the Ohio University during 1928-1933 and of female students at the same university during 1930-1933. Controlling for sex, year of matriculation, and ability, he found that both during the fall and spring terms, freshmen who pledged fraternities and sororities earned a higher grade-point average than did freshmen who did not pledge these groups; however, the difference between the pledgers and nonpledgers was much smaller in the spring term. Equating groups of students at various class levels on sex, year of matriculation, number of hours per week for which each student was enrolled during his first semester on campus, and grade-point average

OTHER STUDIES: (continued)

earned during that semester, Lehman found that the grades for Independents for all semesters after the first were better than those for fraternity and sorority members.

At a college whose name he does not provide, Rigg (1937) found that a sample of freshman students who did not pledge a fraternity had, on the average, higher intelligence scores than did a sample of students who pledged a fraternity. During the first semester, the nonfraternity group was less academically successful than the second group (statistical significance of difference not given). Moreover, the first group declined in grade point during the second term while the second group increased. Reporting a study of fraternity and nonfraternity students at a large number of colleges and universities, one of the conclusions of Kamens (1967a) is as follows: "On the basis of their high school grades students attracted to fraternities are as capable as the rest of the student population. ... Controlling for their ability they are just as likely to achieve high grades [in college] as the others. If anything, fraternity members do a little better than other students, particularly those with poor high school records" (p. 10). At a relatively select, small coeducational college, Wallace (1963) found that for students of high ability, Greeks had higher grade-point averages than did Independents, while just the reverse was true for those of low ability.

Stricker (1964) found no significant differences with respect to cumulative grade-point averages among male and female commuters, dormitory students and off-campus dwellers; neither did students in fraternities or sororities differ from Independents in this area. Comparing a sorority pledge class and an independent group of students (at the University of Kansas) from the fall of 1951 through the fall of 1952, Maduros (1953) did not find a statistically significant difference between the two groups with respect to freshman-sophomore change in grade-point average. This was also the case when each group was divided into four categories with respect to intelligence-test scores. Buckner (1961) divided a group of freshman fraternity pledges and a group of residence-hall freshmen--who were at the University of Missouri in the fall of 1958--into five subgroups according to the level of potential for college scholarship or achievement. At each of these ability levels, no statistically significant difference was found between the first-term grade-point averages of the two groups. At a "residential liberal arts college for men with a student body of about 2,900 undergraduates," Segal (1965) found that a larger percent of non-Jewish Independents than non-Jewish fraternity members had a cumulative average of B or higher, whereas for Jews, a larger percent of affiliated students than nonaffiliates had such an average. Neither set of findings, however, were statistically significant at the .05 level. Halbower (cited in Patterson, 1956) found that two groups of upper division female students--those living in sororities and those unaffiliated--did not differ with respect to scholastic achievement. Carter (1934) found no significant difference in the "average index of achievement" of fraternity and nonfraternity men at Albion College.

Table 8A.--Summaries of studies comparing student and faculty orientations

Harris (1934): The Allport-Vernon Study of Values was filled out by 62 faculty members and by 338 male students at Lehigh University (year not given). Results are given in the original analysis for only four of the six scales.

Allport-Vernon Study of Values	Mean score of faculty	Rank of mean score	Mean score of students	Rank of mean score
Theoretical	36.18	1	30.57	2
Aesthetic	29.35	2	26.16	3
Religious	27.93	3	25.83	4
Political	27.63	4	32.74	1

Students and faculty were significantly different on three of the four values: faculty were higher than students on theoretical and aesthetic but lower on political. In terms of the rank order of the importance of these values, faculty and students were not similar rho = -.20 ($p > .05$, 1- and 2-tailed tests).

Knode (1943): During 1941-1942, 112 faculty members at 28 state universities and 545 students at 16 state universities filled out a questionnaire dealing with a variety of matters. In one part of the questionnaire, students and faculty were asked to rate each of ten "life objectives" on a 3-category continuum (essentially high, medium and low in importance). We have shown the rankings of the "absolute" scores on each item for the faculty and students.

Life objectives	Rank of "absolute" score of faculty	Rank of "absolute" score of male students	Rank of "absolute" score of female students
To live a "good life"	1	3	2
Home and children	2	1	1
Achievement	3	2	3
To leave a recorded heritage (writing, art, music, research, etc.)	4	9	8
To improve social conditions	5	5	4
To attain professional eminence	6	6	7
A good income	7	4	5
To attain prestige and influence	8	8	9
Social life	9	7	6

In terms of absolute score (not shown here) the faculty on the average scored lower than men students on all the life objectives except improving social conditions and leaving a recorded heritage. Faculty scored lower than women students (in absolute scores) on all items except attaining professional eminence and leaving a recorded heritage. (Probability level of results is not given for these absolute differences.) With respect to the ranks of these absolute scores (as shown here), students and faculty were fairly similar: for male students and faculty, rho = +.73 ($p < .05$, 1- and 2-tailed tests); for female students and faculty, rho = +.77 ($p < .01$, 1-tailed test; $p < .05$, 2-tailed test). In terms of these rankings, faculty were higher than students on living a "good life" and leaving a recorded heritage, while students were higher than faculty on home and children, a good income and social life.

Table 8A.--Summaries of studies comparing student and faculty orientations (CONTINUED)

Knode (continued):

In another part of the questionnaire, students and faculty were asked to rate each of thirteen "student honors" on a 3-category continuum (essentially, high, medium and low in importance). Shown here are the rankings of the "absolute" scores on each item for the faculty and students.

Student honors	Rank of "absolute" score of faculty	Rank of "absolute" score of male students	Rank of "absolute" score of female students
Graduation "with honors"	1	3	3.5
Membership in senior scholastic honor society (Phi Beta Kappa, Phi Kappa Phi, etc.)	2	1	1
Student body president	3	2	3.5
Membership in senior honor society such as "mortar Board," "Blue Key," etc.	4	4	2
Editor of the yearbook or university paper	5	5	5
Membership in dramatic, debating, musical, writing or similar organizations	6	11	11
Business manager of a student activity	7	10	10
President of junior class	8	6	6
Captain of athletic or gym team	9	8	8
President of social fraternity or of "Independents" or "Barbs" or "Phrateres"	10	9	9
To be voted the most popular man or woman of senior class	11	7	7
Cheer leader	12	12	12
Drum "major or majorette"	13	13	13

In terms of absolute score (not shown here) the faculty scored lower than both male and female students on all thirteen student honors. (Probability level of results is not given.) With respect to the ranks of these absolute scores (as shown here), students and faculty were quite similar: for male students and faculty, rho = +.82 ($p < .01$, 1- and 2-tailed tests); for female students and faculty, rho = +.83 ($p < .01$, 1- and 2-tailed tests). In terms of these rankings, faculty were higher than students on the following items: (1) graduation with "honors"; (2) membership in dramatic, debating, musical, writing or similar organizations; and (3) business manager of student activity. Students ranked higher than faculty on the following items: (1) membership in senior scholastic honor society; (2) president of junior class; (3) to be voted the most popular man or woman of senior class; (4) captain of athletic or gym team; and (5) president of social fraternity.

For similarities and differences between students and faculty with respect to evaluation of different possible courses of study, judgment of the principle strengths and weaknesses of intercollegiate activities, evaluation of various vocations, and evaluation of different possible avenues for American leadership following the war, see the original reference.

Hall (1951): During the spring of 1950, 76 faculty members and over 1,650 freshman and senior students at Syracuse University took a scale of religious beliefs and a scale of social values (constructed by Hall). Compared to both freshmen and seniors, faculty scored lower on the first scale, indicating that the faculty were less religious and less likely to believe in God. On the second scale, faculty were less egocentric, more sociocentric (concerned for the welfare of others) than were freshman and senior students. (Probability level of results are not given for differences on either scale.)

Table 8A.--Summaries of studies comparing student and faculty orientations (CONTINUED)

Wallace (1963): In November 1959, 519 nonfreshman students (at a small, undergraduate, co-educational, non-denominational college located in the midwest) were asked to choose, in paired comparisons, among eleven characteristics (or values) related to college life. In April 1960, 67 faculty members were asked to choose among these same characteristics (or values) in terms of what they "prefer to see" in male and in female students. In the tables here are given the percentages of students and faculty for whom each of four characteristics are judged first or second in importance among the eleven characteristics. The ranks of these percentages are also given.

Male students

Characteristic (or value)	Percent of faculty judging characteristic of first or second in importance with respect to male students	Rank of percentage	Percent of male students judging characteristic as first or second in importance to them	Rank of percentage
Having close friends and spending time with them	88%	1	80%	1
Making at least an A-minus average	62%	2	42%	2
Having as many dates as one wants with whomever one wants	30%	3	41%	3
Participating in extracurricular activities as much as one would like to	20%	4	36%	4

In terms of percentage endorsement, male students were more likely than faculty to consider dates and extracurricular activities important and less likely than faculty to consider academic achievement and friendship important (probability level not given.) In terms of the rank ordering of these percentages, male students and faculty were highly similar: rho = +1.00 ($p < .05$, 1-tailed test; $p > .05$, 2-tailed test).

Female students

Characteristic (or value)	Percent of faculty judging characteristic of first or second in importance with respect to female students	Rank of percentage	Percent of female students judging characteristic as first or second in importance to them	Rank of percentage
Having close friends and spending time with them	89%	1	89%	1
Having as many dates as one wants with whomever one wants	45%	2	56%	2
Making at least an A-minus average	43%	3	27%	3.5
Participating in extracurricular activities as much as one would like to	18%	4	27%	3.5

In terms of percentage endorsement, female students were more likely than faculty to consider dates and extracurricular activities important and less likely than faculty to consider academic achievement important (probability level not given). In terms of the rank ordering of percentages, female students and faculty were similar: rho = +.95 ($p > .05$, 1- and 2-tailed tests).

Table 8A.--Summaries of studies comparing student and faculty orientations (CONTINUED)

Wilson and Lyons (1961): A sample of faculty and of students at a number of cooperative colleges (those having work-study programs) ranked six goals of higher education in order of importance. The rankings (based on composite rankings across members of a sample) for faculty and students in liberal arts, engineering and business administration programs are given here.

Educational Goal	Liberal Arts Faculty ranking	Liberal Arts Student ranking	Engineering Faculty ranking	Engineering Student ranking	Business Administration Faculty ranking	Business Administration Student ranking
Provide a basic general education and appreciation of ideas	1	1	1	2	1	2
Help to develop one's moral capacities, ethical standards, and values	2	4	3	4	2	4
Provide vocational training; develop skills and techniques directly applicable to one's career	3	2	2	1	3	1
Develop one's abilities and interests for participation in community and civic affairs	4	5	5	5	5	5
Develop one's abilities to get along with different kinds of people	5	3	4	3	4	3
Prepare one for a happy marriage and family life	6	6	6	6	6	6

For both liberal arts and business curricula, the rank-order correlation between student and faculty ranking is +.71 which, although high, is not statistically significant. For engineering faculty and students, the rank-order correlation coefficient of +.89 is statistically significant at the .05 level. For all three programs faculty ranked the goal of developing moral capacities higher than did students, while students ranked the goals of vocational training and developing abilities to get along with different kinds of people higher than did faculty.

Lewis (1967a): A sample of faculty and of students at "a rapidly growing urban institution with an enrollment of over 10,000 full-time day students" were asked to judge the importance of six goals "that some say the ideal public university should emphasize in its undergraduate program." Shown here are the percentages of faculty and of students in each of four fields judging each of five goals to be of highest importance on a five-point scale. The ranks of these percentages are given in brackets. (We have not shown the results for the sixth goal since the metric of comparison--percentage of respondents who think the goal is of "at least considerable importance"--differs from that used for the other five.)

Percent judging each goal as being of highest importance on a five-point scale

Educational Goal of the Ideal Public University	Humanities Fac.	Humanities Stud.	Soc Science Fac.	Soc Science Stud.	Science Fac.	Science Stud.	Engineering Fac.	Engineering Stud.
Provide a basic education and appreciation of ideas	74.2% [1]	57.7% [2]	58.9% [1]	43.6% [2]	60.8% [1]	26.6% [3]	43.8% [1]	25.0% [1.5]
Provide deepening and broadening experiences	48.5% [2]	60.6% [1]	39.3% [2]	50.0% [1]	28.0% [2]	37.6% [1]	15.6% [2]	23.6% [3]
Develop knowledge and interest in community and world problems	31.8% [3.5]	29.5% [4]	26.8% [3]	24.5% [4]	16.1% [3]	14.4% [5]	9.4% [3.5[	13.8% [4]
Develop moral capacities, ethical standards and values	31.8% [3.5]	11.2% [5]	13.4% [5]	19.0% [5]	12.6% [4.5]	16.7% [4]	9.4% [3.5]	12.5% [5]
Provide knowledge and ideas about cultural heritage	47.0% [5]	49.3% [3]	18.8% [4]	41.8% [3]	12.6% [4.5]	27.7% [2]	0.0% [5]	25.0% [1.5]

For the four fields of study, the rank-order correlations between student and faculty rankings are positive, although none are statistically significant. The degree of rank-order agreement between faculty and students differed by major field as follows: social science--rho = +.80; humanities--rho = +.55; science--rho = +.23; engineering--rho = +.20. For all four fields, a higher percent of faculty than students judged the goals of basic education and of knowledge and interest in community and world problems to be of high importance. For all four fields, a higher percent of students than faculty judged the goals of engaging in deepening and broadening experiences and of providing knowledge about cultural heritage to be of high importance. With respect to the goal of developing moral capacities and ethical standards, student endorsement was higher than faculty endorsement in the social sciences, sciences, and engineering but not in the humanities. Other data (not given here), shows that for all four fields, a higher percent of students than faculty judged the goal of providing "vocational training and skills related to career" to be "of at least considerable importance."

For similarities and differences between students and faculty with respect to their view on faculty autonomy (freedom of expression) and on the importance of teaching and research activities of the faculty, see the original reference.

Table 8A.--Summaries of studies comparing student and faculty orientations (CONTINUED)

Pace (1954); Pace and Troyer (1949): During 1947-48, 690 faculty members and roughly 550 students (about equally divided between sophomores and juniors) at Syracuse University were asked to judge the importance of eighteen objectives of general education. Shown here are the percentages of faculty and of students judging each objective as "very important." The ranks of these percentages are also given.

Objectives of General Education	Faculty: Percentage judging as very important	Faculty: Rank of percentage	Students: Percentage judging as very important	Students: Rank of percentage
How to think clearly, meet a problem and follow it to a right conclusion without guidance	87%	1	85%	2.5
Understanding other people	69%	2.5	85%	2.5
Discovering personal strengths and weaknesses, abilities and limitations	69%	2.5	71%	6
Making a wise vocational choice	68%	4	88%	1
Writing clearly and effectively	64%	5	57%	10.5
How to participate effectively as a citizen	61%	6	49%	13.5
Understanding the meanings and values in life	60%	7	65%	8
Preparing for a vocation	59%	8.5	81%	4
Speaking easily and well	59%	8.5	75%	5
Understanding world issues and pressing social, political and economic problems	57%	10	49%	13.5
Developing a personal philosophy and applying it in daily life	55%	11	57%	10.5
Developing social competence and social graces	48%	12.5	63%	9
Developing good health habits	48%	12.5	55%	12
Preparing for a satisfactory family and marital adjustment	46%	14	73%	7
Understanding the basis of personal and community health	38%	15	41%	15
Understanding scientific developments and processes and their applications in society	37%	16	31%	16
Developing an understanding and enjoyment of literature	28%	17	27%	18
Developing an understanding and enjoyment of art and music	23%	18	28%	17

Considering only statistically significant differences, a larger percentage of faculty than students judged the following educational objectives as "very important": writing clearly and effectively; understanding world issues and pressing social, political and economic problems; understanding scientific developments and processes and their applications in society; and how to participate effectively as a citizen. A larger percentage of students than faculty judged the following educational objectives as "very important": preparing for a vocation; making a wise vocational choice; developing a personal philosophy and applying it in daily life; preparing for a satisfactory family and marital adjustment; understanding other people; speaking easily and well; developing social competence and social graces; developing good health habits.

In terms of the rank ordering of the percentages of endorsement of these items, the similarity between faculty and students was fairly high: Spearman's rho = +.79 ($p < .01$; 1- and 2-tailed tests).

Jervis and Congdon (1958): 154 faculty members and over 1000 students at the University of New Hampshire were asked to rank order nine objectives of higher education. The rank order of the median ranks (for faculty and for students) is given here.

Objectives of Higher Education	Rank of median rank of each objective for faculty	Rank of median rank of each objective for students
Intellectual growth	1	4
Self-fulfillment	2	2
Self-understanding	3	3
Vocational preparation	4	1
Informal intellectual activity	5	8
Faculty relationships	6	9
Preparation for life	7	7
"The degree"	8	6
Social growth	9	5

Although there was some similarity between these rankings, the rank-order correlation of +.53 is not significant at the .05 level (1- and 2-tailed tests). Faculty ranked the objectives of intellectual growth, informal intellectual activities and faculty relationships higher than did students. Students ranked the following objectives higher than did faculty: vocational preparation, "the degree" and social growth.

Smith (1933): During March 1932, 37 faculty members and 518 male and female students at Muskingum College filled out a questionnaire constructed by Smith to determine feelings toward war and peace. On this scale, 15% of the faculty scored as "militarists" while 28% of the students so scored (probability level of this result not given).

Table 8A.--Summaries of studies comparing student and faculty orientations (CONTINUED)

University of Vermont (1965): During 1963-1964, 235 faculty members and 861 students at the University of Vermont filled out a questionnaire asking their opinions and attitudes about the Greek-letter system at the university. Shown here are the results on two of the more general items of the questionnaire.

All things considered, what do you think about fraternities as a part of the Univ. of Vermont?	Faculty	Students not in fraternity or sorority	Fraternity or sorority members	All students
Good thing	20%	37%	83%	56%
The good balances the bad	31%	48%	15%	34%
Better if there were none	38%	15%	2%	10%
No response	11%	---	1%	---

If a younger brother (son) asked you about fraternities, how would you advise him?	Faculty	Students not in fraternity or sorority	Fraternity or sorority members	All students
Encourage him to join a fraternity	16%	33%	75%	51%
Not advise him either way	47%	52%	24%	41%
Discourage him from joining	32%	13%	1%	8%
No response	5%	1%	---	---

In general, students (particularly those in fraternities and sororities) manifested a more favorable attitude toward the Greek-letter system than did faculty. (Note, however, that the percentages are not fully comparable because different proportions of students and faculty are in the "no response" category.)

Sherman (1967): 139 faculty members and 866 students at the University of Colorado were asked to complete a 40-item scale measuring attitude toward fraternities (year not given). Shown here are the average scores for fraternity students, sorority students, independent students, and faculty. A score of 120 is considered by the investigator to indicate a "hypothetical neutral" score, while lower scores indicate varying degrees of positiveness towards fraternities and higher scores varying degrees of negativeness towards fraternities.

	Faculty	Fraternity students	Sorority students	Independent students
Average score--indicating attitude toward fraternities	132.72	88.12	101.34	126.94

Both faculty members and independent students were significantly less favorable towards fraternities than were fraternity and sorority students. The mean difference between faculty and independent students, indicating a slightly less favorable attitude toward fraternities on the part of faculty, is not statistically significant.

A second part of this study attempted to determine attitudes toward specific aspects of fraternity life. Here it was found that the greatest faculty concerns were in the area of membership policies (including racial or religious discrimination and financial demands of membership). Independent students did not respond as negatively as the faculty in this area, but did tend to disagree with statements dealing with the advantages of fraternity membership, especially in the areas of scholastic or intellectual contributions of fraternities.

Table 8A.--Summaries of studies comparing student and faculty orientations (CONTINUED)

Beardslee and O'Dowd (1962): During the spring of 1958 72 faculty members and 170 freshmen and seniors at Wesleyan University responded to a questionnaire designed to determine their images of a variety of occupations in terms of the social position of an occupation, the life style and personality associated with members of an occupation, and the style of social participation implied by occupational membership.

The images so determined were found to be highly similar for students and for faculty. Within this basic agreement, there were some differences, however. In general, the faculty had more negative views of the occupations of lawyer, physician, business executive, and school teacher than did students. With respect to school teachers, both groups agreed that members of this occupation were calm and cautious but the faculty rated school teachers lower in worldly success, intellectual potency, sociability, and personal dynamism. The artist was held in the same general regard by both groups, but the faculty rated him less radical and impulsive than did the students, while the students perceived him as somewhat more prosperous and intelligent. The college professor was seen in a less favorable light by faculty than by students, especially freshmen.

Pennsylvania State University (1966b): During the spring of 1965, 196 members of faculty and administration and over 1,300 students of the Pennsylvania State University expressed their feelings in a questionnaire about the responsibility for students' off-campus visitations with members of the opposite sex. Essentially, the questionnaire asked students and faculty to offer an opinion on whether the responsibility for regulating such visits was to be entrusted to one of three sources, as shown here.

Regulation of responsibility for students' off-campus visitations should be:	Faculty and administration	Students
Entrusted to the judgment of parents	38%	33%
A part of the University's continuing function	46%	7%
Delegated to the individual student concerned	16%	60%

About a third of the students and of the faculty felt the regulation of off-campus visitations should be a function of parents. A much larger proportion of faculty than of students felt it should be a function of the university, while a much smaller proportion of faculty than of students felt it should be a function of the individual student.

Hubbell (1966): During 1963-64, 226 faculty members and 590 students at the University of Wisconsin were asked to read ten detailed incidents of misbehavior that had happened recently on the campus: theft, academic dishonesty, heterosexual premarital relations, sexual perversion, traffic violations, disorderly conduct on campus, disorderly conduct off campus, illegal use of alcoholic beverages, violation of disciplinary probation, and violation of housing regulations. The respondents were presented with five possible disciplinary actions (*viz.*, nonjurisdiction, verbal warning, disciplinary probation, suspension, or expulsion) and asked to check one of them for each case with respect (1) to the action they thought the university actually took and (2) the one action they themselves thought ought to have been taken if they had the authority and responsibility.

Comparing the faculty and student groups across the ten cases, it was found that students felt that the university would be more severe than did the faculty. Moreover, on four occasions the majority of the student sample correctly anticipated the original university action while on only one occasion did the faculty do so. Finally the faculty and student groups were quite similar on the action they themselves would have recommended for each of the ten cases. For seven cases, the modal response of the two groups was the same. In two instances, the faculty was more lenient, and in one case less lenient, than were students.

Table 8A.--Summaries of studies comparing student and faculty orientations (CONTINUED)

OTHER STUDIES:

Guthrie (1954) and Maslow and Zimmerman (1956) have shown that there is a fairly substantial--but by no means perfect--agreement between faculty and student ratings or evaluations of specific teachers. There does seem to be a difference in the grounds used for these ratings. Faculty tend to focus on such criteria as scholarly attainments, creativeness, desirability as a colleague. Students focus more on teaching qualities and personality.

Responding to CCI (College Characteristics Index) or to CUES (College and University Environment Scales), faculty and students are in high agreement about the profile of characteristics, opportunities and demands of their schools. That is, the rank-order correlation between faculty and student rankings of the 30 CCI scales and the 5 CUES scales is high--usually in the .80s and .90s. Within this agreement on the relative press of different aspects of the environment, faculty and students do not always agree on the exact level or strength of any particular press. For studies comparing students and faculties on these scales, see Barton (1961); Berdie (1965, 1967a); Brewer (1963); Brown (1966); Chickering (nd[b]); McPeek (1967); Murphy (nd); Pace (1960, 1966a); Pace and Stern (1958); Rowe (1963, 1964); Webb and Crowder (1961a); and Weiss (1964). For research on similarities and differences in the results of factor analyses on CCI scores for faculty and students, see LeBold (1961). For an interesting study on the high relative and absolute similarity between faculty and students at a new college with respect to their hopes of what the environment would be like (in terms of CUES scores), see New College (1964).

Table 8B.--Summaries of studies presenting student ratings of quality of instruction and satisfaction with courses and teachers

REFERENCE, SAMPLE	RESULTS	
Henderson and Northrup (1964). Sample of male and female students (at all class levels) at the Pennsylvania State University. April 1962.	"Penn State is doing a very good job in fulfilling the educational goals I consider important" "Strongly agree" 8% "Agree" 61% "Disagree" 27% "Strongly disagree" 4%	"Of the courses I have taken here, I would consider the following percentage to have been excellent ..." "More than 90%" 6% "Around 75%" 30% "About half" 29% "About one-fourth" 26% "Less than 10%" 9%
	"The academic training which a student obtains from Penn State is ..." "Excellent and exciting" 8% "Adequate and exciting" 35% "Adequate but unexciting" 54% "Inadequate and unexciting" 3%	"I sometimes feel that most of my time in classes is wasted." "Strongly disagreed" 7% "Disagreed" 52% "Agreed" 35% "Strongly agreed" 7%
	"Most of the professors that I have had have been intellectually stimulating." "Strongly agree" 3% "Agree" 42% "Disagree" 50% "Strongly diagree" 5%	"On the whole, my professors have been well prepared for their classes." "Strongly agree" 9% "Agree" 78% "Disagree" 11% "Strongly disagree" 2%
	Other results: To the statement that "in general, I feel that most of my time here [at Penn State] has been wasted," only 7% agreed while 93% disagreed. Seventy-four percent of the students agreed that "the quality of Penn State faculty is on a par with that of other major universities," and 62% agreed that "in general, the faculty at Penn State is doing an excellent job."	
Preu (nd). Sample of male and female students (all class levels) at Florida State University. May 1961.	Rating of general teaching methods Males* / Females* "Excellent" 7% / 3% "Good" 42% / 44% "Fair" 36% / 42% "Poor" 10% / 7% "No opinion" 2% / 1%	Rating of faculty-student relationships Males / Females "Excellent" 16% / 11% "Good" 35% / 50% "Fair" 30% / 29% "Poor" 11% / 5% "No opinion" 8% / 5%
*No explanation is given as to why percentages do not add to 100 percent.	Other results: Two-thirds of the students felt that the quality of education they were receiving in their "majors" was "good" or "excellent," while another 16% felt it was "superior." Eighty-four percent of the men and 89% of the women rated the general quality of the faculty under whom they studied as either "good," "excellent," or "superior." (Further breakdowns are not given.)	
Harry Sharp (personal communication to authors). Random sample of male and female students at the University of Wisconsin. November 1965.	"How satisfied are you with the general quality of teaching throughout the University?" Freshmen and Sophomores / Juniors and Seniors "Very satisfied" 20% / 23% "Moderately satisfied 66% / 61% "Slightly dissatisfied" 10% / 10% "Dissatisfied" 4% / 6%	
Olson (1964b). Random sample of male and female students living in residence halls at Michigan State University. Winter term 1964.	"The quality of the academic program in my major field compares favorably with that in other universities." Males / Females "Agree strongly" 56% / 58% "Agree somewhat" 35% / 31% "Disagree somewhat" 7% / 9% "Disagree strongly" 2% / 2%	
Ellis (1965). Sample of male and female freshmen at the University of Oregon in May 1961, and of those of these students who were still at the university as sophomores in May 1962.	Satisfaction with intellectual level of courses Freshmen / Sophomores "Highly satisfied" 32% / 17% "Fairly satisfied" 50% / 60% "Neutral" 12% / 13% "Fairly dissatisfied" 5% / 10% "Highly dissatisfied" 1% / 0%	Satisfaction with quality of instruction in courses Freshmen / Sophomores "Highly satisfied" 24% / 16% "Fairly satisfied" 54% / 50% "Neutral" 11% / 14% "Fairly dissatisfied" 9% / 16% "Highly dissatisfied" 2% / 4%

Table 8B.--Summaries of studies presenting student ratings of quality of instruction and satisfaction with courses and teachers (CONTINUED)

REFERENCE, SAMPLE	RESULTS
Panos and Astin (1967b). Follow-up sample in the summer of 1965 of original sample of freshmen entering a large number of colleges and universities in the fall of 1961. Results from the 1965 sample have been adjusted by the investigators for the differences between respondents and nonrespondents and for the disproportionate sampling of institutions from the various stratification cells of the original sampling design.	Evaluation of the amount of outlets for creative activities Males / Females "Too much or too many" 1.8% / 1.6% "Just about the right amount" 58.0% / 57.1% "Not enough" 40.2% / 41.3% "What is your over-all evaluation of this college?" Males / Females "Very satisfied" 40.0% / 41.3% "Satisfied" 43.8% / 42.2% "On the fence" 10.1% / 10.7% "Dissatisfied" 4.8% / 4.5% "Very dissatisfied" 1.2% / 1.3%
Goldsen (1951); Goldsen, Rosenberg, Williams, and Suchman (1960). Random sample of male and female students at Cornell University (in the Colleges of Agriculture, Architecture, Arts and Sciences, Engineering, Home Economics, Hotel Administration, and Industrial and Labor Relations) in 1950. Follow-up sample (of juniors and seniors) in 1952.	"Do you ever feel that what you are doing at Cornell is a waste of time?" 1950 Sample Freshmen / Sophomores / Juniors / Seniors "Rarely" 33% / 31% / 30% / 32% "Sometimes" 51% / 55% / 58% / 55% "Often" 16% / 14% / 12% / 13% 1952 Sample Males / Females "Rarely or never" 46% / 32% "Sometimes, not often" 41% / 49% "Yes, often" 13% / 18%
Goldsen, Rosenberg, Williams, and Suchman (1960). Random sample of male students at eleven universities in 1952.	Percent of students who "agree" to the following statement: "Most of what I am learning in college is very worthwhile." Fisk 80% Wesleyan 78% Wayne State Univ. 77% Cornell 77% Yale 76% Harvard 75% Univ. of Michigan 75% Univ. of Texas 74% Univ. of North Carolina 71% UCLA 70% Dartmouth 66%
Harp and Taietz (1964). Random sample of male students in the Colleges of Agriculture, Arts and Sciences, and Engineering at Cornell University. Fall 1962.	"Most of what I am learning in college is worthwhile." "Agree" 64% "Undecided" 18% "Disagree" 18% "I am disillusioned about college life." "Disagree" 76% "Undecided" 12% "Agree" 12%
Katz and Allport (1931). Sample of entire student body at Syracuse University. May 1926.	Chance for self-expression afforded by studies "My studies give me <u>every chance</u> to develop my main interests or show what I am worth" 12% "My studies give me a <u>good chance</u> to develop my main interests ..." 39% "My studies give me a <u>fair chance</u> to develop my main interests ..." 35% "My studies give me a <u>slight chance</u> to develop my main interests ..." 11% "My studies give me <u>no chance whatever</u> to develop my main interests or show what I am worth" 3%
Lehmann and Dressel (1962). Sample of male and female seniors at Michigan State University. Spring 1962.	"Generally, I found my classes pretty interesting." Males / Females "Strongly agree" or "agree" 89% / 90% "Strongly disagree" or "Disagree" 11% / 10%
Birney, Coplin and Grose (1960). Sample of male students at Amherst College in their freshman year (May 1956) and of those of these students who were still at the college as juniors (May 1958).	"Did you have enough opportunity for intellectual activity?" Freshmen / Juniors "Too much" 3% / 3% "Just the right amount" 56% / 41% "Not quite enough" 32% / 46% "Definitely not enough" 9% / 11%

Table 8B.--Summaries of studies presenting student ratings of quality of instruction and satisfaction with courses and teachers (CONTINUED)

REFERENCE, SAMPLE	RESULTS
Weiss (1964). Sample of entire student body at St. Louis University (College of Arts and Sciences, School of Commerce and Finance, School of Nursing and Health Services, Institute of Technology, and Parks College of Aeronautical Technology) during the academic year 1963-64.	"If I could select any college or university in the country for my undergraduate work, I would still choose St. Louis University from the academic point of view." "Agree" 41% "Uncertain" 24% "Disagree" 35%

OTHER STUDIES:

Freedman (1956) reports that almost all of the students at Vassar were highly satisfied with the way of life at Vassar and with the opportunities the school offered. In addition, most of them were "interested, even enthusiastic about at least some of their courses" (p. 15). Morgenstern, Gussow, Woodward, and Russin (1965) report that 85% of a sample of students from a cross-section of America's colleges and universities declared themselves satisfied with college.

DiRenzo (1965) found that on the average students at Fairfield University during the 1963-64 school year had a "moderately positive" image of the faculty (with respect to such things as the quality of the faculty, the standards the faculty demanded, and student-faculty relationships) and a "minimally positive" image of Fairfield with respect to its quality as an academic institution.

In their longitudinal study of 10,000 high school seniors (graduating during 1959) Trent and Medsker (1967) found that approximately 90 percent of those who started and finished college, and 70 percent of those who started but withdrew from college, felt satisfied with intellectual growth as a result of college. Seventy percent of the college persisters and 65% of the withdrawals felt that most of the faculty were intellectually stimulating.

Among the nearly 15,000 student ratings of instructors obtained during the winter quarter in 1949 at the University of Minnesota (College of Science, Literature and the Arts), 34 percent of the students had rated their instructors as "one of the best instructors in teaching ability." another 34 percent as "better than most instructors," and 24% as "about average." Only 6 percent characterized their instructors "not as good as most instructors," and 2 percent as "one of the poorest instructors" (Clark and Keller, 1954).

In 1963, 13 percent of the seniors majoring in science at Mundelein College stated that they were consistently bored in class; the percentage was higher for seniors majoring in psychology/sociology and in English: 21% and 32% respectively (Hassenger, 1965). Sussmann (1960) reports that with the exception of their chemistry lecture, large majorities of freshmen at MIT (in 1957) found their courses, lectures and laboratories either "very interesting" or "fairly interesting."

For a comparison of the satisfaction with college of male veterans and nonveterans in a variety of colleges (just after the end of World War II), see Frederickson and Schrader (1951).

Table 8C.--Summaries of studies showing degree of student contact with faculty outside of the classroom

REFERENCE, SAMPLE	RESULTS
Pennsylvania State University (1966a). Representative sample of male and female students at the Pennsylvania State University. Fall 1965.	"I have visited an instructor with a problem relating to his course" "Very often" 3% "Often" 12% "Occasionally" 29% "Seldom" 40% "Never" 16% "I have visited an instructor to discuss a personal problem" "Very often" 1% "Often" 1% "Occasionally" 3% "Seldom" 16% "Never" 79% "I have hesitated to visit an instructor because his manner was aloof and repelling" "Never" 39% "Seldom" 25% "Occasionally" 20% "Often" 11% "Very often" 5%
Birney, Coplin and Grose (1960). Sample of male students at Amherst College in the sophomore year (May 1957) and of those of these students who were still at the college as juniors (May 1958) and as seniors (April 1959).	Number of yearly contacts with faculty outside of class ... (Sophomores / Juniors / Seniors) "On matters pertaining to classes" Mean contacts 5 / 9 / 10 Median contacts 3 / 6 / 6 % reporting none 12% / 4% / 4% "On matters of interest to you" Mean contacts 2 / 4 / 4 Median contacts 1 / 2 / 2 % reporting none 40% / 20% / 25% "About a personal matter of some importance" Mean contacts 1 / 2 / 3 Median contacts 0 / 1 / 2 % reporting none 59% / 39% / 28% "Chatting informally under spontaneous circumstances" Mean contacts 7 / 9 / 9 Median contacts 3 / 5 / 6 % reporting none 15% / 6% / 7%
Olson (1964b). Random sample of male and female students living in residence halls at Michigan State University. Winter term 1964.	"I visit my instructor's office when I have difficulty in a course" (Males / Females) "Agree strongly" 31% / 40% "Agree somewhat" 36% / 37% "Disagree somewhat" 23% / 17% "Disagree strongly" 11% / 6% "I do not consult my instructors as often as I would like because I find it difficult to communicate with them" (Males / Females) "Disagree strongly" 19% / 27% "Disagree somewhat" 45% / 35% "Agree somewhat" 28% / 29% "Agree strongly" 7% / 9% "Professors often stop to talk when they meet students outside of the classroom" (Males / Females) "Agree strongly" 10% / 14% "Agree somewhat" 32% / 35% "Disagree somewhat" 37% / 30% "Disagree strongly" 22% / 21%
Lehmann and Dressel (1962). Sample of male and female seniors at Michigan State University. Spring 1962.	"Compare how you *thought* your four years at college would be with how you actually found it for contact with faculty" (Males / Females) "More than I thought" 31% / 36% "Same as I thought" 28% / 25% "Less than I thought" 41% / 39%
Weiss (1964). Sample of entire student body at St. Louis University (College of Arts and Sciences, School of Commerce and Finance, School of Nursing and Health Services, Institute of Technology, and Parks College of Aeronautical Technology) during the academic year 1963-64.	"I have found it difficult to consult my teachers outside of class." "Disagree" 63% "Agree" 23% "Uncertain" 14% "I feel that I know at least one faculty member quite well." "Agree" 52% "Disagree" 40% "Uncertain" 8%
Harp and Taietz (1963). Sample of male students (all class levels) in the Colleges of Agriculture, Arts and Sciences and Engineering at Cornell University. Fall 1962.	Proportion of students reporting informal talks with faculty "Frequently" 11% "Occasionally" 32% "Seldom" 42% "Never" 15%
Ellis (1965). Sample of male and female sophomores at the University of Oregon. May 1962.	Number of faculty members with whom students are personally acquainted "More than 4" 20% "3-4" 25% "1-2" 32% "None" 21% "No answer" 2%

OTHER STUDIES:

Among a random sample of students at Columbia University during the spring of 1965, 45% of the seniors, 50% of the juniors, 34% of the sophomores, and 44% of the freshmen reported that they had visited at least three instructors to talk about studies one or more times during that academic year. Fifty-five percent of the seniors, 42% of the juniors, 36% of the sophomores, and 11% of the freshmen said that they knew one or more Columbia instructors on a personal basis (Thielens, 1966).

Table 8D.--Summaries of studies showing degree to which students feel faculty are personally involved with them

REFERENCE, SAMPLE | **RESULTS**

Gaff (1965).

Sample of male and female students at the University of California at Berkeley, University of the Pacific, and Raymond College. Summer 1964.

"About what proportion of the faculty members in the college as a whole would you say are really interested in students and their problems?"

	Berkeley		Univ. of the Pacific		Raymond
	Freshmen*	Seniors	Freshmen	Seniors	Freshmen
"Almost all"	6%	4%	22%	13%	91%
"Over half"	25%	13%	31%	44%	7%
"About half"	18%	22%	32%	23%	2%
"Less than half"	30%	30%	10%	12%	--
"Very few"	13%	30%	3%	6%	--

"Is there any faculty member at your college to whom you have felt particularly responsible and whom you believe feels particularly responsible to you?"

	Berkeley		Univ. of the Pacific		Raymond
	Freshmen	Seniors	Freshmen	Seniors	Freshmen
"Yes, there are several"	5%	11%	9%	19%	46%
"Yes, there is one"	20%	26%	29%	43%	24%
"No, there isn't any"	75%	63%	62%	37%	29%

*No explanation is given as to why percentages do not add to 100 percent.

Goldsen (1951); Goldsen, Rosenberg, Williams, and Suchman (1960).

Random sample of male and female students at Cornell University (in the Colleges of Agriculture, Architecture, Arts and Sciences, Engineering, Home Economics, Hotel Administration, and Industrial and Labor Relations) in 1960. Follow-up sample (of juniors and seniors) in 1952.

"How many of your instructors do you think take a personal interest in their students?"

1950 Sample

	Freshmen	Sophomores	Juniors	Seniors
"All or most"	24%	23%	22%	26%
"About half"	30%	28%	30%	28%
"Few or none"	46%	49%	48%	45%

1952 Sample

	Males	Females
"All of them"	2%	3%
"Most of them"	24%	17%
"About half of them"	24%	24%
"Few of them"	45%	53%
"None of them"	4%	2%

Harp and Taietz (1963).

Sample of male students (all class levels) in the College of Agriculture, Arts and Sciences, and Engineering at Cornell University. Fall 1962.

"Few instructors take genuine interest in my personal welfare."

"Strongly disagree"	3%
"Disagree"	24%
"Undecided"	15%
"Agree"	43%
"Strongly agree"	15%

Henderson and Northrup (1964).

Sample of male and female students (at all class levels) at the Pennsylvania State University. April 1962.

"In many of my classes, I have felt like just another face in the crowd."

"Strongly disagree"	4%
"Disagree"	29%
"Agree"	52%
"Strongly agree"	16%

Weiss (1964).

Sample of entire student body at St. Louis University (College of Arts and Sciences, School of Commerce and Finance, School or Nursing and Health Services, Institute of Technology, and Parks College of Aeronautical Technology) during the academic year 1963-64.

"Most faculty members on this campus show high regard for students as persons."

"Agree"	63%
"Disagree"	19%
"Uncertain"	18%

Harry Sharp (personal communication to authors).

Random sample of male and female students at the University of Wisconsin. November 1965.

"Do you feel education on this campus is not depersonalized, somewhat depersonalized, or highly depersonalized?"

	Freshmen and Sophomores	Juniors and Seniors
"Not depersonalized"	18%	19%
"Somewhat depersonalized"	72%	69%
"Highly depersonalized"	10%	12%

Goldsen, Rosenberg, Williams, and Suchman (1960).

Random sample of male students at eleven universities in 1952.

Percent of students who consider "production line teaching methods" a justified charge pertaining to their school

Wayne State Univ.	37%
Dartmouth	41%
Wesleyan	43%
Fisk	43%
Harvard	45%
Univ. of North Carolina	50%
Yale	52%
Univ. of Michigan	55%
Univ. of Texas	58%
UCLA	63%

OTHER STUDIES:

At Mundelein College in 1963, 16% of the seniors majoring in science felt that no faculty member "cared about" them, while 28% of the seniors majoring in the social sciences and in humanities felt this way (Hassenger, 1965).

Table 8E.--Summaries of studies showing perceived influence of various sources

Prusok (1960): In the fall of 1959, male and female freshman students at the University of Iowa, living in off-campus residence, were asked if they ever needed help with problems or questions in a number of areas, and if so, from what sources they had received assistance. The sources of assistance are listed in rank order, the first being the most frequent. The types of problems brought to each source are also shown, as follows: (1) personal problems; (2) vocational problems; (3) course work--problems concerned with the mechanics of course sequence and requirements; (4) academic major--problems around the choice of major field; (5) social problems; and (6) financial problems. (Adapted from Table 6, p. 5.)

Rank order of varying sources of help in terms of frequency

Male students		Female students	
Other students:	1, 3, 4, 5, 6	Faculty adviser:	1, 2, 3, 4
Instructor:	1, 3, 4, 6	Professor or instructor:	1, 2, 3, 4
Faculty adviser:	2, 3, 4	Parents:	1, 6
Relative:	1, 2, 4, 6	Other students:	1, 3, 4, 5, 6
Dean of men:	1, 2, 4, 6	Student pastor or minister:	1, 4
Adult friend:	1, 2, 4, 6	Univ. Counseling Service:	1, 2, 3, 4
Parents:	1, 2, 4, 6	Student Health Service:	1, 2
Univ. Counseling Service:	2	Office of Student Affairs:	1, 2, 3, 6
Office of Student Affairs:	6	Householder:	1, 3, 4
Fraternity:	1, 2, 3, 4, 5	Family physician:	1, 6
Minister:	1, 2, 4, 6	Adult friend:	1, 3
		Roommate:	1, 3
		Liberal Arts Advisory Office:	3, 4

Collins (1960): During 1952 female students (at all class levels) at Sarah Lawrence College completed a questionnaire dealing with their experience at college. Among other things, they were asked with whom they discussed serious problems and what kinds of experiences at college were their "best" experiences. (Adapted from discussion on pp. 69 and 79.)

Percent of students checking each of several persons as some one with whom they discuss serious problems (Note: since students could check more than one person, percentages add up to more than 100%.)

Person	Percent
A student friend:	79%
Mother:	55%
Don (student adviser):	38%
A male friend:	37%
Father:	36%
A member of family other than mother or father:	25%
A non-student female friend:	22%
Faculty member other than don:	17%
Husband or fiance:	15%

Rank of various college experiences, as determined by percent of students who consider experience as one of the two best in their college lives

Freshmen Experience	Rank	Seniors Experience	Rank
A specific course or teacher:	1	A specific course or teacher:	1
Relationships with people other than faculty (e.g., making friends, meeting different kinds of people):	2	Relationships with faculty:	2
General academic achievement:	3	Relationships with people other than faculty (e.g., making friends, meeting different kinds of people):	3
Methods of working at college:	4	Extracurricular activities	4.5
		General academic achievement:	4.5

Henderson and Northrup (1964): During the spring of 1962, male and female students at all class levels at Pennsylvania State University were asked to select the three most important aspects of their life at Penn State from among seven aspects. (Adapted from the table on p. 16.)

Percent of students checking each of several aspects as one of the three most important aspects of their life at Penn State (Note: since students could check more than one aspect, percentages add up to more than 100%.)

Aspect	Percent
Academic activities such as classes, lectures, and exams:	96%
Casual, interpersonal relations with small groups of students:	72%
Organized social activities sponsored by organizations:	46%
Non-organized social activities such as movies and informal parties:	32%
Cultural activities such as plays, concernts, and art exhibits:	28%
Informal, interpersonal relations with faculty:	15%
Religious activities:	13%

Table 8E.--Summaries of studies showing perceived influence of various sources (CONTINUED)

Katz (1967a): During the spring of 1965, male and female seniors at Stanford and the University of California at Berkeley were asked how much each of eighteen factors contributed to the changes that took place in them during college. (Adapted from Table 61, pp. 113-114.)

Percent of student checking each of several factors as having "much" influence in contributing to the change that took place in them during college

Stanford

Males		Females	
Gaining understanding of myself as a person:	55%	Confrontation with problems and conflicts in myself:	67%
Confrontation with problems and conflicts in myself:	48%	Gaining understanding of myself as a person:	66%
Close relations with friends of the opposite sex:	41%	Close relations with friends of the opposite sex:	66%
Close relations with friends of the same sex:	36%	Close relations with friends of the same sex:	50%
Being away from home:	36%	Being overseas:	46%
Living group:	34%	Crises in my relations with other people:	42%
Being overseas:	33%	Being away from home:	40%
Ideas presented in courses or by teachers:	26%	Confrontation with problems and conflicts with others:	38%
Ideas in books I read on my own:	23%	Ideas presented in courses or by teachers:	34%
Work experience:	23%	Living group:	28%
Crises in my relations with other people:	21%	Work experience:	19%
Confrontation with problems and conflicts with others:	21%	Ideas in books I read on my own:	18%
Close relations with teachers or other adults:	15%	Discovery of the capacity I did not know I had:	18%
Problems in my family:	12%	Close relations with teachers or other adults:	16%
Participation in student organizations, committees, etc.:	11%	Problems in my family:	14%
Discovery of the capacity I did not know I had:	11%	Participation in student organizations, committees, etc.:	9%
Participation in activities directed to social or political improvement:	10%	Lack of academic success:	8%
Lack of academic success:	10%	Participation in activities directed to social or political improvement:	7%

Berkeley

Males		Females	
Gaining understanding of myself as a person:	42%	Gaining understanding of myself as a person:	63%
Being away from home:	38%	Close relations with friends of the opposite sex:	57%
Confrontation with problems and conflicts in myself:	38%	Confrontation with problems and conflicts in myself:	56%
Close relations with friends of the opposite sex:	32%	Being away from home:	48%
Close relations with friends of the same sex:	27%	Close relations with friends of the same sex:	38%
Living group:	26%	Crises in my relations with other people:	36%
Ideas presented in courses or by teachers:	22%	Confrontation with problems and conflicts with others:	31%
Work experience:	18%	Ideas presented in courses or by teachers:	27%
Confrontation with problems and conflicts with others	18%	Work experience:	23%
Crises in my relations with other people:	18%	Problems in my own family:	19%
Ideas in books I read on my own:	15%	Ideas in books I read on my own:	18%
Problems in my own family:	13%	Living group:	18%
Lack of academic success:	9%	Close relations with teachers or other adults:	14%
Discovery of the capacity I did not know I had:	9%	Discovery of the capacity I did not know I had:	13%
Participation in student organizations, committees, etc.:	9%	Participation in student organization, committees, etc.:	10%
Participation in activities directed to social or political improvement:	7%	Participation in activities directed to social or political improvement:	10%
Close relations with teachers or other adults:	6%	Being overseas:	8%
Being overseas:	5%	Lack of academic success:	6%

Table 8[illegible].--Summaries of studies showing perceived influence of various sources (CONTINUED)

Pennsylvania State University (1965): During the spring of 1965, male and female students of all class levels at Pennsylvania State University were asked about the important aspects of their life at Penn State. (adapted from discussion on p. 18.)

Percent of students checking each of several experiences as an important aspect of their life at Penn State

Experience	Percent
Meeting many different kinds of people:	88%
Casual, interpersonal relations with small groups of students:	85%
Cultural activities such as plays and concerts:	44%
Informal, interpersonal relations with members of the faculty and/or staff counselors:	28%
Religious activities:	14%

Lehmann and Dressel (1962): During the spring of 1959, a sample of male and female freshmen at Michigan State University completed an experience inventory. A sample of male and female sophomores were questionnaired during the spring of 1960; juniors during the spring of 1961; and seniors during the spring of 1962.

Freshmen were asked to check from a list of twenty, the five items that were most important experiences to them during their first year at college. The ten experiences receiving the largest percentage-endorsement are given here. (Adapted from Table 54, p. 190.)

Freshmen

Percent of students checking each of several experiences as among the five most important to them

Males		Females	
Friends at school:	66%	Friends at school:	73%
Family:	49%	Person dated:	51%
Athletic events:	44%	Family:	50%
Person dated:	34%	Church:	35%
Extracurricular activities:	33%	Bull-sessions:	31%
Bull-sessions:	32%	Close friend:	30%
Close friend:	30%	Extracurricular activities:	29%
Church:	29%	An instructor:	25%
Where student lives:	22%	Athletic events:	23%
An instructor:	21%	Sorority:	23%

Sophomores at the same school were asked to check from a list of fifty, the three experiences that had had a positive and the three that had had a negative influence upon them. The five most positive and the five most negative influences (in terms of percentage checking) are given here. (Adapted from Table 60, pp. 203-205.)

Sophomores

Percent of students checking each of several experiences as among the three positive influences on them

Males		Females	
Close friends:	26%	Close friends:	42%
A course in major field:	21%	Person dated:	28%
Fraternity:	18%	Being away from home:	22%
Family:	18%	Sorority:	21%
Person dated:	17%	Family:	19%

Percent of students checking each of several experiences as among the three negative influences on them

Males		Females	
Campus regulations:	29%	Campus regulations:	26%
ROTC:	25%	Conduct pattern of students:	25%
Conduct pattern of students:	14%	A course in major field:	17%
A Communicaton Skills instructor:	14%	Natural Science 183:	17%
An instructor other than in the four general education courses or major field:	12%	A course other than one in the general education sequence or student's major field:	13%

Juniors at the same school were asked to check from a list of fifty, the three experiences that had had the most reinforcing effect and the three that had had the most modifying effect on their behavior. The five most reinforcing and the five most modifying experiences (in terms of percentage endorsement) are given here. (Adapted from Table 61a, pp. 213-215.)

Juniors

Percent of students checking each of several experiences as among the three having the most reinforcing effect on their behavior

Males		Females	
An instructor in major field:	20%	An instructor in major field:	22%
A course in major field:	19%	A course in major field:	19%
Close friends:	18%	Family:	19%
Family:	18%	Close friends:	17%
Fraternity:	13%	Sorority:	16%

Percent of students checking each of several experiences as among the three having the most modifying effect on their behavior

Males		Females	
Close friends:	14%	A person dated:	29%
Discussions or "bull-sessions":	14%	Close friends:	26%
ROTC	13%	Discussions or "bull-sessions":	24%
A person dated:	13%	Being away from home:	21%
Campus regulations:	10%	A course in major field:	18%

Table 8E.--Summaries of studies showing perceived influence of various sources (CONTINUED)

Lehmann and Dressel (continued):

Seniors at the same school were also asked to check the three most modifying and the three most reinforcing experiences, with results as given here. (Adapted from Table 61b, pp. 219-221.)

Seniors

Percent of students checking each of several experiences as among the three having the most reinforcing effect on their behavior

Males		Females	
An instructor in major field:	23%	An instructor in major field:	22%
A course in major field:	22%	A course in major field:	21%
Close friends:	16%	Close friends:	20%
Fraternity:	12%	Family:	15%
Person dated:	11%	Person dated:	14%

Percent of students checking each of several experiences as among the three having the most modifying effect on their behavior

Males		Females	
An instructor in major field:	14%	A person dated:	20%
Close friends:	13%	Being away from home:	19%
Being away from home:	13%	Discussions or "bull-sessions":	14%
A person dated:	12%	Close friends:	14%
Employment:	10%	An instructor in major field:	11%

In addition, seniors at this school were asked to pick from a list of seven, the one factor that played the most important part in their career decisions during college. (Adapted from Table 48, p. 165.)

Percent of students checking each of several factors as the one having the most important impact or effect on their career plans

Males		Females	
Discussions with faculty (other than academic adviser):	24%	Discussions with academic adviser:	21%
Discussions with academic adviser:	20%	Discussions with faculty (other than academic adviser):	18%
Advice from parents:	17%	Advice from parents:	18%
Vocational or similar psychological tests:	17%	Vocational or similar psychological tests:	18%
Peers:	13%	Peers:	12%
Advice from family other than parents:	5%	Vocational or guidance counselor:	7%
Vocational or guidance counselor:	4%	Advice from family other than parents:	6%

E. K. Wilson (1966): During May 1960, a sample of male and female seniors at Antioch College were asked how they had changed during their college years and to what "agents" or factors they attributed this change. (Adapted from Table 3.4, p. 88.)

Percent of students attributing perceived change in six areas to each of several agents or factors

	Category of Change					
Agent or Factor of Change	Intel-lectual %	Development of interest in new fields %	World view and personal philosophy %	Person-ality develop-ment %	Social devel-opment %	Career plans and choices %
Course(s)	21	35	17	13	6	22
Self-development, maturation, growing up	15	10	16	16	15	9
Work experience	9	8	11	17	16	30
Fellow student(s)	6	11	11	12	15	4
Teaching faculty	16	6	8	3	4	11
Antioch atmosphere, community program	6	7	6	3	7	2
Family, employer, fellow employee, special project or relationships with others generally	3	2	2	4	9	4
Other (including "don't know" and "not ascertained")	25	21	31	30	29	19
Total	101	100	101	99	101	101

Table 8E.--Summaries of studies showing perceived influence of various sources (CONTINUED)

Weiss (1964): During the fall of 1963, a sample of male and female students at all class levels in the various undergraduate schools of St. Louis University (College of Arts and Sciences, Institute of Technology, School of Commerce and Finance, School of Nursing and Health Services and Parks College of Aeronautical Technology) were asked to check which source of a number of sources made the greatest contribution to their education and which the second greatest. (Adapted from Table 25, p. 115. Only the percentages across the five schools of the University are given; the rank ordering of these courses are nearly always identical for each school considered separately.)

Percent of students checking that each of the following sources made:

"the greatest contribution" to their education		"the second greatest contribution" to their education	
Preparation for courses:	42%	Preparation for courses:	34%
Faculty:	39%	Faculty:	30%
Independent study:	9%	Discussions with other students and friends:	19%
Discussion with other students and friends:	8%	Independent study:	10%
Extracurricular activities:	1%	Extracurricular activities:	4%
Others:	1%	Others:	1%

Wilson (1956): In the spring of 1954, a sample of seniors in fifty colleges and universities widely distributed throughout the United States were asked to indicate the factors that most influenced their ideas and attitudes about international affairs. From a list of twenty possible sources of influences, students were asked to pick the five most influential factors and to rank order these using a priority scale of 5, 4, 3, 2, 1. Shown here is the average rating (total number of points for an item divided by the total number of students in the sample) for the ten most important influences. (Adapted from Table 3, p. 97.)

Average rating given each of several possible influences affecting outlook on world affairs

Influences	Average rating
College courses taken:	2.36
Newspapers:	1.86
Magazines:	1.48
Newscasts:	1.23
Discussions and bull-sessions with friends:	1.21
Ideas and opinions of parents:	1.10
Books:	.96
Lectures:	.89
Travel outside the United States	.68
Faculty members active in world affairs:	.54

Heath (1968): During the early 1960s small samples of male freshmen and seniors at Haverford College were interviewed about the changes they felt they had made with respect to their self-image, values, intellectual skills, and interpersonal relationships. (The changes were subsequently coded into those showing increased maturity and those showing increased immaturity.) They also were questioned about the influence of various factors on these changes. The rankings of various determinants for four change-areas are given here.

Highest ranking factors with respect to importance in determining change (subsequently coded as increased maturity) in four areas

SELF-IMAGE

Freshmen Determinant	Rank	Seniors Determinant	Rank
Male friends:	1	Female friends:	1
Roommates:	2	Male friends:	2
Type of student at Haverford:	3	Roommates:	3
Female friends:	4	Summer vacation:	4
Faculty academic expectations:	5	Intellectual atmosphere:	5
Specific course:	6	Type of student at Haverford:	6
Intellectual atmosphere:	7	Parental relations:	7
Living arrangements:	8	Faculty academic expectations:	8

VALUES

Freshmen Determinant	Rank	Seniors Determinant	Rank
Intellectual atmosphere:	1	Female friends:	1
Social honor system:	3	Roommates:	2
Type of student at Haverford:	3	Intellectual atmosphere:	3
Male friends:	3	Male friends:	4
Academic honor system:	5	Social honor system:	5
Roommates:	6	Parental relations:	6
Freshman English course:	7	Summer vacation:	7
Faculty academic expectations:	8	Type of student at Haverford:	8

Table 8E.--Summaries of studies showing perceived influence of various sources (CONTINUED)

Heath (continued):

Highest ranking factors with respect to importance in determining change (subsequently coded as increased maturity) in four areas

INTELLECTUAL SKILLS				INTERPERSONAL RELATIONSHIPS			
Freshmen		Seniors		Freshmen		Seniors	
Determinant	Rank	Determinant	Rank	Determinant	Rank	Determinant	Rank
Freshman English:	1.5	Intellectual atmosphere:	1	Roommates:	1.5	Female friends:	1
Intellectual atmosphere:	1.5	Faculty academic expectations:	2	Male friends:	1.5	Roommates:	2.5
Faculty academic expectations:	3	Freshman English:	3	Female friends:	3	Male friends:	2.5
Social Science courses:	4	Specific faculty:	4	Type of student at Haverford:	4	Living arrangements:	4
Humanities:	5	Independent project course:	5.5	Living arrange; ments:	5	Summer vacation:	5.5
Roommates:	6.5	A specific course:	5.5	Parental relations:	6	Type of student at Haverford:	5.5
A specific course:	6.5	Natural science courses:	7	Summer vacation:	7	Bryn Mawr College:	6.5
Male friends:	8	Male friends:	8	Bryn Mawr College:	8	Social honor system:	8

MacIntosh (1953): During the fall of 1948, a sample of male students at Haverford College (at all class levels) were interviewed about the effect of various factors on their occupational decisions and plans. (Adapted from Tables 15-18, pp. 44, 47, 49, and 51.)

Percent of students indicating that each of several factors had some effect on their occupational plans and decisions (Note: since students could indicate that more than one factor had an effect, percentages add to more than 100%.)

Factor	Percent
Actual vocational experience:	81%
A specific course:	60%
A specific teacher:	56%
Family and friends:	53%
General college work:	52%
Various vocational conferences:	28%
Adviser:	12%
Dean:	5%

Thielens (1966): Of a sample of 179 students at all class levels at Columbia College during the spring of 1965, 114 had made a decision about their future occupation. Shown here are the perceived percent of these 114 students who felt that each of the listed sources was "a great influence" and the percent who felt each of the sources was "at least some influence." (Adapted from Table 8, p. 70.)

Percent of students saying that each of the following sources of influence on occupational decision was:

"a great influence"		"at least some influence"	
Father:	24%	Father:	60%
College teacher:	18%	Mother:	51%
All other persons:	14%	Close friends:	49%
Mother:	12%	College teacher:	43%
High school teacher:	11%	High school teacher:	42%
Other relatives:	7%	College adviser:	33%
Close friends:	6%	Other relatives:	31%
College adviser:	5%	All other persons:	25%
High school guidance counselor:	4%	High school guidance counselor:	17%

Slocum and Empey (1956): During the fall of 1952, a sample of students at Washington State College were asked to judge which persons had the greatest influence on their occupational choice. (Adapted from Table 10, p. 19. For similar findings on a slightly different sample, see Slocum, 1954, Table 3.)

Percent of students selecting each of the following as the greatest influence on occupational choice

Males		Females	
No one influential:	22%	Parents:	24%
Parents:	21%	No one influential:	19%
All others:	11%	Don't know:	17%
Close friends:	11%	Teachers:	15%
Teachers:	10%	Close friends:	10%
Don't know:	10%	All others:	6%
Advisers or counselors:	9%	Prominent acquaintances:	5%
Prominent acquaintances:	6%	Advisers or counselors:	4%

Table 8E.--Summaries of studies showing perceived influence of various sources (CONTINUED)

Study	Findings
Austin (1965, 1966): A sample of male seniors at five mid-western liberal arts colleges were asked who most influenced their career choice. (Adapted from Table 3, p. 18, in Austin, 1966.)	<u>Percent of students indicating that each of the following most influenced their career choice</u> Faculty: 39% None: 17% Parents: 17% Others: 16% Friends: 11%
Newton (1962): During the spring of 1960, a sample of male seniors from 31 colleges located in the south were asked to rank order six possible sources of influence in terms of their importance in helping them to make their decision about their present major field. (Adapted from Table 4, p. 56.)	<u>Percent of students indicating that each of the following was of first importance in their choice of major field</u> Friends or relatives in occupation student plans to enter: 28% College teacher: 21% Parents: 18% High school teacher: 17% Fellow students: 12% College vocational counselor: 5%
Katz and Allport (1931): During May 1926, nearly two-thirds of a sample of male and female students in the College of Liberal Arts at Syracuse University indicated that they had experienced some change in their religious convictions during their college life. These students were then asked to check from a list of influences the one or two influences that were the most important in bringing about this change. (Adapted from Table 83, p. 313.)	<u>Percent of students checking each of several influence-factors as the one or two most important with respect to religious change</u> (Note: since students could check more than one factor as important, percentages add to more than 100%.) Teaching in certain courses: 72% Contacts with fellow students: 46% General process of becoming more mature: 38% Reading outside of courses: 30% Personal influence of professors in classes: 21% Other influences outside of college life: 20% Personal influence of professors outside of courses: 8% Religious services in churches of the city: 7% A minister not associated with the University: 6% Student pastor: 3% University YMCA or YWCA: 2%
Arsenian (1943): During the early 1940s, samples of senior students in a "men's college in New England' were asked what factors in and outside college had influenced their attitude toward religion (either favorably or unfavorable). (Adapted from Table 5, p. 344.)	<u>Absolute number of students choosing each factor as influencing their attitude toward religion</u> Professors and courses: 58 Schoolmates: 57 Reading: 45 Church: 44 Parents: 33 Summer camps: 29 College clubs and organizations: 22 Clubs and organizations outside of college: 21 Sisters and brothers: 18 Relatives: 17

Table 8E.--Summaries of studies showing perceived influence of various sources (CONTINUED)

MacGregor (1967): During 1960-1966, samples of male and female students (at all class levels) at Brooklyn College of the City University of New York indicated the degree to which each of a number of factors affected their thinking on religion. (Adapted from Table 4, p. 4.)

Percent of students indicating that each of several factors either "very much" or "moderately" affected their thinking on religion

Factor	%
Informal conversation:	48%
Outside reading:	42%
History:	40%
Literature:	40%
Science:	40%
Philosophy:	37%
Religious organizations:	30%
Psychology:	22%
Sociology-Anthropology:	21%
Specific teachers:	20%
Any others:	6%

Educational Reviewer (1963): During 1961-1963, samples of male and female students at all class levels in twelve colleges completed a questionnaire dealing with political and religious matters. The twelve colleges were: Sarah Lawrence College (SL); Williams College (Wms); Yale University; Marquette University (Marq); Boston University (BU); Indiana University (IU); South Carolina University (SC); Howard University (Hwd); Reed College; Davidson College (Dav); Brandeis University (Bran); and Stanford University (Stan). As part of the questionnaire, students were asked if they had changed their political view since entering college. Those students who had changed their views were asked to check from a list of factors those two or three that were the most important influences. (Adapted from Table 27, p. 288.)

Percent of students checking each of several influence-factors as among the two or three most important with respect to political change (Note: since students could check more than one factor as important, percentages add to more than 100%.)

	SL %	Wms %	Yale %	Marq %	BU %	IU %	SC %	Hwd %	Reed %	Dav %	Bran %	Stan %
Increased thinking about political questions:	92	81	83	87	79	80	62	45	67	54	51	54
Increased independent reading:	46	18	43	55	54	46	35	29	47	32	30	27
Lectures and/or assigned reading:	46	65	47	37	53	41	32	33	27	20	36	27
Influence of friends:	23	46	34	29	23	34	17	9	29	30	27	23
Independence from parental ideas:	7	14	8	13	12	9	12	7	5	12	10	14
Personal contact with faculty members:	7	16	11	4	9	10	8	9	8	6	6	7
Other:	15	--	4	4	4	3	3	2	5	4	4	2

Students at these schools were also asked if they had reacted while in college either partially or wholly against the religious tradition in which they were raised. Those who had were asked to check from a list of sources those two or three that were the most important influences. (Adapted from Table 9, p. 286.)

Percent of students checking each of several influence-factors as among the two or three most important with respect to religious change (Note: since students could check more than one factor as important, percentages add to more than 100%.)

	SL %	Wms %	Yale %	Marq %	BU %	IU %	SC %	Hwd %	Reed %	Dav %	Bran %	Stan %
Increased thinking about religion and related problems:	100	86	75	69	81	77	65	73	100	65	69	78
Influence of friends:	33	13	40	17	31	37	40	9	60	34	30	35
Independence from parental ideas:	33	26	16	17	31	28	44	25	20	21	23	30
Courses dealing with religion:	--	20	18	15	13	10	15	20	20	78	15	30
Increased reading in religion:	--	6	8	15	18	13	6	23	60	39	15	19
Personal contact with faculty members:	--	--	8	2	2	4	1	3	20	--	7	5
Other:	--	6	8	20	8	10	14	6	--	4	7	5

Table 8E.--Summaries of studies showing perceived influence of various sources (CONTINUED)

OTHER STUDIES:

Denzin (1966) asked a samll sample (N=67) of college students enrolled in an introductory sociology class at a large midwestern state university to list those persons or groups of people whose evaluation of them as a student concerned them most. The most frequently appearing was faculty: 84% of the students mentioned faculty. Sixty-nine percent mentioned friends, 43% family members, and 39% other students. On the other hand, when asked to list those persons or groups of people whose evaluation of them as a person concerned them most, 79% mentioned friends, 62% family, 48% faculty, and only 12% other students.

In a study by Regan and Thompson (1965), most freshman students at the University of California at Davis said that they would seek advice first from their parents. Friends at college were the second source of assistance. Eight percent said they would turn first to their minister, another 5% to the faculty, and less than 5% to the Dean's office.

At the University of Michigan in the early 1960s, 86% of a sample of second-semester male freshmen and sophomores rated the discussions and intellectual exchanges with friends and other students as being at least of "some importance" to them in their life at Michigan; only 27% so rated "relationships with faculty outside of class" (Gurin and Newcomb, 1964).

Heist (1963) states that in a survey of sophomore students on a number of campuses, approximately two-thirds or more of them indicated that other students had been more important, or second only to some faculty member, as a major educational influence in their lives.

Male and female students at Washington State College (Slocum, 1954) were asked what aspect of college they thought would be most helpful in preparation for their life work. Sixty-three percent checked "courses"; 13%, "personal contacts"; 7%, "certain personal experiences"; and 5%, "social life." Seven percent were undecided and the remainder designated aspects other than those just listed.